Christian Heritage Rediscovered

The Series, as the name suggests, is meant to focus on Christian Faith & Living vis-à-vis topics like Literature & Poetry, Indigenous Philosophizing, Ethical response towards Agriculture, Health & Healing, Science & Technology, Eco-feminist Theology, Sociological approach towards Human Rights, Law & Politics, Arts, History of Ideas, Ancient Civilizations, Cultural Contiguity, Religious Cosmologies & Mysticism, Footsteps of famous Theologians, World Peace & Harmony, Global Capitalism, Network Marketing, Cybertheology, Population & Demographics, Epigraphic Studies, Contextualized Education, and many others. We welcome a Mss. on any topic/s mentioned, whether they are original works, scholarly monographs, collections of conference papers, revised dissertations, or translations of historical documents. Through the Series we, the Publishers, are striving to put forward published works that may help Institutions, Academic Bodies, Researchers, Scholars and the World at large in furthering their respective knowledge and understanding on the concerned subject. We welcome your comments on our efforts and further suggestions on how we can foster the upcoming thought provoking theologically grounded books.

Christianity among the Meiteis in Manipur

Christian Heritage Rediscovered - 61

Christianity among the Meiteis in Manipur

A Missiological Perspective

L. Bimol

CWI

Christian World Imprints™

First Published in 2018 by

Christian World Imprints(TM)
Christian Publishing & Books from India
H-12 Bali Nagar, **New Delhi-110015**
info@christianworldimprints.com
www.ChristianWorldImprints.com
Phone: +91 11 25465925

ISBN: 978-93-5148-258-1 (HB) ISBN: 978-93-5148-259-8 (PB)

Cataloging in Publication Data--DK
Courtesy: D.K. Agencies (P) Ltd. <docinfo@dkagencies.com>

Bimol, L., 1973- **author.**
Christianity among the Meiteis in Manipur : a missiological perspective / L. Bimol.
pages cm. -- (Christian heritage rediscovered ; 61)
Includes bibliographical references.
ISBN 9789351482581 (HB)
ISBN 9789351482598 (PB)

1. Meitheis (Indic people)--India--Manipur--Religion. 2. Christianity--India--Manipur. 3. Missions--India--Manipur. 4. Vaishnavism--India--Manipur. 5. Manipur (India)--Church history. I. Title. II. Series: Christian heritage rediscovered ; 61.

LCC BR1156.M36B56 2018 | DDC 275.417 23

Printed in India

DEDICATION

This work is dedicated to my wife and son who have always stood by me and dealt with all of my absence from many family occasions with a smile.

The book in its original form is the thesis submitted
to the Senate of Serampore College (University),
towards the Doctor of Theology degree and
is published with written permission.

The Candidate is responsible for the title,
contents and opinion expressed in it.

Contents

Acknowledgement

At the outset, I would like to take this opportunity to first and foremost thank God, the Almighty, for His showers of blessings throughout my research work. Without Him, I would not have had the wisdom or the physical ability to do so.

The book in its original title "Christianity among the Meiteis in Manipur Valley: An Analysis of the Causes for Rejection" is a dissertation submitted to the Senate of Serampore College (University) in fulfillment of the requirement for the degree of Doctor of Theology.

This book appears in its current form due to the assistance and guidance of several people. I would therefore like to offer my sincere thanks to all of them.

I owe my deepest gratitude to Dr. D. Arthur Jayakumar, my research supervisor for his valuable suggestions, corrections and advices throughout the research programme. This research work would have remained a dream without his guidance.

I express my gratitude to The Tamilnadu Theological Seminary, my research centre and SATHRI for giving me an opportunity to do the research work. I would also like to thank the principals and deans of the Seminary, past and present, for their valuable help extended during my study.

It gives me great delight in acknowledging the financial support extended to me during my research work. I would like to thank KIA, ATEN, Rev. Rachel, Pual, Maddy, Dr. Leslene, Roman, Naong, Ebom and Brojen for their support. This work would not have been accomplished without their support.

I wish to gratefully acknowledge the library staff of The Tamilnadu Theological Seminary; State Central Library, Imphal; Manipur University; Meitei Baptist Association; Manipur Baptist Convention; Council of Baptist Churches in North East India, Guwahati; North-Eastern Hill University, Shillong; Eastern Theological College, Jorhat; United Theological College, Bangalore; Union Biblical Seminary, Pune; Papal Seminary, Pune and various individuals for providing the research materials. I would also like to express my sincere thanks to all the people who have contributed by responding to the letters, in the interview and in the questionnaire.

I would also like to thank the Mizoram Presbyterian Mission Field Centre, Imphal, Manipur for their hospitality extended during my empirical study.

My sincere thanks go to all the people who have supported me to complete the research work directly or indirectly.

Last but not the least, I would like to give my special thanks to Dr. Nyimang and Manna, my wife and son for their love, patience and encouragement throughout the research work.

28 December, 2017 **Dr. L. Bimol**

Foreword

It is indeed heartening to hear of a seminal work by Dr. L. Bimol coming out as a book entitled **Christianity among the Meiteis in Manipur: A Missiological Perspective.**

So far people have written on the history of Christianity in Manipur in a general way and that too about Christianity in the Hills rather than in the valley of Manipur. Since none has analysed the causes for rejection of Christianity by the Meiteis in general in Manipur valley, this becomes a seminal work and path-finder for mission and ministry.

Christianity was presented to the Meiteis, known also as Manipuris, in 1894 by William Pettigrew who came through the Arthington Aborigines Foreign Missionary Society. But then the political crisis in the Kingdom of Manipur made his work difficult. In such a situation the Manipur tribal Christian converts of William Pattigrew took the Gospel to the Meiteis of the Manipur Valley. Yet the number of Christians among the Meiteis stood at 5000 only of whom 75% are from schedule caste *Loi* Meiteis, and that made Dr. L. Bimol Meitei, a Meitei himself to analyse the causes for poor response, even rejection of Christianity by the Meiteis of Manipur Valley, for which he had used the historical analytical methodology. His analysis has been objective.

Dr. L. Bimol analyses the causes for rejection under three headings viz Sanskritisation of Meiteis, a revival of traditional religion and British colonialism in Manipur (1891-1947). Each of these causes is dealt with lucidly and with clarity, using relevant documents including Government sources. The author's purpose viz to disseminate the causes for rejection are very effective and illuminating. He explains them in such a way that even a non-Manipuri/Meitei could understand them very easily and ponder over them. I came to know more about the traditional religion of the Meiteis viz. Sanamahism through this work. It is very revealing to hear how British Colonialism in Manipur was a cause for the rejection of Christianity since British Colonialism was exploitative, cruel and inhuman in nature, contrary to the Christian Gospel of love.

Dr. L. Bimol Meitei's book is timely when the Meitei Christians are faced with persecution. This work will certainly encourage other researchers to pursue such an analytical methodology.

I thank Dr. L. Bimol for having given me this opportunity to write the foreword for his seminal work. I am sure this publication will be well received and made use of by one and all.

Best wishes to the author Dr. L. Bimol Meitei.

Oct.1, 2017

Rev. Dr. D. Arthur Jeyakumar
Chennai-600044

Glossary

Amangba	:	polluted or untouchable
Apokpa	:	ancestor
Areppa Laining	:	determined worship
Asheeba	:	another name of Sanamahi
Bhajana, sanshya vandana & *nagarakirtan*	:	twilight prayer usually performed with songs
Chadar	:	seat for learned nobles
Chahi Taret Khuntakpa	:	Seven Years' Devastation
Chak-Umba	:	eating rice
Chandan	:	pottu mark
Chatpa	:	adherent or follower
Chaudries	:	*Zamindars* or landowners
Chawkidar	:	in charge
Cheiraoba	:	traditional religious ritual cum celebration
Cheitharol Kumbaba	:	Chronicle
Ching Tam Potlanba	:	exchange of gifts between the hills and the valley
Ching-Tam Lai Marup	:	the hill and valley religious association
Chongkhaba hanjaba	:	in charge of umbrellas
Choop-saba	:	a ritual
Erat or Eratpa	:	worship
Gunja	:	the front tuck of dhoti
Hats	:	markets
Heikru Hidongba	:	a traditional festival
Hellois	:	beautiful female deity

Hingchabis	:	witch
Ima Keithel	:	mother's market
Imung lai	:	household deity
Ingen	:	June-July
Iraileima	:	goddess of water
Irum	:	name of a deity
Ishing	:	water
Kaba	:	climbing up
Kacha	:	male court
Kalen	:	April-May
Kangla Sha	:	the State Emblem
Kanglei Leima	:	the chief queen
Keirungba	:	in charge of the royal godown
Khoriphaba	:	name of an event
Khurailakpa	:	minister of law and order
Khurumba	:	bowing down or worship
Khwairamband	:	Bazaar or marketplace
Kirtan or sankirtan	:	devotional song
Kubera	:	name of a deity
Kwak-tanba	:	a traditional festival
Lai	:	god
Lai haraoba	:	fertility rite or pleasing of god
Lainingthau	:	king of deities
Lairembi	:	goddess
Laisang	:	god's abode
Lakpa	:	trainer or supervisor
Lallup	:	war organization
Lam	:	outdoor or land or place
Leiching purel	:	leaders who lead people forward
Leikai	:	locality or village
Leikai Lakpa	:	in charge of locality or village
Lma Leimarel Sidabi	:	immortal mother deity
Loi	:	schedule caste Meitei

Loisangs	:	cultural and ethical institutions
Lugul	:	sacred thread
Maiba	:	priest
Maibis	:	priestess
Maichaow	:	Meitei scholar or foreteller
Mandapas	:	a place for social gathering
Mangang Salai	:	royal family clan
Mangba-Sengba	:	clean and unclean
Marjing	:	name of a deity
Meiteilon	:	Meitei language
Ngamus	:	a variety of fish (often used in ritual)
Ningol Lakpa	:	tutor for the royal maidens
Ningthou	:	king
Ningthou pongba tara	:	ten learned nobles
Ningthouja	:	a Meitei clan
Nommai Petanga	:	a traditional festival
Nong laoba	:	words for social condemnation
Nongin	:	the State bird
Nongthomba	:	prime minister's post
Nungshit	:	air
Nupi lan	:	women's war
Pacha	:	female court
Pana anjaba	:	a name of the post at the palace
Pannaha	:	division
Panthoibi	:	goddess of love and courage
Pari	:	land (one *pari* is 2.50 acre)
Pattas	:	land ownership record
Phairel	:	February – March
Phambal kaba	:	coronation
Phamdoms	:	nobles
Phanek	:	sarong (female traditional dress)
Phathi	:	Learned men
Phauoibi	:	goddess of paddy

Phiroi	:	first death anniversary
Phunganai	:	servant
Phung-ga	:	traditional fire place
Phung-ga Lairu	:	god of *Phunga*
Piba	:	eldest living male of a clan
Pongba tara	:	ten old men with great knowledge
Pukhramba	:	minister of food and supplies
Puyas	:	ancient Meitei religious scripts
Sagei	:	clan
Sanamahi	:	the trinity God
Sanamahi *Laihi*	:	words of Sanamahi
Sanamahism	:	the worship of Sanamahi
Sangai	:	State Animal
Sareng	:	a kind of fish
Sa-roi-nga-roi	:	evil spirits
Shanglen lakpa	:	head of the administrative unit
Shorarel	:	sky
Sidaba Mapu	:	*immortal God*
Singloop	:	club
Tairen	:	Cedrela toona
Tangbal loi	:	the highest title
Taoroinai	:	name of a deity
Thouni	:	asking blessing
Umanglai	:	forest deity
Urik	:	ritual necklace made out of tulsi beads
Utra	:	specific place
Wakching	:	December – January
Wangbaral	:	name of a deity
Yaibirel Sidaba	:	supreme soul
Yaosang	:	holy festival
Yeks	:	clans
Yim-Chau	:	big house

Introduction

1. Statement of the Problem

Christianity among the Meiteis[1] in Manipur[2] valley[3] has been a challenging phenomenon ever since the coming of Christianity in 1894. Out of approximately 1.3 million Meiteis in Manipur valley alone, there are around 5000[4] believers only, even after more than a century of missionary endeavor.[5] This fact has made the writer raise questions on the rather slow growth of Christianity among the Meiteis. Realizing that there is a problem in the midst of the Meiteis regarding the acceptance of Christianity, the writer made a study of this problem among the Meiteis in Manipur valley. In order to be specific in his study, the writer zeroed in on the analysis of the causes for the rejection of Christianity among this group of people. He believes there are historical causes to the problem for the rejection of Christianity which need to be probed into and analyzed. Other authors have written on the history of Christianity in Northeast India, but none have touched

[1] The Meiteis also known as Manipuris are the main inhabitants of the Manipur valley. Often the Manipur valley and the Meitei are usually taken as synonymous. The *Lois* (scheduled caste Meiteis) scattered throughout the valley are interspersed with the Meiteis. Thomas C. Joshua, "Christian Impact and Conflict Resolution in Manipur," in *Impact of Christianity on North East India,* edited by J. Puthenpurakal (Shillong: Vendrame Institute Publications, 1996), 492.

[2] The name Manipur was given to this land after the declaration of Hinduism as the State religion during the time of the great king of Manipur, Pamheiba (Garibaniwaza), in the beginning of the 18th century. Kh. Ratan Kumar, *Lai Haraoba of Manipur: Indigenous Festival of the Meitei: A Socio-Historical Perspective* (Imphal: Smt. Ph. Pratima Devi, Mayang Imphal Konchak, 2001), 1.

[3] There are four different districts in Manipur valley. They are: i) Imphal West, ii) Imphal East, iii) Thoubal and iv) Besenpur Districts. The Manipur map gives the details. The map can be seen at the Appendix-1 of Chapter -2.

[4] Out of these 5000 believers, 75% of them are from schedule caste (not general Meitei), the number of Meitei Christians who have accepted Christianity from general background is much fewer. Ph. Dhaneswor Singh, Executive Secretary, Meitei Baptist Association, Wangjing, Manipur, letter to the author, 20 November, 2010.

[5] Chaoba Singh, Mission and Evangelism Secretary, Meitei Baptist Association, Wangjing, Manipur, letter to the author, 9 January 2010.

on the problem of rejection of the religion. Therefore, this work is the study and analysis of the problem of rejection of Christianity among the Meiteis in Manipur valley.

2. Elaboration of the Problem

2.1. Christianity in Manipur

William Pettigrew, the first Christian missionary to Manipur, came to India under the sponsorship of a private society called Arthington Aborigines Foreign Mission Society (AAFMS).[6] He was a member of the Church of England. Pettigrew came to West Bengal in 1890 to propagate Christianity. It was during the time when the kingdom of Manipur was going through a serious political crisis. This political crisis led to the outbreak of a palace revolt which resulted in the massacre of seven British officials. The shocking news of the massacre spread across the country and beyond and this was the key factor for Pettigrew in deciding to go to Manipur:[7]

> The massacre of 1891, in which seven British officials were killed by the Manipuris, attracted his attention to Manipur. ... He applied for permission to enter the State to work among the Manipuri Hindus, but it was not until January, 1894, that permission was granted.

His interest in Manipur grew stronger when he met Meiteis in Cachar, Assam in 1891 but he could not enter Manipur at that time as British power was not completely established in the State.[8] Therefore, he had to stay for another three years at Silchar[9] to wait for an opportunity. While waiting, he had plenty of time to get training and learn Meiteilon[10] for the mission work that he was about to begin for the people of Manipur. He mastered Meiteilon to a considerable extent.[11] Thus, Pettigrew was able to prepare himself for the new field where he was going to work and looked for divine guidance to open a way with great hope and zeal.

---

[6] Lal Dena, "Christian Proselytism 1894-1949," in *History of Modern Manipur, 1826-1949,* edited by Lal Dena (New Delhi: Orbit Publishers & Distributors, 1991), 105–6.

[7] Johan M. Solo and K. Mahangthei, complied, *Forty Years Mission in Manipur: Mission Reports of Rev. William Pettigrew* (Imphal: Christian Literature Centre, 2006), viii.

[8] Frederick S. Downs, *History of Christianity in India: North East India in the Nineteenth and Twentieth Centuries,* vol. v, part 5 (Bangalore: The Church History Association of India, 1992) 84.

[9] One of the towns of Assam which is not far away from the Manipur border.

[10] Meiteilon is the official language of the State of Manipur, India. It is the mother tongue i.e. the first language, of the ethnic group Meitei. Meiteilon has been recognized as the Manipuri language by the Indian Union and has been included in the list of scheduled languages. Meiteilon is taught as a subject up to the Post-graduate level (Ph.D.) in Universities of India, apart from being a medium of instruction up to the undergraduate level in Manipur. "Translation Services in Meitei," http://www.tridindia.com/translat-ion-services-in-meitei/ (18 Mar 2013).

[11] T. Luikham, *A Short History of the Manipur Christians* (Ukhrul: North East Christian Association, 1948), 10.

William Pettigrew, having waited for around three years, had received permission to work in Imphal from A. Porteous, the acting political agent during the absence of Maxwell (chief political officer). Thus Pettigrew, an English Christian missionary arrived in Imphal on 6th February 1894 to start Mission work through education—that is how Christianity came to Manipur.[12]

When he saw Meiteis in Manipur valley, he began to think that his call was to work among these people. So, he became anxious to preach the gospel among them. After working only for six months, the British authorities who were then administering the area on behalf of the minor Raja decided against his work in Imphal due to objections raised concerning his preaching, and the baptism of the first Meitei boy, Angom Porom Singh.[13] However, Major Maxwell suggested that he could remain in the State, if he wished to work in the hill areas, which were also under British control.[14] He willingly accepted the suggestion and decided to establish a mission centre at Ukhrul.[15] But he was disappointed once again by the refusal of Arthington Mission to support his mission any longer because of the mission policy, which was not to establish a permanent mission station in any particular place. Therefore, having no alternative, he applied for membership in the American Baptist Missionary Union in Assam, and suggested taking over the Manipur field. His petition was accepted and formally made a resolution in January 1896, saying that Pettigrew should take over the work in Manipur.[16] Thus, William Pettigrew, who prepared himself for three years in learning Meiteilon in Assam and also who confessed to be the messenger of God to the Meiteis of Manipur valley shifted his vision and mission to the hilly region of Manipur.

As soon as Pettigrew received permission, on 10th February in the same year, he began his work at Ukhrul.[17] He constructed a mission bungalow in Ukhrul, and started a teaching ministry.[18] Soon the Mission work bore its first fruit with the conversion and Baptism of twelve schoolboys of both Kuki and Naga

---

[12] L. Leiren Singh, "Reverend William Pettigrew and Modern Education in Manipur," in *Rev. William Pettigrew: A Pioneer Missionary of Manipur* (Imphal: Fraternal Green Cross, 1996), 7.

[13] N. Debendra Singh, "A Study on the Introduction and Growth of Christianity among the Meiteis of Manipur" (Bachelor of Divinity thesis, Senate of Serampore College, 1992), 23.

[14] Frederick S. Downs, *The Mighty Works of God: A Brief History of the Council of Baptist Churches in North East India: The Mission Period, 1836-1950* (Guwahati: Christian Literature Centre, 1971), 76.

[15] Ukhrul is one of the hill districts in Manipur and is occupied by tribal people. The dominant tribal group is Tangkhul.

[16] H. Maxwell, Political Agent in Manipur, Monday, "30. 12. 1895, Government of Manipur, Secretariat Library," (unpublished diary) Imphal.

[17] R. K. Ranjit, "Emergent Ethnic Processes in Manipur," in *Manipur: Past and Present,* vol. I., edited by Naorem Sanajaoba (Delhi: Mittal Publications, 1988), 87.

[18] Narola Imchen, *Remembering Our ForeMothers: The Influence of the American Woman's Movement on American Baptist Women Missionaries in North East India,* women study series no. 2. (Jorhat, Assam: Women Study Department ETC, 2003), 133.

communities on September 19th, 1901. The following year, three more members were added with their Baptism on February 23rd, 1902, and the first Baptist Church in Manipur was established in Ukhrul.[19]

The arrival of U. M. Fox in Ukhrul in 1911 assisted Pettigrew in his work. Soon Christianity began to spread in the western part and *Sadar* Hills. Mainly the credit goes to Lungkhobel Kom and the first converts of Kukis, whose ardent efforts bore fruit with the establishment of several churches in the area. With the widespread growth of Christianity, the Manipur Christian Association was formed in November 1916, and the first convention was held at Ukhrul in 1917.[20] Pettigrew also spent most of his time in learning the local dialect and doing translation work. He also gave out medicine, in addition to assisting the State officials in the day-to-day administration of the hill areas.[21]

But his work in Manipur suddenly came to an end in 1943, due to his wife's illness. The couple went to the United States for medical treatment but unfortunately she did not recover. For some reason, perhaps connected to his wife's death, he did not return to Manipur. [22]

William Pettigrew's mission among the Meiteis of Manipur valley was not fruitful even though he came to Manipur with a great vision to evangelize this group of people in particular. Nevertheless, his mission was revived by his followers, who had become Christians through his evangelistic work done in the hills of Manipur. Those tribal Christians who were converted by Pettigrew became instruments to evangelize the Meiteis of Manipur valley. Even though Pettigrew was unable to do significant work for Meiteis, he had a conviction that one day the tribal people of the hills of Manipur would evangelize the Meiteis of Manipur valley. In this regard, Pettigrew comments:[23]

> There is the hope of a certain number being found willing, capable, and intelligent enough to accept the training needed to make them the leaders of their several Christian communities, and to be of help to the missionaries in establishing the Christian Church in Manipur in such a way that they themselves in the years to come will rejoice with those who have laid the foundations in seeing a self-propagating, self-supporting, and self-administering body of men and women in

---

[19] Milton S. Sangma, *History of American Baptist Mission in North-East India, 1836-1850,* vol. I (Delhi: Mittal Publications, 1987), 274-75.

[20] Lal Dena, "Christian Proselytism 1894-1949," 107.

[21] Temsu Jamir, "Christianity and Tribal Ecumenism in the North East India with Special Reference to Nagaland" (Master of Theology thesis, Senate of Serampore College, 2004.) 40-41.

[22] R. Constantine, *Manipur Maid of the Mountains* (New Delhi: Lancers Publishers, 1981), 249.

[23] William Pettigrew, "Manipur State 1932-1981," *The Baptist Missionary Review,* vol. III, No. 11 (November, 1982): 449-50.

their evangelistic and elementary education work, freed from the supervision and control of the missionaries.

As presumed, essentially in 1960s, the gospel was brought back into the valley by the tribal missionaries and the Manipur valley was evangelized, however the outcome was very insignificant. In spite of great efforts made by tribal missionaries, a majority of Meiteis continued to oppose Christianity. Today, the Meitei Baptist Association (MBA) is the primary Meitei-led and Meitei-staffed mission organization which was established in order to resume the missionary work among the Meiteis, yet it is still unable to do a fruitful ministry.[24] The rejection of Christianity among the majority Meiteis in Manipur valley continues.

In order to review the coming and establishment of Christianity in Manipur, we need to recall the following main events.

- Christianity came among the Meiteis in Manipur valley in 1894.
- The first Meitei Christian who accepted Christianity was Angom Porom Singh.
- Christianity was opposed by the general Meiteis and was expelled from Manipur valley in 1896.
- Christianity came back to the valley again in 1960s but could not grow due to opposition and rejection.
- MBA was established in 1982 in order to resume and to do missionary work among the Meiteis yet it is still unable to do a fruitful ministry due to rejection.

Thus, Christianity is still being rejected by the majority of Meiteis in the valley of Manipur. Therefore, the research work is a study of the causes for rejection of Christianity among the Meiteis. These causes are to be looked at in depth in this study and are briefly stated below.

They are:

- Sanskritization of Meiteis
- Revivification Movement and
- British Colonialism in Manipur.

2.2. Sanskritization of Meiteis: Principal Cause for Rejection of Christianity

The Meiteis, also known as Manipuris,[25] are the dominant ethnic group of the Manipur[26] State in North East India. Although, they speak the Tibeto-Burman

[24] Ph. Dhaneswor Singh, Executive Secretary, Meitei Baptist Association.

[25] The terms Meitei and Manipuri are synonymous terms used by most of the prominent authors.

[26] The original names are Kangleipak, Meitrabak, Poirei, etc., Gangmumei Kabui, "Socio-Religious Reform Movement," in *History of Modern Manipur, 1826-1949*, edited by Lal Dena, (New Delhi: Orbit Publishers, 1991), 92.

language, they differ culturally from the surrounding hill tribes by following Hinduism. Before the forceful conversion into Vaishnavism[27] they were one of the tribal ethnic groups in the State,[28] who were animists; they used to eat meat, sacrifice cattle and practice headhunting.[29] Valley and hill people of the State had intimate relations until Vaishnavism was forcefully introduced.[30] But now Meiteis abstain from all these customs and practices because of the conversion into Vaishnavism.

Sanskritization of Meiteis had a great socio-religious and socio-political impact. The impact of Vaishnavism was considerable upon the Meiteis since the religion was followed first by the kings, the *pibas*[31] and the nobles. It gained ground among the common people because it was enforced on them. Soon after becoming an official religion in Manipur, Vaishnavism enlisted the full support of the priests and the common people as is evidenced from the history of temples, land-grants, and endowments towards the establishment of religious centres.[32]

Under the influence of Vaishnavism certain weaknesses crept into the minds of the Meiteis. Idolatry, caste division, the sati system and untouchability crept into Meitei society and self-identity and self-consciousness and traditional values were gradually lost.[33] With the coming of Vaishnavism, the relationship between the people of hills and valley ceased due to caste division and untouchability introduced by Vaishnavism. This gap became more visible when the majority of the hill tribes accepted Christianity, as there is always enmity between Hinduism and untouchable people (tribal people) and Hinduism and Christianity. Thus, Meitei Hindus in Manipur detested Christianity[34] and its followers.

---

[27] Vaishnavism is also called *Vishnuism,* or *Visnuism, Sanskrit Vaisnavism,* worship of the god Vishnu and of his incarnations, principally as Rāma and as Krishna. It is one of the major forms of modern Hinduism – with Śaivism and Shaktism (Śāktism). *Encyclopædia Britannica,* 2007 edition. s. v; "Vaishnavism," CD-ROM.

[28] The Meiteis, the Nagas and the Kuki-Chins had inbuilt affinities in the course of the ethnogenetic process. In the living folk traditions of the Meiteis, Nagas and Kukis, they are said to be brothers. Naorem Sanajaoba, "The Roots: South East Asian Personality," in *Manipur: Past and Present,* vol. I., edited by Naorem Sanajaoba (Delhi: Mittal Publications, 1988), 11.

[29] R. P. Athparia & S. S. Data Choudhury, "Socio-Religious Transformation Among the People of Manipur," in *Religion in North-East in India,* edited by Soumen Sen (New Delhi: Uppal Publishing House, 1993), 33-34.

[30] Maharajkumar Priyobrata, "Reminiscences of the First and Last Chief Minister: Under Manipur State Constitution," in *Manipur: Past and Present,* vol. I., edited by Naorem Sanajaoba (Delhi: Mittal Publications, 1988), 141.

[31] The male chiefs of the clans – traditionally, *pibas* – were highly regarded.

[32] L. Bimol Singh, "Meitei Christian Identity: Problems and Prospects," *The Sathri Journal: Journal of Contextual Theology,* 3/1 (May 2009): 56.

[33] Maharajkumar Priyobrata, "Reminiscences of the First and Last Chief Minister", 142.

[34] Ph. Dhaneswor Singh, Executive Secretary, Meitei Baptist Association.

By the time Christianity reached in 1894 to Manipur valley, Meiteis were already deeply rooted into Hindu religious doctrine and its philosophy[35] and they were unable to perceive anything beyond Hinduism, for their minds were closed to other religious doctrines.[36] For this reason, Sanskritization of Meiteis which will be dealt with in detail later on is considered as the principal cause for the rejection of Christianity among Meiteis in Manipur valley.

2.3. Revivification Movement: A Major Cause for Rejection of Christianity

Another cause for the rejection of Christianity among the Meiteis in Manipur valley is the revivification movement which proved popular particularly among the youth.[37] During the reign of King Churachand (1891-1941) in the thirties, a revivification movement of the traditional religion called Sanamahi[38] started in a Meitei village in Cachar in Assam. The key leader of the movement was Naorem Pullo,[39] commonly known as Laininghol Naoria.[40] So, although the real reform spirit was not from proper Manipur yet the wave of the reformation movement had a great impact on the Sanskritized Meiteis in Manipur.

People began asking about their own identity. They raised the question about their own traditional religion, culture, scripts, language and literature etc. This inquisitiveness led them towards a great reformation movement. Meiteilon, which is the official language of the government of Manipur, was included in the 8th schedule of the Indian Constitution on August 20, 1992.[41] By the 71st amendment of the Constitution, the ancient Meitei scripts had been revived. Most of the Manipur valley schools have introduced the ancient Meitei scripts as a preliminary programme. Meitei scripts have been appearing on the signboards and other official public places.[42]

At the close of the 20th century Sanamahism gained a strong foothold owing to the coming of modern education, increase in population and many other social

---

[35] Gangmumei Kabui, *History of Manipur: Pre-Colonial Period*, vol. I (New Delhi: National Publishing House, 1991), 58.

[36] Th. Kumar, the First Executive Secretary, Meitei Baptist Association, Wangjing, Manipur, letter to the author, 23 January, 2010.

[37] Th. Kumar, the First Executive Secretary, Meitei Baptist Association.

[38] Sanamahism is the worship of Sanamahi, the Creator aspect of *Sidaba Mapu*, the trinity God of the Meiteis. Sanamahism is one of the oldest sects of South Asia. It originated in Manipur and is mainly practiced by the Meiteis.

[39] The names Naorem Pullo and Laininghol Naoria will be used interchangeably.

[40] R. Constantine, *Manipur Maid of the Mountains*, 73-74.

[41] Ng. Kangjia Mangang, *Revival of a closed Account: A Brief History of Kanglei Script and the Birth of Phoon (Zero) in the World of Arithmetic and Astrology* (Imphal West: Sanamahi Laining Amasung Punsiron Khupham, 1969), 15.

[42] L. Thoihenba, General Secretary, Meitei Thang-Ta Lup, Kurai, Imphal East, Manipur, letter to the author, 11 January, 2010.

factors. The gap of untouchables between Sanamahism and Hinduism became closer. During this period the impact of Sanamahism became more and more embedded in the hearts and minds of the people in general. As a result, it gave a new hope and dimension in the process of the revivalist's movement of Sanamahism. Old beliefs and religious bindings were put aside and the beliefs of the emerging movement began to take their place.[43] Today, the followers of Sanamahism are pressing all the Meiteis to give up Hinduism and follow Sanamahism.[44] So, it is obvious that the followers of the revivification movement are comfortable with and contented with their traditional religion. They are against any form of new religious system being introduced into Meitei society[45] including Christianity.[46] Therefore this is taken as another major cause for rejection of Christianity among the Meiteis in Manipur valley.

2.4. British Colonialism in Manipur: A Lesser Cause for Rejection of Christianity

The last cause, which is regarded as a lesser cause for rejection of Christianity among the Meiteis in Manipur valley, is British colonialism. The British rulers in their aggressive quest for more and more territories played off one tribe against another and conquered the whole of the northeastern region.[47] The people of Manipur fought against the British colonialists' aggressive designs on their land. In 1891, the brutally independent Senapati Tikendrajit Singh was tried along with others by the British on the charge of waging a war against the British-India government. The accusers made a mockery of the trial and passed the death sentence on Tikendrajit and Thangal General.[48] There was a custom in the Meitei society that anyone sentenced to death could be reprieved if a large number of women appeared to intercede for him. This showed that women were held in high esteem in Meitei society. On 13th August 1891—the day the order was announced—gallows were erected on the polo ground in Imphal and thousands of women dressed in white assembled there hoping that the age-old

[43] Sairem Nilabir, "The Revivalist Movement of Sanamahism," in *Manipur Past and Present: The Ordeals and Heritage of a Civilization*, vol. 2, edited by Naorem Sanajaoba (New Delhi: Mittal Publications, 1991), 116.

[44] L. Thoihenba, General Secretary, Meitei Thang-Ta Lup, Kurai. Nilabir also gave the same remarks. Sairem Nilabir, "The Revivalist Movement of Sanamahism," 118.

[45] The followers of the revivification movement do not oppose Christianity being practiced by other ethnic groups in Manipur. Their main concern is for Meiteis and its society. W. Kaboklei, General Secretary, Ima-lup, Laipham Khunnao, Imphal West, Manipur, letter to the author, 4 February, 2010.

[46] Th. Kumar, The First Executive Secretary, Meitei Baptist Association.

[47] R. C. Majumdar, ed, *The History and Culture of the Indian People: British Paramountcy and Indian Renaissance* (Bombay: Bharatiya Vidya Bhavan, 1970), 48.

[48] N. Joykumar Singh, *Social Movement in Manipur*, second edition. (New Delhi: Mittal Publications, 2005), 26.

custom would still prevail. However, the hope was misplaced. When they were hanged in broad daylight, thousands of people cried and wailed.[49] The British occupation of Manipur and the execution of Tikendrajit and Thangal General created a great sensation among the Meiteis.[50] The stand taken by Tikendrajit and his martyrdom continued to be a source of inspiration in Manipur valley. The establishment of colonial authority in Manipur since then signaled the beginning of the long struggle of the Meiteis for dignity and independence.[51]

In 1904, hundreds of thousands of women demonstrated in Imphal to protest and disobey the orders of the British superintendent of Manipur that people should supply bamboo, timber, cane etc. to reconstruct the house of the assistant superintendent which had been destroyed by fire. This event came to be known as First *Nupi lan* or the 'war of women' in Manipur.[52] During the colonial (1891-1947) period, British exploited, tortured and killed people of Manipur.[53] Because of all these, people of Manipur still have ill feelings towards the British and also towards their religion. Their feelings against Christianity were because Christianity was brought and introduced by William Pettigrew soon after Manipur was colonized by the British in 1894. In the minds of the people, Pettigrew entered Manipur with full support from a British official called Mr. A. Porteous.[54] British colonial power and Christian missions in Manipur were linked together.[55] Even though Christianity offered spiritual and sympathetic missions, the exploitative nature of the British overshadowed the work contributed by Pettigrew and other Christians.[56] As a result of these, Meiteis still have ill feelings towards the British and towards Christianity dating from the colonial period in Manipur.[57] Therefore this factor is considered as a lesser cause for the rejection of Christianity among the Meiteis in Manipur valley.

---

[49] Gangmumei Kabui, "The Anglo-Manipur War of 1891," in *History of Modern Manipur, 1826-1949*, second edition, edited by Lal Dena (New Delhi: Orbit Publishers & Distributors, 1991), 68.

[50] Robert Reid, *History of Frontier Areas Bordering on Assam, 1883-1941* (New Delhi: Eastern Publishing House, 1983), 60.

[51] R. K. Tamphasana Devi, History Lecturer, G.P. Women College, Imphal West, Manipur, letter to the author, 21 January, 2012.

[52] "Nupi Lan, 1939," *Lamyanba* 5/51 (December 1973): 6.

[53] E. W. Dun, *Gazetteer of Manipur* (Delhi: Vivek Publishing House, 1981), 61-62.

[54] Debendra Meitei, Former Executive Secretary, Meitei Baptist Association, Kakching, Manipur, letter to the author, 28 April, 2012.

[55] Lal Dena, *Christian Missions and Colonialism: A Study of Missionary Movement in Northeast India with Particular Reference to Manipur and Lushai Hills, 1894-1947* (Shillong: Vendrame Institute, 1988), xii.

[56] Th. Kumar, The First Meitei Executive Secretary, Meitei Baptist Association.

[57] Debendra Meitei, Former Executive Secretary, Meitei Baptist Association.

3. Importance of the Study

The Study of the causes for rejection of Christianity among the Meiteis in Manipur valley is crucial at this point of time as the rejection of Christianity in this community is increasingly obvious. Indeed, rejection has brought persecution to the minority Meitei Christians. Concerning this Kh. Chaoba Singh, State Secretary, All India Christian Council (AICC) remarks:[58]

> Manipur repeats the burning of Churches in valley after five years. Two churches reported burnt down and one attempted to destroy in Imphal West District of Manipur. A new communal force is suspected to be behind the serial attacks on Churches. There is report of an uprising Hindutva like communal force in Manipur, which has started targeting Meitei Christian minorities. To save from communal riots like Gujarat 2002 and Kandhamal, all civil society must resist and oppose the uprising neo communal force in Manipur.

Looking at the historical fact, Christianity is not supposed to be an alien one to the majority of Meiteis but due to lack of historical findings and proof, they continue to hold wrong conceptions.

A majority of the Meiteis think that Christianity is for tribal people (i.e., Nagas and Kukis) as they are the ones who have been mostly Christianized. But as stated above the historical reality is that during the time of King Surachandra Singh, the first Christian missionary, William Pettigrew, arrived in Imphal on the 6th February 1894 to start Mission work through education, and he started his work amongst the Meiteis.[59] The gospel of Jesus Christ was not first preached to the Nagas nor Kukis but to the Meiteis. So, it is hoped that this work will also enable majority Meiteis to understand the historical reality, and thereby a positive attitude towards Meitei Christians and Christianity will be developed.

This work has also helped towards creating a platform for a possible dialogue between minority Meitei Christians and majority Meiteis. Due to lack of historical facts and findings, there is great hatred towards Christianity and Christians among the dominant Meiteis in Manipur valley. And this study will further help to initiate a wider inter-religious dialogue among the followers of various religions viz. Christianity, Hinduism, Sanamahism, Buddhism. The socio-political, socio-religious and socio-economic conditions of present day Manipur are in a chaotic situation, and at this juncture, to have a common platform for inter-religious dialogue would be meaningful and helpful.

---

[58] Kh. Chaoba Singh, State Secretary, All India Christian Council, Imphal, Manipur, letter to the author, May 12, 2009.

[59] L. Leiren Singh, "Reverend William Pettigrew and Modern Education in Manipur," 7. cited in. Lal Dena, "Christian Proselytism, 105.

The feeling of dislike towards Christianity and Christians by the dominant Meiteis in Manipur valley has resulted in persecution of the minority Meitei Christians. Mr. Sam Paul of AICC writes about some of the incidents that recently took place in Manipur valley.[60]

> Now, we are very much concerned that Meitei Christians are in panic of recent series of attacks by some fanatic groups belonging to the fundamentalists, promoting the divisive Hindutva philosophy. On 11 May 2009, a Baptist church at Phumlou, and a catholic church at Phayeng, Imphal West district were set on fire by some unknown fanatics.
>
> On May 10, 2009 an unknown person suspected to be a member of a newly formed group, allegedly backed by an outlaw outfit has warned Church members to stop Church building construction in Lamshang in Imphal West district.
>
> From these series of attacks on Meitei Christians, there is a growing fear that an organized attack on Christians to intimidate, frighten and harass by the fanatic groups seems to be emerging. They are targeting to destroy the peace and harmony among all religious groups by attacking minority Meitei Christians.

The study will also enable Meitei Christians to understand the historical problems which have resulted in the rejection of Christianity among this group of people and suggest how they may be able to find an acceptable strategy in their missionary venture.

4. Scope and Limitation

As far as Christianity among Meiteis in Manipur valley is concerned, the research work is limited to the Baptist works based on Meitei Baptist Association (MBA),[61] which will cover the period from 1982 to 2008.[62] It is an expression of historical connection; it does not imply a lack of acknowledgement of those Meitei churches associated with other denominations in the Manipur valley; these also have been neglected by the majority Meiteis, nor does it involve a disregard for the history of Christianity among the Meiteis in Manipur valley. Nevertheless, this research will have implications for all the Meiteis including those Meiteis in Assam, Tripura, Burma and other parts of the World.

---

[60] Sam Paul, National Secretary-Public Affairs, The All India Christian Council, Secunderabad, Andra Pradesh, letter to the author, May 14, 2009.

[61] The Meitei Baptist Association is situated at Wangjing of Thoubal district, which is one of the districts in Manipur valley.

[62] MBA was established in 1982 and 2008 was the year of silver jubilee. So the researcher will limit the study within the passage of 25 years of its existence.

The Factors for Choosing Meitei Baptist Association (MBA):

1) Baptist mission was the first Christian mission established in Manipur through the activities of William Pettigrew, the English Christian missionary who arrived in Imphal on the 6th February 1894 to start Mission work, but who later joined the American Baptist Missionary Union and took over the Manipur field.
2) MBA was established with the help of Baptist churches which were planted by William Pettigrew and his followers under the American Baptist Missionary Union.
3) MBA is a primarily Meitei-led and Meitei-staffed Baptist mission organization that functions exclusively amongst the Meiteis in Manipur valley.
4) And MBA is the only Meitei Christian organization directly affiliated to the Manipur Baptist Convention (MBC), which is one of the conventions of the Council of Baptist Churches in North-East India (CBCNEI). CBCNEI is the biggest Baptist body in India.

5. Previous Research

While several writers, including Lal Dena, F. S. Downs, C. T. Luikham and N. Debendra Singh, have written on the history of Christianity in Manipur, no work has been done, to this researcher's knowledge, on the study of the causes for the rejection of Christianity among the Meiteis in Manipur valley.

1) Lal Dena's book,[63] *Christian Missions and Colonialism: A Study of Missionary Movement in Northeast India with Particular Reference to Manipur and Lushai Hills* is a significant study and evaluation of the Christian missionary movement in Northeast India. This work is an analysis within the framework of the various modes of interactions between Christian missions and colonial powers in Africa and Asia. It is an attempt to examine and evaluate the missionary movement in Manipur and Lushai hills during the latter part of the 19th century and the 1st half of the 20th century from the colonial perspective.
2) Frederick. S. Downs' book, *The Mighty Works of God: A Brief History of the Council of Baptist Churches in North East India* is an excellent one as far as CBCNEI is concerned. The book gives a narrative description of the American Baptist Missionary Union and its efforts in missionary endeavor and establishment of various mission centers in most of the Northeastern States in India.[64] The book touches on the mission work of CBCNEI in Manipur.

---

[63] Lal Dena, *Christian Missions and Colonialism.*

[64] Frederick. S. Downs, *The Mighty Works of God*, 156-83.

3) T. Luikham in his book,[65] *A Short History of the Manipur Christians* focuses on early Christians and their mission efforts mainly done by the tribal people in the hilly region of Manipur. The author has also brought out some of the adventurous missional efforts done by the pioneering Christians and has supported an opinion that the growth of Christianity among the tribal people in the hilly region of Manipur is credited to those pioneering Christians and to William Pettigrew.
4) N. Debendra Singh in his B.D. thesis,[66] *A Study on the Introduction and Growth of Christianity among the Meiteis of Manipur* has dealt briefly on the coming and growth of Christianity among the Meiteis but was unable to bring out the proper picture about the growth as there had never been a significant growth of Christianity among the Meiteis in Manipur valley.

An answer to the problem for rejection of Christianity among the Meiteis in Manipur valley is yet to be found; this research work is therefore breaking new ground in its efforts to suggest the causes to the problem.

6. Structure of the Study

This work is divided into six chapters. Chapter one is this general introduction. Chapter two gives an overview on the present context and condition of Manipur.. The coming and establishment of Baptist missions in Manipur with particular reference to MBA is dealt with in chapter three. Chapter four focuses on the Sanskritization of Meiteis in Manipur valley which is shown to be the principal cause for rejection of Christianity. The other major cause found for rejection of Christianity is considered in chapter five: the revivification movement which. The last chapter deals with British colonialism in Manipur which is ascertained as a lesser cause for rejection of Christianity amongst the Meiteis. The study ends with a brief retrospect.

---

[65] T. Luikham, *A Short History of the Manipur Christians.*

[66] N. Debendra Singh, "A Study on the Introduction and Growth of Christianity among the Meiteis of Manipur" (Bachelor of Divinity thesis, Senate of Serampore College, 1992).

Chapter 1

Manipur: An Overview

Introduction

The first part of this chapter is geographical background of Manipur where topography, climatic condition, latitude and longitude, population and administrative aspects are some of the main things which will be highlighted. The second part of this chapter is anthropological background. Here, various tribal ethnic groups of Manipur are briefly described. The main focus of the anthropological background is on Meiteis. Consequently, an elaboration of the origin of Meiteis, the early Meitei State and their traditional and cultural values are discussed in this chapter.

1. Geographical Background

Manipur[1] is situated in the northeastern[2] part of India. Manipur[3] is a gateway of

---

[1] Appendix 1, a geographical map of Manipur. "Manipur Map," *Maps of India.Com* (12 Jan 2012): http-://www.mapsofindia.com/maps/manipur/ (2 Mar 2013).

[2] North-East India refers to the easternmost region of India consisting of the contiguous Seven Sister States, Sikkim, and parts of North Bengal (districts of Darjeeling, Jalpaiguri, and Koch Bihar). North-East India is ethnically, linguistically and culturally very distinct from the other States of India. This region is officially recognized as a special category of States. The North East Council (NEC) was constituted in 1971 as the nodal agency for the economic and social development of the eight States, the North Eastern Development Finance Corporation Ltd (NEDFL) was incorporated on August 9, 1995 and the Ministry of Development of Northeastern Region (DONER) was set up in September 2001. Of these, Sikkim became an Indian protectorate in 1947 and a full State in 1975. "Where and what is northeast India," http://www.north-east-india.com/information/what_where.html (2 Mar 2013).

[3] The name Manipur was given to this land after the declaration of Hinduism as the State religion during the time of the great king of Manipur, Pamheiba or Garibaniwaza, in the beginning

India to South-East Asia.[4] The State is surrounded by ranges of hills. It is one of the beauty spots on the earth and rightly called "the Jewel of India," by Nehru; "Switzerland of India," by Lord Iwin and "A flower on lofty heights", given by certain Japanese soldiers.[5] Manipur is also known by a variety of names in the neighbouring areas. People from Myanmar called it 'Ka-the,' and the Shan and other tribes east of the river Chindwin 'Kase.' By the inhabitants of the Cachar district in Assam it was termed 'Mogli,' and those of Assam proper 'Mekheli' or 'Mogalou.'[6]

The State capital is Imphal. The State lies at latitude of 23°83'N - 25°68'N and longitude of 93°03'E - 94°78'E. The total area covered by the State is 22327 sq. km[7] and the total population of the State is 2,721,756.[8] It is bounded by Nagaland in the north, Mizoram in the south, Assam in the west, and by the borders of the country Myanmar in the east. The State has its own emblem, bird and animal. The State Emblem is Kangla Sha. The State Bird is Nongin and the State Animal is Sangai. When India became independent in 1947, the Manipur Constitution Act of 1947 was passed due to which Manipur had the democratic form of Government with Maharaja as an executive head and an elected legislature. The State of Manipur was merged with the Indian union on October 15, 1949. On 21 January, 1972 Manipur became a full-fledged State of India.[9]

The State has two main physiographic regions, the valley[10] and a huge surrounding tract of mountainous region. The valley, some 690 square miles, runs north-south and lies at an elevation of 2,600 feet. Its main physical feature is Logtak Lake, covering about 40 square miles, which is the source of the Manipur River.[11] The river flows southward through the valley into Myanmar. The hill ranges, connected by spurs and ridges run generally north-south.[12] These ranges include

of the 18th century. Kh. Ratan Kumar, *Lai Haraoba of Manipur: Indigenous Festival of the Meitei: A Socio-Historical Perspective* (Imphal: Smt. Ph. Pratima Devi, Mayang Imphal Konchak, 2001), 1.

[4] Gangmumei Kabui, "Glimpses of Land and People of Ancient Manipur," in *Manipur: Past and Present,* vol. I., edited by Naorem Sanajaoba (Delhi: Mittal Publications, 1988), 3.

[5] Jyotirmoy Roy, *History of Manipur* (Calcutta: K.L. Mukhopadhyay, 1958), 1.

[6] Ravindra Pratap Singh, *Geography of Manipur* (New Delhi: National Book Trust, 1982), 1.

[7] M. T. Laiba, *The Geography of Manipur* (Imphal: N. Priyokumar Singh, 1992), 84.

[8] According to 2011, Manipur has a population of 2,721,756. Of this aggregate, 58.9% live in the valley and the other 41.1% in the hilly locales. http://indiapopulation2017.in/population-of-manipur-2017.html

[9] N. N. Acharyya, "Manipur in the Eye of Foreign Historians," in *Manipur: Past and Present,* vol. I., edited by Naorem Sanajaoba (Delhi: Mittal Publications, 1988), 40.

[10] It is also called Imphal valley which is one of the Himalayan midlands like the Kathmandu and Kashmir valley. It is a large basin, about 60 km long and 30 km broad, enclosed by the Eastern and the Western Hills of Manipur. Ravindra Pratap Singh, *Geography of Manipur,* 20-21.

[11] W. Yumjao Singh, *An Early History of Manipur* (Imphal: W. Lalmani Singh and other Brothers, 1966), 1-3.

[12] Kh. Ratan Kumar, *Lai Haraoba of Manipur: Indigenous Festival of the Meitei*, 2-3.

the Naga Hills to the north, the East Manipur Hills along the eastern Myanmar border, the Mizo and Chin Hills to the south, and the West Manipur Hills to the west.[13] Average elevations vary between 5,000 and 6,000 feet, although the hills in the north rise to more than 9,500 feet. In the west the Surma River, known as the Barak River in Manipur, has cut a narrow, steep-sided valley through the West Manipur Hills as it flows to join the Meghna River in Bangladesh.[14]

The climate is moderate in the valley and cold in the hills. Rainfall is abundant, with about 65 inches (1,650 millimetres) of precipitation occurring yearly. The hills are densely covered with mixed forests containing stands of bamboo and teak. Other trees include oak, magnolia, and chinquapin. The Luzon pine grows in the Naga Hills. Among the State's notable plants are rhododendrons, primroses, and blue poppies.[15] Animal life includes the Asiatic elephants, tigers, leopards, and wild buffalo. The rhinoceros is hunted for its horn, which, when ground, is valued as an aphrodisiac. The brow-antlered deer is in danger of extinction. Gaurs are the largest wild bison in the world; the mithan (or gayal), the domesticated form, is widely distributed in the State.[16]

1.1. Districts of Manipur

There are nine districts in Manipur, they are: 1) Imphal East district, 2) Imphal West district, 3) Thoubal district, 4) Bishnupur district, 5) Senapati district, 6) Tamenglong district, 7) Ukhrul district, 8) Chandel district and 9) Churachandpur district.[17]

Each district is headed by a Deputy Commissioner (DC) who is over-all in charge of the administration in the particular district. The DC has to perform triple functions as DC, the District Magistrate (DM) and the Collector. As a DC, the person is the executive head of the district with wide ranging responsibilities. As the DM, the person is responsible for maintaining the law and order situation in the district. As the Collector, the person is the Chief Revenue Officer of the district, responsible for revenue collection and recovery. The Police administration in the district is under the control of a Superintendent of Police.[18] Details of the nine districts are listed below.

---

[13] Jyotirmoy Roy, *History of Manipur,* 2.

[14] Ravindra Pratap Singh, *Geography of Manipur*, 5-6.

[15] Sipra Sen, *Tribes and Castes of Manipur: Description and Select Bibliography* (New Delhi: Mittal Publications, 1992), 3-4.

[16] Barbara A. Standley and Deryck O. Lodrick, "Manipur," in *Encyclopædia Britannica,* 2002 edition. CD-ROM.

[17] The Manipur map of Appendix 1, gives the nine geographical district boundaries.

[18] Indra Kumar Telem, comp., *General Knowledge of Manipur 2010: Complete & Comprehensive* (Imphal: Sharmila Telem, 2010), 29.

1.1.1. Imphal East: Imphal East district as its name signifies is situated in the eastern part of the State with headquarters at Porompat.[19] The district came into existence on 18th June 1997. It occupies an area of 469.44 sq. km with a total population of 394,876 according to 2001 census. It has rich flora and fauna. There are many valuable trees in this district. A wide variety of medicinal plants are also grown in both plain and hilly areas. Some important attractions of this district are: Kaina, Jiribam, Poirou Pat, Shree-Shree Govindajee Temple, Hanuman Temple at Mahabali.[20]

1.1.2. Imphal West: Imphal West district has its headquarters located at Lamphelpat.[21] The district surrounds Senapati District in the north, Imphal East district in the east, Thoubal district in the south and Senapati and Bishnupur Districts in the west." The Imphal West District comes under the Manipur valley region. It is a tiny plain at the centre of Manipur surrounded by Plains of other districts. Imphal City, the State capital is the centre of all important activities of Manipur. Some important historical places of this district are: Shree Shree Govindajee Temple, Ima Keithel,[22] War Cemeteries, Manipur Zoological Gardens, Manipur State Museum, Shaheed Minar, Lanthabal, Khongampat Orchidarium, Nupi-lal Memorial, Kangla.[23]

1.1.3. Thoubal: Thoubal district's headquarters is at Thoubal town.[24] The district occupies the bigger portion of the eastern half of the Manipur Valley and takes the shape of an irregular triangle. It is bounded in the north by Imphal district, in the east by Ukhrul and Chandel districts, in the south by Chandel and Churachandpur districts and on the west by the districts of Imphal and Bishnupur. Some important places in this district are: Khongjom, Sugnu, Waithou, Kakching, Thoubal, Pallel etc.[25]

1.1.4. Bishnupur: Bishnupur headquarters is located at Bishnupur town.[26] The district is bounded in the north by Imphal West District, in the south by Churachandpur District, in the east by Imphal and Thoubal districts. The

---

[19] Indra Kumar Telem, comp., *General Knowledge of Manipur 2010*, 29.

[20] M. T. Laiba, *The Geography of Manipur*, 88.

[21] Indra Kumar Telem, comp., *General Knowledge of Manipur 2010, 29.*

[22] Ima Keithel—the only market place run and controlled by women in the world can be seen in Manipur valley. It is one of the oldest markets. More than 3,000 women congregate to sell fresh vegetables, fish, grain, handicrafts and other household utensils. The uniqueness of Ima Keithel is that one could not find a single man doing business in the market; all stalls are managed and run by women alone. "Things to do in Manipur," http://www.thrillophilia.com/blog/things-to-do-in-manipur/ (13 Mar 2013).

[23] M. T. Laiba, *The Geography of Manipur*, 88.

[24] Indra Kumar Telem, comp., *General Knowledge of Manipur 2010*, 29.

[25] M. T. Laiba, *The Geography of Manipur*, 88.

[26] Indra Kumar Telem, comp., *General Knowledge of Manipur 2010*, 29.

original name of Bishnupur was Lumlangdong.[27] Bishnupur is popularly known as the 'land of the dancing deer'. Keibul Lamjao National Park, Loktak Lake, INA Memorial, Phuballa Resort, Loukoipat Ecological Park are some attractions of this district.[28]

1.1.5. Senapati: Senapati district has its headquarters at Senapati town.[29] The district is bounded in the south by Imphal District, in the east by Ukhrul District, in the west by Tamenglong District and in the north by the State of Nagaland. The district is home to a variety of tribes. Their main occupation is cultivation. Shifting cultivation has been practiced since ancient times. The major rivers of this district are Iril, Imphal, Barak, Ithai and Irang. Besides Senapati town, Mao gate and Makhel are two important places in this district.[30]

1.1.6. Tamenglong: Tamenglong district is endowed with hills, ranges, narrow valleys and forests with rich variety of flora and fauna. The district is located along the western boundary of the State. Its administrative seat is situated at Tamenglong town which is also the centre of all commercial activities in the district.[31] The attractions of this district are: Tharon cave, Barak River, Seven waterfalls, Zeilad Lake at Makoi, Buning (N-piulong).[32]

1.1.7. Ukhrul: Ukhrul district headquarters is at Ukhrul town.[33] The district shares international border with Myanmar in the east and is bounded by Chandel District in the south, Imphal East and Senapati Districts in the west and Nagaland State in the north. The topography of the district is hilly all through with the highest point of 3114 m at Khayang Peak. The district has got a number of important places, they are as follows: [34]

- Shirui Kashung (Shiroi Peak), the floral garden of Shirui Lily
- Khankhui Cave
- Hundung Mangva Cave
- Dilily Water Fall near Khayang Phungtha
- Azoa Jenephiu Magi Lake near Kachouphung
- Cold Water Fishery Project near zero point Phangrei, Shirui
- Saline Springs at Rajai Kl and Kn, Marem, Maramphung, Kalhang, Luireishimphung

---

[27] Now the place is known as Lamangdong meaning 'open-air field'.

[28] M. T. Laiba, *The Geography of Manipur*, 88.

[29] Indra Kumar Telem, comp., *General Knowledge of Manipur 2010*, 29.

[30] M. T. Laiba, *The Geography of Manipur*, 89.

[31] Indra Kumar Telem, comp., *General Knowledge of Manipur 2010*, 29.

[32] M. T. Laiba, *The Geography of Manipur*, 89.

[33] Indra Kumar Telem, comp., *General Knowledge of Manipur 2010*, 29.

[34] M. T. Laiba, *The Geography of Manipur*, 89.

- Longpi Pottery at Longpi
- Khayang Peak
- Chingjui Matza
- Phangrei Picnic Spot
- Nillai Tea Estate on the way to Tolloi
- MATA Industrial Complex, Lungpha

1.1.8. Chandel: Chandel district headquarters is situated at Chandel town.[35] The district is located in the south-eastern part of Manipur. It shares common borders with Myanmar (erstwhile Burma) in the south, Ukhrul district in the east, Churachandpur district in the south and west, and Thoubal district in the north. The Moreh town, the international trade center of the State lies in the southernmost part of the District. When the Trans-Asian Super Highway comes into existence, Chandel district will be one of the gateways to the Asian countries.[36]

1.1.9. Churachandpur: Churachandpur district headquarters is located at Churachandpur town.[37] This is one of the fast growing hill districts of the northeastern region. The district is situated in the southwestern corner of the State bordered by the States of Assam and Mizoram and international border with Myanmar.[38]

2. Anthropological Background

One of the stunning hilly States of northeastern India, Manipur houses quite a number of tribes besides Meiteis. These tribes may be broadly divided into two categories i.e., Naga and Kuki.[39] There are many tribes in the two categories, and though each tribe is small numerically, they have all contributed to an uniqueness in socio-cultural exuberance of the whole of the Indian subcontinent. Festivals and fairs also are integral part of the life of the tribes of Manipur. To celebrate the festivals in proper spirit and enthusiasm, all the tribes have incorporated special dance forms and musical melodies. The tribes are still staunch believers in many superstitions and prejudices and this fact has been emphasized time and again by the anthropologists. Artistic endeavors of these tribes of Manipur, mainly farmers, are shown in the products like weaving clothes and potteries. Society is mainly matrilineal and cross cousin marriages are widely prevalent. Rice is the staple food

---

[35] Indra Kumar Telem, comp., *General Knowledge of Manipur 2010*, 29.

[36] M. T. Laiba, *The Geography of Manipur*, 89.

[37] Indra Kumar Telem, comp., *General Knowledge of Manipur 2010*, 29.

[38] M. T. Laiba, *The Geography of Manipur*, 89.

[39] Tilak Bagchi and K. Jonathan, "Ethnicity and Inter-Tribal Relation in the Hills of Manipur," in *State, Development and Identity in South Asia: A Search for Alternative Paradigms*, edited by R. Vashum & Prakash Louis (New Delhi: Indian Social Institute, 2002), 61.

and the tribes also grow large quantities of cash crops.[40] Even though our main focus is on Meitei, it will be helpful to look briefly at various tribal ethnic groups of Manipur.

2.1. Various Tribal Ethnic Groups of Manipur

Aimol: The Aimol is one of the small tribes living near Loktak Lake and in Chandel District of Manipur.[41] In search of better opportunities and livelihood, a handful of Aimol tribes have settled down in other regions like Mizoram and Tripura.[42] Following the tradition of most of the tribes of the Indian subcontinent, Aimol tribes have taken up agriculture as their key occupation. Paddy is the main agricultural product and all the Aimol farmers farm them in huge quantities. Apart from this, other products like sesame, maize, soya bean, pumpkin, gourd, ginger, tomato, chilly and groundnut are also popular and are largely cultivated among them. Aimol people also love animals and nourish them with great care and affection. They domesticate animals like mithan or water buffalo, pig, ox and chicken. They celebrate festivals with great vivacity and color. Music and dance are integrated in these festivals, thereby exhibiting the richness of their cultural customs and practices.[43]

Anal: The Anal is one of the tribal communities in Manipur mostly settled in Chandel and also a handful of them are in Thoubal and Churachandpur districts.[44] The Anal tribe has a rich cultural heritage. During festivals and special occasions they used to wear colourful traditional dresses. The Anal community is one of the ancient inhabitants of the mountainous areas in Manipur State.[45] Like many other tribal communities of the Indian subcontinent, the Anal tribe adopts agriculture as their main occupation and their main economy. However, following the trends of modern times, Anal people are now slowly accepting a few customs and practices of modern society, thus moving themselves towards their own betterment. Young people especially are going to schools and colleges, which in the process increases the literacy rate of the Anal society.[46]

Angami: The Angami is one of the recognized tribal communities in Manipur even though they are mostly settled in Nagaland.[47] The life style of Angami people is simple, typical of any other agrarian society of Indian tribal communities,

---

[40] Tilak Bagchi and K. Jonathan, "Ethnicity and Inter-Tribal Relation in the Hills of Manipur," 62-65.

[41] Indra Kumar Telem, comp., *General Knowledge of Manipur 2010*, 34.

[42] "Aimol Tribe, Manipur," http://www.indianetzone.com/7/aimol.htm (13 Mar 2013).

[43] Sipra Sen, Tribes and Castes of Manipur, 44.

[44] Indra Kumar Telem, comp., *General Knowledge of Manipur 2010*, 34.

[45] "Anal Tribe, Manipur," http://www.indianetzone.com/7/anal_manipur.htm (13 Mar 2013).

[46] Sipra Sen, Tribes and Castes of Manipur, 45.

[47] Indra Kumar Telem, comp., *General Knowledge of Manipur 2010*, 34.

with agriculture as their chief occupation. A unique feature of their cultivation practices is that the Angami tribes carry on cultivation of wet rice on the hilly terrains. Due to this, the intricate irrigational system has transformed the steep barren hills into picturesque paddy and rice fields.[48] Angami women are experts in weaving the customary clothes. Their sense of artistry is also reflected in the décor of Angami houses. They maintain a conventional house style with all the paraphernalia that highlight their ennobled status. Festivity is part of their life. During those festive seasons, one can observe the fantastic carved panels, crossed roof struts and mithan skulls thus displaying and maintaining their own culture. Just like any other tribe, the Angami people too have similar cultural elements.[49]

Chiru: The Chiru tribe is an ethnic group which resides in various regions, including Tamenglong, Senapati and Bishnupur.[50] The word 'Chiru' has an etymological significance. It implies 'the seed of a plant'. Over the years, the Chiru tribe developed a tradition of musical recitals, dancing, quite integrated into the entire culture of Manipur. In this manner, the Chiru tribe maintains a similarity with the other tribes of the State.[51] The Chiru tribe is also one of the branches of Komrem. Komrem is a united banner which includes, apart from Chiru, four other tribes called Aimol, Purum, Koireng and Kom. Chiru tribes have become farmers, and this supplies their daily needs. For practicing mainly shifting and wet farming, rugged terrains of the mountains are ideal. The Chiru people of Manipur have also proved their fine skill and artistry in weaving, carpentry and manufacturing of musical instruments.[52]

Chothe: The Chothe,[53] one of recognized tribes of Manipur, live in Chandel district.[54] Literally, the word has originated from the term 'Kachohte', which means, 'to bring or to hold a boy.' They also practice agricultural activities to a wide extent. However, trading is also regarded to be an important profession amongst various people of these Chothe tribes. They have established trading links with all the other tribes and communities. Products like woven clothes, exquisite

[48] "Angami Tribe, North East India," http://www.indianetzone.com/8/angami.htm (13 Mar 2013).

[49] Sipra Sen, *Tribes and Castes of Manipur*, 46.

[50] Indra Kumar Telem, comp., *General Knowledge of Manipur 2010*, 34.

[51] "Chiru Tribe, Manipur," http://www.indianetzone.com/8/chiru_tribe.htm (13 Mar 2013).

[52] Sipra Sen, *Tribes and Castes of Manipur,* 47.

[53] Nowadays, Puram tribe is nowhere. Instead of Puram, they now call themselves as the Chothe. But, this Chothe tribe was there also when the Puram tribe was reported long back in the census of India in 1931. From 1971 in the census of India no mention is made of this tribe. Sipra Sen, *Tribes and Castes of Manipur*, 60.

[54] Indra Kumar Telem, comp., *General Knowledge of Manipur 2010*, 34.

crafts are made for selling in the market places.[55] There is no lack of festivals and fairs—in fact, throughout the whole year, they celebrate various festivals adding their own fervour and liveliness. Folk music and dance are inseparable things of the festivals of Chothe tribes, thus demonstrating the exuberance of their spirit and enthusiasm.[56]

Gangte: The Gangte tribe is one of the tribes of Manipur who are scattered in different parts of southern Churachandpur district.[57] This tribal community is a sub group of the Chin-Kuki-Mizo tribes. The word is named after the place carrying the name Ganggam, the word Gangte means 'person from Ganggam.'[58] Primitive practices and rituals are some of the identifiable traits of Gangte society. Killing of animals like mithan, and goats and also singing and dancing are an integral part of the Gangte festivals.[59]

Hmar: The Hmar tribe has gained recognition as one of the scheduled tribes as per the Sixth Schedule of the Constitution of India.[60] Belonging to the Chin-Kuki-Mizo group of tribes, Hmar tribes mostly reside in the southern area of Manipur State, especially in the districts of Churachandpur. Apart from Manipur the Hmar tribes are also settled in some parts of Mizoram, Assam Meghalaya and Tripura.[61] Cultural embellishes are being identified in the Hmar tradition of revering dance forms, festivals and music. They show their expertise in traditional folk dances and folk songs that beautifully represent scenes of adventure, battle, love, victory, and other experiences throughout history.[62]

Kabui: The Kabui tribe refers to those people who are found in the four Kabui villages of Sawombung, Tarungkhun, Sangaiporou and Langthabal.[63] This tribal community is one of the scheduled tribes of India.[64] In fact, Kabuis shared very good relations with other communities such as Meiteis, Pangals. Kabuis have their different and distinctive socio-cultural, traditional and linguistic variants and

[55] "Chothe Tribe, Manipur," http://www.indianetzone.com/8/chothe_tribe.htm (13 Mar 2013).

[56] Sipra Sen, *Tribes and Castes of Manipur,* 47-48.

[57] Indra Kumar Telem, comp., *General Knowledge of Manipur 2010*, 34.

[58] "Gangte Tribe, Manipur," http://www.indianetzone.com/8/gangte_tribe.htm (13 Mar 2013).

[59] Sipra Sen, *Tribes and Castes of Manipur*, 48-49.

[60] Indra Kumar Telem, comp., *General Knowledge of Manipur 2010*, 34.

[61] "Hmar Tribe, *Tribes of Manipur,*" http://www.indianetzone.com/8/hmar_tribe.htm (13 Mar 2013).

[62] Sipra Sen, *Tribes and Castes of Manipur*, 49-50.

[63] Sawombung, Tarungkhun, Sangaiporou and Langthabal are located among the Meiteis in Manipur valley. Kabuis have been staying along with Meiteis for a long time.

[64] Indra Kumar Telem, comp., *General Knowledge of Manipur 2010*, 34.

also genetic identity. They wear a lot of ornamentation. Both men and women have pierced ears. While the males usually wear feathers in their ears, the women traditionally wear brass rings.[65] Celebrations are part of their lives; various festivals are closely linked to their physical habitat and are also a celebration of religion. The celebrations usually reflect the different agricultural stages and include an expression of physical prowess and talents. Agriculture is the main source of livelihood for the people. They are greatly skilled in bamboo wood, blacksmithing and pottery works.[66]

Kacha Naga: The Kacha Naga tribe comprises the Liangmei and Zeme tribes. Although later these two liked to identify themselves by their original names, in the list of schedule tribes of the Indian Constitution, they are known as Kacha Naga.[67] The Kacha Naga tribal name has etymological significance and is derived from an Angami word 'Ketsa' which means dense forest.[68] Like any other tribes, these Kacha Nagas take up the profession of agriculture, mainly living in 'pile dwelling houses' having thatched roofs. Separate dormitories are made for young Kacha Naga boys and girls. It becomes a hub of teaching moral discipline and other training in handiworks like basket making and wooden craft. Here, the girls contribute voluntary services like collection of firewood and water for the poor and desolate widows. They are also taught trading skills like spinning and weaving. Like other tribes, they also observe various festivals.[69]

Koirao: The Koirao is another of the tribes in Manipur.[70] This tribal people are also known as Thangal. They have settled mostly in Sadar Hill areas of the Senapati district. The major occupation of the Koiraos is agriculture. Majority of them practice wet farming and shifting cultivation is also practiced. Women folk too are engaged in various cottage industries, especially weaving.[71] The Koirao society is a monogamous one following the tradition of a nuclear family. Festivals are as many as there are days in the calendar of the Koirao society. Most of these festivals commemorate various socio-religious rituals and customs related to farming.[72]

Koireng: The Koireng is one of the small tribal groups in Manipur.[73] They live mostly in foothills surrounding the Imphal valley. Koireng has an etymological

[65] "Kabui Tribe, Manipur," http://www.indianetzone.com/8/kabui_tribe.htm (13 Mar 2013).

[66] Sipra Sen, *Tribes and Castes of Manipur,* 50-51.

[67] Indra Kumar Telem, comp., *General Knowledge of Manipur 2010,* 34.

[68] "Kacha Naga Tribe, Manipur," http://www.indianetzone.com/8/kacha_naga_tribe.htm (13 Mar 2013).

[69] Sipra Sen, *Tribes and Castes of Manipur,* 51-53.

[70] Indra Kumar Telem, comp., *General Knowledge of Manipur 2010,* 34.

[71] "Koirao Tribe, Manipur," http://www.indianetzone.com/8/koirao_tribe.htm (13 Mar 2013).

[72] Sipra Sen, *Tribes and Castes of Manipur,* 53-54

[73] Indra Kumar Telem, comp., *General Knowledge of Manipur 2010,* 34.

significance. It has been derived from two words, 'Kol', meaning east and 'ren' which means men. Later they were known as 'Korem'. However, they are listed in the Indian Constitution as Koireng.[74] The people of this community mostly cultivate maize, potato, sesame, paddy, arum and ginger. And also Koireng people practice fishing. Rituals, festivals and other customs also embellish the culture of the Koireng.[75]

Kom: The Kom tribe is one of the recognized tribes mainly found in Senapati and Churachandpur districts of Manipur.[76] They share the same language of other tribes like Aimol, Koireng, Chiru. They also share a close affinity with the Hmar tribe.[77] The Koms are farmers, practicing mainly shifting and wet cultivation. Rice is the staple food. Also they produce potatoes, millets and maize. Koms domesticate several animals like pigs, fowls, goats, cows, buffaloes and mithan. Festivals, both of social and religious nature, are an integral part of culture of Kom.[78]

Lamgang: The Lamgang is one of the small tribal communities in Manipur.[79] Their dialect is quite similar to Anal, Moyon and Monsang of the Kuki-Chin group of languages of the Tibeto-Burman family. They address themselves as Kasen. Hiroi Lamgang was a Meitei name used to address them for they made boats (hi) for the Meitei kings.[80] They have settled mostly in the Southern districts of Manipur near Chakpikarong, Kakching Khunou and are scattered in twenty-four villages. They still lack literacy compared to Moyon, Monsang and other tribes.[81]

Mao: They inhibit the hill ranges to the extreme north of Manipur on national highway No. 39. Mao the name of the village and the people are Maomei or Imemei. The Angamis of Kohima call them as Shipfumei. The literacy rate of the Mao tribe is high. They actively participate in politics.[82] They are considered to be one among the major tribes in the State.[83] Most are agriculturists and cultivate terraced paddy fields. They rear cows, buffalos, pigs and fowls. At present the

---

[74] "Koireng Tribe, Manipur," http://www.indianetzone.com/8/koireng_tribe.htm (13 Mar 2013).

[75] Sipra Sen, *Tribes and Castes of Manipur,* 54.

[76] Indra Kumar Telem, comp., *General Knowledge of Manipur 2010,* 34.

[77] "Kom Tribe, Manipur," http://www.indianetzone.com/8/kom_tribe.htm (13 Mar 2013).

[78] Sipra Sen, *Tribes and Castes of Manipur,* 54-55.

[79] Indra Kumar Telem, comp., *General Knowledge of Manipur 2010,* 34.

[80] "The People of Manipur," http://themanipurpage.tripod.com/culture/peopleofmanipur.html (13 Mar 2013).

[81] Sipra Sen, *Tribes and Castes of Manipur,* 55.

[82] "The People of Manipur."

[83] Indra Kumar Telem, comp., *General Knowledge of Manipur 2010,* 34.

regional potato farm is located at Mao and assists the nearby villages in growing more potatoes through modern techniques. Mao is also a commercial center and station for tourists in the State.[84]

Maram: The Maram, another of the tribal groups of Manipur, is scattered in two main areas of Senapati district, i.e., Tadubi Sub-division and Kangpokpi area.[85] Their villages are divided into '*Sadung*' or '*Khel*' (sector). Each *Khel* has derived its individual name from a common ancestor, Rangnamei, meaning descendants of Rang.[86] The majority of them are farmers, widely practicing shifting as well as wet cultivation. Rice is their main food. Like many other tribal communities of Manipur, they observe a number of festivals. During festivals, they love to sing songs. Both males and females take part, with great exuberance and enthusiasm.[87]

Maring: The Maring tribe is mainly situated in the hilly villages of the Tengnoupal subdivision in the Chandel district in Manipur.[88] The term Maring is derived from 'Mei' which means fire and 'ring' which means start or produce. Moreover, anthropologists have made an inference that this tribal community has got close association with the Meitei Kings.[89] Marings practice farming and irrigation. They are also experts in handicraft especially in bamboo and cane. Traditional cultures are highly preserved in their original form. Fun, merrymaking, feasting, dancing and singing play an integral part in various festivals that these Maring tribal communities celebrate with great vivacity.[90]

Lushai: The Lushai tribe has drawn the admiration of many eminent anthropologists. This tribal community is said to be one of the primitive tribes of India.[91] Though the Lushais are also settled in Mizoram, they are found especially in every nook of the hilly provinces of Manipur State.[92] The etymological meaning of this tribe is 'head cutters'. Lushais have developed expertise in swimming and hunting. They are good archers, apparent from the fact that they can expertly

---

[84] Sipra Sen, *Tribes and Castes of Manipur*, 56.

[85] Indra Kumar Telem, comp., *General Knowledge of Manipur 2010*, 34.

[86] "Maram Tribe, Manipur," http://www.indianetzone.com/8/maram_tribe.htm (13 Mar 2013).

[87] Sipra Sen, *Tribes and Castes of Manipur*, 55-56.

[88] Indra Kumar Telem, comp., *General Knowledge of Manipur 2010*, 34.

[89] "Maring Tribe, Manipur," http://www.indianetzone.com/8/maring_tribe.htm (13 Mar 2013).

[90] Sipra Sen, *Tribes and Castes of Manipur*, 56-57.

[91] "Lushai Tribe, Manipur," http://www.indianetzone.com/8/lushai_tribe.htm (15 Mar 2013).

[92] Indra Kumar Telem, comp., *General Knowledge of Manipur 2010*, 34.

handle 'Sairawkher.'[93] The way they dress shows that Lushais have got aesthetic sense.[94]

Monsang: The Monsang tribe is mainly found in the Chandel district that lies in the south-eastern part of Manipur.[95] The name of the tribe is the derivative of the name of a village, named Mosang where the Monsangs are located in large numbers.[96] The Monsang tribe is divided into two major clans, namely Simputi and Rinheti. Socio cultural norms too are quite ennobled as depicted in its plethora of festivals and joyful functions. The majority of them are cultivators.[97]

Moyon: The Moyon tribe is concentrated in the south-eastern part of Manipur, particularly in the Chandel district.[98] The word Moyon is named after a village, i.e., Moyon Khullen. It is known as Bujuur. The social structure and pattern of the tribe is quite similar to other major tribal groups in the State.[99] Festivals, rituals, ceremonies too are integrated into the Moyon tribal community, resulting in their culture becoming really enriched. Amongst various festivals which the tribe celebrates in great splendor are Sachii ichii and Buren Iimpeh. Sachii ichii is the sowing festival of this tribal community, while the latter is a special festival of harvesting.[100]

Paite: The Paite tribe belongs to the Kuki-Chin-Mizo group of Tibeto-Burman family. The Paites are one of the scheduled tribes, mainly settled in Lamka town of Churachandpur district.[101] The word Paite is a combination of two terms, i.e., 'pai' which stands for marching, while 'te' means people. As a whole, Paite means 'a group of people marching.'[102] Besides Manipur, Paite tribes also inhabit Mizoram. Dances, songs, tales, all are linked to everyday life. Thus, they dignify tradition and culture. Zangtalam is a popular dance style performed by this community. Both males and females actively take part in it. Although, the Paite tribes are mainly cultivators, many of them have achieved remarkable feats.[103]

---

[93] It is an indigenous bow made locally that is distinguished by its use of clay shots instead of arrows.

[94] Sipra Sen, *Tribes and Castes of Manipur,* 57.

[95] Indra Kumar Telem, comp., *General Knowledge of Manipur 2010,* 34.

[96] "Monsang Tribe, Manipur," http://www.indianetzone.com/8/monsang_tribe.htm (15 Mar 2013).

[97] Sipra Sen, *Tribes and Castes of Manipur,* 58.

[98] Indra Kumar Telem, comp., *General Knowledge of Manipur 2010,* 34.

[99] "Moyon Tribe, Manipur," http://www.indianetzone.com/8/moyon_tribe.htm (15 Mar 2013).

[100] Sipra Sen, *Tribes and Castes of Manipur,* 58.

[101] Indra Kumar Telem, comp., *General Knowledge of Manipur 2010,* 34.

[102] "Paite Tribe, Manipur," http://www.indianetzone.com/8/paite_tribe.htm (15 Mar 2013).

[103] Sipra Sen, *Tribes and Castes of Manipur, 58*-60.

Poumai: The Poumai[104] tribe is one of the biggest tribes, predominantly inhabiting the Senapati District of Manipur.[105] The word Poumai is derived from two syllables 'Pou' and 'Mai'. Pou is the name of the ancestor and his descendants are known as Poumai. The literal meaning of Poumai means "People of Pou."[106] They have their own unique and enriched culture and traditional customs. The language of the Poumai is called 'Poula'; it has a myriad ways of expression and humour in communicating with each other. Poula is unique and is a very rich language. They have a number of festivals, songs, dances and other performing arts. Poumais are well known for their bright and colorful traditional attire and costumes with wonderful designs. Their accessories are also considered to be some of the best among the Nagas. Like other tribal groups, cultivation is their main occupation.[107]

Ralte: The Ralte is one of the small tribal communities; they inhabit in Churachandpur district of Manipur[108] but are mainly settled in the neighboring State of Mizoram. They belong to the kuki-chin group of people. They have their own dialect which is different from the Lushai language. The majority of them are agriculturists and they rear animals like cows, buffalos and pigs.[109]

Sema: The Sema[110] tribe is a recognized community in Manipur.[111] They belong to the Naga community. Only a handful of Semas reside in Manipur as their main settlement is in Zunhiboto, Dimapur and Wokha districts of Nagaland. There are also Semas in Assam and Arunachal Pradesh. Like any other tribal community in India, their main occupation is cultivation.[112]

Simte: The Simte is one of the tribal ethnic groups in Manipur.[113] They belong to kuki-chin family. Most of the Simtes are settled in Churachandpur district; there are also Simtes in the neighboring State of Mizoram. According to their tradition,

---

[104] The Poumai tribe was recognized as a separate tribe by the Central Government of India under the Constitution of Scheduled Caste and Scheduled tribe Order (Amendment) Act 2002. Before this they were known as Mao. The Poumai is considered an important tribe in Manipur since times immemorial. "Poumai Naga Socio-cultural Aspects," http://thohepou.wordpress.com/category/poumai-naga-socio-cultural-aspects/ (15 Mar 2013).

[105] Indra Kumar Telem, comp., *General Knowledge of Manipur 2010*, 34.

[106] "Poumai Naga Socio-cultural Aspects."

[107] "Poumai.com," http://poumai.tripod.com/ (15 Mar 2013).

[108] Indra Kumar Telem, comp., *General Knowledge of Manipur 2010*, 34.

[109] Sipra Sen, *Tribes and Castes of Manipur*, 61.

[110] The name Sema has been changed into Sumi however people continue to use the old name particularly in the government offices.

[111] Indra Kumar Telem, comp., *General Knowledge of Manipur 2010*, 34.

[112] Sipra Sen, *Tribes and Castes of Manipur*, 61.

[113] Indra Kumar Telem, comp., *General Knowledge of Manipur 2010*, 34.

cultivation is the main occupation; however, these days educated youth are not interested in it.[114]

Tangkhul: The Tangkhul[115] tribe is one of the biggest tribal communities who inhabit Ukhrul district in Manipur.[116] Most of the people of this community pierce their earlobes. Stunning and colourful dresses add to the embellishment of the culture and tradition of the whole of Tangkhul society. Following the tradition of almost all the tribal communities of the north-eastern hilly States of India, they are also engaged in agriculture which naturally makes their economy an agrarian one. They produce a lot of rice, cotton, millet, maize, arum, chilli, sesame, ginger, tomato, pumpkin, cucumber and beans. They also rear various animals.[117]

Tarao: The Tarao is a small tribal community. They inhabit Chandel and Ukhrul districts of Manipur.[118] Their villages are situated near the Burma border. They belong to the old Kuki group. Linguistically, they are closely allied with the Lushai tribe.[119] Their main occupation is cultivation. They do not eat or sacrifice mithan and dog but they do sacrifice and eat pigs and fowls. They are lovers of music—their main musical instruments are drum, cymbal and gong. Traditional Tarao group dance is well known.[120]

Thadou: The Thadou is one of the tribes among the list of tribal communities which are scattered in different parts of Manipur.[121] The Thadou people are rich in their culture and tradition with its plethora of folk tales, songs, dance and verses. Beautiful dresses add to the embellishment of the culture and tradition of the whole of Thadou society.[122] Their attire becomes the style marks of Thadou people. Their traditional dresses include a standard black shawl with red borders. Just like other tribes of the north-eastern States, the Thadous too have adopted agriculture as their chief occupation.[123]

---

[114] Sipra Sen, *Tribes and Castes of Manipur,* 62.

[115] Another remarkable feature of this Tangkhul tribal society is that they are revered by all the anthropologists for being the most learned tribes in the whole of Manipur region. The Tangkhul tribes can again be subdivided into several sub tribal groups, each having distinctive languages and variants. "Tangkhul Tribe, Manipur," http://www.indianetzone.com/8/tangkhul_tribe.htm (16 Mar 2013).

[116] Indra Kumar Telem, comp., *General Knowledge of Manipur 2010,* 34.

[117] Sipra Sen, *Tribes and Castes of Manipur,* 61-62.

[118] Indra Kumar Telem, comp., *General Knowledge of Manipur 2010,* 34.

[119] "Tangkhul Tribe, Manipur."

[120] Sipra Sen, *Tribes and Castes of Manipur,* 57-58.

[121] Indra Kumar Telem, comp., *General Knowledge of Manipur 2010,* 34.

[122] "Thadou Tribe, Manipur," http://www.indianetzone.com/8/thadou_tribe.htm (16 Mar 2013).

[123] Sipra Sen, *Tribes and Castes of Manipur,* 62-63.

Vaiphei: The Vaiphei is a tribal community. They mainly inhabit the Churachandpur district in Manipur.[124] Apart from this State, they have also settled in different parts of Mayanmar and Bangladesh.[125] As far as their adaptability to any profession is concerned, the Vaipheis are mainly agriculturists. They use forest products like timber for numerous occasions. Like other tribal communities, they do rear animals for meat as well as for cultivation[126]

Zou: The Zou[127] tribe is considered as one of the scheduled tribes within the State of Manipur as per the modifications of the Constitution of India, done in the year 1956.[128] The name Zou means 'human being.'[129] The Zou tribal community populace is being centralized in districts, such as Churachandpur and Chandel. Hunting and agriculture are the major occupations of the Zou tribal people.[130]

2.2. The Origin of Meitei

We now look at the Meitei community in more detail. There are two distinct beliefs popular among the Meiteis with regard to their origin i.e., Meitei as tribal origin and the other one is Meitei as of Hindu descent. British administrators and well known scholars like McColloch, Damant, Johnstone, Hodson, Pembertone, and Brown are inclined to trace the origin of the Meitei in Manipur valley from an agglomeration of Naga-Kuki Tibeto-Burman who surrounded the valley.

As far as Hindu descent is concerned, P. V. Bhattacharyya remarks that the Meiteis claim their descent from 'Babhruvahan,' the son of Arjuna of Mahabharata.[131] Looking into genealogy examining the origin of the Rayal Clan, T. C. Hodson finds that excepting Pakhangba, all other names are the Sanskritic names. Based on this fact he remarks that the tale of that account for the origin of the Royal Clan is ruined by the influence of Hinduism.[132] Hodson's position is also supported by Gait. He mentions that the degraded Brahmans who served

---

[124] Indra Kumar Telem, comp., *General Knowledge of Manipur 2010*, 34.

[125] "Vaiphei Tribe, Manipur," http://www.indianetzone.com/8/vaiphei_tribe.htm (16 Mar 2013).

[126] Sipra Sen, *Tribes and Castes of Manipur*, 63-64.

[127] The Zou language has become one of the major Indian languages of India. It has achieved the status of being incorporated in the study curriculum of the high schools and also some of the higher secondary schools of the State of Manipur. "Zou Tribe, Manipur," http://www.indianetzone.com/8/zou_tribe.htm (16 Mar 2013).

[128] Indra Kumar Telem, comp., *General Knowledge of Manipur 2010*, 34.

[129] "Zou Tribe, Manipur."

[130] Sipra Sen, *Tribes and Castes of Manipur*, 64-65.

[131] Padmanath Vidyavinod Bhattacharyya, *Mr. Gait's History of Assam: A Critical Study* (Allahabad: The Indian Press, 1908), 17.

[132] T. C. Hodson, *The Meitheis* (London: McMillan & Co, 1908), 4-5.

Meiteis invented a legend that the people were the descendants of Arjun.[133] Rejecting the claim of Hindu descent Pemberton concluded that the Meiteis are the descendants of emigrants from a Tartar colony who came through North-West borders of China.[134] Ethnologically Hodgson acknowledges that the Meiteis belong to Moi section of the Tai (Moitai = combined name of Kachin Chinese 'Moi' and Siamese 'Tai').[135]

The ideas of both the authors, i.e. Pemberton and Hodson, have been criticized by later scholars from the point of view of language, culture and tradition of the people. According to Hodson, the socio-political influence of the Shan rather than that of the Tai races has greater impact on the culture and politics of Manipur.[136] G. H. Damant remarks that from the peculiarities found in the grammar of all the three languages, namely Naga, Kuki and Meitei, as well as Lushai language, it is probable that they were derived from the same stock.[137] Hodson observes that structure and vocabulary of the Meitei language is similar to those of the Tibeto-Burman races.[138] Grierson places the Meitei language into Tibeto-Burman family under the Kuki-Chin group of languages. Thus, a relationship of the Meitei and the hill tribes is evident in the writing of the above scholars in linguistic context.[139]

W. McColloch deals with the tradition prevalent among both the Meitei and the Naga-Kuki tribes of the hills. He concludes that the Meiteis are a conglomeration of several distinct tribes.[140] Damant in line with McColloch gives the conclusive view that Meiteis are a combination of several distinct tribes.[141] McColloch further states that the Manipur valley was originally occupied by several tribes i.e., 'Koomul' (Khumal), 'Looang' (Luwang), 'Moirang', 'Meithei' (Meitei)—who came from different directions. The Moirang came from the south, the direction of 'Kookies' (Kukies), the 'Koomal' from the east, the direction of the 'Muring', and 'Meitei' and 'Looang' from the north-east, the direction of 'Koupooes' (Kabuis). The off-shoots of these tribes who are very similar to those of the Kabui, Kuki and Maring living on the hills, became dominant in the valley

---

133 Edward Gait, *A History of Assam* (Calcutta: Thacker Spink & Co, 1926), 270.

134 R. Boileau Pemberton, *Report of the Eastern Frontier of British India* (Guahati: Government of Assam, 1966), 37-38.

135 B. H. Hodgson, "On the Indo-Chinese Borders and their Connection with the Himalayans and Tibetans," *Journal of the Asiatic Society of Bengal.* vol. xxii / no. 1 (June, 1875): 1-25.

136 T. C. Hodson, *The Meitheis*, 10.

137 G. H. Damant, "Notes on Manipuri Grammar," *Journal of the Asiatic Society of Bengal.* vol. XLIV/part 1, no. ii, (June, 1875): 173-181.

138 T. C. Hodson, *The Meitheis*, 10.

139 G. A. Grierson, *Linguistic Survey of India*, vol. v, part 1 (Delhi: Motilal Banarasidass, 1967), 7.

140 W. McColloch, *Account of the Valley of Manipur and of the Hill Tribes with a Comparative Vocabulary of the Munnipore and other Languages* (Calcutta: Bengal Printing Co. Ltd., 1859), 4.

141 G. H. Damant, "Notes on Manipuri Grammar," 176.

at different times one after another. At one time Khuman became most powerful, on another occasion the Moirang. But ultimately the Meitei subdued all the others and gradually the name Meitei became applicable to all the tribes that got settled in Manipur valley.[142]

Based on the above traditions, R. Brown arrived at a noteworthy speculation. According to Meitei tradition, the Manipur valley was at one time covered entirely by water. In line with it, Brown hypothesises that when even a small part of the valley skirting the hills became suitable for cultivation, the hill-people bordering the area used to come down and cultivate and returned to their mountain homes after reaping the harvest. Gradually when the land mass increased some of them settled permanently in the valley. Later on various tribes from diverse ethnic groups who were residing around the valley came down and settled in different parts of the valley as the life in the valley was more comfortable. On the other hand, enmity and war amongst various ethnic groups for supremacy and ownership of land began in the valley. After struggling for supremacy and ownership of the land, *Ningthouja* tribe (a Meitei clan) ultimately overpowered and conquered the entire valley. Thus, those defeated tribes were compelled to pay tributes to *Ningthouja* tribe. Subsequently, in the course of time, they became part of *Ningthouja* society. Eventually an ethnic group developed which is now known as Meitei.[143]

As far as homogeneousness is concerned, McColloch , James Johnstone and Brown on the basis of dress[144] and Hodson from the point of other aspects of culture, especially marriage rule, finds a homogeneity between the Meitei and the Naga-Kuki tribes of the hills. The coronation ceremony of the Meitei was performed in Naga dress and the existence of *'Yim-Chau'* (big house) in the Naga style in the palace, the dress of the participants in the boat race are examples of some of these traditional customs that the Meiteis continue to preserve. Hodson remarks that two hundred years ago in internal organization, particularly in the system of exogamous divisions, religious practices, habits and manners, Meiteis were like those of the hill people. Gradually they developed from primitive culture into a relatively higher civilization, coming in contact with Shan, Burmese, Vaishnavism and eventually the rule of the British.[145]

Looking at the above stated two distinct beliefs popular among the Meiteis with regard to their origin, it is probable that Meiteis are of tribal origin. As far as the historical account of the origin of Meiteis as of Hindu descent is concerned,

---

[142] W. McColloch, *Account of the Valley of Manipur*, 4-5.

[143] R. Brown, *Statistical Account of Manipur* (Delhi: Sanskaran Prakashak, 1975, 1st edition 1874), 9.

[144] W. McColloch, *Account of the Valley of Manipur*, 4. cf James Johnstone, *My Experiences in Manipur and Naga Hills* (London: Marston and Company, 1896), 82-83. cf R. Brown, *Statistical Account of Manipur,* 10.

[145] T. C. Hodson, *The Meitheis*, 11.

it is a made-up theory brought by the Hindu missionaries in order to convert Meiteis into Hinduism. Hence, Sanskritization of Meiteis in Manipur valley will be dealt with in chapter four in detail.

2.3. The Early Meitei State (Mythology)

The Meiteis do not perceive history merely in terms of the factual, chronological events of the past but go back to the very origin of the Meitei being. It is hard to make out whether the kings, the leaders or the learned people were superhuman beings or mythical or sacred ancestors. Nevertheless, to Meiteis, the past is an integral part of the present. For every ritual that they perform, they invoke the spirit of their ancestors, arrange specified seats for them, offer food, and also bid them farewell at the end of the ritual. They remember their origin at every festival. They consider their God as supreme ancestor from whom they claim descent. Here in this section we shall be looking briefly at the mythological background.

2.3.1. Creation Story

According to Meitei mythology, there is a supreme being called Atingkok. He along with his consort Amamba (left-side of Atingkok) told Atiya Sidaba (Immortal Sky Father) and his consort Leimaren Sidabi[146] (Mother Earth) to create the World on earth.[147] Atiya Sidaba had two sons Asiba and Konchin Tingthokpa. Atiya Sidaba then told the two sons to go around the universe seven times to attain knowledge. While Asiba (the elder son), being physically stronger, literally went around the universe seven times. Konchin Tingthokpa (the younger one), on being advised by his mother, went around his father's throne seven times. Atiya Sidaba (Father), was pleased with his younger son's wisdom, and hence conferred the title Pakhangba[148] on him. Later he became the complete incarnation of his father. Since then, he is also referred to as Atiya Sidaba.[149]

The elder son Asiba was told to create the physical world. Asiba created nine highlands and nine lowlands,[150] the moon, stars and rivers. He is also considered to be the founder of agriculture. He was also named Sanamahi and became a household deity for protection from evils.[151] For creating human beings, Atiya Sidaba sought the help of Atingkok the Supreme Being. Atingkok opened his mouth and showed him (Atiya Sidaba) the world of living beings. With great joy, Atiya Sidaba drew out the living beings from inside the mouth of Atingkok. Another mythical version says that, when the task of creating the world was

---

[146] According to their belief, Mother Earth lives seven layers below the earth.

[147] N. Vijaylakshmi Brara, *Politics, Society and Cosmology in India's North East* (Oxford: Oxford University Press, 1998), 47.

[148] The one who knows his father and the one who does the wishes of his father.

[149] M. T. Laiba, *The Geography of Manipur*, 2.

[150] Nine highlands and nine lowlands are *Nonglen mapal* and *Leirol mapal* in Meiteilon.

[151] M. T. Laiba, *The Geography of Manipur*, 3.

complete Atingkok wanted humans to be made in his own image residing in it. Atiya Sidaba made an exact replica of Atingkok. Asiba then went inside it and gave life to it, while directional deities,[152] also considered as guardian spirits, took their places inside this body. Thus a man was created who acknowledged the supreme authority of Atingkok and venerated it.[153] In yet another version, Atingkok manifested himself in two beings—his right side became Lainingthou[154] and his left side became Lairembi.[155] They became the supreme *Pa* and *Pi*[156] for the whole world.[157] Later, the sky, water and other living beings were created; thus this universe came to exist.[158]

2.3.2. The Early Meitei Kings and their Administrative Roles

There are certain outstanding features of the rule of various Meitei kings. Some important kings remembered most by the people are as follows.

2.3.2.1. Nongda Lairen Pakhangba: Nongda Lairen Pakhangba was the first Meitei ruler who reigned in A.D. 33-154. He is remembered as the conqueror, since it was he who subjugated the other clans under his rule.[159] Pakhangba was the title given to him, because he was considered the ideal ruler. He also set up *Kacha* (male court) of which he himself became the head and *Pacha* (female court) and made his wife Laisana its head. Another eminent thing for which he is known is having divided the land into four *Pannas*[160] (four administrative units).[161]

2.3.2.2. Khuyoitompok: Nongda Lairen Pakhangba's son Khuyoitompok succeeded his father and reigned 110 years (A.D. 154-264).[162] He was the Meitei *Piba* (chief). He introduced the concept and class of nobility. He created 64 posts of *Phamdoms* (nobles), two advisory institutions under the control of *Phathi* (Learned men), introduced the post of *Keirungba* (in charge of the royal godown),

---

[152] Directional deities are *Koubru, Marjing, Wangbaren and Thangjing*. They are placed into four different directions.

[153] N. Vijaylakshmi Brara, *Politics, Society and Cosmology*, 48.

[154] It literally means king of gods, who is also known as Atiya Sidaba.

[155] Lairembi means divine queen.

[156] *Pa* and *Pi*—it means father and mother. It can also be understood as male and female in terms of gender.

[157] N. Vijaylakshmi Brara, *Politics, Society and Cosmology*, 48.

[158] R. K. Jhaljit Singh, *A Short History of Manipur: From 33 A.D. to the Present Time* (Imphal: The O.K. Store, 1965), 12.

[159] R. K. Jhaljit Singh, *A Short History of Manipur*, 13. Pakhangba reigned for 120 years. "History of Manipur," http://www.iitg.ernet.in/rcilts/phaseI/his_mnea.html (28 Feb 2013).

[160] It is administrative unit—four *pannas* were four different administrative units, namely Ahallup, Naharup, Laipham and Khabam.

[161] N. Vijaylakshmi Brara, *Politics, Society and Cosmology*, 52.

[162] R. K. Jhaljit Singh, *A Short History of Manipur*, 15.

the post of *Leikai Lakpa* (in charge of locality) and post of *Ningol Lakpa* (tutor for the royal maidens).[163]

2.3.2.3. Naokhamba: For the first time the term *Ningthou* (king) was introduced during the reign of *Naokhamba* (in A.D. 411-438).[164] This indicates the transition from a clan structure to a State structure, where the chief of a clan became the head of all the seven clans. This was a terminological addition that signified a status higher than that of the term chief.[165]

2.3.2.4. Naophangba: Naophangba (in A.D. 428-518) is recalled for his ethical administration. His authoritative declaration was that the *Kanglei Leima* (the chief queen) should not at any point make two contradictory statements and the king should not make two decisions for any one case. He further stated that, both justice and discipline should be maintained among the Meiteis. Whenever the *Maichous* (the learned ones) learnt of something said about the king or the nobles, they were to inform the king. The hands of thieves were to be cut off. Those with an evil eye on the king's wife were to be blinded. Those involved in treason were to be killed.[166]

2.3.2.5. Naothingkhong: King Naothingkhong (in A.D. 663-763) had nine wives, out of whom, three were childless. In a famous legend known as Naothingkhong *phambal kaba* (coronation of Naothingkhong), he encounters various regions, starting with the Langmais in the eastern hills and the Khumans, the Moirangs and the Luwangs in the valley are described.[167] He used to consult his nobles once every twenty days. Within the social customs and convention, he was capable of forcing his will on to the nobles. In consultation with the nobles, he used to award the *tangbal loi,* the highest title of the land to a warrior who had the capacity to arrest one hundred enemies.[168]

The further administrative roles of king Naothingkhong can be seen as follows. *Pongba tara*[169] (ten old men with great knowledge) were appointed by the king. The post was not hereditary. They were popular with the people and were also called *leiching purel* (leaders who lead people forward). He created a prime

---

[163] N. Vijaylakshmi Brara, *Politics, Society and Cosmology*, 52.

[164] N. Vijaylakshmi Brara, *Politics, Society and Cosmology*, 52.

[165] Ranajit Kumar Saha, *Valley Society of Manipur: A Cultural Frontier of Indian Civilization* (Calcutta: Punthi Pustak, 1994), 94-95.

[166] N. Vijaylakshmi Brara, *Politics, Society and Cosmology*, 53.

[167] R. K. Jhaljit Singh, *A Short History of Manipur*, 17.

[168] N. Vijaylakshmi Brara, *Politics, Society and Cosmology*, 54.

[169] *Pongba* means learned man with good reputation and *tara* means ten. In brief it is known as "ten old men with great knowledge"—they were to help the administrative works of the king.

minister's post called *nongthomba*, who was the head of the revenue department and the royal treasury and was given power to pass judgment in civil cases.[170]

Another important post was the administrative one of food and supplies which is known as *pukhramba*. Under the leadership of *pukhramba* the management and distribution of food was done and that was appreciated by the people.[171] *Khurailakpa*[172] was responsible for maintaining law and order in *khurai* by keeping watch over delinquent youth. He also acted as the guardian for social customs and conventions in that region. *Shanglen lakpa* (head of the administrative unit) were selected to look after each administrative unit. Out of these four, two were made part of the *ningthou pongba tara* (ten learned nobles) according to seniority of age. *Chongkhaba hanjaba* was responsible for selecting umbrellas of different kinds, for deities and senior dignitaries. The leaders of the seven clans had different coloured umbrellas. He had to check to see which of the officials and relatives of the king were entitled to sit on the red carpet, which ones on the *chadar* (seat for learned nobles) and which ones on the cushion.[173]

Piba (head of the clan) besides having physical strength and a knowledgeable mind also had to fulfill the criterion of not being born of the remarriage of a widow or a widower or of a foreign father or mother.[174] According to tradition, kingship was not always hereditary. Any powerful man within the *ningthouja* clan could become the king. The person had to be capable of receiving respect and veneration from the people. The council of ministers was the king maker. They were also the intermediary link between the king and the people and were much more popular with the people than the king himself.[175]

These were some of the elements of the early Meitei history as collected by old people. It was narrated from the knowledge that was passed on from generation to generation and from their own experience and perception of the rule of these kings and eventually written down. Later on in chapter four, we shall be looking at socio-political and religious conditions of Manipur valley before the entry of Vaishnavism, which will continue to highlight the early Meitei State from socio-political and religious backgrounds.

2.4. Traditional and Cultural Values of Meitei

There are changes and developments in tradition and culture of every society due to the impact of a number of forces that work in its history. Yet in the midst of changes and development, humans try to retain some of the basic age-old beliefs,

[170] N. Vijaylakshmi Brara, *Politics, Society and Cosmology*, 54.

[171] Ranajit Kumar Saha, *Valley Society of Manipur*, 119.

[172] *khurai* was a region—at present it is located in the eastern part of Imphal, which was an important administrative area during the time of king Naothingkhong. *Lakpa* means leader.

[173] R. K. Jhaljit Singh, *A Short History of Manipur*, 13.

[174] N. Vijaylakshmi Brara, *Politics, Society and Cosmology*, 54-55.

[175] Ranajit Kumar Saha, *Valley Society of Manipur*, 115-16.

customs, conventions, traditions and norms, unless the whole system is completely changed due to some social and political revolution (as in the case of Soviet Russia and China). Meitei society in Manipur valley is not an exception to change. The present-day Meitei society, for instance, has undergone rapid changes, due to modernization and other elements. But in spite of the changes, some elements of tradition persist in respect of beliefs, customs and institutions. This section in this study is neither comprehensive nor exhaustive but rather exploratory. It is based on the general observation of the traditional and cultural values perceptible in the traditional Meitei society. Some of the common values are as follows:

2.4.1. Kinship: In Meitei society, some of the social values are implanted in kinship relations. Value may be regarded as a variable in the kinship relation among members of the family. Thus, respect for the husband by the wife and of the parents by the children is a value relation to kinship. Wives carefully avoid calling their husbands by their names even at the cost of extreme disadvantage. They are generally loyal to the husband—loyalty being considered as one of the good qualities of a devoted wife in Meitei society.[176]

2.4.2. The Role and the Status of Women: Meitei women of Manipur, from time immemorial, have been taking important roles in the society—in the context of economy of the State, critical social issues and political sphere and in the framework of religious affairs. These practices flow down from the ancient bravery, patronage of culture, dedication, hard work and sense of responsibility bred into the Meitei women. They have been cultivated with the sense of responsibility and strong determination. Meitei women conduct most of the trades in the valley and enjoy high social status.[177] Captain E.W. Dun in his book '*The Gazetteer of Manipur*' wrote thus, "they are very industrious—most of the work of the country except the heaviest is performed by them. It would be difficult to find a more industrious woman in India than the Meitei women."[178] Mrs. Grimwood also spoke of Meitei women in her book '*My Three Years in Manipur,*' "The Meiteis do not shut up their women, as is the custom in most parts of India, and they are much more enlightened and intelligent in consequence."[179] Meitei women thus played a major role in the productive process of the society. In the political sphere Meitei women stood in the forefront of every movement.[180] A similar

[176] S. Shyamkishor, "Observations on the Value-System of the Traditional Meitei Society," in *Manipur: Past and Present*, vol. 2., edited by Naorem Sanajaoba (Delhi: Mittal Publications, 1991), 138.

[177] Chongtham Budhi, "The Ethnonym Meitei," in *Manipur: Past and Present*, vol. I., edited by Naorem Sanajaoba (Delhi: Mittal Publications, 1988), 72-73.

[178] E. W. Dun, *The Gazetteer of Manipur* (Delhi: Vivek Publishing House, 1957), 17.

[179] E. Grimwood, *My Three Years in Manipur* (Delhi: Vivek Publishing House, 1975), 58-59.

[180] Kh. Bimola Devi, "Manipuri Women: A Study," in *Manipur: Past and Present*, vol. I., edited by Naorem Sanajaoba (Delhi: Mittal Publications, 1988), 168-170.

feature can also be seen in the area of religious matters. The role and the status of Meitei women may very well be described as a mother politically, a wife socially, a hardworking daughter economically and a spiritual mentor religiously. The contribution of Meitei women in the above cited areas make the Meitei society a lively and meaningful one. It is generally understood that the women in this community have never remained complacent but are always active and vigilant towards the causes of family, society, community and State as a whole.

2.4.3. Solidarity and Cohesion: The solidarity and cohesion of the family is a highly desirable value. The father as the head of the family unifies the family. Obedience to the parents is a value on the part of the children. In Meitei society a cohesive and harmonious family is respected by all.[181]

2.4.4. Fertility: As per their tradition, people are expected to lead the life of householder. A man with many sons is respected in the society. The social status of a woman who is blessed with sons and daughters is high. Indeed, fertility is a biological survival value in this society. Aged bachelor and spinsters are not respected much. If an unmarried adult dies, a ritual known as '*choop-saba*'[182] is performed, so that the spirit of the deceased may not come back to the family and hence the person may not find rebirth in the family.[183]

2.4.5. Cooperation: In Meitei society, cooperation among the members is highly desirable. The spirit of cooperation is considered as a social value. A sociable person is appreciated and an unsociable one is universally condemned. An unsociable person is sometimes the target of an institutionalized form of social condemnation known as *'Nong laoba'*, which is a mode of denouncing a person's behaviour calling him/her by bad name. Such custom is practiced at the night preceding the Meitei festival called *'Yaosang'* (holy festival) in which everyone is expected to participate in the social work.[184]

2.4.6. Towards Sick, Old and Weak People: Another important aspect is the care for the sick, the old and the weak people. This aspect is generally regarded as a social value in Meitei society. Every '*leikai*'[185] has a *'singloop'* (club) to look after and also to perform the last rite for the deceased.[186] Regarding the '*singloop*', McColloch rightly remarks:[187]

---

[181] S. Shyamkishor, "Observations on the Value-System of the Traditional Meitei Society," 138.

[182] The demise of an unmarried adult in a Meitei family is considered bad omen, therefore the ritual known as '*choop-saba*' is a must so that such misfortune does not come back to the family.

[183] S. Shyamkishor, "Observations on the Value-System of the Traditional Meitei Society," 138.

[184] S. Shyamkishor, "Observations on the Value-System of the Traditional Meitei Society," 138.

[185] *Leikai* means locality. A big village can be divided into three *leikais,* i.e., *awang leikai* means northern locality; *mayai leikai* means central locality and *makha leikai* means southern locality.

[186] S. Shyamkishor, "Observations on the Value-System of the Traditional Meitei Society," 138.

[187] W. McColloch, *Account of the Valley of Manipur*, 18.

> Whether civilization in its advance proportionately increases the happiness of individuals may be questioned. It certainly tends to their isolation. A person in London might die all alone of sickness without its being known to or even much cared for, by his next door neighbor. This could not well happen in Manipore (sic). Each district divides itself into neighborhoods, who again divide into *'singloops'* or 'wood clubs'. The elders of the neighborhood settle all minor disputes occurring in it, and in case of illness of a member they tell off individuals to attend on the sick person, whilst should die, the wood club to which he belongs brings the wood for his funeral pyre. The sympathy of his neighbours and their attentions must have a soothing and beneficial effect upon the sick persons, and the depression of spirit to which, more especially in epidemics weighs down a people, must be considerably alleviated.

James Johstone also comments in relation to it, he says, "…the attitude of all classes was such as to excite admiration, there were no cases of sick being deserted and everyone appeared calm and collected."[188]

2.4.7. Language: Meitei language, which is called Meiteilon, has a rich vocabulary of polite and ceremonious words. Formal behaviour is one of the values of a cultured person. So, traditional Meiteis are polite and ceremonious in their dealings with the elders and superiors.[189] In this regard McColloch observes, "… Manipoories (sic) are ceremonious. They address one another by the name of the office they may hold, or may have held, or as younger or elder brothers."[190]

2.4.8. Hospitality: The traditional Meiteis are eager to entertain guests to their heart's content. This is evident from the social and religious feasts organized by the Meiteis at their homes. They do not hesitate to spend whatever they have on such occasions. Some of the feasts, organized by people in high social status are very elaborate. Such grand feasts bring reputation to the family.[191]

2.4.9. Reciprocity: Customary Meiteis, in their social interactions, observed some norms of reciprocity, some of the common ones are: i) One should not injure those who have helped them, ii) one should try to help those who have helped them, iii) one should avoid fighting with the juniors and the inferiors as far as possible, iv) one should not be rude to the weak, the infirm and the invalid.[192]

---

[188] James Johnstone, *My Experiences in Manipur and Naga Hills,* 194.

[189] S. Shyamkishor, "Observations on the Value-System of the Traditional Meitei Society," 139.

[190] W. McColloch, *Account of the Valley of Manipur*, 22.

[191] S. Shyamkishor, "Observations on the Value-System of the Traditional Meitei Society," 139.

[192] S. Shyamkishor, "Observations on the Value-System of the Traditional Meitei Society," 139.

2.4.10. Cleanliness: Meiteis attached great importance to cleanliness in personal habits. They take bath daily before taking meals, they usually put on clean white cloths, and they are also very particular about keeping their surroundings neat and clean. A dirty person is looked down upon in the society. Cleanliness is highly valued; therefore, they take great pains to keep themselves clean.[193]

2.4.11. Dance and Music: Meiteis are lovers of natural beauty. They are creative as well as appreciative. Their works of fine art give ample evidence of creativity. Majority of Meiteis were experts in dance and music. E. W. Dunn thus mentions that according to 1881 census, there were 5000 professional musicians in a population of little more than one lakh Meiteis in the valley of Manipur.[194] Learning dance and music was almost compulsory especially for the girls.

The present-day Meitei society is in the process of change. There is change in the structure of the society and corresponding change in the comprehensive standard which is called value. Yet in the midst of the process of change, we find in the modern Meitei society the processes that tend to maintain and revive the traditional and cultural values. The pace of modernization, however, is very fast and it is gradually sweeping away the elements of these traditional values from their society. As a part of the continuation of this section, traditional and cultural values of Meitei will be dealt with further in chapter five.

---

[193] S. Shyamkishor, "Observations on the Value-System of the Traditional Meitei Society," 141.

[194] E. W. Dun, *Gazetteer of Manipur*, 27.

Chapter 2

Christianity in Manipur (1894-1943)

Introduction

Manipur is a land of various communities all with varied practices and dialects. There are around thirty-two different communities settled in the State, divided broadly into two groups, namely the Meiteis and the tribals.[1] The tribal people of Manipur are classified under two major tribal groups – the Nagas and the Kuki-Chin.[2] Generally the tribals followed Christianity, whereas the Meiteis who occupied the valley were Sanskritized in the 18th century, and through a royal decree in 1705 *Vaishnavite* Hinduism was established as the principal religion in the State.[3] It was in this *Vaishnavited* society, that an English Christian missionary by the name William Pettigrew landed in Imphal on 6th January 1894 to start Mission work through education, and that was the beginning of Christianity in Manipur.

For historical connectivity and better deliberation, this chapter is divided into five subsections. They are: North-East India before the coming of Christianity; the early missional activity in Northeastern region; Christianity in Manipur; the genesis and endeavour of Meitei Baptist Association; an appraisal and finally the chapter ends with a brief conclusion.

---

[1] B. B. Kumar, *The Tribal Societies of India: A Macro Perception* (New Delhi: Omsons Publications, 1998), 201.

[2] J. N. Das, "Rights Over Land Among Tribes of North-East India" in *Tribal Situation in North-East India: Tribal Studies of India Series T. 170,* edited by Sarthak Sengupta (New Delhi: Inter-India Publications, 1994), 98.

[3] K. B. Singh, "Social Stratification and Mobility in Manipur" in *North East India: A Sociological Study*, edited by S. M. Dubey (Delhi: Concept Publishing Company, 1978), 62.

1. North-East India before the Coming of Christianity

The People of North East India (NEI), specially the tribals, have gone through a critical period of an unavoidable transition. This section attempts to give a synoptic view of the NEI and its people (particularly tribals) in transition with the inception of Christianity.

During the pre-Christian period, the people of the region were isolated from the rest of the world, having their own respective distinct cultures, customs, administration and religions. There were minimal contacts with the outside world in the long course of history. These contacts were made either while migrating from place to place before settling in the present respective settlements, or while raiding and invasions. There were exceptional cases of the emergence of a new dynasty in Assam and sanskritization in the plains of Assam, Tripura, and Manipur and insignificantly in the Khasi-Jaintia[4] hills. O.L. Snaitang affirms that the tribals' geographical setting was one of the reasons that made them isolated from each other.[5] According to S. M. Dubey, it was the consequences of ecological, historical and geographical factors that caused the rural and tribal communities and the different ethnic groups in NEI to remain isolated from each other for centuries.[6] There were some tribes like Khasis, Semas, Konyaks and Mizos who practiced chieftainship and had inter-village alliances. But most of the tribes were confined to their own village-world and governed the village independently.[7]

There were rare cases of inter-marriages, or political allegiance either for political refuge or coalitions to raid a fierce and strong village. But mostly they were hostile to each other and engaged in inter-village raiding. The driving force behind this raiding was not for the expansion of geographical territory, but to avenge for earlier misdeed by other village(s), for political reasons like subjugating smaller villages to make them tributaries, and most importantly for head trophies, which was regarded as the most prestigious trophy a man could achieve in a life time to show his valor and achieve certain social status. In this regard F. S. Downs comments:[8]

> Each of the many small tribes has traditionally lived in isolation from the others, and each has its own distinct history which is often quite

[4] Khasi and Jaintia people are mainly settled in Meghalaya.

[5] O. L. Snaitang, *Christianity and Social Change in Northeast India: A Study of the Role of Christianity in Social Change among the Khasi-Jaintia Hill Tribes of Meghalaya* (Shillong: Vendrame Institute, 1993), 39.

[6] S. M Dubey, "Inter-Ethnic Alliance, Tribal Movements and Integration in NorthEast India," in *Tribal Movements in India*, vol. 1, edited by K. S. Singh (New Delhi: Manohar Publications, 1982), 1.

[7] Wati Longchar, *The Tribal Religious Traditions in North East India: An Introduction* (Jorhat: Author, 2000), 104.

[8] F. S. Downs, *History of Christianity in India: North East India in the Nineteenth and Twentieth Centuries,* vol. v, part 5 (Bangalore: The Church History Association of India, 1992), 5.

> different from that of other tribes. Consequently, each tribe has its own culture and social structure. The situation is further complicated by the fact that among most tribes the village was an autonomous unit, a kind of village-State, which was often in conflict with neighbouring villages of the same tribes. Hence, among tribes like the Tangkhuls of Manipur, each village developed its own dialect which was intelligible to people of the same tribe belonging to distant villages.

The tribals, especially those residents of the hilly regions were isolated from the outside world. However, one observes their occasional contacts with them. The Nagas, especially the Lothas, Aos, Phoms and Konyaks, had occasional wars and peace treaties with the Ahoms,[9] a Shan community of Mongoloid stock from Burma who occupied Assam in around 1226 AD and ruled it till the British colonial government incepted in 1826.[10] There are oral traditions and folk songs that narrate the Ao Nagas going to the Ahom kings to settle certain disputes, which the village court could not solve. There are also traditions of intermarriage between the Ahom king Godabhar Singh and a very beautiful Ao Naga girl Sentishila of Nokpu village.[11] The Khasi-Jaintias also frequently married women from the plains. Snaitang admits that it is not known when intermarriages started and how they could marry women from the plains. But he also assumes that the women were part of the "loot" of the raids, which Khasi-Jaintia warriors often made on the plains.[12]

There was minimal contact with Hinduism, Buddhism and Islam, with little or no significant impact on the socio-religious life of the people, except in Arunachal and Sikkim where Buddhism made major impact, and in Assam, Tripura and Manipur valley which were impacted by Hinduism. The tribals continued to profess the traditional religion. M. Kipgen gives the account of the insignificant impact of the other religious communities upon the Zos of Mizoram, though the inhabitants of the territories bordering Mizoram were Hindus, Buddhists and Muslims.[13] Through commercial and marital contacts the Khasi-Jaintias also came into contact with the plain people and their Hindu religion. But it did not have significant impact.[14]

---

[9] Bendangangshi, *Glimpses of Naga History* (Mokokchung: Naga Patriots from Soyim, 1993), 4.

[10] S. N. Ratha, "Migration into Assam – The Past History, the Present Realities and Future Implications," in *Ethnic Groups Cultural Continuities and Social Change in North East India,* edited by Indira Barua, Sarthak Sengupta and Deepanjana Dutta Das (New Delhi: Mittal Publications, 2002), 49.

[11] Bendangangshi, *Glimpses of Naga History*, 4-11.

[12] O. L. Snaitang, *Christianity and Social Change in Northeast India*, 38.

[13] Mangkhosat Kipgen, *Christianity and Mizo Culture* (Aizawl: Mizo Theological Conference, 1996), 47-54.

[14] O. L. Snaitang, *Christianity and Social Change in Northeast India*, 39.

Surya Kumar Bhuyan,[15] in his book *Studies in the History of Assam* gives an account of the inter-relationship between Ahoms and the tribals living in the hills (mainly the Khasi-Jaintias, Garos, Lushais, Miris and Mikirs, Akas Duflas, Abors, Khamptis, Singphos, Mishmis and Nagas) and in the plains (Bodos). Though living in isolation, there was certain inter-dependence between them. Bhuyan in his account notes that the salt that came annually from the Naga Hills amounted to about 650 mounds.[16] But in the later period it was the Nagas who bartered their goods especially ginger and other vegetables for salt. Mackenzie in his reports gives the account of a staple trade of cotton between the Garos and the Bengali merchants under the supervision of the *Chaudries* (*Zamindars*) of the plains at principal *hats* or markets. In return the *Chaudries* realized their dues from both the parties. Cotton trade was one of the main enterprises of the Garos.[17] In most cases, the *Chaudries* oppressed and extorted the Garos to which they retaliated by incursions in the plains. As an act of punishment for the continual raids and offence, in 1852 the *hats* were closed down by order of the government. A complete exclusion from the plains was pronounced. Regarding this William Carey comments:[18]

> The measure did to some extent prove successful. It was found that the trade in cotton had become so materially a source of profit to the Garos, that the closure of the *hats* was felt as severe punishment.

We see that, though living in isolation, certain inter-dependence on each other existed. However, this inter-dependence did not give them any sense of solidarity. The inter-tribal contact also did not have any significant impact; it did not lead to a feeling of a sense of solidarity or accepting each other, rather each treated the other as strangers and regarded as taboo to accept a stranger. Even with the closest kin tribal groups, there were no sound relationships. In the case of the Ao Nagas and those left behind (the Sangtams, Changs, Yimchungers, Phoms etc) beyond Dikhu river in the process of migration,[19] instead of maintaining the kinship, there was constant inter-tribal warfare.

---

[15] Surya Kumar Bhuyan was the former Vice-chancellor of the Guwahati University; he is a well known Historian.

[16] Surya Kumar Bhuyan, *Studies in the History of Assam* (Gauhati: Srimati Laksheswari, 1965), 43-45, 52.

[17] Alexander Mackenzie, *The North-East Frontier of India* (New Delhi: Mittal Publications, 1994), 245-47.

[18] William Carey, *The Garo Jungle Book* (Tura: Tura Book Room, 1993, first published in 1919), 45.

[19] I. Bendangangshi & I. T. Apok Aier, *The Religion of the Ao Nagas* (Guwahati: Bendangangshi, 1997), 10.

1.1. The Beginning of British Supremacy

Since Assam[20] is the gateway not only for Manipur but also for most of the States in the northeastern region, it is essential for us to understand something about the administrative role of British in the State. Assam was under the rule of Ahom kings[21] for nearly six centuries. In the thirteenth century, the Ahoms under the leadership of Prince Sukapha entered Assam through Patkai range and established their kingdom in upper Assam after expelling the original inhabitants of the region. They slowly adopted the Hindu religion and customs (mainly caste system) and also the language of the natives. They developed a peculiar system of administration and their reign was prosperous and peaceful.[22]

During the last three decades of the 18th century, Gaurinath Singha was ruling the lower Assam at Guwahati. During his reign, a vassal chief Krishnanarayan raided his territory with the help of a band of mercenaries known as Burkandaz and subjugated part of the lower Assam. Seeing the threat of the invaders, Gaurinath Singha sought help from the British at Bengal. Since the Company had always wanted to establish trade relations with Assam, the company willingly assisted the Ahom king in driving out the invaders in 1772. In 1794, a non-interference policy adopted by the Company resulted in withdrawing the British troops immediately from Assam. And the consequence was the resurrection of the Burkandaz. Gaurinath Singha died in 1794 a defeated man. His successors Kamaleswar Singha and Chandrakanta Singha were mere puppets under the Prime Minister Purnananda Bura Gohain, who brought the whole situation under control. He also took measures to discipline Badan Chandra Bar Phukan, the viceroy at lower Assam for his oppressive behaviour and gross exaction. But sensing the plot against him, the viceroy fled to Bengal and sought help from the British but the request was turned down flat. He then approached the Burmese[23] king. The monarch, who had an intention to extend his control as far as the Brahmaputra valley, agreed and toward the end of 1816, a strong contingent of Burmese troops was sent to Assam. Thus, the invasion and subjugation of Assam (and even Manipur) under the Burmese monarch began. To be specific,

---

20 Assam is one of States in north-east India with its capital at Dispur located in the city of Guwahati. Located south of the eastern Himalayas, Assam comprises the Brahmaputra and the Barak river valleys along with the Karbi Anglong and the North Cachar Hills with an area of 30, 285 square miles. "Ahom," http://www.absoluteastron-omy.com/topics/Ahom (25 Feb 2013).

21 Appendix I, The Ahom Kingdom (1228-1826) was a medieval kingdom in the Brahmaputra valley in Assam that maintained its sovereignty for nearly 600 years and successfully resisted Mughal expansion in North-East India. "Ahom Dynasty," http://www.absoluteastronomy.com/topics/Ahom_Dynasty (24 Feb 2013).

22 Rebati Mohan Lahiri, *The Annexation of Assam, 1824-1854* (Calcutta: Firma K. L. Mukhapadhyay, 1975), 1.

23 The names Burma and Myanmar are used interchangeably.

the Burmese dominated and virtually ruled Assam from 1819 to 1824 during which mass killing and dreadful atrocities were widespread throughout Assam.[24]

The British came to the rescue to prevent the tyranny of Burmese troops. The British formally declared war against the King of Ava on March 5, 1824.[25] In the war, Ava armies were driven out of Assam, Arakan, and Manipur. British forces occupied southern Myanmar and advanced toward the capital, Amarapura (near present-day Mandalay). The Anglo-Burmese war ended with the defeat of the Burmese, who were compelled to accept the terms of peace by the Treaty of Yandaboo[26] concluded on February 24, 1826.[27] The Ahom princes were reinstated according to the proposal of David Scott, the Political Agent to the Governor General. He was well aware of the Assamese sentiment that they would not immediately accept the foreign ruler. But the Ahom Princes were mere tools in the hands of the British. And British Rule was imposed in Assam beginning from 1826. However, after two years of the expulsion of Burmese, there were several insurrections of rebellion against the British sovereignty over Assam.[28]

2. The Early Missional Activity in Northeastern Region

Stephen Cacella and John Cabral were the first Christian missionaries to tour the Brahmaputra valley of Assam in 1627.[29] They were Jesuit[30] Missionaries and their main purpose was exploratory, ostensibly to find a route into China and

[24] Hemeswar Dihingia, *Assam's Struggles Against British Rule: 1826-1863* (New Delhi: Asian Publication Services, 1980), 13-15.

[25] King Bagyidaw was an ineffectual king, but his general, Maha Bandula, influenced him to follow Bodawpaya's policy of aggressive expansion in north-eastern India. He conquered Assam and Manipur, making them Myanmar tributaries. The border with British India thus extended from Arakan on the Bay of Bengal northward to the foot of the Himalayan Mountains. "King Bagyidaw," http://www.journeysm- yanmar.com/historical_timeline.htm (25 Feb 2013).

[26] Appendix 2, the account statement of the Yandaboo treaty gives information about Britain's role in northeastern region. "King Bagyidaw." http://www.journeysmyanmar.com/historical_timeline.htm (24 Feb 2013).

[27] Hemeswar Dihingia, *Assam's Struggles Against British Rule*, 15-17.

[28] Rebati Mohan Lahiri, *The Annexation of Assam*, 59-60.

[29] Wessels, C. *Early Jesuit Travellers in Central Asia: 1603-1721* (Delhi: J. Jetly, 1997, first print in 1924), 131-32.

[30] Member of the Roman Catholic order of religious men called the Society of Jesus. First organized by St. Ignatius of Loyola in 1534 at the University of Paris, the order was approved by Pope Paul III in 1540. It discontinued many practices of medieval religious life, such as obligatory penances and fasts and a common uniform, and instead focused on military-style mobility and adaptability. Its organization was characterized by centralized authority, probation lasting many years before final vows, and special obedience to the pope. The Jesuits served as a preaching, teaching, and missionary society, actively promoting the Counter-Reformation, and by the time of Ignatius's death in 1556 their efforts were already worldwide. "Jesuit," http://www.answers.com/topic/jesuit (25 Feb 2013).

Tibet.[31] Later there grew up two Catholic churches; one dedicated to 'our Lady of the Rosary' and the other to 'our Lady of Guadelopce' at the Moghul garrison at Rangamati in Goalpara district of lower Assam in 1696. Very little is known about the early life of these two missionaries. The former was born at Aviz in the diocese of Evora,[32] became a Jesuit at the age of nineteen and sailed for India in 1614. On completing his studies he was at least for some time in Cochin.[33] The companion of his Tibetan journey, John Cabral, was his junior by fourteen years, a native of Celorico in the province of Beira;[34] he had joined the Society of Jesus in 1615 and came to India in 1624.[35] Basing his proposition on C. Wessel's *'Early Jesuit Travellers in Central Asia'*, F.S. Downs has maintained that the Christians in these two places might have come with the Moghul army of 63,000 men that Aurangzeb had sent against the Ahoms in 1669 or be the first fruit of the sixteenth and seventeenth century Jesuit mission to the Moghuls.[36] However, it is recognized that there were no permanent churches, and even the first Christian communities in these two places disappeared soon after Goalpara was surrendered to the East India Company by the Moghuls in 1765.[37]

2.1. Serampore Mission

After closing the episode of Jesuit mission, the first noteworthy missionary contact with North-eastern region was made by the Serampore mission of the Baptist Missionary Society[38] in the early part of the 19th century. Interestingly, the proposal for starting missionary enterprise came from the government officials.

---

[31] S. K. Bhuyan, *Early British Relation with Assam* (Shillong: Department of Historical and Antiquarian Studies in Assam, 1948), 3.

[32] Évora is situated in Alentejo (south of Portugal). It is the chief city of the district and capital of Alto Alentejo Province. The city was wrested from the moors by Geraldo the Fearless (Sem Pavor) in 1166 and flourished as one of the most dynamic cities in the Kingdom of Portugal during the Middle Ages.

[33] Kochi, formerly known as Cochin (the erstwhile colonial name), is a major city in the Indian State of Kerala. The city is one of the principal seaports of the country and is located in the district of Ernakulam, about 220 kilometres (137 mi) north of the State capital, Thiruvananthapuram.

[34] A port city in eastern Mozambique on the Mozambique Channel.

[35] Wessels, C. *Early Jesuit Travellers in Central Asia,* 121.

[36] F. S. Downs, "Early Christian Contacts with North-East India," *Indian Church History Review*, 5/1 (June, 1971): 69-70.

[37] Lal Dena, *Christian Missions and Colonialism: A Study of Missionary Movement in Northeast India with Particular Reference to Manipur and Lushai Hills 1894-1947* (Shillong: Vendrame Institute, 1988),18

[38] Appendix-3, a brief historical background of the Baptist Missionary Society. "Record of the Baptist Missionary Society – Collection 223," *Billy Graham Centre Archives.* http://www.wheaton.edu/bgc/-archives/GUIDES/223.htm (24 Feb 2013).

Clearly they expected that what could not be achieved by the power of armed forces could be gained by the message of the love of Christ.[39]

The officials in Assam also felt that Assam and its hills, inhabited by various communities who were not in the least influenced by Hinduism or Islam, offered the most promising field for the spread of the love of Christ.[40] Attracted by their simplicity of manners, and void of prejudices which were perhaps common among the plains people, the official believed that they could be rendered of importance to the British India. In order to achieve this objective, they reiterated the need for the spread of Christianity and to educate the people in the region.[41] James Johnstone, the then political agent of Manipur also thought in terms of the stabilisation of the British Empire and regarded Christianisation of the people as the only efficient means for reciprocally attaching them to the government. He therefore, resolved that a large number of Christians between Assam and Burma would be a valuable prop to the British administration.[42]

In December 1813, on the invitation from the British magistrate of Sylhet (now in Bangladesh),[43] William Carey of Serampore mission sent Krishna Chandra Pal, the first Serampore convert, to work among the Khasis in Sylhet who were evidently refugees from inter-tribal wars within the neighbouring Khasi kingdom[44] Over-enthusiastic, the magistrate even recommended outright baptism of these fugitives prior to proper religious teaching. The prospect was too rosy for Carey who had already undertaken the translation work of the Bible into Khasi language in Bengali script[45] with the help of a Khasi Pandit. Carey was thus confident that Krishna Chandra Pal could have no language problem and would be the right person to carry the gospel of Jesus Christ among the Khasis. Krishna Chandra Pal continued his ministry in Sylhet for eight months during which two Khasis and five natives of Assam were baptised.[46] The newly converted Christians

---

[39] S. K. Barpujari, "Early Christian Missions in the Naga Hills: An Assessment of their Activities," *Journal of Indian History*, vol. 48. (April, 1970): 427.

[40] N. K. Barooh, *David Scott in the North-East India, 1802-1831: A Study in British Paternalism* (New Delhi: Munshiram Manoharlal, 1970), 188.

[41] S. K. Barpujari, "Early Christian Missions," 427.

[42] James Johnstone, *Manipur and Naga Hills*, reprinted (New Delhi: Gyan Publishing House, 1971), 43-44.

[43] Sylhet is now in Bangladesh and is a major city in north-eastern part of the country. It is the main city of Sylhet Division and Sylhet District, and was granted metropolitan city status in March 2009. Sylhet is located on the banks of the Surma River and is surrounded by the Jaintia, Khasi and Tripura hills. "Sylhet: The Home of Saints and Tea Gardens," http://www.betelco.com/bd/sylhet/sylhet.html (25 Feb 2013).

[44] F. S. Downs, "Early Christian Contacts with North-East India," 70.

[45] Before the inception of Christianity, the influence of Bengali script among the hilly people in the region was considerably visible but with the coming of Christianity, this had been replaced by the Roman script.

[46] F. S. Downs, "Early Christian Contacts with North-East India," 70.

became the core group of the Christian community later brought into existence at Cherrapunji. Coincidentally, Cherrapunji that stood in the hills just above Sylhet became the first place of British administration in the district.

Meanwhile, David Scott, Chief Commissioner of Assam, in his epistolary communication to Bayley, Secretary to the Government of India on 17th April 1825, made a novel plan to the Calcutta council to invite missionaries to start humanitarian services among the people of Assam.[47] While thus seeking permission to negotiate with Bishop Heber at Calcutta for such missionary assistance, Scott argued that nothing permanently good could be obtained by any means other than by the gospel of Christ. It does not mean that Scott had genuine concern for the spread of the gospel; he perhaps took it only as a means for cultivating the ungovernable situation.

Reasonably optimistic about the success of missionary effort, Scott thus powerfully pleaded that even if government's support was not instantly forthcoming he himself would personally finance the missionary endeavour. The government according to the request gave Scott the necessary permission to contact Christian missionaries in his private capacity. But deeply impressed by the prospect of missionary work, particularly among the tribal people, he later on instructed the local officials in Assam to invite the Christian missionaries to undertake what they called a mission of civilization to humanise the uncivilised tribes of the North-East Frontier, stating that the government could give not only financial assistance but also salary to the people who might be employed in their capacity as missionaries.[48] Further to give surety of local officials' support, the Baptist Missionary Society (BMS)[49] opened a centre at Guwahati in 1829.

David Scott had not only helped the mission to establish a school but also deputed a British officer in the person of James Rae, the superintendent of public works for Assam to manage the newly established mission station in Guwahati. Soon Rae began to think that he was called to serve as a missionary. Hence, he resigned the company's service. But, aware of his incompetency, he went to Serampore for theological training for a year. Despite having received theological education and assistance from Ramchandra Nath, a native worker,

---

[47] Alexander Mackenzie, *North-East Frontier of India* (Delhi: Mittal Publications, 1989), first published in 1884, entitled, *History of the Relation of the Government with the Hill Tribes of the North-East Frontier of Bengal,* 253-54.

[48] N. K. Barooh, *David Scott in the North-East India, 1802-1831*, 177.

[49] The Baptist Missionary Society (BMS; originally known as the Particular Baptist Missionary Society for Propagating the Gospel among the Heathen) was established in 1792, largely at the instigation of the Northamptonshire Baptist Association. It was the first Protestant society to be founded specifically for the purpose of overseas mission, and its earliest mission was that founded by William Carey, Joshua Marshman and William Ward in Serampore, Bengal (now West Bengal, India), in 1793 the Serampore Mission separated from its parent society in 1827, reuniting in 1837. "Mundus: Gateway to Missionary Collections in the United Kingdom", http://www.mundus.ac.uk/cats/10/1092.htm (25 Feb 2013).

Rae's evangelistic work among the Bengali and Assamese inhabitants was hardly a success.[50] The Church which he had established did not fare well from the very outset. It was virtually dead. The arrival of a new missionary in the person of Rev. William Robinson failed to improve the existing situation. Eventually, finding no other alternative, Rae and Robinson left evangelistic work for government services.[51] Possibly they did not have a strong conviction which could ensure they could endure the hard reality in their mission endeavour.

Not disheartened by the failure of James Rae and William Robinson in the Brahmaputra valley, the Serampore Mission endeavoured to strengthen the work which had been started by Krishna Chandra Pal at Cherrapunji. In 1833, Alexander B. Lish, an Anglo-Indian missionary, followed by other missionaries landed at Cherrapunji.[52] The Khasi field was the twenty-first mission centre that Serampore Mission had opened in India when the mission was no longer financially sound. Evangelistic work and education side by side, Lish and Roe opened three schools in different places which were definitely beyond their means. Because of the financial constraint and inadequacy of human-power followed by the death of Joshua Marshman, one of the Serampore trio, the Serampore Mission decided to give up both the Khasi and Assam fields.[53] In 1841, the American Baptist Mission which had established a station in upper Assam took over the lower Assam, and the Welsh Presbyterian Mission stepped into the Khasi Area.

2.2. American Baptist Foreign Missionary Society

Ironically, the American Baptist Foreign Missionary Society (ABFMS)[54] in NEI was at first established not to evangelize the inhabitants of the NEI, but to make them strategic outposts in a campaign to evangelize the Shan tribes of Northern Myanmar and Southern China.[55] However, in the process, the Mission work turned out more favorably for the people of NEI. ABFMS wanted to open a mission field in China hence the society was looking for an opportunity to enter China. The society's interest in China had been greatly aroused by the publication

---

[50] F. S. Downs, "Early Christian Contacts with North-East India," 72-73.

[51] F. S. Downs, "Early Christian Contacts with North-East India," 73.

[52] F. S. Downs, "Early Christian Contacts with North-East India," 74.

[53] J. H. Morris, *The History of the Welsh Calvinistic Methodists' Foreign Mission: To the End Year of 1903*, reprinted (Delhi: M.L. Gidwani, Indus Publishing Company, 1996), 75.

[54] American Baptist Missionary Union (also known as the American Baptist Foreign Mission Society and today, American Baptist International Ministries) is an international Protestant Christian missionary society founded in 1814 in the United States. The Union is the oldest Baptist missionary organization based in North America. "American Baptist International Ministries celebrates New Baptist Covenant," *International Ministries* (8Feb 2008): http://www.internationalministries.org/read/4870-american-baptist-international-ministries-celebrates-new-baptist-covenant (25 Feb 2013).

[55] F. S. Downs, *The Mighty Works of God: A Brief History of the Council of Baptist Churches in North East India: The Mission Period, 1836-1950* (Gauhati: Christian Literature Centre, 1971), 14.

of Charles Gutzlaff's *Journal of Two Voyages along the Coast of China,* in 1834.[56] As part of central Asian strategy, ABFMS began to develop a strong interest in China. ABFMS subsequent involvement in Northeastern part of India was only an accident of being at most a part of this 'Asian strategy'. But ABFMS was not clear as to how the plan of China Mission was to be carried out. Their approach to China through their mission station in Bangkok being not practical, they started to carry out this project through the Shan mission field which was based in the northern part of Myanmar.[57]

William H. Pearce of Baptist Missionary Society at Kolkata (formerly known as Calcutta) informed the government that his mission had recently opened two fields at Cherrapunji and Gauhati[58] and therefore was not in a position to undertake a new mission field. He however suggested that the government should invite ABFMS from Myanmar.[59] Jenkins, Trevelyan and Pearce thus jointly appealed to the ABFMS in Myanmar stressing the great opportunities a mission station at Assam would provide. From time to time Jenkins would correspond even to the home board in America by making proposals for new work with offers of financial assistance. Jenkins thus exercised tremendous influence upon the working of the ABFMS in its initial period. On the other hand, the mission also had benefited from the support of government officials.[60]

The ABFMS readily accepted the offer because they saw in it the prospect of opening the gateway to the Celestial Empire at no distant future. According to them, the proposed station, which was hoped to act as a highway to Tibet and Western China, would enhance its value from a missionary as well as from a political and commercial point of view.[61] They hoped to accompany the government team to China via the Assam route to make enquiry about the culture of the tea-plant and then carry the gospel to the Chinese people under the protection afforded by the East India Company. It was this double interest both in the China Mission and Shan Mission which ultimately dragged them to open a station at Sadya at the extreme eastern part of the Brahmaputra valley of Assam.[62]

Consequently, the ABFMS immediately designated two of their missionary families, in the persons of Nathan Brown and Oliver Cutters for the Sadya mission station. The latter was a person trained in printing work, hence Jenkins provided two thousand rupees for the ministry of the printing work. The main objective of

---

[56] F. S. Downs, "Early Christian Contacts with North-East India," 74.

[57] Gammel, W.A.M. *History of American Mission in Asia, Africa, Europe and North America* (Boston: Gould, Kendall and Lincoln, 1849), 214.

[58] Gauhati and Guwahati—these terms are used interchangeably.

[59] Dana M. Albaugh, *Between Two Countries: A Study of Four Baptist Fields-Assam, South India, Bengal-Orissa and South China* (Philadelphia: The Judson Press, 1935), 50.

[60] F. S. Downs, "Early Christian Contacts with North-East India," 75.

[61] Dana M. Albaugh, *Between Two Countries: A Study of Four Baptist Fields-Assam,* 49.

[62] Gammel, W.A.M. *History of American Mission in Asia,* 216.

the mission was thus to use Sadya station as a base because of its connection with Yunnan in China. It is to be observed that the Sadya station was only a part of the Asian Strategy for evangelizing the Shans and then the Chinese.[63]

The vision of a coordinated evangelistic enterprise extending throughout central Asia made it difficult for the missionaries to sensibly organise the much humbler work of evangelizing the people of Assam at that point of time. Unaware of the realistic situation, they were more concerned with the Shan or Chinese in the distance than the people of Assam with whom they were interacting daily.[64] The Asian strategy was ill-planned because the Singphos (a tribe)[65] and the Khamtis (a tribe)[66] among whom they started working, had hardly any contact with Myanmar. Moreover, the Singphos and the Khamtis could not come to terms with the British. Therefore, political instability on the Assam-Myanmar borders greatly disrupted Brown's hope and made him think that the whole strategy seemed to be unsuccessful.[67] Because of the unfriendly attitude of the Singphos and the Khamtis, Rev. Mile Bronson began to look towards the tribal people of Tirap division of North East Frontier Agency.[68] That was indeed a fortunate move towards the tribal communities who were living in the forest without proper civilisation. Thus, Christianity began spreading throughout the north-eastern region.

2.3. The Further Spread of Christianity in the Region

It is crucial for us to have an overview on the further spread of Christianity upon the major communities in the North-eastern region before we take up Manipur. For this, the researcher has deliberately selected Khasi-Jaintia and Garos of Meghalaya, Aos of Nagaland and Mizos of Mizoram.

[63] Gammel, W.A.M. *History of American Mission in Asia,* 211-12.

[64] F. S. Downs, "The Establishment of the American Baptist Mission in Assam, 1836-1841," *Indian Church History Review,* 5/1 (June, 1972): 71-74.

[65] Singpho is one of the powerful tribes living in the plains and hills of Assam and Arunachal Pradesh. Their abode was in the hills Singra-Boom in Tibet and from there formed several groups. Out of these groups, one went to China, one to Burma (now Myanmar), and the rest came over to India and settled in the hilly region. During the first three decades of the 19th century, the continuous invasion of the Manns particularly in the conflict of the Sadiya Saikhowa battle most of the Singpho returned to their original home land Burma and few of them stayed back in the Patkai-foot hills. "Singpho," http://www.srimanta-.net/contents_l3.php?q=3&-ID=1&ID3=11&link_caption=Singphos (25 Feb 2013).

[66] Khamti is a tribe of the north-east frontier of India, dwelling in the hills bordering the Lakhimpur district of Assam. They are of Shan origin, and appear to have settled in their present abode in the middle of the 18th century. In 1839 they raided the British outpost of Sadiya, but they have since given no trouble. In 1901 the number of speakers of Khamti was returned as only 1490, they are now mostly in Burma. "Khamtis," http://www.1911encyclopedia.org/Khamtis (25 Feb 2013).

[67] Dana M. Albaugh, *Between Two Countries: A Study of Four Baptist Fields-Assam,* 52.

[68] F. S. Downs, *The Mighty Works of God,* 23.

Khasi-Jaintia: The inception of Christianity in the Khasi-Jaintia Hills of Meghalaya dates back to the early 19th century. The first Christian mission that worked among the Khasi-Jaintias was the Serampore Baptist Mission in 1813. As stated above, Krishna Chandra Pal of the Serampore Baptist Mission stationed himself at Pandua, a marketing center of the Cherrapunji Syiemship (Chieftainship/kingdom) in the plains under the protection of the British.[69] That same year in April, K. C. Pal. baptized the first two Khasi converts, U Duwan and U Anna.[70]

Garo: Like many other mission fields, Christianity in Garo Hills did not go very smoothly at the initial stage. The first Christian contact with the Garos was made by David Scott, the Commissioner of Koch Bihar, whose fervent enthusiasm for evangelization was motivated by William Carey when he studied under him at Fort William College in Calcutta (Kolkata). After he left Garo Hills for his new assignment as Civil Commissioner and the Agent of the Governor-General in 1823, he made arrangement for three Garo youths to study and sent them to Serampore College at his own expense. He also tried to get a missionary for the Garos, which could not be achieved due to the untimely death of Bishop Heber, the Anglican Bishop of Kolkata with whom the correspondence for Garo evangelization project was undertaken. At the instigation of David Scott, a school was opened for the Garo children at Singimari in 1828. Valentine William Hurley, an assistant apothecary at Chunar was appointed schoolmaster of the Garo School. But he soon resigned due to his inability to conduct the enterprise. He was replaced by Mr. Fermie, a junior teacher of English and geography in the Hindu College at Calcutta in July 1828. However, it was also disappointedly closed down with the death of Mr. Fermie in November.[71]

The next contact, after David Scott's futile attempt, was initiated by Capt. Jenkins. In 1837 he appealed to American Baptist Missionaries to establish a mission station at Guwahati especially meant to reach out to the Garos.[72] The appeal was turned down since BMS was technically at that time committed to the Shan work. In 1847, Jenkins established a government school at Goalpara for the Garo Children. Omed W. Momin and Ramkhe W. Momin both from Watrepara village were among others who enrolled in it. Omed and Ramkhe in later years played vital roles in the pioneering work of evangelism.[73] Regarding

[69] F. S. Downs, *History of Christianity*, 66. cf. O. L. Snaitang, *Christianity and Social Change in Northeast India*, 65.

[70] S. Pearce Carey gives the account of four sepoys, two Khasis and an Assamese baptized by K. C. Pal. S. Pearce Carey, *William Carey* (London: Hodder and Stoughton Limited, n.d.), 332.

[71] William Carey, *The Garo Jungle Book*, 38-41.

[72] Panichikkal, "The Garos," 253.

[73] M. K. Kuriakose, comp., *History of Christianity in India: Source Materials* (Madras: Christian Literature Society, 1982), 209.

their conversion Downs comments that the Missionaries themselves had nothing to do with the conversion of the first Garo Christians, Omed and Ramhke.[74]

Omed and Ramkhe were baptized by Dr. Miles Bronson on February 8, 1863 on the Sukhewar Ghat, Guwahati; along with them were an Assamese Bhupati, brother in-law of Kandura Smith, the pastor of Guwahati Church and a Kachari couple Kandura Bairagi and his wife.[75] The following year in March 1864, both Ramkhe and Omed obtained dismissal from the government jobs and committed themselves to propagate the newfound religion among the Garos. Within a few months of their work they won over a handful of people. Omed led them in establishing a new village called Rajasimla, while Ramkhe started a school at Damr; hence Christianity grew among this group of people.[76]

Ao: As far as Naga Hills of Nagaland is concerned, the first Christian missionaries to come into contact with the Nagas were with the Namsangheas. Miles Bronson and his group established the Namsang Mission which was however short-lived. After the abandonment of the mission in 1841, as early as 1847 a Naga named Hubi, whose tribal identity is not known, was baptized at Sibsagor. But unfortunately he died of cholera within a month of baptism. The next convert was an Ao Naga named Longjanglepzük of Merangkong village who was baptized at Sibsagor in 1851. But he was killed during a raid on his village to which he returned to visit after two years.[77] The permanent establishment and the first Christian mission in the Naga Hills (Nagaland) began with the coming of Godhula,[78] Rufus Brown and Edward Winter Clark. Clark, who came to Sibsagor to work among the Assamese in 1869, became interested in the Ao Nagas who frequently attended the Sibsagor bazaar. He, along with an Assamese evangelist, Godhula, who shared the same interest to evangelize the Nagas, thus became the pioneers of the gospel to the Nagas.[79]

Mizo: When the British government was gradually gaining control over the Mizo Hills, the Zo people were prepared to embrace Christianity through visions and dreams of two persons namely Selkhuma and Darphawka. According to this tradition, the dreams were about the true religion, which would be preached

---

[74] F. S. Downs, *The Mighty Works of God*, 47.

[75] William Carey, *The Garo Jungle Book*, 79.

[76] Milton S. Sangma, *History of American Baptist Mission in North-East India, 1836-1850,* vol. I (Delhi: Mittal Publications, 1987), 189-90.

[77] F. S. Downs, *History of Christianity*, 82.

[78] "Godhula, an Assamese evangelist, was the first to undertake a successful Christian work among the Nagas. After an exploratory journey into the hills occupied by the Ao Nagas in the winter of 1871,... There he gathered the first Naga Christian congregation...." M.K. Kuriakose, comp., *History of Christianity in India,* 213.

[79] F. S. Downs, *The Mighty Works of God*, 63-64. cf. Mary Mead Clark, *A Corner in India* (Philadelphia: American Baptist Publication Society, 1907), 10-15.

by men of white colour. It was this preliminary preparation that made the evangelization easier.[80]

The first missionary that entered Mizo Hills was William Williams, a young Welsh Presbyterian missionary working at Shella in Khasi Hills in April 1891.[81] He returned back after observing the possibility of evangelizing the Zo people. He appealed to the Home Board in Liverpool, which favourably approved. In 1892, the General Assembly of the Welsh Calvinistic Methodists formally adopted Mizo Hills as a mission field.[82]

3. Christianity in Manipur

To begin the history of Christianity in Manipur, it is worth looking first at the situation in brief. As has been stated earlier, there are around thirty-three different communities inhabiting Manipur which are broadly divided into two groups, the Meiteis and the tribals[83] of Manipur.[84] The tribal people of Manipur are categorized under two tribal groups, the Nagas and the Kuki-Chin.[85] The hill tribals and the valley Meiteis were put under different administrative blocks by the British. The king and the State Durbar had administrative power limited to the valley. Under the Manipur State Constitution Act, 1947, the hills and valley of Manipur were brought under a common administrative structure.[86] It is significant to note that the Meiteis who occupied the valley were Sanskritized[87] in 18th century by a Hindu missionary, Santidas Adhikary (Goswami) and through a royal edict in 1705, the *Vaishnavite* Hinduism was accepted as a principal religion.[88]

---

[80] Mangkhosat Kipgen, *Christianity and Mizo Culture*, 188-91. cf. Matthew Mattumana, *Christianity in Assam and Inter-faith Dialogue: A Study on the Modern Religious Movements in North East India* (Pune: Satprakashan Sanchar Kendra, 1984), 34.

[81] Chittan Rajan Nag, *The Mizo Society in Transition* (New Delhi: Vikas Publishing House Pvt. Ltd., 1993), 98.

[82] Mangkhosat Kipgen, *Christianity and Mizo Culture*, 191-92.

[83] There are thirty-two recognized tribal ethnic groups in Manipur. Indra Kumar Telem, comp., *General Knowledge of Manipur 2010: Complete & Comprehensive* (Imphal: Sharmila Telem, 2010), 34.

[84] Indra Kumar Telem, comp., *General Knowledge of Manipur 2010,* 33-34.

[85] B. B. Kumar, *The Tribal Societies of India: A Macro Perception* (New Delhi: Omsons Publications, 1998), 201.

[86] Ksh. Shyamkanhai Singh, "Hill Administration under the Manipur Constitution," in *Proceedings of North East India History Association*, Fourth Session (Shillong: North-Eastern Hill University, 1983), 216.

[87] The Sanskritization of Meitei of Manipur valley will be dealt with in detail in chapter five.

[88] K. B. Singh, "Social Stratification and Mobility in Manipur," 62. cited in. Lal Dena, *Christian Missions and Colonialism,* 31.

3.1. Accord with the British

The first contact with the British was in 1862,[89] when the kingdom of Manipur faced constant Burmese attacks. It was also a time of the threat from the deposed King, Ajit Sai, who was taking refuge at Tippera[90] and was trying to avail himself of the British help.[91] The King, Jai Singh, sent his Vakil, Haridas Gossain, on his behalf and signed an accord with Mr. Harry Verelst, Chief of Chittagong Factory on behalf of the British on September 4, 1762. The articles of the Treaty contained defensive alliance and trade between the two groups.[92]

The conditions of the Treaty could not be fulfilled till it was revived again in 1824–1825, when the Burmese authorities threatened the British frontier in the North-East India,[93] which resulted in the Anglo-Burmese War in 1825, which ended in February, 1826. A peace treaty known as the accord of Yandaboo[94] was signed between British and Burma authorities.[95] Under this accord, Article 2 provided Manipur the status of an independent country, with Gambhir Singh as the King.[96] In 1833 and 1834, two Treaties, Jiri Treaty and Kubo[97] Valley Treaty were made between the Manipur State and the British Government.[98] After the death of Gambir Singh in 1834, there were a number of unpleasant incidents on the matter of succession that took place.[99] This had further weakened the Meitei kingdom in Manipur Valley.

The first British Political Agent was selected in 1835, and from 1836, the Political Agency in Manipur was put under direct control of the Government of

---

[89] We are not looking in detail concerning the first contact with British here as it will be dealt with in Chapter Six later on.

[90] The name 'Tippera' is an old name, now it is known as Tripura, one of the States in North East India.

[91] K. Ibochuba, "Anglo-Manipuri Relations 1762-1947," in *Manipur: Past and Present,* vol. I, edited by Naorem Sanajaoba (Delhi: Mittal Publications, 1988), 98.

[92] "Articles of a Treaty between Hurray Das Gussein, acting on behalf of Jai Singh and Mr. Harry Verelst, Chief of Chittagong Factory on behalf of the British – dates the 4th September 1762 (Home Dept. Public 1762, 4 Oct., Nos. 2-3)" in *Manipur: Past and Present,* vol. I., edited by Naorem Sanajaoba (Delhi: Mittal Publications, 1988), 472.

[93] K. Ibochuba, "Anglo-Manipuri Relations 1762-1947," 99-101.

[94] Appendix- 4, "Accord of Yandaboo, February 24, 1826," in *Manipur: Past and Present,* vol. I, edited by Naorem Sanajaoba (Delhi: Mittal Publications, 1988), 471.

[95] V. I. K. Sarin, *India's North-East in Flames* (New Dellhi: Vikas Publishing House, 1980), 110.

[96] "Treaty of Yandaboo, February, 24, 1826," 471.

[97] Appendix- 5, "Agreement Regarding Compensation for the Kubo Valley, 1834," in *Manipur: Past and Present,* vol. I, edited by Naorem Sanajaoba (Delhi: Mittal Publications, 1988), 468.

[98] Alexander Mackenzie, *The North-East Frontier of India* (New Delhi: Mittal Publications, 1994), 151-52.

[99] V. I. K. Sarin, *India's North-East in Flames*, 110-112.

India. When the Assam Chief Commissionership was formed, the Agent and the officers of Manipur were placed under the control of the Chief Commissioner.[100]

3.2. Administrative Supremacy of the British

Following the demise of King Chandra Kirti, the son of Gambir Singh, in 1886, a dispute among the sons of the expired King over succession became a strong political issue. On September 21, 1890, Surchandra Singh, the eldest son who succeeded to the throne could not assert his authority and took refuge at the residency of the Political Agent. On the order of the Government of India, Mr. Quinton, the Chief Commissioner of Assam, led a strong contingent and visited Manipur to settle the disordered matter. But tragically, Quinton along with five officers were killed in March 1891.[101] That same year, an expedition was carried out and reached the capital on April 27, 1891. The supremacy of the British Government was re-asserted. The British did not capture the State as a mark of mercy but the State was granted to a native king, Churachand Singh. However, all powers of administration were centralized in the hands of British officers.[102] In regard to it, Ibochuba remarks:[103]

> It is evident that the entry of British forces into the State was due to the feuds and dissentions among rival princes of the State in their lust for power. It was in 1890-91 that the British appeared. Had there been unity and co-operation among them, the unhappy situation might have been averted.

The British occupation of the State resulted in establishing its cantonment in the heart of Imphal town. As a result, British civil power came to exist in Manipur and continued to control Manipur till 1947.[104]

3.3. Factors for Choosing Baptist Mission

As far as the coming of Christianity in Manipur is concerned, there are two major denominations i.e., Baptist and Presbyterian. The former was brought by William Pettigrew, the first Christian missionary in Manipur, and the latter was established under the leadership of Watkins R. Roberts. Pettigrew's work was in the northwest, northeast and in the valley while Roberts did his work in southwestern Manipur. The projected research work is focused on the Baptist work. We have chosen Baptist mainly because for the following reasons:

---

[100] Alexander Mackenzie, *The North-East Frontier of India* , 152.

[101] J. Bimal Devi & Dilip K. Lahiri, "Manipur: Palace Politics and Administration," in *Proceedings of North East India History Association,* Fourth Session (Shillong: North-Eastern Hills University, 1983), 126-29.

[102] J. Bimal Devi & Dilip K. Lahiri, "Manipur: Palace Politics and Administration," 128-129.

[103] K. Ibochuba, "Anglo-Manipuri Relations 1762-1947," 107-08.

[104] K. Ibochuba, "Anglo-Manipuri Relations 1762-1947," 111.

1) Baptist mission was the first Christian mission established in Manipur and William Pettigrew, the English Christian missionary who arrived in Imphal on the 6th January 1894 to start Mission work through education was the first Christian missionary to come to Manipur.
2) Meitei Baptist Association (MBA) was established with the help of Baptist churches which were planted by William Pettigrew and his followers under the American Baptist Missionary Union.
3) MBA is primarily Meitei-led and Meitei-staffed mission organization that functions among the Meiteis in Manipur valley.
4) MBA is the only Meitei Christian organization directly affiliated to the Manipur Baptist Convention (MBC), which is one of the conventions of the Council of Baptist Churches in North-East India, which is also the largest Baptist body in India.

Therefore, it is an expression of historical connection; it does not imply a lack of acknowledgement of those other denominations in Manipur which have also rendered valuable services nor does it involve an ignoring of the other history of Christianity in Manipur.

3.4. An Attempt to Establish Christian Mission

Compared to other neighbouring States in the northeastern region, the Christian gospel in Manipur was supposed to reach there much earlier. The American Baptist mission in Burma made the first attempt to establish their mission station in Manipur in 1836. Due to opposition from both the ruling princes of the State and the British Political Agent, no missionary was allowed to enter Manipur during this time.[105] In 1840, Rev. Jacob Tomlin, a former missionary of London Missionary Society in India suggested three places where the Welsh Calvinistic Methodist Foreign Mission Society, Liverpool, could send their missionaries and Manipur was one of them.[106] The unsettled political situation in the State was the main factor which prevented the missionaries from entering it.[107] Moreover the people who had accepted the Bengal Vaishnavite Hinduism during the early 18th century resisted the entrance of Christianity in this princely State.[108] At this juncture people in Manipur were extremely conscious of the social atmosphere and they were motivated by a hierarchical legacy of Hinduism from the earliest

[105] Narola Imchen, *Remembering Our ForeMothers: The Influence of the American Woman's Movement on American Baptist Women Missionaries in North East India*, Women Study Series No. 2, (Jorhat, Assam: Women Study Department ETC, 2003), 132.

[106] Lal Dena, "Christian Proselytism 1894-1949," in *History of Modern Manipur, 1826-1949*, edited by Lal Dena (New Delhi: Orbit Publishers & Distributors, 1991), 105.

[107] N. Basanta, *Socio-Economic Change in Manipur, 1891-1947* (Imphal: N. Basanta, 1998), 83.

[108] Lal Dena, *Christian Missions and Colonialism:* 31.

period of Indian history among themselves.[109] Because of all these results, it was not possible to establish a Christian Mission centre at that time in Manipur.

3.5. William Pettigrew the First Christian Missionary

The first American Baptist Missionary in the State of Manipur was neither an American nor a Baptist. F. S. Downs writes, "American Baptists became involved in Manipur by accident. A most fortunate accident perhaps, but an accident nonetheless … ."[110]

On 6th January 1894, William Pettigrew, the first Christian missionary, arrived in Imphal to start his Mission work with a school.[111] He was sponsored by a private society called Arthington Aborigines Mission Society (AAMS).[112] The political situation of Manipur was in a state of unrest at the time of his arrival. It was a time when King Surachandra Singh overthrew his kingship due to conflict among the royal family members. William Pettigrew was British, born in Edinburgh, Scotland on 5th January, 1859 and educated in Livingstone College, London.[113] He was at first a member of the Anglican Church but later on he was convinced of the inadequacy of infant baptism and therefore accepted believer's baptism from R. Wright Hay,[114] in Dacca,[115] Bangladesh, while he was working there as a Missionary under the Arthington Aborigines Mission. However, he remained an Anglican and worked under the same Mission till he joined the American Baptist Church at Sibsagar in 1896. Not long after he joined the Baptist Mission he was called and ordained to the Gospel Ministry. The same year in November 13, he was married to Alice Gorehame of Brighton, England. The marriage took place in the Lower Circular Baptist Church, Calcutta.[116]

---

[109] Lal Dena, "Christian Proselytism, 105.

[110] F. S. Downs, *The Mighty Works of God,* 73.

[111] L. Leiren Singh, "Reverend William Pettigrew and Modern Education in Manipur," in *Rev. William Pettigrew: A Pioneer Missionary of Manipur* (Imphal: Fraternal Green Cross, 1996), 7. cf. Lal Dena, "Christian Proselytism, 105.

[112] Appendix–6, Arthington Aborigines Mission was a private mission society of English millionaire named Robert Arthington of Leeds, England. Brian Stanley, "Robert Arthington," in *Biographical Dictionary of Christian Mission,* edited by Gerald H. Anderson (Michigan/Cambridge: William B. Eerdmans Publishing Company, 1999), 30. cited in. Elungkiebe Zeliang, *A History of the Manipur Baptist Convention* (Imphal: Manipur Baptist Convention, 2005), 19-20.

[113] Lal Dena, "Christian Proselytism, 105.

[114] R. Wright Hay was a Baptist missionary working in Dacca. Robert Fletcher Moorshead, *Heal the Sick: the Story of the Medical Mission Auxiliary of the Baptist Missionary Society* (Oxford: Oxford University, 1929), 35.

[115] During the British regime in India it was a part of India. After Indian independence in 1947 it became part of East Pakistan when it was divided into India and Pakistan. And in 1971 Bangladesh became a sovereign State and now Dacca is the capital of Bangladesh.

[116] Johan M. Solo and K. Mahangthei, comp., *Forty Years Mission in Manipur: Mission Reports of Rev. William Pettigrew* (Imphal: Christian Literature Centre, 2006), vi-vii.

Alice Gorehome, William Pettigrew's wife was born in London, England, on 20th December 1869. Pettigrew was born in the first month of the year and Alice in the last month of the same year. She stood four feet eleven inches only but was a beautiful girl with a strong faith in God. She had graduated from the Missionary Training School, West Brighton, England, that signified her preparatory training for the mission work which was to begin in the near future. Their marriage was not a sudden arrangement but a result of a long relationship and plan. Pettigrew and Alice first met when they were in the high school standard. Since then their relationship grew from strength to strength culminating in their marriage in November 1896 in Calcutta. Just before Pettigrew sailed for India on December 16, 1890, they spent time together about which he made an entry in his diary of the day, "We spent a quiet day. The Lord giving us strength to help us part! Alice was so beautiful and kept up bravely. God bless her."[117]

When Pettigrew arrived in West Bengal in 1890, his desire was to propagate Christianity among the Indians. However his interest in Manipur started when he met Meiteis in Cachar, but unfortunately he could not enter Manipur until A. Porteous, the Acting Political Agent, permitted him to open a school at Imphal, the Capital in 1894.[118]

3.6. Missionary to Meiteis

Pettigrew came to Cachar, Assam in 1891 when he met some Meiteis. So he was convinced to go to Manipur, but at that time the British power had not been fully established in the State. So he had to stay for another three years at Silchar to wait for the opportunity. While waiting, he had plenty of time to get training and learn Meiteilon for the mission work that he was about to begin for the people of Manipur. He mastered Meiteilon to a high level.[119] Thus, Pettigrew was able to prepare himself for the new field where he was going to work, and he was looking for divine guidance to open a way with great hope and zeal.

3.7. The First Meitei Christian

Pettigrew had received permission to work in Imphal by A. Porteous, the acting political agent during the absence of Maxwell. When he saw Meiteis in Manipur valley, he began to think that his call was to work among these peoples. So he became anxious to preach the gospel among them. After working for only six months, the British authorities, who were then administering on behalf of the minor Raja, decided against his work in Imphal, due to objections raised

---

[117] Johan M. Solo and K. Mahangthei, comp., *Forty Years Mission in Manipur,* vii.

[118] Frederick S. Downs, *History of Christianity in India: North East India in the Nineteenth and Twentieth Centuries,* vol. v, part 5 (Bangalore: The Church History Association of India, 1992), 84.

[119] T. Luikham, *A Short History of the Manipur Christian* (Ukhrul: North East Christian Association, 1948), 10.

concerning his preaching, and the baptism[120] of the first Meitei boy, Angom Porom Singh.[121] However, Major Maxwell, the Chief Political Officer, suggested he should remain in the State, working in the Hill areas, which were also under the British control.[122] He accepted the suggestion and decided to establish a Mission Centre at Ukhrul. But he was disappointed once again by the refusal of Arthington Mission to support his Mission any longer because of the Mission policy, which was not willing to establish a permanent Mission station in any particular place. Therefore, having no alternative, he applied for membership of the American Baptist Missionary Union in Assam, and to take over the Manipur field. His petition was accepted and a formal resolution was made in January 1896 to take over the mission field in Manipur.[123]

3.8. From Imphal to Ukhrul

As soon as William Pettigrew received permission, on 10th February, 1896, he began his work at Ukhrul.[124] He constructed a mission bungalow in Ukhrul, and started his teaching ministry.[125] Soon the Mission work bore its first fruit with the conversion and Baptism of twelve schoolboys of both Kuki and Naga communities on 19th September, 1901. The following year, three more members were added with their Baptism on 23rd February, 1902, hence the first Baptist Church in Manipur was established in Ukhrul.[126]

The arrival of U. M. Fox in Ukhrul in 1911 relieved Pettigrew by assisting in his work. Pettigrew spent most of his time in learning the local dialect and doing translation work. He also gave out medicine apart from assisting the State officials in the day-to-day administration of the hill areas.[127] As a result, he could not give

---

[120] Appendix 7, According to the personal record of Rev. Angom Porom Singh, he was baptized on 3rd January, 1896 at Imphal River by Rev. W. Pettigrew. Perhaps because of this, Pettigrew was asked to leave Imphal valley. Had he not been involved in preaching and baptismal work, people would not have objected to his stay in the valley as his educational work was appreciated by the people and he was a well-liked teacher. Therefore, many Christians particularly among the Meiteis believe that Mr. Porom Singh must have been the first person baptized by William Pettigrew in Manipur. Angom Moses Singh, former Mission and Evangelism Secretary, MBA, letter to the author, 24 March 2011.

[121] N. Debendra Singh, *A Study on the Introduction and Growth of Christianity among the Meiteis of Manipur* (B.D. thesis, Senate of Serampore College, 1992), 23.

[122] F. S. Downs, *The Mighty Works of God*, 76.

[123] H. Maxwell, *Unpublished Diary*, Political Agent in Manipur, Record of the Government of Manipur, 1895, 12.

[124] R. K. Ranjit, "Emergent Ethnic Processes in Manipur," in *Manipur: Past and Present,* vol. I., edited by Naorem Sanajaoba (Delhi: Mittal Publications, 1988), 87.

[125] Narola Imchen, *Remembering Our ForeMothers,* 133.

[126] Milton S. Sangma, *History of American Baptist Mission in North-East India*, 274-75.

[127] Tamsu Jamir, "Christianity and Tribal Ecumenism in the North East India with Special Reference to Nagaland" ((M.Th. thesis, Senate of Serampore College, 2004), 40-41.

himself to preaching. Meanwhile the State government appointed Pettigrew as superintendent of the first census of the hill territory (1910–1911) since he was the only man who knew the language of the hill tribes.[128] In early 1912 Pettigrew left for England.

Soon Christianity began to spread in the western part and Sadar Hills. The main credit goes to Lungkhobel Kom and the first converts of Kukis whose ardent efforts bore fruit with the establishment of several churches in the area. With Christianity becoming widespread, the Manipur Christian Association (MCA) was formed in 1916,[129] and the first convention was held at Ukhrul in 1917.[130]

As the number of Christians increased due to the missionary activities, William Pettigrew came back from England and continued his missionary work in Manipur. But his work in Manipur suddenly came to an end in 1943, due to his wife's illness. The couple went to the United States for medical treatment but unfortunately she did not recover. For some reason, perhaps connected to his wife's death, he did not return to Manipur.[131]

3.9. Other Mission Agencies

Even though our focus is on the mission and endeavour of the first Christian Baptist missionary William Pettigrew, it is helpful to look in brief at a few other Christian agencies, which have also rendered valuable ministry in uplifting the people, particularly among the tribals in the southern part of Manipur.

As the whole of Manipur hills was claimed to be the exclusive mission field of American Baptist Mission, other Christian missions of individual missionaries were looked upon as intruders, including Watkins R. Roberts[132] accompanying Dr. Peter Fraser, who came to Lushai hills in the southern part of Manipur in December 1908 and started a new Christian mission field. Thus, the claim of the American Baptist Mission came to an end.[133]

In the beginning, Roberts did not wish to be considered himself as a missionary[134] but undertook to act as dispenser and private helper of Dr. P. Fraser

---

[128] Lal Dena, *Christian Missions and Colonialism,* 34-35.

[129] Pettigrew was a member of the Church of England. Even after his baptism by T. Wright in India he remained as an Anglican. Yet he was associated with American Baptist Mission. So accordingly MCA was neither an Anglican nor a Baptist organisation at the time of its formation. Of course, MCA became Baptist in the later period.

[130] Lal Dena, "Christian Proselytism," 107.

[131] R. Constantine, *Manipur Maid of the Mountains* (New Delhi: Lancers Publishers, 1981), 249.

[132] Watkins R. Roberts was a Welsh Missionary who came first to Mizo Hills in 1908. cf. Lal Dena, *Christian Missions and Colonialism,* 49.

[133] Lal Dena, *Christian Missions and Colonialism,* 49.

[134] Watkin Roberts was never on the staff of the Welsh Presbyterian Mission but later on was deeply interested in its work. "Hmar Gospel Centenary: Southern Manipur Gospel Centenary (1910-2010)," http://hmargospelcentenary.blogspot.in/2011/11/birth-of-christianity-in-hmar-tribe.html (20 Mar 2013).

at the Welsh mission medical clinic in Aizawl. The turning point for him was in 1909 when invitation came from the chief of Senvon village, Kamkholen Singson, who had previously refused permission for Pettigrew to start mission work there. In response to this invitation Roberts visited the village together with some students from Aizawl. Later three Aizawl students[135] were sent to begin permanent work at Senvon. In the meantime Roberts organized what was called the Indo-Burma Thado-Kookie Pioneer Mission to sponsor this work.[136] His own mission was apparently not prepared to take it up, possibly because Manipur was recognized as an American Baptist Mission comity area.[137] Those three students arrived at Senvon in May 1910, in spite of the fact that the political Agent had not yet given them the permission Roberts had sought. For reasons which are not entirely clear that chief changed his mind again and asked the students to leave his village at once. They refused to go back and somehow managed to stay until 1913. During their three years of stay there, they were able to witness for Christ; as a result of their work, some 70 villagers became Christians and hence a church came to emerge at that village.[138]

In the same year, in 1913, under the initiation of Roberts, pastor Dala was sent to look after the newly formed church but he was ordered to leave the place by the political Agent. This action was taken at the request of Pettigrew who claimed Manipur to be solely the mission field of American Baptist. After extended but not very friendly discussions it was decided to draw the boundary between the Baptist and Welsh mission area at the Manipur-Cachar road.[139] Thus, Welsh mission work, in the southern part (bordering to Mizoram) of Manipur expanded and that is why we do not see a Baptist church in that area today.[140]

In spite of many controversies over the legal rights of possession claimed by the American Baptist Mission and the pressures laid on Roberts to discontinue his work, the Pioneer Mission (as it was known) began to grow with the efforts of the local workers. In 1919, Roberts renamed the pioneer mission as the North-East India General Mission.[141] With the change of time, other missions like the Roman Catholic, the Seventh Day Adventist, Pentecostal Church and other independent Christian churches came to exist in the State and most influential

---

[135] Three Aizawl students were: Vanzika, Taitea and Senvon. F. S. Downs, *The Mighty Works of God*, 166.

[136] F. S. Downs, *The Mighty Works of God*, 166.

[137] Lal Dena, *Christian Missions and Colonialism,* 49.

[138] F. S. Downs, *The Mighty Works of God*, 166.

[139] F. S. Downs, *The Mighty Works of God*, 167.

[140] L. Jeyaseelan, *Impact of the Missionary Movement in Manipur* (Delhi: Scholar Publishing House (P) LTD., 1996), 64.

[141] Lal Dena, *Christian Missions and Colonialism,* 50-53.

spread of Christianity took place among the tribals of Manipur.[142] With this brief background, we shall now continue by looking at the Baptist work in Manipur.

3.10. Christian Mission Strategy

Like in most of the Christian mission fields in other parts of India, Mrs. and Rev. Pettigrew also adopted various mission strategies in their endeavor. Some of the crucial areas that they undertook were: a) Christian mission through educational activity; b) empowerment of women in leadership through education; c) mission through physical healing; and d) mission through literary work. We shall now look briefly at each of these.

3.10.1. General Education

For the Christian missionaries, education and evangelism were inseparable.[143] In this regard D. Arthur Jeyakumar, a well-known scholar, remarks thus, "It is no exaggeration to say that it was the Christian missionaries who brought the modern system of education to India and made it available for all people irrespective of caste, colour, creed or status."[144]

Even before his entry into Manipur, William Pettigrew learned Meiteilon at Cachar. When he was allowed to enter Manipur after the Anglo-Manipur war of 1891, Pettigrew opened a school[145] at Moirang Khom in Imphal on 6th February, 1894.[146] In those days there were no schools. Even the children of government officials received only tutorials. The school founded by Pettigrew offered a kind of private tuition in its initial stage.[147] Six months later the school began to run officially. In consultation with the State officials Pettigrew began to formulate the educational policy for the State. Maxwell, the Political Agent, later on appointed Pettigrew as honorary inspector of schools by entrusting him with the power to draw up the whole educational budget for the entire State.[148] The schools were practically State sponsored schools, all expenditure being paid by the State.

---

[142] Sipra Sen, *Tribes & Castes of Manipur* (New Delhi: Mittal Publications, 1992), 28.

[143] Peter Haokip, "A Response to Dr. Thomas C. Joshua: Christian Impact and Conflict Resolution in Manipur," in *Impact of Christianity on North East India*, edited by J. Puthenpurakal (Shillong: Vendrame Institute Publications, 1996), 506.

[144] D. Arthur Jeyakumar, *History of Christianity in India: Selected Themes,* revised and enlarged edition, (Madurai: Author, 2007), 37.

[145] This school was named after Sir James Johnston and it came to be known as Johnston Middle School but now this has been upgraded to Higher Secondary, it is now known as Johnston Higher Secondary School. Jamini Devi, *Education in Manipur* (Imphal: Rai Pravina Brothers, 1989), 36.

[146] William Pettigrew, *Ukhrul Mission School* (Rangoon: American Baptist Mission Press, 1922), 14.

[147] F. S. Downs, *The Mighty Works of God*, 67.

[148] N. Basanta, *Socio-Economic Change in Manipur, 1891-1947,* 84.

3.10.2. Women's Education

Ever since Mrs. Alice Pettigrew arrived in Manipur, women's education was one of her main concerns for which she fought against conservative attitudes of the time. Females were meant for a life of drudgery in the home and in the field. Mrs. Alice Pettigrew took fourteen years to make any appreciable impression upon the attitude of the people, even when the parents had become Christians.[149] She remarked concerning the hardship of women's education in Manipur, "If the parents and the entire community looked with suspicion upon any attempt to educate their sons, how much more strongly they opposed the education of their daughters."[150] Even though attempts among the men to educate their sons were tough at the initial stage, it grew in due time, but women's education was strongly opposed.[151]

It was in 1908–1909 that she was able to interact with the girls. She walked from door to door, urging the parents to permit their daughters to attend the night school after the day's work was done. She used her bungalow as night school for the girls. Later she took the elementary education to the girls' dormitory. This was one of the greatest breakthroughs in her endeavours in the field of the women's education.[152] But in the valley among the Vaishnavite Meitei women, the privilege was delayed due to a policy of the Darbar. William Pettigrew in his account, "*Forty Years in Manipur*," remarks: [153]

> As for the Manipuri (Meitei) Hindus of the valley, it was not until the hill girls had progressed so far as to be ready for training at Nowgong, Golaghat and Gauhati that their opposition to educate girls began to decrease; only within the last three years have the Darbar members of the State reorganized female education and allowed girls to enter the schools established for boys, and then willing to allow villagers to establish girls' schools in the valley. As the women dominate the men in many ways, especially in their business transactions, we look for a great awakening among the Manipuri (Meitei) Hindus now that there has been this first break with custom.

Sina Khayi, concerning Meitei women of the valley comments:[154]

---

[149] Sina Khayi, "Contribution of Mrs. Alice Pettigrew in the Field of Women's Education in Manipur: 1896-1933," in *Rev. William Pettigrew: A Pioneer Missionary of Manipur* (Imphal: Fraternal Green Cross, 1996), 26. cf. Johan M. Solo and K. Mahangthei, comp., *Forty Years Mission in Manipur,* 89.

[150] Johan M. Solo and K. Mahangthei, comp., *Forty Years Mission in Manipur,* 89.

[151] Johan M. Solo and K. Mahangthei, comp., *Forty Years Mission in Manipur,* 90.

[152] Sina Khayi, "Contribution of Mrs. Alice Pettigrew," 27.

[153] Johan M. Solo and K. Mahangthei, comp., *Forty Years Mission in Manipur,* 90.

[154] Sina Khayi, "Contribution of Mrs. Alice Pettigrew," 31.

The Meitei women of the valley who embraced education much later than hill people, in spite of their rigid society came forward to embrace Christianity. A lone girl Ms. Kaboklei who was baptized by the missionary in 1916 in the capital town Imphal was a source of blessing. She had her previous teaching in the Welsh Mission in lower Assam. She carried on a little school for boys and girls in the capital and helped to form and encourage the group of Christians gathered from all parts. Later, she joined Mrs. Pettigrew in Kangpokpi Mission, teaching the primary students.

It is evident that the empowerment of women leadership through education which was brought by the missionaries in Manipur is remarkable.[155] D. Arthur Jeyakumar rightly points that "Christian missions were pioneers in the field of women's education. Since 1870, a large number of schools and colleges were established for women by the protestant missions/churches throughout India."[156] Likewise, it was Christian missionaries who have initiated modern education in Manipur.[157] To those women, it was like a daylight that brightens the dark corner of their lives—not only to be able to see their world but also to be able to take part in building their society with responsibility and leadership.

3.10.3. Freedom and Growth

In so far as the hill people were concerned, the government did not raise any objection to Christian truth being taught in the schools. On 10th February, 1897, the first school in the hill was opened at Ukhrul with 24 boys, whose ages ranged from 7 to 14 years. Pettigrew himself was the headmaster, head teacher and head in everything. Another 20 boys from a nearby village four miles south of Ukhrul entered the school later.[158] With the help and encouragement of the Political Agent, Col. J. Shakespeare, village schools were opened on a three-year basis in about a dozen villages of the tribe, and led by young men whose salaries were paid by the State. These students in the central school who were diligent and earnest enough to continue their studies and long enough to warrant their being made teachers, village writers, and *Iambus* (peons) for the State were given such posts as the need arose.[159] A large number of the boys who went to Ukhrul were content with the three years course which enabled them to get through, and owing to the phonetic system of spelling used in the school text books which had been

[155] L. Jeyaseelan, *Impact of the Missionary Movement in Manipur,* 60.

[156] D. Arthur Jeyakumar, *History of Christianity in India,* 46.

[157] Jamini Devi, *Education in Manipur*, 39.

[158] William Pettigrew, *Ukhrul Mission School,* 1-2.

[159] Lal Dena, "Christian Proselytism," 112.

prepared, they were able to write in their own dialect and used it for their own purposes in their own villages.[160]

Till 1912, no Kuki or Anal boys entered the Ukhrul Mission School. During 1912, Pettigrew managed to prepare two primers in the Thadou Kuki language with the help of two Kuki boys who were baptized in 1910.[161] The first convert among the Kuki groups was Longkhobel Kom, second clerk in the Sub-Divisional Office of the South-West area, who was very highly thought of by his superior officer Gasper; S. D. O. Teba Kilong was another convert who was the head clerk in the Sub-Divisional Office at Ukhrul. Another Thado Kuki boy brought up in the Ukhrul school was Sheijalut, who was for some time teacher at the new Secondary School at Kangpokpi and was also third clerk in the same office at Ukhrul. Ngulhao, an influential Thado Kuki, trained and taught at Kohima Middle English School, was another early convert who helped Pettigrew at Ukhrul School for some time and then took up evangelistic work in North-West area.[162] The educational work grew more and more among the hill people. Through this many came to know the living God and they became instrumental for mission work in Manipur.[163]

So far the Christian missions had emphasised only elementary education. Justifying this stand, Pettigrew indicates:[164]

> The rigid clannishness of the people, their great ignorance coupled with gross superstition, and their fatalistic beliefs in their animistic worship; the environment and shut-offness and shut-upness of the whole country, valley included, from the world outside, decided us on a policy of an elementary education.

Pettigrew further comments:[165]

> It is not necessary for such people as we have to deal with to have anything higher than a Middle English school grade. The great majority will for many years to come be content with an education that will enable them to write and read in their own vernacular. In spite of this conviction, however, there is the hope of a certain number being found willing, capable, and intelligent enough to accept the

---

[160] N. Basanta, *Socio-Economic Change in Manipur, 1891-1947,* 85.

[161] F. S. Downs, *The Mighty Works of God*, 33.

[162] Lal Dena, *Christian Missions and Colonialism,* 90-92.

[163] S. Jonah M. and K. Mahangthei, ed., *Forty Years in Manipur, Assam: An Account of the Work of W. Pettigrew, the First Foreign Missionary in Manipur Landed in 1894* (Imphal: Christian Literature Center, 1986), 7.

[164] Pettigrew, "Manipur State 1932-1981," *The Baptist Missionary Review, vol. III, no. 11* (November, 1932): 449.

[165] Pettigrew, "Manipur State 1932-1981," 449-450.

> training needed to make them the leaders of their several Christian communities, and to be of help to the missionaries in establishing the Christian Church in Manipur in such a way that they themselves in the years to come will rejoice with those who have laid the foundations in seeing a self-propagating, self-supporting, and self-administering body of men and women in their evangelistic and elementary education work, freed from the supervision and control of the missionaries.

One of the dreams dreamt by Pettigrew can now be seen in the form of Manipur Baptist Convention High School that makes a solid contribution to the educational efforts of the convention.[166]

3.10.4. Physical Healing Work

Wherever mission stations were established, hospitals also inevitably were established. The opening of the new mission station at Kangpokpi was another milestone. Concerning the work of the Christian medical service, D. Arthur Jeyakumar further remarks:[167]

> Medical work came to occupy an outstanding position in the ministry of almost all the Christian Missions which landed in India as well as of the Indian church. The terrible inadequacy of medical facilities in India induced Christian agencies to start hospitals and dispensaries both in cities and villages.

Medical mission work in Manipur was initially begun by Mrs. Alice Pettigrew even though later on other well-known medical doctors joined the work. Mrs. Alice Pettigrew, in her missionary training had included a course in medicine and nursing at Sussex County Hospital, England and she soon found use for all the knowledge and skill she possessed. Malaria fever, cholera, dysentery, tuberculosis, yaws, leprosy, smallpox, chickenpox, bronchitis, pneumonia—not to mention wounds from spears, axes and knives—all were widespread in Manipur especially in the hilly region.[168] At first Nagas, while willing to accept ointments for external application, were afraid to take any medicine internally, lest they offend the evil spirit; but little by little Mrs. Alice Pettigrew won their confidence. Her long, patient and very successful nursing of a young Naga blacksmith, who had been terribly burned in an explosion, did much to convince them of the efficacy of her treatment as well as of the love and devotion that lay behind her ministry. Thus, her medical ministry eventually came to be recognised by the people.[169]

---

[166] L. Jeyaseelan, *Impact of the Missionary Movement in Manipur,* 61.

[167] D. Arthur Jeyakumar, *History of Christianity in India,* 47.

[168] Johan M. Solo and K. Mahangthei, comp., *Forty Years Mission in Manipur,* 89.

[169] Johan M. Solo and K. Mahangthei, comp., *Forty Years Mission in Manipur,* 90.

There was a request made to the State government for allowing a second foreign missionary to be active in the State but permission was refused for many years. But the missionary and his people prevailed and ultimately the Manipur State Durbar granted permission for a second missionary family to come to Manipur on condition that the missionary must be a doctor.[170] At the request of Pettigrew, Dr. G.G. Crozier and his wife came to Manipur in 1918 from Tura, Assam and took charge of the newly established dispensary.[171] The mission centre was transferred from Ukhrul to Kangpokpi, a leprosy hospital,[172] and a dispensary was established. In the leper asylum many were healed.[173] Dr. Crozier brought a medical assistant from Tura, a Garo named Aban H. Momin, who later married a Tangkhul girl.[174] Pertaining to the growth and service of Christian medical work in Manipur, K. M. Singh writes:[175]

> After Dr. Crozier had severed all connections with the leper settlement at Kangpokpi, Pettigrew was much worried about a proper supervisor of the institution which was of course put under a temporary inspection of the civil surgeon until a new medical missionary was to arrive in October 1931. On the 10th November Pettigrew reported to Mr. Higgins that Walter R. Werilive, MD, who was the new Medical Missionary and his wife had arrived at Kangpokpi, as already understood by the Manipur State Darbar.

In this way the work grew in the State. Some selected young men and women of the hill tribes were given medical training from this dispensary for public health care and nursing. Hence bringing people into Christianity through medical work became an effective ministry. Many people accepted Christianity through the physical healing ministry. Later on this dispensary developed into a full-fledged hospital. After Dr. Crozier, Dr. Werilivs took up the medical work and many people were healed through their benevolent service. Another medical missionary who worked in the hospital was Dr. Ahlguist who was an eye-specialist.[176] Today, this hospital is known as the Kangpokpi Christian Hospital. Dr. A. Hrahsel

---

170 Government of Manipur, *Proceeding of the Manipur State Durbar,* (R), no. 4, 1917, 9.

171 N. Basanta, *Socio-Economic Change in Manipur, 1891-1947,* 93. cf. Johan M. Solo and K. Mahangthei, comp., *Forty Years Mission in Manipur,* 90.

172 Which was also known as "Leper Asylum."

173 J. Champhang, *Christian Life in a Tribal Context: In Manipur* (Ukhrul: J. Champhang, 1919), 50.

174 Lal Dena, *Christian Missions and Colonialism,* 105-107.

175 K. M. Singh, *History of Christian Mission in Manipur and Other Neighbouring States* (New Delhi: Mittal Publications, 1991), 345-346.

176 Lal Dena, "Christian Proselytism," 114-115.

worked as a Medical Superintendent for several years. Later on Dr. Gangte took up the responsibility of the Kangpokpi Christian Hospital.[177]

3.10.5. Literary Work

The missionaries considered the translation and literary work as a medium of communicating the Christian faith and also as the foundation of the future prosperity of the Church in any place. Consequently, Pettigrew never lost sight of the importance of translation and literary work.[178] He was actively engaged from the beginning in the preparation of religious as well as secular literature.[179] In 1896, two years after his arrival at Imphal, he translated the Gospel of St. John into Meiteilon and 500 copies were distributed among the Meiteis in the valley. Along with a host of text-books and catechism, the Gospel of St. Luke was printed in 1898. Later on, the translation of the Gospels of St. Matthew and St. Mark, the Epistles to the Romans and the Corinthians were done by arrangement with the British and Foreign Bible Society.[180]

After his transfer to Ukhrul, Pettigrew soon mastered the Tangkhul language and undertook the translation of the New Testament in that language by an arrangement with the Bible Society. In 1926, the Tangkhul New Testament was published, perhaps the first in a tribal language of Manipur.[181] Later on, Pettigrew studied the Thadou-Kuki language also and soon mastered it. In 1928, in recognition of his translation work of scripture in Meiteilon, Tangkhul and Thado-Kuki, Pettigrew was made an honorary member of the British and Foreign Bible Society.[182]

Besides this translation work, Pettigrew devoted himself to linguistic studies and research in Meiteilon.[183] When in 1923 George Grierson, Director of the Linguistic Survey of India, suggested that materials be collected and a monograph be published in archaic Meiteilon, the Political Agent in Manipur had to ask Pettigrew to supervise this research work. A vocabulary of nearly 1000 words of Meiteilon, a grammar of about 50 pages and the translation of two selected scripts—one from historical sources and another from linguistic sources, were prepared. In appreciation of his research in the languages of Manipur and archaic Meiteilon, Pettigrew was made one of the members of the Royal Asiatic Society of Bengal in 1930. Later, the General Secretary of the Society commented that

---

[177] Interview with P. Haokip, Kangpokpi Mission Hospital Chaplain, Kangpokpi, Manipur, 10th May 2010.

[178] S. Jonah M. and K. Mahangthei, ed., *Forty Years in Manipur, Assam,* 23.

[179] Lal Dena, *Christian Missions and Colonialism,* 107-109.

[180] Jajo Champhang, *The Indigenisation and Contextualisation of Christian Life in a Tribal Context: In Manipur State of North-East India* (Ukhrul: C. Jajo, 1990), 27.

[181] N. Basanta, *Socio-Economic Change in Manipur, 1891-1947,* 96.

[182] Lal Dena, "Christian Proselytism," 115-116.

[183] Jajo Champhang, *The Indigenisation and Contextualisation*, 26.

Pettigrew's work in Manipur was a great contribution to philological science.[184] Although, the mission centre was in the hill area of Manipur, Pettigrew did not neglect the evangelistic work in the valley areas. He continued to endeavour to win the Meiteis to Christ as well. Thus, early in 1916 a church in tribal areas was established. Soon the second Baptist church (Meitei Baptist Church) in Manipur was organised by Pettigrew at Kaisamthong in Imphal. However, this church did not grow, because the Meiteis already adhered to the philosophy of Hinduism.[185] There were only five Christian families in Imphal at that juncture. Later, seeing the condition of the decline of evangelism work among the Meiteis in the valley, Pettigrew and other local Christians focused their attention more on the hill people.[186]

4. The Genesis and Endeavour of Meitei Baptist Association (1982-2008)[187]

With the arrival of, and the work of, foreign missionaries in Manipur most of the tribal people in the districts of Ukhrul, Senapati, Tamenglong and Chandel accepted Christianity. But among the Meiteis, except Angom Porom Singh and his family, there was no other Meitei Christian family. From 1958–1960, K. Mingthing and Angom Dharma Singh[188] initiated evangelistic work among the Meiteis in Manipur valley. In fact, two of them were pioneers in the work of evangelism among the Meiteis. From 1960–1961, the Council of Baptist Churches in North East India (CBCNEI) sent Masangthei as a valley Missionary and he was based at Wangjing mission centre[189] in Thoubal District. He was an energetic preacher of the Christian gospel; spending most of his time in preaching and teaching the Bible.[190] After toiling for around ten years, Paonam Bihari Singh of Wangjing became a Christian in 1970. In the meantime, with the help of CBCNEI, Wangjing Mission Centre was able to own a piece of land and that was indeed a remarkable achievement.[191]

Wangjing having become the main Mission Centre for Meiteis, evangelistic work was continued in various places in the valley for a considerable amount

---

184 Lal Dena, *Christian Missions and Colonialism,* 107-108.

185 N. Basanta, *Socio-Economic Change in Manipur, 1891-1947,* 87.

186 R. R. Lolly, *The Baptist Church in Manipur* (Imphal: R.R. Lolly, 1985), 39.

187 Meitei Baptist Association was established in 1982 and celebrated its silver jubilee in 2008. Hence, our main focus on Meitei Christianity in Manipur valley is within this period.

188 Angom Dharma Singh is a son of Angom Porom Singh, who is considered to be the first Christian in Manipur. According to Angom Moses Singh, a son of Dharma Singh, Dharma Singh was a sincere and hard working person. Angom Moses Singh, Mission Coordinator, Manipur Baptist Convention, Imphal, letter to the author, 26 March 2010.

189 Wangjing mission centre became the centre for Meitei Baptist Association (MBA) later on. The present MBA still stands at Wangjing.

190 Elungkiebe Zeliang, *A History of the Manipur Baptist Convention,* 177.

191 *Souvenir: Meitei Baptist Association Silver Jubilee Celebration, 1982-2008* (Khurai Lomlong Keithel: MBA, 2008), 7.

of time. But the response was negative in nature.[192] In 1982 Masangthei retired from the missionary work.[193] In 1960–1982 during his leadership and evangelistic work, seven Meitei churches emerged. All the emerged Meiteis churches were like a small house fellowship, consisting of about seven to fifteen members each and most of the members were not from the general Meiteis.[194] After toiling for more than 20 years exclusively among the general Meiteis, the nature of the response of Christianity was rejection.[195]

Even though Meitei Christians were few in number, they wanted to have their separate Association which they thought would be effective in evangelistic work in the valley.[196] Therefore, Meitei Christian leaders came together to have a discussion concerning the formation of a separate Meitei Baptist body.[197] Hence, on 21st November, 1982, Meitei Christians assembled at Wangjing Mission Centre and discussed the matter. The assembly unanimously decided to form a separate association for Meiteis. As an upshot of the assembly, in the same year Meitei Baptist Association (MBA) officially came into existence.[198]

Until this time the Wangjing Mission field was looked after by CBCNEI by sending Missionaries. Soon CBCNEI felt the need to hand over the responsibility to the Manipur Baptist Convention (MBC). Consequently, Meitei Mission field has become an official field of MBC. In January, 1983 during the MBC Executive assembly Th. Kumar Singh of Langthabal Lep Makha-leikai[199] was selected to be the first field secretary of MBA. In the same year, in the month of February, during the CBCNEI Executive meeting, the installation service of Th. Kumar Singh was held.[200]

4.1. First Ministerial Team of Meitei Baptist Association

As an association, the first ministerial team of Meitei Baptist Association started its mission and evangelism work among the Meiteis in 1983. The below mentioned

---

[192] Masangthei, Retired Missionary, Council of Baptist Churches in North East India, Panbazar, Guwahati, letter to the author, 29 January 2010.

[193] Elungkiebe Zeliang, *A History of the Manipur Baptist Convention*, 177.

[194] *Souvenir: Meitei Baptist Association,* 8.

[195] Masangthei, Retired Missionary, Council of Baptist Churches in North East India. cited in. Thiyam Kumar. *Manipurgi Christian Lamyanba / The Christian Pioneer of Manipur*. Khurai Lamlong: MBA, 2008, 3.

[196] Paonam Bihari Singh, Early Meitei Christian and Deacon, Wangjing Centre Baptist Church, Wangjing, letter to the author, 13 February 2010.

[197] Masangthei, Retired Missionary.

[198] *Souvenir: Meitei Baptist Association,* 8. cf. Elungkiebe Zeliang has wrongly put the year of establishment. Elungkiebe Zeliang, *A History of the Manipur Baptist Convention*, 177.

[199] A Meitei locality, located in the South-Western part of Imphal West district, which is around 8 kilometers away from Imphal.

[200] *Souvenir: Meitei Baptist Association*, 8.

office bearers served from 1983-1993.[201] This was indeed a historic beginning for Meitei Christians because for the first time in the history of Meitei Christianity—they could see their own association and that it was led by their own people.[202] However there were only 214 Christian members[203] at that time.[204]

Office Bearers[205]

Designation	Person	Duration
Field Secretary	Th. Kumar Singh	1983-1993
Treasurer	N. Nobin Singh	1983-1993
President	A. Thaningjao Singh	1983-1993
Office Assistant Cum-Youth Secretary	Kh. Chaoba Singh	1983-1993
Vice President	H. Devendro Singh	1983-1993

In spite of the disappointment, MBA under the supervision of MBC did not give up the hope of winning general Meiteis for Christ in the valley. Thus, they continued to toil among this group of people.[206] Some of the key leaders and evangelists who directly got involved in the task were: Th. Kumar Singh, A. Thaningjao Singh, H. Devendro Singh, N. Nobin Singh, Kh. Chaoba Singh, N. Woleng, Hormi Makhangwo, Honpam Zimik, Ngaranmi Risom etc.[207]

4.2. Second Ministerial Team of Meitei Baptist Association

In 1993, Meitei Baptist Association was given full-fledged association by the Manipur Baptist Convention. Thus, the post of field secretaryship was changed into executive secretary. Along with this, other departments were also added. The following chart gives the detail.

[201] Th. Kumar Singh, Former Field Secretary, Meitei Baptist Association, Wangjing, letter to the author, 8 March 2010.

[202] Paonam Bihari Singh, Early Meitei Christian and Deacon. cited in. Thiyam Kumar. *Manipurgi Christian Lamyanba,* 4.

[203] According to Elungkiebe Zeliang, number of Meitei Christians at that time was just 200. Elungkiebe Zeliang, *A History of the Manipur Baptist Convention*, 177.

[204] *Souvenir: Meitei Baptist Association*, 8. Thiyam Kumar. *Meitei Baptist Association*. Wabagai: A. Lakhop & S. Beikul, 1993, 6.

[205] *Souvenir: Meitei Baptist Association*, 9.

[206] A. Thaningjao Singh, Former President, Meitei Baptist Association, Wangjing, letter to the author, 25 February 2010.

[207] Th. Kumar Singh, Former Field Secretary.

Office Bearers of the Full-fledged MBA[208]

Designation	Person	Duration
Executive Secretary	Th. Kumar Singh	1993-1997
Mission and Evangelism Secretary	Hormi Makangwo	1993-1997
women Secretary	Mrs. Dharmeshwari	1993-1997
Youth Secretary	N. Deben Singh	1993-1997
Finance Secretary	M. Madhuchandra K. Rajamohon Agnom Moses	1993 1994 1995-1997
Centre Pastor	Honpam Zimik	1992-1997

The newly formed team, under the leadership ofTh. Kumar Singh continued the mission and evangelism work throughout Manipur valley. Full of enthusiasm, they, along with local Christians, performed open-air preaching and many forms of evangelism, including door to door, personal, literary and audiovisual, in all the important places, but unfortunately instead of responding positively to the gospel, those evangelists were harassed and often persecuted.[209]

4.3. Third Ministerial Team of Meitei Baptist Association

Towards the end of 1997 total estimated number of Meitei Christians was around 1500.[210] Due to the human power, financial involvement and duration, people, particularly the tribal Christian leaders, expected much more than the figure given above. As they were the main sponsoring body of MBA and her ministry,[211] most of the people thought that due to poor leadership, Christianity was not growing as expected; therefore, they proposed new leadership at the MBA level. Thus, leadership of MBA was changed in 1998.[212] New MBA leaders were led by N. Debendra Singh—following chart gives the detail of new leadership.

---

[208] Souvenir: Meitei Baptist Association, 9. Thiyam Kumar. *Meitei Baptist Association*, 6-8.

[209] Hormi Makangwo, Former Mission and Evangelism Secretary, Meitei Baptist Association, Wangjing, letter to the author, 14 March 2010.

[210] Most of the Meitei Christians were not from the general caste. Th. Kumar Singh, Former Field Secretary.

[211] Ngaranmi Risom, Former Mission and Evangelism Secretary, Manipur Baptist Convention, Imphal, letter to the author, May 2008.

[212] Hormi Makangwo, Former Mission and Evangelism Secretary.

Third Ministerial Team Members[213]

Designation	Person	Duration
Executive Secretary	N. Debendra Singh	1998-2008
Mission and Evangelism Secretary	Angom Moses	1998-2008
Women Secretary	Th. Mema Devi Th. Susila Devi	1998-2000 2000-2008
Youth Secretary	K. Rajamohol Meitei Ksh. Dilip O. Bimol Singh	1998-2003 2003-2006 2006-2008
Finance Secretary	M. Ibohanbi Meitei Y. Premchandra	1998-2000 2000-2008
Centre Pastor	Honpam Zimik	1992-1997
Caretaker	L. Khami W. Surjit	1998-2005 2006-2008

Under the leadership of N. Debendra Singh, MBA was able to function in its administrative work but could not do effective mission and evangelism work due to opposition and rejection by the general Meiteis.[214] Like the former ministerial team, his team also could not achieve significant ministry. In 2005, MBA had around 2500 members.[215]

In 2008, MBA celebrated its silver jubilee at MBA mission compound, Wangjing, Thoubal District. By the time of the silver jubilee celebration, MBA had around 2600 members. Out of this, most of them were from the *Loi*[216] background; a few of them were migrated Christians, some of them were born Christians and still some of them were job-oriented members.[217] We may recall here the arrival of the gospel among the Meiteis when William Pettigrew the first missionary started working among these people as soon as he landed in 1904 in Imphal valley. Nevertheless, the response of the general Meiteis to the gospel is still rejective.

---

[213] Souvenir: Meitei Baptist Association, 9-10.

[214] N. Debendra Singh, Former Executive Secretary, Meitei Baptist Association, Wangjing, letter to the author, 17 January 2010.

[215] Elungkiebe Zeliang, *A History of the Manipur Baptist Convention*, 178.

[216] *Lois* are schedule caste Meiteis in Manipur. General Meiteis consider *lois* as backward group of people in education, economy and in social status. Ranaji Kumar Saha, *Valley Society of Manipur: A Cultural Frontier of Indian Civilization* (Calcutta: Punthi-Pustak, 1994), 62-63.

[217] N. Debendra Singh, Former Executive Secretary.

4.4. Fourth Ministerial Team of Meitei Baptist Association

As the time went by, the third ministerial team was replaced by the fourth ministerial team after the celebration of the silver jubilee in 2008. The chart below shows the details of the fourth ministerial team.

Office Bearers of the 4th Ministerial Team[218]

Designation	Person	Duration
Executive Secretary	Ph. Daneshower Singh	2008 -
Mission and Evangelism Secretary	Ksh. Chaoba	2008 -
Women Secretary	Th. Shushila Devi	2008 -
Youth Secretary	O. Bimol Singh	2008 -
Finance Secretary	M. Nanda Meitei	2008 -
Centre Pastor	S. Chengai	2008 -
Caretaker	E. Birsingh	2008 -

According to Daneshower Singh, the present Executive Secretary of MBA, the response of the *loi* is hopeful even though it is very slow in accepting the gospel but response of the general Meiteis remains the same. They still reject the gospel of Christ.[219]

5. An Appraisal

As far as the traditional educational system is concerned, Meiteis maintained an educational system of their own. Even though the traditional system of education aimed at over-all development of every individual, later on, with the coming of the western education, that system was broadened.[220] One of the most striking features of the impact of Christianity on the social life of Meiteis is the introduction of modern, western education. William Pettigrew from the very beginning of his work in Manipur started focusing on the value of education; as a result he was occupied in opening schools and in translation and literary works. The educational work extended by the Christian missionaries with limited objectives, widened its scope and soon influenced the people. It was instrumental

[218] The 4th and current ministerial team started in March 2008; right after the silver jubilee celebration and the entire team is expected to continue till March 2012. Ph. Dhaneswor Singh, Present Executive Secretary, Meitei Baptist Association, Wangjing, letter to the author, 11 September, 2010.

[219] Ph. Dhaneswor Singh, Present Executive Secretary.

[220] Jamini Devi, *Education in Manipur*, 38.

in bringing English-medium education and western type learning that resulted in a new beginning.

The Johnston Middle English School[221] at Moirang Khom in Imphal was established on 6th February 1894 and this became the first school in the State. This was upgraded by stages later. Slowly, the number of school-going Meitei children increased. High schools, Higher Secondary schools and colleges came up step by step. Thus, the education system in the State grew.

Now there are 2514 primary schools, 557 middle schools, 501 high schools, 55 higher secondary schools, 28 government colleges, 6 aided colleges, 30 private colleges and one university located at Canchipur on the southern side of Imphal along the Indo-Burma Road.[222] Even though the number of Christians among the Meiteis would be just a handful compared to Nagas and Kuki-Chin yet the impact of Christianity upon Meitei society is great. It is mainly because of educational institutions placed in and around Imphal where Meiteis are settling. Rev. Gangte the then Principal of M.B.C. Higher Secondary School Imphal says that, "Almost 90% of the students are Meiteis and they are non-Christians."[223] Even though they are not Christians they are interested to get good education from Christian mission schools. Most of the government top officers were at one time in Christian mission schools as a student. Roman Singh's father was given English education during his youth. But unfortunately he was insulted by orthodox Hindu families for getting English education, as this kind of education was considered in those days to be untouchable and polluted. Therefore he was not allowed to enter the house with the uniform that was used in the school. As a result he used to keep a hanger outside the house in order to hang the clothes used in the school. All these kinds of wrong doctrines were impressed upon the Meiteis so that Meiteis would be kept under the control of Brahmanic Hinduism. But modern education was an eye opener for the Meiteis, when they saw the discrimination and humiliation practiced by the Brahmans, although this was a bold step for the pioneers.[224]

Modem education provided social mobility. Soon the new educated local influential groups emerged. What was important was the change in their mental outlook. They began to look upon Europeans as models and tended to become pro-western in taste and attitude.[225] They also began to regard themselves as

---

[221] "The Johnston Middle English School" at Moirang Khom, Imphal now has been upgraded to the level of Higher Secondary. At present, it is known as "The Johnston Higher Secondary School."

[222] Jamini Devi, *Education in Manipur*, 39.

[223] Interview with Rev. S. Gangte Principal MBC Higher Secondary School Chingmeirong, MBC Compound, Imphal, 8th May 2010.

[224] Roman Singh, Deacon Phaknung Baptist Church, Imphal East, letter to the author, 27 September, 2010.

[225] Gulab Khan Gori, *Changing Phase of Tribal Area of Manipur* (Delhi: B.R. Publishing Corporation, 1984), 99.

belonging to more or less different categories and assumed a new leadership in politics and religion. In this way, the appearance of new elite groups strengthened the structure of traditional social organisation values and provoked the thoughts for self-consciousness and self-identity among the Meiteis.[226] In fact, there arose a conflict between the two groups—the Sanskritised Meiteis upholding the existing Vaishnavite institutions and practices and the modern elites tending to uphold traditional values and democratic practices. Nevertheless, the impact of western education on both the groups was immense. With the rise of socio-political consciousness, both the groups began to question their rights, privileges and identity. This was mainly due to the western education which had broadened their worldview.[227]

Like in many other places, the Christian missions followed the colonial expansion in Manipur. This was mainly because of the private policy of the colonial rulers which was further deepened by the act of inner line regulation in Manipur. Thus, the Christian missions had, by force of circumstances, to seek or to depend on the goodwill of the officials for their very existence, not only of their works. But on the whole, the government officials had a benevolent attitude towards Christian missions and there is not the slightest doubt that such friendly relations between officials and missionaries were considered important because each partner got tangible benefits out of it. As long as the Missionary Movement did not pose a threat to the colonial occupation, the officials served to reinforce the missionary efforts, particularly through the system of grants-in-aid to educational institutions and other humanitarian or philanthropic works. This seeming benevolent attitude often served as an effective means for legitimization of their rule. On the other hand, so long as the support from the government helped the Christian missions in achieving their main aim—the propagation of the Christian faith—the missionaries also extended a natural helping hand to the government. Such being the attitude of the two partners, stresses and strains arising between them tended to be compromised and solved for the sake of maintaining the system.

At most the missionaries were conservative innovators. While their works in terms of education and literature acted as instruments of social change and modernization, their overall impact contributed, at the best, to the reinforcement of the existing colonial structures. Being ethnocentric like the officials, they tended to have no genuine sympathy for the basic essentials of tribal society. As a result, many of the valuable and precious tribal cultures disappeared. Inevitably, their work on education provided the material basis for the emergence of Westernized and articulate elites who became critical of the colonial rule. In course of time, the missions evolved numerous institutions such as district level church councils, presbyteries and assemblies through which the native leadership was trained in

[226] Lal Dena, "Christian Proselytism," 116-117.

[227] N. Basanta, *Socio-Economic Change in Manipur, 1891-1947,* 100-101.

the techniques of self-administration with a view to realising their proclaimed goal of an independent indigenous Church which was to be self-propagating, self-supporting and self-governing.

The missions in Manipur did not originate in-group consciousness among the different ethnic groups, but they did sharpen it by fostering feelings of linguistic and ethnic exclusivity and hence the innumerable community-based church groups. In spite of all these defects, the greatest strength of Christian missionaries lay in their own character, dedication and sincerity, which alone endeared them to the people in the service of whom some of them laid down their lives while others spent the best part of their lives. In fact, true Christianity could release its true and creative power only when it was based on itself and not on outside forces.

Conclusion

Over and above; Rev. and Mrs. Pettigrew were pioneer missionaries who brought the gospel of Christ into Manipur. They were great teachers in the field of the modern and western education in the State. They were humanists who advocated the principles of humanism which were concerned with the interests and welfare of the people in Manipur. General Meiteis rejected William Pettigrew, the first Christian missionary—they still continue to refuse to accept Christianity.[228] After more than a century of Christianity, this is the response given by the general Meiteis in Manipur valley. The rejecting nature of this community towards Christianity was very obvious from the very beginning. This rejection is based on historical experiences and so we shall be looking at the causes for rejection from the historical analytical perspective in the next three chapters.

---

[228] Th. Shushila Devi, Women Secretary, Meitei Baptist Association, Wangjing, letter to the author, 21 September, 2010.

Chapter 3

Sanskritization of Meiteis
The Principal Cause for Rejection of Christianity

Introduction

We may begin with the question to be pondered throughout this chapter: how and why the Sanskritization[1] of Meiteis in Manipur valley[2] is regarded as the principal cause for the rejection of Christianity among this community. To do this, the current chapter is divided into eight parts. The first part gives a brief background of the beginning of Hinduism in Manipur valley. The second section highlights the immigration of Brahmins beginning from the time of King Kiyamba through King Garibniwaj.[3] The third part deals with the rise of Vaishnavism which later on became the State religion. The fourth section discusses neo-Vaishnavism in Manipur. The fifth section looks at religious syncretism between traditional Meitei religion and Vaishnavism. Success of Vaishnavism in Manipur is in the

---

[1] The Sanskritization of Meiteis can be understood in the explanation given by M. N. Srinivas. According to him, Sanskritization is the process by which a "low" Hindu caste or tribal or other group changes its customs, ritual, and ideology and the way of life in the direction of a high and frequently "twice-born" caste. Generally such changes are followed by a claim to higher position in the caste hierarchy than that traditionally conceded to the claimant caste by the local community. The claim is usually made over a period of time, in fact it is a generation or two before the "arrival" is conceded. M. N. Srinivas, *Social Change in Modern India* (New Delhi: Orient Longmans, 1972), 6. cf. Windy Doniger, *The Hindus: An Alternative History* (New Delhi: Penguin Viking, 2009), 5-6.

[2] Manipur valley consists of four districts, they are: 1) Imphal West district 2) Imphal East district 3) Thoubal district and 4) Bishnupur district. The geographical map of Manipur in Appendix-1 of chapter-2 gives the detail features of Manipur valley.

[3] Both Garibniwaj and Garib Niwaz are used by authors but his Meitei name is Pamhaiba; so these three names may be used interchangeably. Gangmumei Kabui, *History of Manipur: Pre-Colonial Period,* vol. I (New Delhi: National Publishing House, 1991), 237.

sixth part of this chapter. Section seven is an appraisal, dealing with the impact of Vaishnavism among the Meiteis in Manipur valley. The chapter ends with concluding remarks.

A Brief Background

The history of the origin of Hinduism in Manipur is still shrouded in mystery, which may be attributed to manifold reasons. In this regard, it is worthwhile to point out that the conspicuous absence of trustworthy historical accounts of the early period does not help us much in presenting an accurate description of the subject under discussion. Nor do some mythological accounts given in our classical Indian literature give us any positive results. The conflict between mythology and history stands, sometimes, of course, as a barrier in our way of reconstruction of the history of the distant past. However, we can overcome this problem by using the stamp of historicity and some popular beliefs and credible traditions, which attest to literary evidence, some archaeological data and other reliable contemporary accounts.

The issue under treatment finds only little reflection joined with prima-facie comments in the monographs of both native and western scholars. They have portrayed the picture in an anachronistic style. Some of them have mythologized even the reliable historical portions of our ancient historical tradition and created the impression that all the Chronicles ascribed to the post-Hindu period in Manipur are well-embellished with details of glorification of the past and tinges of Hinduism. This impression led some scholars to believe that nothing is worthy of credence that deals with Hinduism in early Manipur. Likewise, some savants, while making an attempt to trace the lineage of the Meiteis to the epic and puranic[4] traditions and to establish their Vedic[5] antiquity in the field of religion, have failed to examine the subject critically, objectively and dispassionately. Thus, the results obtained so far from the line of enquiries conducted by oriental and occidental scholars, do not appear to be very satisfactory.

The demolition and collapse of old souvenirs, records and monuments bearing the positive marks of Hindu culture and civilization in the wake of frequent Burmese invasions of Manipur before 18th century A.D. and the Chinese invasions, between 13th and 16th century A.D., together with other occurrences, might have possibly created vacuums in the knowledge of earlier historians.

[4] Hindu literature written in Sanskrit—a body of 18 works written between the first and 11th centuries and incorporating legends and speculative histories of the universe and myths and customary observances.

[5] (From the Sanskrit word for 'knowledge') any of the most ancient sacred writings of Hinduism written in early Sanskrit; traditionally believed to comprise the Samhitas, the Brahminas, the Aranyakas, and the Upanishads.

Because of his religious bigotry, Garibniwaj[6] (1709 to 1748 A.D.) destroyed many icons of the local deities worshipped by the people in the past, many valuable Puyas[7] written by various Maichaow[8] of Manipur, and also various other temples of indigenous deities and other relics. This destruction created several gaps in the early religious history of Manipur.[9] This is why the details are lacking about the old religious beliefs of the people in Manipur valley. The antiquity of some epigraphical and numismatic data of dubious nature has further proved to be an obstacle in our way of dealing with the subject with a great amount of confidence and certainty.

The incorrect impression that the history of Hinduism in Manipur anterior to Garibniwaj is blank has also stood as a barrier in the way of further verification of the subject. We note that some attempts have been made by native scholars to restore the missing links of the obscure period in the history of Manipur by placing their reliance basically on native Chronicles bearing a historical character and other indigenous sources. Notwithstanding the progress hitherto achieved in the field of historical reconstruction relating to the foundation of Hinduism in Manipur valley, its cultural ethnography and antiquity are not very satisfactory. Therefore there is a need for making a realistic evaluation of the subject along scientific lines. Romila Thapar, a classical historian has correctly remarked thus:[10]

> A realistic assessment of the past is more than just historical value. Such an assessment involves questioning the stereotypes, which have been current in recent centuries.... This process of questioning often results in new perspectives or reveals new insights, particularly when fresh evidence becomes available and leads to a refashioning of the image of the past.

Without doubt in the absence of authentic records of a purely historical nature of the hoary past the task of illumining the dark corner of ancient history of Manipur valley with regard to the rise of Hinduism becomes a little complicated. Nevertheless, here every possible attempt has been made to present in historical outline a new account of the various processes involved in the foundation and development of Hinduism in this valley, maintaining the chronological

---

[6] Garibniwaj was the 50th King of Manipur who reigned for 39 years altogether. N. Tombi Singh, *Manipur and the Mainstream* (Imphal: Chitrebirentombichand Khorjeirup, 1975), 47.

[7] These are ancient Meitei religious scripts. More extensive explanation of the term 'Puya' will be given later on.

[8] It is an honorary title in Manipur given to a Meitei scholar. Maichaow also played a priestly role in ancient Meitei society.

[9] N. Khelchandra Singh, *Ariba Manipuri Sahitya Itihas* (*Old literary History of Manipur*) (Imphal: Ningthoujam, 1969), 32-37.

[10] Romila Thapar, *The Past and Prejudice* (Delhi: National Book Trust, 1967), 21-22.

sequence, as far as practicable, on the basis of literary evidence, native Chronicles, archaeological evidence, historical texts and other classical and collateral sources.

1. Beginning of Hinduism in Manipur Valley

The process of the influence of Aryans, which began in the valley of Manipur in the remote past, is a crucial aspect to look at in brief, as it is proved to be a milestone towards the establishment of Hinduism in Manipur. Several elements of the Aryan culture, which were introduced in the valley of Manipur, served as the base of Hinduism. Till today there is a good deal of controversy among scholars regarding the exactitude of the period during which the foundation of Hinduism was laid. However, the primaeval antiquity of Manipur as an independent Kingdom[11] can be established, and various factors, which proved to be helpful in the introduction of Hindu culture in the State of the early period, can be examined. Some evidence can be furnished for indicating the fact that some section of the Indo-Aryan race claiming their descent from both Brahmins and Kshatriyas[12] passed along the Gangetic and Brahmaputra valley in successive waves in order to penetrate into the remote part of Burma through the territory of Manipur, which possibly might have set the stage for the Aryan colonization of its picturesque valley.[13]

1.1. Pre-historic View

The assertions made by some authorities on the history of Manipur, that the Meiteis came in touch with the Aryans in pre-historic times, can be fairly disputed. But while making such observations they brought to light some facts which are worth considering. Captain E. W. Dun has observed:[14]

> There can be no reasonable doubt that a great Aryan wave of very pure blood passed through Manipur into Burma in pre-historic times. I see traces of this in the finely cut features seen now and then among the Manipuris. The Hinduism of those remote times was probably free from caste prejudices and very different from which it now; but I think it is extremely probable that a tradition of it remained when the missionaries from Bengal arrived. These later for their own

---

[11] Appendix-1. From the ancient time onwards, Manipur was an independent Kingdom reigned over by Kings. According to the historical record, the first King was Nongda Lairen Pakhangba, whose reign started at 33 A.D. N. Tombi Singh, *Manipur and the Mainstream*, 45-48.

[12] Kshatriya is a member of the second highest of the four castes of traditional Indian society, responsible for upholding justice and social harmony, and including people in governing and military positions. "Kshatriya," http://www.answers.com/topic/kshatriya (22 Feb 2013).

[13] W. Yumjao Singh, "Report on the Archaeological Studies," in *Manipur Bulletin* 1/1 (January, 1935): 6.

[14] B. C. Allen, *Assam District Gazetteers: Naga Hills and Manipur*, vol. ix (Calcutta: Baptist Mission Press, 1905), 15.

> purpose distorted the history of Manipur; the Burmese invasion put the finishing touch and killed off the old tradition.

The above statement gives some substratum of truth, so far as Hinduism among the Meiteis in Manipur of that remote time is concerned. Similarly, Abdul Ali,[15] R.K. Jhalajit Singh[16] and James Johnstone[17] have also referred to the Aryan contacts with the Meiteis in the pre-historic period.

1.2. Proto-historic Period

According to this, the antiquity of the influence of Aryans[18] in the valley of Manipur can be pushed back to the proto-historic period, beginning with the Vedic age. The Aryan expansion in the whole eastern belt can conclusively be proved by the Rig-Vedic text.[19] It can be safely assumed that those branches of Indo-Aryans who migrated from Mithila[20] and settled in the Brahmaputra valley in the later Vedic age might have pushed towards the valley of Manipur through Surma and Barak valley.[21] This information can be further directly corroborated by the statement recorded in the works of native and other scholars. Atombapu Sharma, a Meitei scholar, has tried to prove on geographical, astronomical and philological grounds that the Aryans came from Mithila or Videha[22] and were in Manipur in the Vedic age. He has profusely quoted references from the Rig-Vedic

---

[15] Abdul Ali, "Note on the Early History of Manipur," in *Bengal Past and Present*, vol. xxvi, part 2, no. 52 (Calcutta: Calcutta Historical Society, 1923), 3.

[16] R. K. Jhalajit Singh, *A Short History of Manipur: From 33 A.D. to the Present Time* (Imphal: O. K. Store, 1965), 24.

[17] James Johnstone, *My Experiences in Manipur and the Naga Hills*, 1st print, London, 1896 (Delhi: Vivek Publishing House, 1971), 80-81.

[18] Aryans are a group of people who called themselves Arya and who spoke the Indo-European Sanskrit language, are known from the *Rigveda* and other early Indian historical sources. They probably invaded India from the northwest during the 2nd millennium BC, spreading east and south over the succeeding centuries. "Aryans," http://www.answers.com/topic/aryans (22 Feb 2013).

[19] Rig-Veda is an important Hindu scripture which consists of a collection of poems dating from before 2000 BC. Shri Ram Sharma Acharyya, *Rig Veda* (original Sanskrit text with trans.) Mandala 10: Sukta 131.

[20] Mithila was a city in ancient India the capital of the Videha Kingdom. The name Mithila is also commonly used to refer to the Videha Kingdom itself, as well as to the modern-day territories that fall within the ancient boundaries of Videha. The city of Mithila has been identified as modern day Janakpur in Dhanusa district of Nepal. "Mithila," http://www.britannica.com/search?query=Mithila (22 Feb 2013).

[21] V.R.R. Dikshitar, "Aryanisation of East India," *IHQ.*, 1945, vol. xxi, 29-33. cf. James Johnstone, *My Experiences in Manipur,* 130. cf. R. Brown, *Statistical Account of the Native State of Manipur and the Hill Territory Under Its Rule*, 1st print, Calcutta, 1873 (Delhi: K.M. Mittan Sanskaran Prakashak, 1975), 21.

[22] This place was the main center from where the expansion of Aryan culture in Eastern India took place.

text in support of his arguments. Likewise, W. Yumjao Singh, a Meitei academic, while exhaustively dealing with this aspect of the subject has also stated that the Aryan influence in Manipur can be traced back to the Rig-Vedic age.[23]

Atombapu Sharma and W. Yumjao Singh, while establishing the Vedic antiquity of the religious system of Manipur, provided some historical accounts. So far as the Aryan influence on the primitive animistic religious system of Meiteis in Manipur valley is concerned, it can be further substantiated by the statements of the other native scholars.

L. Ibungohal Singh with considerable amount of confidence claimed that in the Vedic period several groups of Aryans came to Manipur and settled in the valley. They were absorbed into the primitive Meitei society.[24] R.K. Jhalajit Singh, another native historian also gives a corresponding statement that the Aryan settlement in the valley of Manipur assisted the diffusion of Vedic culture and civilization.[25]

Another affirmative evidence of early Aryan settlement in Manipur valley is through archaeology. The archaeological evidence also confirms the occurrence of Aryan culture and faith in the valley of Manipur. The discovery of sculptured images of Vedic gods like Indra[26] seated on an elephant in anthropomorphic form and Agni[27] in a seated posture on the Vahana depicting two heads, three legs and seven hands kept on the display in Mutua Museum, Imphal also prove the existence of Vedic Aryans in the valley.[28]

This justifies the claim in support of the Aryan settlement and culture in Manipur valley which provided contacts of the native peoples with those Aryans. These were Aryans who were advancing towards Burma and Indo-China through Manipur, which was one of the principle routes for penetrating further into India in those days. The utilization of Manipur as a route for Indian contacts with China and South-East Asia, and the foundation of Indian colonies and political Kingdoms in Burma, South East Asia and neighbouring lands by the people, who migrated through Manipur proved to be a turning point in the history of the influence of Aryans. On the basis of both Indian and foreign sources it can be positively affirmed that traders from Gangetic India and other parts of the country started passing through Manipur from 2nd century B.C. and possibly came into contact with the indigenous people of Manipur, bringing them within

---

[23] W. Yumjoa Singh, *Religious Belief of Ancient Manipur* (Imphal: W. Yumjoa Singh, 1966), 64.

[24] L. Ibungohal Singh, *An Introduction to Manipur*, 3rd print (Imphal: The Saraswati Printing Works, 1987), 15-17.

[25] R. K. Jhalajit Singh, *A Short History of Manipur*, 22-24.

[26] Indra is the chief Hindu god of the Rig-Veda; god of rain and thunder. WordWeb, 2012 ed, version 6.75, s.v; "Indra."

[27] Agni is (Hindu) the god of fire in ancient and traditional India; one of the three chief deities of the Vedas. WordWeb, 2012 ed, version 6.75, s.v; "Agni."

[28] "Sculpture of Manipur," *Bulletin of Mutua Museum,* no. 2 (December, 1982): 23-24.

the pale of a new culture.[29] From the merchandising point of view, it is said that right from the 2nd century B.C. the traders started going through a land route to China via Manipur, Upper Burma and Yunnan.[30]

From the forgoing brief analysis, it can be affirmed that Hinduism touched Manipur at a very early period even though it was not strong or popular. The coming of Aryans into the valley or the going of Aryan traders through Manipur is a crucial aspect to be taken into account as far as the genesis of Hinduism in Manipur is concerned.

Successive bands of colonists, traders, adventurers and missionaries flowed into Eastern countries from India through this valley of Manipur when there was no facility of going by the sea. As early as the 6th century B.C. Indian princes from Kapilavastu settled in Manipur. Thus, as a result of the coming of Indian emigrants to Manipur in successive waves, the culture, religion, language and tradition of the people in the valley of Manipur came under the Aryan influence.[31] That is why Hodson has quoted rightly J. Lyall Charles' remarks:[32]

> Manipur valley is a singular oasis of comparative civilization and organized society set in the midst of a congeries of barbarous people… while Burma had accepted the mild and gentle religion of Buddha, Manipur had been taken into the pale of Hinduism and imposed upon itself a burden of some restrictions of caste and ritual from which its greater neighbor is happily free.

Ibungohal further comments that during the period of first millennium B.C. to the beginning of the Christian era several branches of Aryan princes from northern India, while coming by land route to Burma must have influenced the Indo-Aryan culture and belief of the people in the valley of Manipur.[33] This might well have set the stage for the advent of early Hinduism in Manipur. Hence, the beginning of Hinduism in Manipur was an ancient phenomenon.

2. Immigration of Brahmins

The second crucial aspect of the Sanskritization of Meiteis in Manipur valley is the immigration and settlement of Brahmins.[34] The influence and spread of

---

[29] Prabodh Chandra Bagchi, *India and China: A Thousand Years of Cultural Relations* (New York: The Philosophical Library, 1951), 16.

[30] D. C. Sircar, *Studies in the Geography of Ancient and Medieval India* (Delhi: Motilal Banarsidass, 1971), 323.

[31] W. Yumjao Singh, *An Early History of Manipur* (Imphal: W. Yumjao Singh 1966), 32-33.

[32] T. C. Hodson, *The Meitheis,* 1st print 1908 (Delhi: Low Price Publication, 1984), xx-xxi.

[33] L. Ibungohal Singh, *An Introduction to Manipur*, 56.

[34] Brahmins are the members of the highest of the four Hindu varnas and Brahmanism is the religious beliefs of ancient India as prescribed in the sacred Vedas and Brahmanas and Upanishads. S. S. Kumar & V. Dey, "Brahman and Brahmanism," in *Encyclopedia of Oriental Philosophy and*

Hinduism was not done by a few Brahmins on one or two occasions but by many on different occasions and periods. One of the reasons for Vaishnavism[35] in Manipur was the continual influence of the immigrant Brahmins. It was because of their efforts that Manipur remained the stronghold of Vaishnavism since 18th century. This is taken to be another factor for their resistance to other religions. Therefore, we shall be looking at various stages in this development.

The later part of the 15th century A.D. constituted a significant landmark in the history of Brahmin colonization of the valley of Manipur. The earliest recorded account of the immigration of Brahmins from different parts of India during the reign of renowned King Kiyamba, (alias Chintaamani,) is available in the chronicle popularly known as "Bamon Khunthoklon". The King Kiyamba promoted the process of Sanskritization.[36] During his time Brahmins from different parts of the country came to Manipur in successive waves, settled down in different parts of the State, received royal patronage and married local women, whose offspring became the progenitors of many Brahmin families of Manipur of today.

It is generally accepted that a large number of Brahmins came to Manipur towards the end of 15th century, but it does not mean that there was no settlement of Brahmins in Manipur prior to the 15th century. With regard to this, W. Yumjao Singh is of the opinion that the movements of Brahmin immigrations, who were later absorbed in the Meitei population, can be traced back to the 4th century A.D.[37] This can be further confirmed by the statement of an indigenous scholar R.K. Jhalajit Singh that during the reign of Pengsiba,[38] who ascended the throne of Manipur in 379 A.D. and ruled for 15 years, some Brahmins arrived but were merged with the local population.[39]

It is very difficult to say what was the pattern of settlement of Brahmins in Manipur before the 15th century and from how many parts of the country such immigrations took place. However, using the various statements made by different sources referred to in the previous section, we know that the period preceding the 15th century was not completely blank, so far as the spread of Brahminical culture is concerned. The most important reason for the absence of any clear and authentic account of the Brahmin migration before the 15th century is their

---

Religion: Hinduism, vol. I, edited by N. K. Singh and A. P. Mishra (New Delhi: Global Vision Publishing House, 2005), 114-16.

[35] Worship of Vishnu one of the 3 chief gods of the Hindu pantheon. E. C. Dimock, "Vaishnavism," in *Abingdon Dictionary of Living Religions,* edited by Keith Crim, Roger A. Bullard Larry D. Shinn (Nashville: Abingdon Press, 1981), 781-82.

[36] N. Tombi Singh, *Manipur and the Mainstream,* 48.

[37] W. Yumjao Singh, *An Early History of Manipur,* 34.

[38] Pengsiba, 5th King of Manipur ruled from 379 to 394 A.D. N. Tombi Singh, *Manipur and the Mainstream,* 46.

[39] R. K. Jhalajit Singh, *A Short History of Manipur,* 44.

merger with the local population. Further they did not leave behind much impact on the socio-cultural history of Manipur in the period up to the 15th century.

2.1. Immigration of Brahmins during the Period 1467–1748 A.D.

The history of the settlement and influence of Brahmins from the time of King Kiyamba[40] is well attested because Brahmins who came during his time settled permanently in Manipur and attained both social and legal status. Noticeably, their impact on the religious and cultural history of Manipur post-fifteenth century proved to be more effective.

(a) Reign of King Kiyamba (1467–1508 A.D.)

King Kiyamba himself was a more enlightened ruler than his predecessors and kept a regular account of the Brahmin immigrations and changes that were witnessed in several fields. That is why the history of the settlement and influence of Brahmins in Manipur, beginning with the 15th century A.D. appears to be more trustworthy and convincing.

The names of the Brahmins who arrived during the period 1467–1508 A.D., and the place from where they migrated and settled in Manipur valley, are given in the Cheitharol Kumbaba[41] (Chronicle)[42] and other sources.[43] There are 17 listed and the places are: Takhel,[44] Gujarat, Nepal side, Tekhao,[45] West Bangal, Nadia, Tripura, Kanpur, Sylhet.[46]

These settled in Manipur valley but subsequently they were absorbed into Meitei community, mostly by marrying Meitei women. This matrimonial relationship hastened the process of the assimilation of the Brahmin community into the Meitei society.

---

[40] Kiyamba, 38th King of Manipur, 1467-1508 A.D. ruled for 41 years. N. Tombi Singh, *Manipur and the Mainstream*, 46.

[41] Cheitharol Kumbaba is an important book in ancient Meitei script containing accounts of the Kings of Manipur. It was rendered into current script and edited by Lairenmayum Ibungohal Singh and N. Khelchandra Singh and first published in 1967 by the Manipur Sahitya Parishad, Imphal.

[42] H. Ibopishak Meitei, ed., *Bamon Khunthoklon* (Imphal: Manipur Sahitya Parishad, 1987), 1-3.

[43] W. Ibohal Singh, *The History of Manipur: An Early Period* (Imphal: 1986), 574-576, 606-607; cf., L. Ibungohal Singh, *An Introduction to Manipur*, 207; cf., R. K. Jhalajit Singh, *A Short History of Manipur*, 82.

[44] The place Takhel roughly stands for a place in the ancient Tripura. P. Lalit, "A Brief History of the Meitei of Manipur," http://themanipurpagm/history/puwarimeitei.html (22 Feb 2013).

[45] Assam proper was known as Tekhao by the Meiteis in those days.

[46] Sylhet is now in Bangladesh, formerly part of India and then part of Pakistan; it achieved independence in 1971. "Sylhet," http://www.britannica.com/search?query=Sylhet (22 Feb 2013).

(b) Reign of King Nonginphaba (1523–1524 A.D.)

The process of settlement and influence of Brahmins in Manipur went on, in a long and continuous process. Mentioned in the Chronicle is King Nonginphaba,[47] during whose reign two Brahmins came to Manipur,[48] one coming from the northern part of Hao.

(c) Reign of King Chalamba (1545–1562 A.D.)

During the time of King Chalamba[49] two Brahmins came and settled in Manipur as recorded in the Chronicle[50] and sources,[51] coming from Gaurdesa, West Bengal and Utter Pradesh. Besides these two Brahmins, some Kshatriyas also came and settled in Manipur during the reign of King Chalamba.[52]

(d) Reign of King Khagemba (1597–1652 A.D.)

The reign of Khagemba[53] constituted a prosperous period in the socio-religious and socio-cultural history of Manipur. This period witnessed the immigration and settlements of large numbers of Brahmins in the State. During this period 10 Brahmins came to Manipur as stated in the Chronicle[54] and other references.,[55] coming from Gaurdesa, West Bengal, Ghosal-Para of Assam, Kumilla, East Bengal, Assam.

(e) Reign of King Paikhomba (1666–1697 A.D.)

The period extending from the latter half of the 17th century A.D. to the closing decade of the 18th century A.D. appears to be eventful, so far as the growth of Hinduism in Manipur through immigration of Brahmins is concerned. The Brahmin names continue to be furnished in the Chronicle.[56] Six Brahmins came

---

[47] Nonginphaba, 41st King of Manipur, 1523-1524 A.D. N. Tombi Singh, *Manipur and the Mainstream*, 46.

[48] H. Ibopishak Meitei, ed., *Bamon Khunthoklon,* 3.

[49] Chalamba, 44th King of Manipur, 1545-1562 A.D, reigned for 17 years altogether. N. Tombi Singh, *Manipur and the Mainstream*, 46.

[50] H. Ibopishak Meitei, ed., *Bamon Khunthoklon,* 3-4.

[51] W. Ibohal Singh, *The History of Manipur: An Early Period*, 576; cf., R.K. Jhalajit Singh, *A Short History of Manipur,* 90; cf., L. Ibungohal Singh, *An Introduction to Manipur*, 207-08.

[52] R. K. Jhalajit Singh, *A Short History of Manipur,* 16.

[53] Khagemba, 46th King of Manipur, 1597-1652 A.D., reigned for 55 years. N. Tombi Singh, *Manipur and the Mainstream*, 46.

[54] H. Ibopishak Meitei ed., *Bamon Khunthoklon,* 4-5.

[55] W. Ibohal Singh, *The History of Manipur: An Early Period*, 577; cf., L. Ibungohal Singh, *An Introduction to Manipur*, 208-09; cf., R.K. Jhalajit Singh, *A Short History of Manipur,*104.

[56] H. Ibopishak Meitei ed., *Bamon Khunthoklon,* 6-7.

during the reign of King Paikhomba,[57] coming from Prayang, Bengal, Bengal, Tekhel, Tripura, Gujarat.[58]

(f) Reign of King Charairongba (1697–1709 A.D.)

From the above data it is quite evident that the process of Sanskritization was making considerable progress even before the formal acceptance of Vaishnavite faith among the Meiteis in Manipur valley. It can be proved that the Brahmin influence through migrations was very helpful in the rise and growth of Hinduism during the medieval period. The presence of Brahmins in Manipur made the path of Sanskritization very smooth even before the time of Charairongba.[59]

During the time of King Charairongba 15 Brahmins came and settled in Manipur as recoded in the Chronicle[60] and other sources,[61] coming from Tekhel, Jagananath, Puri, Mathura, Mathura, Tripura, Orissa.

From the Chronicles we also gather that the different categories of Brahmins included monks, Pandits and astrologers, who found their place in the society, and won the favour of the King. So, the reign of Charairongba was no doubt a turning point in the religious history of Manipur. Hinduism became the dominant religion of the State during his time because of his active support and patronage. However, he did not make any serious attempt to establish Hinduism as a State religion, nor did he neglect the worship of the traditional god (*lai*) and goddess (*lairembi*).[62] We shall be looking at the reign of King Charairongba later on in chapter 3.

(g) Reign of King Garibniwaj (1709–1748 A.D.)

It was after the conversion of the Meiteis into Hinduism, under the influence of one Shantidasa, a Brahmin from Sylhet, during the reign of King Garibniwaj,[63] that the culture and practice underwent a process of Sanskritization. The traditional religious books were burnt, temples to the old Sanamahi[64] God were

---

[57] Paikhomba, 48th King of Manipur, 1666–1697 A.D., reigned for thirty-one years. N. Tombi Singh, *Manipur and the Mainstream*, 46.

[58] W. Ibohal Singh, *The History of Manipur: An Early Period,* 578; cf., L. Ibungohal Singh, An Introduction to Manipur, 210; cf., R.K. Jhalajit Singh, *A Short History of Manipur,* 106.

[59] Charairongba, 49th King of Manipur, 1697–1709 A.D., reigned for twelve years. N. Tombi Singh, *Manipur and the Mainstream*, 46.

[60] H. Ibopishak Meitei, ed., *Bamon Khunthoklon,* 7-9.

[61] W. Ibohal Singh, *The History of Manipur: An Early Period,* 578-580; cf., L. Ibungohal Singh, *An Introduction to Manipur,* 210-11; cited in., R.K. Jhalajit Singh, *A Short History of Manipur,* 115.

[62] Lairenmayum Ibungohal Singh and N. Khelchandra Singh, ed., *Cheitharol Kumbaba* (Imphal: Manipur Sahitya Parishad, 1967), 65-58.

[63] Garibniwaj, 50th King of Manipur, 1709–1748 A.D., reigned for thirty-nine years. N. Tombi Singh, *Manipur and the Mainstream*, 47.

[64] Sanamahism is the worship of Sanamahi, the creator aspect of *Sidaba Mapu*, the trinity God of the Meitei. Sanamahism is one of the oldest sects of South Asia. It originated in Manipur and is

destroyed, and the Bengali script was imposed. This was done despite the strong opposition by the traditional priests and courtiers. The Meitei Kings started claiming that they were descendants of Arjun's son and they got integrated with the great traditions. We shall be looking at it further later on as it is a crucial episode in the history of Manipur as far as Sanskritization is concerned.

There were 11 Brahmins who came and settled in Manipur during the time of King Garibniwaj given in the Chronicle[65] and other sources,[66] coming from Kanyakubja, U.P., Sylhet, Tripura, Assam, and other places not given.

2.2. Summary

On the whole, the above mentioned information gives us a picture of the successive waves of migration of Brahmins from different parts of Assam, Tripura, Bengal, Bangladesh, Orissa, Utter Pradesh, Gujarat, Kanauj and Western Punjab and their expansion and settlement in different parts of Manipur between the 15th and the early part of the 19th centuries. As most of the Brahmins settled at Brahmapur, this area became famous as Bramapur Bamon Leikai.[67] It is evident that most of them came from Tripura and Bengal because of their geographical contiguity. According to the records, those Brahmins entered into marriage relationships with the local women, settled down permanently and left behind their descendants. They became an integral part of Manipur society and contributed their own share in the socio-religious development.

The Chronicle and other sources concerned do not clearly mention the cause of the migration of Brahmins to Manipur from far-off places. However, it can be safely presumed that the migration of Brahmins from one place to another in ancient and medieval period was a regular phenomenon in India. More specifically it can be stated that one of the primary causes of their migration from Bengal, and other parts of Eastern and northern India was the persecution of Brahmins by the Muslim rulers.[68] The royal patronage extended to the Brahmins and land granted to them for their permanent settlements in Manipur facilitated the spread of Brahminic culture among the people of Manipur. As a result a large section of Meiteis came within the area of Brahminic civilization in Manipur valley.

---

mainly practiced by the Meiteis, Kabui, Zeliangrong and other communities who inhabit Manipur, Assam, Tripura, Uttar Pradesh, Myanmar, and Bangladesh with small populations in the United Kingdom, United States and Canada. "Sanamahism," http://www.answers.com/topic/sanamahism (22 Feb 2013).

[65] H. Ibopishak Meitei ed., *Bamon Khunthoklon,* 9-10.

[66] W. Ibohal Singh, *The History of Manipur: An Early Period*, 580-81; cited in., L. Ibungohal Singh, *An Introduction to Manipur,* 212; cited in., R.K. Jhalajit Singh, *A Short History of Manipur*, 138.

[67] It means Brahmin's colony of Bramapur.

[68] Markandey Katju, "Muslim Rulers Deliberately Projected as Intolerant," *The Hindu*, 18 April 2011, 7.

Over time, the religious and social system of Brahminism[69] became stronger and wider. This led to the introduction of several changes in social, religious, cultural, literary and artistic fields. The impact of the Brahminic religion and culture can be seen in the art and architecture, sculpture and iconography, music, dance, drama, literature and various other aspects of the social, political and religious life of the people. The ancient traditional beliefs of Meiteis were modified to a considerable extent by the Brahminic faith. It also shows the establishment of a new Brahminic tradition in Manipur.

3. The Rise of Vaishnavism as the State Religion

The rise of Vaishnavism among the Meiteis in Manipur valley went through various stages under the royal patronage of various Kings. Different schools of Vaishnava[70] cult of Hinduism expanded during the period extending from the second half of the 15th century to the early part of the 19th century. During this long journey, many changes took place, some of which were a transformation of the traditional society, religion and culture, manners and customs, language and literature, art and architecture. In other words, the Hinduism in Manipur is not an infant religion but one that has grown up and matured. The religion is fully secured and protected by its followers and so other religions such as Christianity are unable to penetrate into it. In this section we shall be looking at various phases of the rise of Vaishnavism among the Meiteis in Manipur valley.

3.1. Initial Vishnu Worship

The antiquity of Vaishnavism has been much debated by scholars. However, as far as Manipur is concerned, the earliest available evidence about the introduction of Vishnu worship is the copper plate inscription of King Khongtekcha (763–773 A.D.).[71] In this epigraphic record "Shri Hari" i.e., Vishnu with Lakshmi, has been exalted as the supreme god.[72] If it is true that this copper plate inscription was issued by King Khongtekcha, it can be affirmed that it was his reign which marked the beginning of Vishnu worship in Manipur. However, some scholars do not subscribe to this view based on the period of his reign. Therefore, it is difficult to pin point the exact beginning of Vishnu worship in Manipur.

---

[69] The religious beliefs as prescribed in the sacred Vedas and Brahmanas and Upanishads. WordWeb, 2012 ed, version 6.75, s.v; "Brahminism."

[70] Worship of Vishnu as the supreme deity, as well as of his incarnations, mainly Rama and Krishna. Vaishnavism is one of the major forms of modern Hinduism. "Vaishnavism," http://www.britannica.-com/search?query=Vaishnavism (22 Feb 2013).

[71] Khongtekcha was the 12th King of Manipur, who reigned for ten years, i.e., 763–773 A.D. N. Tombi Singh, *Manipur and the Mainstream*, 45.

[72] W. Yomjao Singh, "Report on the Archaeological Studies in Manipur," *Manipur Bulletin* 2/1 (January-June, 1935): 7; cf., R. K. Sanahal, "Vaishnava Religious Movement in Manipur," in *Souvenir of Manipur Rajya Hindu Sammelan* (Imphal: Manipur Rajya Hindu Sammelan, 1981), 4-6.

3.2. Early Vaishnava form of Hinduism

On the basis of all the available evidence it can be affirmed that it was the reign of Kiyamba (1467–1508),[73] which in fact witnessed the appearance of Vaishnava form of Hinduism in Manipur. It is believed that the Vishnu image was worshipped in Manipur as the family god of the ruling prince earlier but Choupha Khak-Khomba or Khikhomba, the King of Pong, the flourishing State in upper Burma, took it away as the war trophy after having conquered Manipur, and he used it as an instrument for scratching his itches to insult the King and people of Manipur. But he returned this small image of Vishnu to Kiyamba at the time of concluding the friendly treaty with him. After having received the image of Vishnu, King Kiyamba requisitioned the service of one Brahmin to begin the regular worship of Vishnu.[74] Thus, the worship of Vishnu resumed in the State. It is also said that some Brahmins well acquainted with the art of worshipping Vishnu were already there. Under the leadership of King Kiyamba, a Vishnu temple of bricks was built at Bishnupur lying eighteen miles to the south-east of Imphal, for the purpose of propitiation of the image Vishnu.[75] This temple still exists today.[76] As far as the existence of Vishnu worship in Manipur is concerned, this historical monument is an important example.

Visible evidence about the Vishnu worship during the time of King Kiyamba is the image riding on the neck of Garuda[77] and holding the usual weapons and the lotus. It is about five inches high, is now covered with gold on all sides except on the back, and is installed in the temple of Govinda[78] at the palace complex of the Maharaja in Imphal.[79] L. Ibungohal further affirms:[80]

> It is historically recognized that modern form of Vaishnavism was professed by the King and his subjects in 1467 A.D. … But it is not

[73] N. Tombi Singh, *Manipur and the Mainstream,* 46.

[74] Hamlet Bareh, "Manipur," in *Encyclopaedia of North-East India*, volume iii, 1st ed., 2001 (New Delhi: Krishna Mittal for Mittal Publications, 2007), 94-95.

[75] R. K. Jhalajit Singh, *A Short History of Manipur,* 82-84.

[76] Appendix-2. "Bishnupur: The Land of the Dancing Deer," http://bishnupur.nic.in/history.htm. (21 Feb 2013).

[77] Hindu deity, a supernatural eagle-like being that serves as Vishnu's mount. Garuda traveled with the spread of Hinduism to Nepal and to Southeast Asia, where he is frequently depicted on monuments. He is associated with royalty in many Southeast Asian countries. "Garuda," http://www.britannica.com-/search?query=Garuda (22 Feb 2013).

[78] Govinda and Gopāla are names of Krishna referring to his youthful occupation as a cowherd. He is regarded as the Supreme Godhead in the Vaishnava tradition and also by much of the pan-Hindu tradition. The ancient text Sri Brahma Samhita (5.1) describes him as the source of all that is and the original cause of all causes. "Govinda," http://www.answers.com/topic/govinda (22 Feb 2013).

[79] R. K. Jhalajit Singh, *A Short History of Manipur,* 84.

[80] L. Ibungohal Singh, *An Introduction to Manipur*, 31.

clear in what form it was worshipped before this (1467).... In about 1467 Mitaya Manipuris belonged to Bishnuswami sect of Vaishnavism in the reign of King Kiyamba.

While affirming the introduction of Vishnu worship in Manipur in the 15th century, S.K. Chatterji has also stated that during the time of King Kiyamba both Siva and Vaishnava forms of Hinduism were common among the people.[81] He is of the firm opinion that definite evidence of Sanskritization through the spread of the worship of Vishnu is found in Manipur, as early as the 15th century, when King Kiyamba ruled over the Meiteis.[82]

Even though the worship of Vishnu had become a common religious phenomenon during the time of King Kiyamba, he did not formally initiate Vaishnavism. However, the worship of Vishnu gradually became widespread. The image of Vishnu returned by the Pong King to Kiyamba was handed down to the succeeding Kings. The initiative taken by Kiyamba in the field of Vishnu worship was further followed by his successors. The only change noticed in the later period was an intense devotion of the Kings to Vishnu.

3.3. Continuation of Vishnu Worship

On the basis of some available evidences it can be pointed out that during the reign of Khagemba[83] (1597–1652 A.D.) also the Vishnu worship was prevalent to some extent. This can be proved by two crucial events which took place during his reign: [84]

1) The first one was the introduction of a new feature in 1635, which was added to the boat race festival connected with the worship of Vishnu. It is said that from that year onwards a boat was kept apart for the image of Vishnu, presented by the King of Pong to Kiyamba. According to mythological belief the deity (Vishnu) used to witness the boat race. The poplar tradition also confirms it.
2) Another remarkable event was that a copy of Bhagavad-Gita[85] was brought from Tripura, which shows the influence of Hinduism during his reign.

[81] Sunil Kumar Chatterji, "Kirata-Jana-Krti: The Indo-Mongoloids, their Contribution to the History and Culture of India," *Journal of the Asiatic Society of Bengal*, 16/2 (June, 1950): 151-52.

[82] Sunil Kumar Chatterji, "Kirata-Jana-Krti: The Indo-Mongoloids," 144.

[83] Khagemba was the 46th King of Manipur, he reigned for 55 years. N. Tombi Singh, *Manipur and the Mainstream*, 45.

[84] H. Ranbir Singh, "Vaishnavism in Manipur: It's Advent." *Manipur Sahitya Parishad*, 2/1 (April, 1985): 2-3.

[85] (Hinduism) the sacred 'song of God' composed about 200 BC and incorporated into the Mahabharata (a Sanskrit epic); contains a discussion between Krishna and Arjuna on human nature and the purpose of life. WordWeb, 2012 ed, version 6.75, s.v; "Bhagavad-Gita."

Like King Kiyamba, he also did not initiate a formal Vaishnavism in Manipur; however, the above stated evidence shows that there was worship of Vishnu in the early 17th century. Nevertheless, the religious phenomenon of Vishnu was not formal among the Meiteis in Manipur valley at that point of time.

3.4. Formal Appearance of Vaishnavism

During the reign of Charairongba (1697-1709 A.D.) the 49th King of Manipur, the Meiteis passed to the period in which Vaishnavism became the dominant religion in Manipur, but it was not a smooth process.[86] The era of Charairongba marked the transition from Vishnuswami sect to Nimandi Vaishnavism of Madhvacharyya sect[87] in which the worship of Radha-Krishna image was emphasized. Vishnu was kept as King Charairongba's family god.[88] As far as Vaishnavism is concerned, Charairongba was the first King of Manipur to have formally initiated Vaishnavism.[89] In 1704 in *Sajibu* (April-May), a Brahmin named Krishnacharyya alias Rai Vanamali, arrived from Stweta Ganga, Puri and initiated King Charairongba into Vaishnavism.[90] The Brahmin Krishnacharyya was accompanied by his wife, another Brahmin and two Shudras.[91] After the formal conversion, Charairongba adopted the Sanskritized name of Pitambar Singh.[92] Thereafter the King started extending an imperial patronage to Vaishnavism, and so it began to flourish in the valley. Parratt further observes thus, "although the King himself formally took the sacred thread, he did not attempt to establish Vaishnavism as the State religion, nor did he neglect the worship of the traditional

[86] Gangmumei Kabui, "Socio-Religious Reform Movement," in *History of Modern Manipur*, edited by Lal Dena (New Delhi: Orbit Publishers, 1991), 90-91.

[87] The Madhvas are Vaishnavas. They are known as Brahma Sampradayins. The founder of the Nimandi Vaishnavism sect is Madhvacharya, otherwise called Ananda Tirtha and Purna-Prajna. He was born in 1199. He was a great opponent of Sankaracharya's Advaita system of philosophy. He is regarded as an incarnation of Vayu or the Wind-God. He erected and consecrated at Udipi the image of the Lord Krishna. Hence, they give emphasis to Lord Krishna. Sri Swami Sivananda, "Madhava," http://www.dlshq.org/saints-/madhva.htm (22 Feb 2013).

[88] L. Ibungohal Singh, *An Introduction to Manipur*, 32.

[89] As far as the formal initiation of the coming of Vaishnavism in Manipur valley is concerned, it is commonly accepted by most of the eminent historians of Manipur that it was roughly in April 1704 A.D. that King Charairongba was formally initiated into Vaishnavism by a Brahmin named Krishnacharyya. Saroj Nalini Parratt, *The Religion of Manipur: Belief, Ritual and Historical Development* (Calcutta: Firma KLM Private Limited, 1980), 134-35.

[90] Lairenmayum Ibungohal Singh and N. Khelchandra Singh, ed., *Cheitharol Kumbaba,* 56; cf., R. K. Jhalajit Singh, *A Short History of Manipur,* 115-116.

[91] Saroj Nalini Parratt, *The Religion of Manipur*, 135.

[92] The name Charai Rongba and Pitambar Singh will be used interchangeably.

lai."[93] He died five years after his conversion to Vaishnavism and not much was achieved in the spread of the new religion among the Meiteis in Manipur valley.[94]

The school of Vaishnavism to which Charairongba belonged laid emphasis on the worship of Shri Krishna as the supreme deity. In fact, this was not very much in contrast to the worship of Vishnu that had been going on since the time of King Kiyamba in the 15th century A.D. The fact remains that Shri Krishna has been widely accepted as the full incarnation of Vishnu. In order to popularize this cult of Vaishnavism, he constructed a temple at Brahmapur Aribam Leikai in 1707 A.D. and dedicated the temple to Sri Krishna.[95] This indicates that Vaishnavism faith was accepted by the King, his family members and possibly many others in the palace. Sri Krishna worship by the gurus (religious leaders) of the King is still worshipped by their descendants, who are now known as Guru Aribam Brahmins which means religious leaders of the old Brahmins.

Further, it is important to note that Charairongba was profoundly influenced by the philosophy, which was preached by the followers of the school of Nimbarka,[96] who flourished in the 15th century. He also followed Ramanuja, whose exposition qualifies monism and brought Vaishnavism to the public eye. The worship of Radha and Krishna, the two important Hindu deities became popular because of the impact of the basic doctrines of Bhakti as emphasized by Nimbarka. The Nimbarka's concept of Bhakti in connection with the worship of Krishna and Radha greatly helped the growth of Vaishnavism in Manipur valley.[97]

3.5. Further Growth of Vaishnavism

The reign of Garibniwaj (1709-1748 A.D.)[98] witnessed a change from Madhavacharyya sect of Vaishnavism to Chaitanya Vaishnavism.[99] His reign

---

[93] Saroj Nalini Parratt, *The Religion of Manipur*, 135.

[94] R. K. Jhalajit Singh, *A Short History of Manipur*, 115.

[95] Lairenmayum Ibungohal Singh and N. Khelchandra Singh, ed., *Cheitharol Kumbaba*, 59.

[96] Nimbarka was a Hindu philosopher and commentator. Nimbarka's philosophical position is simultaneous duality and non-duality. He defines three categories of existence, God (*Isvara*), souls (*cit*) and matter (*acit*). God exists independently and by Himself, but the existence of souls and matter is dependent upon God. Souls and matter have attributes and capacities which are different from God, but at the same time they are not different from God because they cannot exist independently of Him. God is both the efficient and material cause of the universe. Creation is a manifestation of His powers of soul and matter. "Nimbarka," http://www.newworldencyclopedia.org/entry/Nimbarka (22 Feb 2013).

[97] R. G. Bhandarkar, *Viashnavism, Saivism and Minor Religious Systems* 1st print 1913 (New Delhi: Asian Educational Service, 1965), 62; cf., Charles Eliot, *Hinduism and Buddhism: An Historical Sketch*, vol. 3 (London: Edward Arnold, 1957, 1st print 1921), 230.

[98] N. Tombi Singh, Manipur and the Mainstream, 46.

[99] Gaudiya Vaishnavism (also known as Chaitanya Vaishnavism and Hare Krishna) is a Vaishnava religious movement founded by Chaitanya Mahaprabhu (1486–1534) in India in the 16th century. "Gaudiya" refers to the Gauda region (present day Bengal and Bangladesh) with Vaishnavism meaning "the worship of Vishnu." Its philosophical basis is primarily that of the

proved to be the blooming period for the efflorescence of Vaishnavism in Manipur. The two schools of Vaishnavism known as Chaitanya's school and the Ramanandi[100] school prospered side by side during this period. This can be considered as an important historic occurrence, so far as the introduction of the Vaishnavism form of Hinduism in Manipur is concerned. This was the period of both progress and protest. Both forms of Vaishnavism were being propagated by the followers of these two different schools. King Garibniwaj himself embraced both the sects of Vaishnavism. Like his father Charairongba, Garibniwaj also appointed a preacher named Gopaldash as his Guru, who got him initiated to Vaishnavism in 1717, in the month of October, as recorded in the chronicle.[101] The form of Vaishnavism, which he mainly accepted, was Chaitanya school of Vaishnavism, which laid great emphasis on the worship of Sri Krishna as the supreme deity. Not only the King but other people were also initiated into this form of Vaishnavism. Guru Gopaldash, after having initiated the King and his followers to Chaitanya cult, returned to his native place. Nevertheless, the arrival of other Brahmins continued, which facilitated the proselytization of the people. As a result, this new faith further progressed. According to the doctrines propounded by Chaitanya school of Vaishnavism, Sri Krishna was looked upon as the full incarnation of Vishnu and worshiped as the supreme god. This god was worshipped in accordance with the principles laid down in Shrimad Bhagavata. The Bhakti[102] cult of the devotion became the basis of this form of Vaishnavism. It is understood that the King followed this form of Vaishnavism for nearly twenty years; it was practiced on a large scale during his reign and a large number of Brahmins and pilgrims tracked into Manipur.

Chaitanya[103] was a great Vaishnava preacher of that period. He preached the worship of lord Krishna to all classes of people, his main aim being to popularize the worship of Krishna through Bhakti cult, and in this he was successful. He carried with him the tradition which was maintained at Sylhet, which was an important centre for Vaishnavism. After his arrival in Bengal the number of followers of Ramanandi school of Vaishnavism began to decrease. Instead of Ram,

---

Bhagavad Gita and Bhagavata Purana, as well as other Puranic scriptures and Upanishads. The focus of Gaudiya Vaishnavism is the devotional worship (*bhakti*) of Radha and Krishna and their many divine incarnations as the supreme forms of God. "Gaudiya Vaishnavism," http://www.answers.com/topic/gaudiya-vaishnavism (22 Feb. 2013).

[100] Instead of Ramanandi, some writers spelt as Ramandi, therefore these terms may be used interchangeably.

[101] Lairenmayum Ibungohal Singh and N. Khelchandra Singh, ed., *Cheitharol Kumbaba,* 66.

[102] (Hinduism) loving devotion to a deity leading to salvation and nirvana; WordWeb, 2012 ed, version 6.75, s.v; "Bhakti."

[103] Chaitanya, also called Gauranga, original name Vishvambhara Mishra (born 1485, Navadvipa, Bengal—died 1533, Puri, Orissa), Hindu mystic whose mode of worshipping the god Krishna with song and dance had a profound effect on Vaishnavism. "Chaitanya," http://www.britannica.com/EBchecked/-topic/88591/Chaitan-ya (22 Feb 2013).

Krishna acquired more popularity as the supreme deity. Many Meiteis under the influence of the King were also devoted to the worship of Krishna and Radha at that time. The religion and culture of Manipur still bears the stamp of Chaitanya's Vaishnavism.

In regard to this, C. Eliot comments that Chaitanya's doctrine was not original. The concept of the worship of Krishna based on Bhakti, which he preached was nothing new. However, it cannot be denied that Krishna was exalted to a supreme position during his time. That is why the followers of his school were greatly devoted to Krishna in the 18th century.[104] A striking similarity can be noticed between the teachings of Chaitanya and that of Nimbarka. Both of them popularized the worship of Krishna and his consort Radha. The worship of god Krishna accompanied by song and dance became widely prevalent in many places in India. So also, under the power of the King, the concept of Krishna distinctly emerged in the valley society of Manipur as a result of the Vaishnava preaching of this school. The devotees of both Nimbarka and Chaitanya schools of Vaishnavism began to popularize the Krishna-Radha cult more and more, and started putting the ritualistic (sectarian) marks on the forehead.[105]

3.6. Imposition of Vaishnavism as the State Religion

The forceful conversion of Meiteis into Vaishnavism began only in the 18th century during the reign of King Garibniwaj, even though there had been a long process in the development of this religion. This indicates that there was no imposition of religion by King Charairongba and other forerunners. But after the end of the reign of King Charairongba, his son Garibniwaj became his successor and reigned over the people of the State.[106] He imposed Vaishnavism as the official religion of the State.[107] Regarding this imposition of religion, Parrat comments:[108]

> We have reached a stage where Vaishnavism became the official religion of the State. A serious attempt was made to impose it upon the people as a whole, and punishments were prescribed for those indulging in blatant non-Hindu activities.

Because of this royal imposition, Meiteis were forced to follow Hinduism. and they were not permitted to resume their traditional faith and worship openly.

---

[104] Charles Eliot, *Hinduism and Buddhism: An Historical Sketch,* 253.

[105] S. K. De, *Early History of the Vaisnava Faith and Movement in Bengal* (Calcutta: General Printers and Publishers, 1942), 34-35; cf., R. G. Bhandarkar, *Vaishnavism, Saivism and Minor Religious Systems,* 82.

[106] Ravindra Pratap Singh, *Geography of Manipur* (New Delhi: National Book Trust, 1982), 3-4.

[107] K. B. Singh, "Social Stratification and Mobility in Manipur," in *North East India: A Sociological Study,* edited by S. M. Dubey (Delhi: Concept Publishing Company, 1978), 62.

[108] Saroj Nalini Parratt, *The Religion of Manipur,* 135.

This brought a great change in socio-religious organization.[109] It was in the first quarter of the eighteenth century during the reign of Garibniwaj, that the Vaishnava missionary, Shantidasa Goshai[110] converted the King to Hinduism.[111] Hence, the King declared Vaishnavism as the State religion and advised his subjects to accept it.[112] The declaration of Vaishnavism as the State religion is a crucial event in the religious history of Manipur. Therefore, it will be good for us to look at more about the Vaishnava missionary Shantidasa as well as his religious strategy through which he managed to convince the King.

It was about 1720 A.D.[113] that Shantidasa came to Manipur from Sylhet[114] to popularize the worship of Ram (Rama)[115] and Hanuman.[116] He, for the first time, conceived of Ram and Sita as the dual incarnation of Vishnu. In the beginning, the King did not show much favour to this form of Vaishnavism preached by Shantidasa but his persuasive arguments, forceful logic and persistence won the heart of the King, and convinced the King about the importance of this form of Vaishmanvism. He also tried to prove that Garibniwaj belonged to the royal family of Manipur, whose lineage is traced to the Hindu creation story. So, in order to convince the King, the Brahmin invented the genealogy of *Mangang Salai* (royal family clan),[117] to Brahma of the Hindu Trimurti. Accordingly the genealogy of the royal family is as follows:[118]

> The Brahmadev (The creating God of the Universe) had sprung out from the Navel lotus of Narayan (the Protecting God of the Universe), Marichi Muni (a Hindu sage) was born from the limbs of Brahmadev. Marichi's son, Kosshop Muni (a Hindu saint); Kosshop Muni's son,

---

[109] R. K. Saha, "An Ethnic Movement in Manipur Valley," in *Tribal Movement in India,* vol. I, edited by K.S. Singh (New Dellhi: Ramesh Jain Manohar Publications, 1982), 99.

[110] His name is also known as Santidas Adhikary, Saroj N. Parratt, *The Religion of Manipur*, 136.

[111] M. McCulloh, *Valley of Manipur* (Delhi: Gian Publications, 1980), 5-7.

[112] Ng. Kangjia Mangang, Revival of a Closed Account: A Brief History of Kanglei Script and the Birth of Phoon (Zero) in the World of Arithmetic and Astrology (Imphal West: Sanamahi Laining Amasung Punsiron Khupham, 1969), 12.

[113] According to Some other writers, Shantidasa Goshai from Sylhet arrived in Manipur valley in 1728 A.D., however in general it is referred to at 1720 A.D.

[114] The place Sylhet is at present in Bangladesh—it was an important religious centre during that time.

[115] Avatar of Vishnu whose name is synonymous with God; any of three incarnations: Ramachandra, Parashurama or Balarama. WordWeb, 2012 ed, version 6.75, s.v; "Rama."

[116] In Hinduism, the monkey god and helper of Rama; god of devotion and courage. WordWeb, 2012 ed, version 6.75, s.v; "Hanuman."

[117] Mangang Salai (Mangang clan) later more popularly known as the Ningthouja Salai (Ningthouja clan) or the Meitei. Saroj Nalini Parratt, *The Religion of Manipur*, 134-137.

[118] T. C. Hodson, *The Meitheis* (London: Mac Millan & Co., 1908), 5.

Surja (Sun); Surja's son, Shaborna Muni; Shaborna's son, Indoo Muni; Indoo Muni's son, Chitra Ketoo; Chitra Ketoo's son, Chitradhaja; Chitradhaja's son, Chitrabija; Chitrabija's son, Chitra Sarba; Chitra Sarba's son, Chitra Rat; Chitra Rat's son, Chitra Vanoo; Chitra Vanoo had no son, only a daughter named Chitranggada; Chitranggada's son, Babrubahan; Babrubahan's son, Sooprabahoo; Sooprabahoo's son, Pakhangba (Jobista). Jobista or Pakhangba was the first ruling King of Manipur.

On this invented genealogy of the origin of the Meitei royal family, T. C. Hodson further comments, "Such tales are obviously tainted by the influence of Hinduism and appearance of non-Hindu names seems to mark the beginning of native legend."[119] A Meitei scholar, Kunj Bihari Singh, has pointedly commented on such a deliberate attempt by the Brahmins and later by the Meitei intellectuals: "These tales are manifestly post-Hindu, and invented by the Brahmins to flatter the pride of the newly converted Meitei King and Kinglets who would connect their origin with the great Kings of India."[120]

Shantidasa also promised not to hurt the sentiments of the King and the subjects and to regard Sri Chaitanya as an incarnation of lord Krishna. But he expressed the doubt that the masses may not be able to follow the teachings of Chaitanya based on the cult of Bhagavatism. Ultimately, the King was moved and made up his mind to accept this form of Vaishnavism. Thus, the King shifted his allegiance from Chaitanya Vaishnavism to the Ramanandi sect (worship of Ram and Sita) that stood in direct contrast to Nimbarka sect (worship of Krishna and Radha).[121]

Throughout the period between 1729 and 1737 A.D., the King and his three hundred followers were initiated to Ramanandi school of Vaishnavism. Thereafter this form of Vaishnavism received royal backing and it was propagated to a considerable extent. Having accepted this form of Vaishnavism, the King founded the images of Rama, Lakshaman, Bharat and Satrughana and began to worship. These images are still worshipped by the people of Wangkhei Leikai, Imphal.[122] He also built a temple of Hanuman at Mahabali on the left bank of the Imphal River. The King also carved an image of Hanuman out of a big slab of stone and installed it at the temple for its worship in 1729 A.D.[123] Today this image of Hanuman is still being worshipped in the Mahabali temple. Ramandi

[119] T. C. Hodson, *The Meitheis*, 6.

[120] K. B. Singh, "The Meiteis of Manipur," (Ph. D. Thesis of Bombay University, 1962), 112-114.

[121] R. K. Jhalajit Singh, *A Short History of Manipur*, 134-36.

[122] Lairenmayum Ibungohal Singh and N. Khelchandra Singh, ed., *Cheitharol Kumbaba*, 83.

[123] R. K. Jhalajit Singh, *A Short History of Manipur*, 136; cf., Lairenmayum Ibungohal Singh and N. Khelchandra Singh, ed., *Cheitharol Kumbaba*, 77-78.

cult of Vaishnavism was popular and official during the time of King Garibniwaj. Concerning this Gunindra Singh remarks, "Some of the bell metal coins of Garibniwaj in both Nagari and Bengali scripts depicting "Je Sri Ram," "Jay Ram," and "Ram" undoubtedly proved the existence of Ramandi cult of Vaishnavism during the time of King Garibniwaj."[124]

The followers of the Ramandi school of Vaishnavism worshipped Sri Rama as the principal deity. However, the Chaitanya cult of Vaishnavism which was followed by Garibniwaj's father Charairongba continued in various corners of the State.

As a mark of reaction against the so-called forcible Sanskritization as carried out by Garibniwaj, the followers of the old faith, prevalent in pre-Vaishnava period, did not extend much support to the new faith. As a result of this development one is bound to face a crisis in dealing with the progress of Hinduism. Garibniwaj had to face the opposition from two sides at the same time, one from rival Vaishnavite sects and the other from the protagonists of the Meitei traditional religion. Because of this there was religious persecution from 1740 to 1742 in Manipur.[125]

In order to put down the revolt of the followers of the Meitei traditional religion who were against the forceful declaration of Vaishnavism as the State religion, Garibniwaj in pursuit of his religious fanaticism burnt a large number of *puyas*[126] and destroyed innumerable traditional gods and goddesses together with their temples.[127] In spite of facing all kinds of opposition, Garibniwaj continued to extend royal support to the propagation of Vaishnavism, which percolated down to the lowest level and in later centuries it also enjoyed the patronage of his successors.

From the time of Charairongba to Garibniwaj the Chaitanya school of Vaishnavism acquired more popularity than any other school of Vaishnavism. Even though for some time Charairongba's son Garibniwaj shifted his allegiance from Chaitanya sect to Ramanandi sect of Vaishnavism, at heart he stood more for Chaitanya school of Vaishnavism. Later on the successors of Garibniwaj did not pay any attention to religious reforms. It is said that most of the succeeding Kings of Manipur were in favour of Chaitanya school of Vaishnavism.[128] Thus

---

[124] P. Gunindra Singh, *Manipur Numismatic* (Imphal: Mutua Museum, 1983), 29-33.

[125] Lairenmayum Ibungohal Singh and N. Khelchandra Singh, ed., *Cheitharol Kumbaba*, 79, 83.

[126] Appendix 3. The burning of *Puya* (ancient Meitei religious texts) in front of Kangla Uttra by the then King Pamheiba (Garibniwaj) at the behest of Hindu missionary leader Shantidasa Gosai on the 17th day of Manipuri month of *Mera* in the year 1732 is observed every year in Manipur and also outside of Manipur. "Puya Meithaba Observed," *The Sangai Express* (Imphal), 26 October 2010; cf., "Burning of Puya Commemorated as Black Day by ACOAM," *Imphal Free Press*, 26 October 2010; cf., "Puya Destruction Remembered on Black Day," *The Sangai Express* (Imphal), 19 January 2009; cf.,"Puya Meithaba Date Fixed," *The Sangai Express* (Imphal), 9 October 2008.

[127] Lairenmayum Ibungohal Singh and N. Khelchandra Singh, ed., *Cheitharol Kumbaba*, 72-75. cited in. Ph. Atombapu Sharma, *History of Manipur* (Imphal: Manipuri Sahitya Parishad, 1976), 55.

[128] R. K. Jhalajit Singh, *A Short History of Manipur*, 165.

Chaitanya school of Vaishnavism continued to grow among the Meiteis in Manipur valley. As has been discussed, the origin of Vaishnavism in Manipur is not a recent phenomenon but centuries old. During this long journey, Hinduism in Meitei society has become deeply rooted. This is the principal cause for their rejecting the introduction of new religions in their society.

4. Neo-Vaishnavism in Manipur

In this section we shall be dealing in brief with a few Kings who were sincerely dedicated to Vaishnavism and its propagation among the Meiteis in Manipur valley.

4.1. Neo-Vaishnavism under the Patronage of King Chourajit

Chourajit[129] the 59th King of Manipur was a religious King who dedicated his life to the growth and propagation of neo-Vaishnavism among his people. The chronicle records that he went on pilgrimage to the Ganges and returned to Manipur. He also accompanied his father to the religious centers of Vaishnavism.[130] He celebrated a formal coronation ceremony: Mayang Kunjadas sprinkled the water of Radhakunda over his head on the abhishek ceremony[131]. He was ceremoniously bathed by one hundred and eighty Brahmin virgins. The King feasted all the people and made presents among the recluse.[132] He did penance and meditation under the shade of trees. He constructed a temple for Sri Govindji and distributed a lot of money to those Brahmins. He also constructed seven cultural institutions.[133] King Chourajit rejoiced in devotion to lord Chaitanya and Nityanandai. He donated gold to the temples in Puri, Nabadwip[134] and Vrindavan.[135] Thus he secured the

---

[129] Chourjit, 59th King of Manipur, reigned for ten years, i.e., 1803-1813. N. Tombi Singh, *Manipur and the Mainstream*, 47.

[130] Lairenmayum Ibungohal Singh and N. Khelchandra Singh, ed., *Cheitharol Kumbaba*, 155.

[131] *Abhisheka* (also *abhiseka, abhishek, abhiṣeka*) is a Sanskrit term comparable to *puja*. *Abhisheka* is the name given to a late Vedic rite of anointing government officials, particularly heads of State, at the time of their taking power or to mark a signal achievement. It is also the bathing ceremony and anointing performed on certain festival days for the temple deities. "*Abhisheka*," http://www.answers.com/topic-/abhisheka (22 Feb 2013).

[132] Lairenmayum Ibungohal Singh and N. Khelchandra Singh, ed., *Cheitharol Kumbaba*, 179.

[133] Lairenmayum Ibungohal Singh and N. Khelchandra Singh, ed., *Cheitharol Kumbaba*, 194.

[134] Nabadwip (also Navadwip, Navadvipa or Nabadwipdham) is a city and municipality in Nadia district in West Bengal. Its name means "9 islands" in Bengali. It is a place of many *lilas* (or "pastimes of God" in Hinduism) of Sri Chaitanya Mahaprabhu. "Nabadwip," http://www.answers.com/topic/nabadwip (23 Feb 2013).

[135] Vrindavan (alternately spelled Vrindaban, Brindavan, Brindavana, or Brundavan) also known as Vraj (as it lies in the Braj region) a town in the Mathura district of Uttar Pradesh. It is the site of an ancient forest which is the region where Lord Krishna spent his childhood days. "Vrindavan," http://www.an-swers.com/topic/-vrindavan (23 Feb 2013).

good will of the Vaishnavas. It was for the first time, during his reign, that Meiteis started settling at Nabadwip for religious purposes.[136]

4.2. Neo-Vaishnavism under the Patronage of King Gambhir Singh

One of the striking things to remember about Gambhir Singh[137] is courage. He was truly a very courageous King who fought various battles. He brought back the stolen idol of Sri Govindaji and consecrated it at the temple of Langthabal.[138] Under his arrangement, temporary houses were built in all thanas. The road from Vishnupur to Langthabal was decorated with plantains. The litter carrying the idol was set with gems and accompanied by rows of people bearing flags, bells and umbrellas. Many musicians and *Maibis* (traditional priestesses) entertained the people. Parched rice and flowers were thrown over them. The music and dance maddened the Meitei devotees who had been denied the sight of Govindaji for some years. This was an important episode in the religious history of Manipur. King Gambhir Singh also constructed many Hindu temples. He extended great hospitality to Vaishnava saints and the Brahmins who had met with persecutions in other parts of India. Another historic event during his time was the visit of three descendants of disciples of Chaitanya; they were Mahasay Thakura (a descendant of Nishiram Acharya), Nabakishor Gosai (a descendant of Advaita) and Gosai of the family of Nityananda. The King received them warmly and extended monetary help for the spread of Vaishnavism work.[139]

4.3. Neo-Vaishnavism under the Patronage of King Nara Singh

Nara Singh,[140] who acted as the regent of the minor prince Chandrakirti from 1834 and later became King of Manipur, is stated to be a good Vaishnava. His reign was marked by the revival of religious activities after the Burmese war.[141] It was marked by the cultivation of nine modes of bhakti and an infusion of religious fervour into the daily life of the people. Manipur feels the impact of his influence even today. On the full-moon day of the Kalen (April-May) 1845,

---

[136] A. C. Banerjee, *The Eastern Frontier of British India,* 1784-1826 (Calcutta: A. Mukerjee & Co., 1946), 329-30. cited in., Lairenmayum Ibungohal Singh and N. Khelchandra Singh, ed., *Cheitharol Kumbaba,* 188.

[137] Gambhir Singh, 63rd King of Manipur, reigned for six months in 1821. N. Tombi Singh, *Manipur and the Mainstream,* 48.

[138] Langthabal is located in southern part of Imphal. The Langthabal temple was an important one during his time.

[139] Lairenmayum Ibungohal Singh and N. Khelchandra Singh, ed., *Cheitharol Kumbaba,* 224, 26, 34.

[140] Nara Singh, 70th King of Manipur, reigned for six years, i.e., 1844-1850. N. Tombi Singh, *Manipur and the Mainstream,* 48.

[141] Appendix-4. It is important to look at the wars between Meitei Kings and the Burmese for our background knowledge in brief. "History of Manipur," http://www.answers.com/topic/history-of-manip-ur#-Anglo-Burmese_Advents (21 Feb 2013).

he organized the Manipuri Jalakeli on the model of the Jala-yatra festival of Radha-Krishna. Because of its local colouring, it had an immediate appeal to the people. He patronized music, religious discourse and the Vaishnava practice of the people. During his stay in Cachar[142] King Nara Singh had thoroughly mastered the devotional songs under the instruction of Krisnadas Thakur, a scholar of the time. He composed two songs, one in praise of Radha and another in praise of Chaitanya. He was indeed a musician, who loved devotional songs.[143]

Another significant work was the encouragement of *bhajana, sanshya vandana* (twilight prayer) and *nagarakirtan.*[144] These groups, apart from occasional meetings, join the temple procession. They go around the street singing early in the morning. They brave the chill and dew of the winter.[145] King Nara Singh's service and dedication in the field of religious costume is significant. The King gave instructions that the persons who participated in the *kirtan* (*sankirtan*)[146] should use huge turbans[147] and the front tuck dhoti.[148] The King often arranged periodical religious guidance for the propagation of Vaishnavism. Like his predecessors he was kind to the mendicants coming from Puri, Sylhet, Nabadwip and other places.

King Nara Singh contributed much towards architecture and art. Temple renovation was the most valuable work done by him in his time. Reinstallation of various images was done by him. He reinstalled the image of Ramchandra Prabhu at a temple of Khwairamband Bazar. He performed the *abhishek* (installation) ceremony of Govindaji, Nityananda and Chaitanya. He also brought the images of Sanamahi and Pakhangba from Cachar and reinstalled them in proper places in Imphal.[149] His reign indeed was distinguished by the revival of religious activities.

---

[142] Cachar is now in Assam. It was one of the territories of Manipur.

[143] Lairenmayum Ibungohal Singh and N. Khelchandra Singh, ed., *Cheitharol Kumbaba*, 261, 75-78.

[144] This is a form of religious service conducted by a leader with the assistance of a small group in which sacred songs are sung.

[145] Lairenmayum Ibungohal Singh and N. Khelchandra Singh, ed., *Cheitharol Kumbaba*, 262.

[146] Kirtan: a Hindu devotional song, typically about the life of Krishna, in which a group repeats lines sung by a leader. "Kirtan," http://www.answers.com/topic/kirtan (23 Feb 2013).

[147] A traditional headdress consisting of a long scarf wrapped around the head. WordWeb, 2012 ed, version 6.75, s.v; "Turban."

[148] A long loincloth worn by Hindu men usually. WordWeb, 2012 ed, version 6.75, s.v; "Dhoti."

[149] Lairenmayum Ibungohal Singh and N. Khelchandra Singh, ed., *Cheitharol Kumbaba*, 276, 278-88, 91.

4.4. Neo-Vaishnavism under the Patronage of King Chandrakirti

King Chandrakirti (1850-1886 A.D.)[150] was another remarkable personality in Manipur. In his early life he lived in Cachar and Surma valley for some time where he was greatly helped by Gosai Radha Vallahap Chakravarti of Mursidabad. When he became King, the Gosai was his friend, philosopher and guide in complicated problems; consequently, he wielded a great influence over the King and the people. A significant place was assigned to Gosai and his family members in the Court.[151]

Bhagavata Saptaha[152] was held at the palace by the order of the King in 1867. During the night in the King's dream, the two deities, Rama and Krishna appeared and asked the King to install their images in the temple of Govindaji. Next morning, the King summoned Chungkham Lolang Singh a *pana anjaba* (the name of the post) of Brahmapur and asked him to prepare four images of Rama and Krishna and two images of Gopaladeve. On Ingen (June-July) 5, 1868, the *abhisehk* (installation) ceremony of the images was celebrated at the palace by the King. Seven sankirtan parties sang successively in connection with the ceremony. The King himself acted as the main singer of Rama-Krishna *Arati*. The images are worshipped to this day. The King shifted the idols of Rama, Bharata, Sita etc. to their original abode in Ningthempukri from Uripo.[153] The chronicle says the King set up many images and distributed them to different centers. This act evoked religious devotion and encouragement among the common people.[154] Some of the religious centers which were established by him are still popular today in Morang and Ningthoukhong.[155]

King Chandrakirti performed many good deeds and put the religious teachings into practice. He treated the Brahmin experts and promoters of Bhakti-rasa cult. He dedicated two bells to Sri Govindaji in 1875. One of them was extant till 1933. The damaged bell is now found at the south-west corner of the temple of Sri Govindaji. He set up images of Hanuman and Garuda and kept them as gate-keepers in the temple of Sri Govindaji. He organized various religious fairs.

---

150 Chandrakirti, 72nd King of Manipur, reigned for thirty-six years altogether. N. Tombi Singh, *Manipur and the Mainstream*, 48.

151 Lairenmayum Ibungohal Singh and N. Khelchandra Singh, ed., *Cheitharol Kumbaba*, 28.

152 Bhagavata-saptaha: a seven-day series of lectures on Srimad-Bhagavatam given by professional reciters to a paying audience. "ISKCON Desire Tree-Devotee Network," http://www.iskcondesiretree. -net/profiles/blogs/bhagavatasaptaha-1 (18 Mar 2013).

153 Ningthempukri is located in the northern part of Imphal and Uripo is in the western part of Imphal. During his reign, the former was considered to be the original abode, hence shifting took place.

154 Lairenmayum Ibungohal Singh and N. Khelchandra Singh, ed., *Cheitharol Kumbaba*, 362, 75, 452, 58.

155 Morang and Ningthoukhong are located in south-west. The former is 45 kilometers away from Imphal and the latter is 25 kilometers.

It was an occasion to display creative works. The mela was held each year for five days from 3rd to 7th Kalen (April-May) in the latter part of his reign.[156]

One of the attention-grabbing efforts made by the King as far as the propagation of Vaishnavism in Manipur is concerned is the sending of devoted Meitei scholars in search of rare manuscripts that could not be found in Manipur. The King used to send them to Nabadwip in west Bengal and Vrindavana in U.P. These two places were renowned for their Sanskritic and Vaishnava works. It was because of their efforts that the cultural renaissance of Vaishnavism in Manipur reached its climax. The Loisangs (cultural and ethical institutions) contained a number of sacred books. The Vaishnava Gosvami and latter Bengali preacher produced the Rasa literature, of which Meitei pundits made copies. They carried with them the sacred writings like precious gems. Many people ceaselessly studied them. This work is closely connected with the dissemination of Vaishnava education. During his reign also Brahmins and the pilgrims from various places came to Manipur. Some were worshippers of Rama others were the followers of Gauddiay Vaishavism. The King adopted a liberal religious view and gave attention to various sects i.e., Saivism,[157] Saktism,[158] Tantrism[159] and *Umanglai* cults.[160] He is reported to have introduced worship of Devi.[161] At Nommaiching hill[162] he also consecrated Kundas (receptacles for the sacred fire) to Lakshmi[163]

---

[156] Lairenmayum Ibungohal Singh and N. Khelchandra Singh, ed., *Cheitharol Kumbaba*, 437-39.

[157] Shaivism or Saivism is the name given to a group of religious traditions which regard Lord Siva, also spelled as Shiva, as the highest Supreme Self or Brahmin and worship Him accordingly. It is considered to be one of the oldest, if not the oldest, sect of Hinduism, whose antiquity is rooted in the prehistoric traditions of ancient India, dating back to the Indus Valley civilization (5000 BC) or even earlier. Jayaram V., "Know All About Saivism," http://www.saivism.net/ (23 Feb 2013).

[158] The religion followed by those who worship the Supreme as the Divine Mother - Shakti or Devi - in Her many forms, both gentle and fierce. Shaktism is one of the four primary sects of Hinduism. "Shaktism," http://www.experiencefestival.com/shaktism (23 Feb 2013).

[159] Tantrism is a movement within Buddhism combining elements of Hinduism and paganism. Doctrine of enlightenment as the realization of the oneness of one's self and the visible world; combines elements of Hinduism and paganism including magical and mystical elements like mantras and mudras and erotic rites. "Tantrism," http://www.philtar.ac.uk/encyclopedia/hindu/devot/tant.html (23 Feb 2013).

[160] Appendix 5. It gives the explanation of *umanglai* cult. Khomdon Singh Lisam, *Encyclopaedia of Manipur*, vol. 3 (Delhi: Kalpaz Publications, 2011), 335-37.

[161] Hindu mother goddess; supreme power in the universe; wife or embodiment of the female energy of Siva having both beneficent and malevolent forms or aspects.

[162] This was a great center of Saivism in the eastern part of Imphal valley, it was popularized by him.

[163] Goddess Lakshmi means Good Luck to Hindus. The word 'Lakshmi' is derived from the Sanskrit word "Laksya", meaning 'aim' or 'goal', and she is the goddess of wealth and prosperity, both material and spiritual. Lakshmi is the household goddess of most Hindu families. Although she is worshipped daily, the festive month of October is Lakshmi's special month. Lakshmi Puja

and Saraswati.[164] His attitude towards those people who followed other sects was tolerant. His respect for the rights, opinions or practices of others made him more popular.[165]

Besides the above works, King Chandrakirti is valued in the local legends and books as the upholder of primitive cults. Syncretisation, which was inaugurated by the former Kings, reached its perfection in his reign. A close affinity between Hindu gods and ancient Meitei gods was established. The text of Sanamahi Laihi[166] is one such. The hearing of this book took place at the altar of Sanamahi. In Ingel (June-July) 1822, the King was personally present at this function. He dedicated a big bell to Pakhangba after two days of the function. He worshipped the images of Govindaji, Nomsaba, Pakhangba and Sanamahi simultaneously. The King performed religious functions through Brahmin pundits, maiba and nobles.[167] The ritual practice of *Umanglai* involved some financial burden. So the King himself granted money yearly from his pocket to some temples of *Umanglai* to meet their recurring expenses.[168]

The worship of Pakhamba, Sanamahi and *Umanglai* had been adopted in Cachar, Tripura, Lamka, Sylhet etc., by the Meitei settlers, in the course of their sojourn there during the Burmese war. In fact, one can see in these places the temples dedicated to the *Umanglai* of Manipur. They have not only preserved their religion, but also their nationality. They exercised a great cultural influence in these areas. The King had to look into the maintenance of these places through agents from time to time. It became more or less necessary for him to help the people of these places to realize their religious ambition and to remove obstacles which prevented them from discharging their religious function.[169]

---

is celebrated on the full moon night of Kojagari Purnima. Subhamoy Das, "Lakshmi: Goddess of Wealth and Beaty," http://hinduism.about.com/od/-hindugoddesses/p/lakshmi.htm (23 Feb 2013).

164 Saraswati is the Hindu goddess of knowledge, music and all the creative arts. Saraswati is called the Mother of the Vedas and the repository of Brahma's creative intelligence. Saraswati is also called Vak Devi, the goddess of speech. Dressed in white, Saraswati holds a mala and a palmleaf scroll, indicating knowledge. Saraswati usually rides a swan and sometimes a peacock, while playing music on a veena.

"Saraswati," http://www.sanatansociety.org/hindu_gods_and_goddesses/saraswati.htm (26 Mar 2013).

165 Lairenmayum Ibungohal Singh and N. Khelchandra Singh, ed., *Cheitharol Kumbaba*, 313-14.

166 Sanamahi Laihi means the words of Sanamahi, which is considered as an important religious aspect among the followers of Sanamahism.

167 Lairenmayum Ibungohal Singh and N. Khelchandra Singh, ed., *Cheitharol Kumbaba*, 383-84.

168 Lairenmayum Ibungohal Singh and N. Khelchandra Singh, ed., *Cheitharol Kumbaba*, 447.

169 Lairenmayum Ibungohal Singh and N. Khelchandra Singh, ed., *Cheitharol Kumbaba*, 448.

5. Religious Syncretism

The Vaishnavism in Manipur borrowed many local elements and associated itself with pre-Vaishnavite gods. This form of religious syncretism[170] was a unique phenomenon that took place among the Meiteis, and was one of the grounds for the further development of Vaishnavism in Manipur. Therefore, it is important for us to briefly consider the religious syncretism. It was the policy of most of the Meitei Kings to unite the conflicting interests of ancient Meitei religion and Vaishnavism. There was mutual compromise which can be observed in the synthesis of the Meitei religion with its gods and goddesses and traditions, its myths and rituals, its legends and traditions, its social customs and practices and its priests and Brahmins.

5.1. Rejection of Nimandi and Ramandi Cults

Although, the people of the valley are mostly said to be the followers of Chaitanya Vaishnavite Hinduism, yet people have not completely forsaken their original beliefs and practices.[171] Religious syncretism which took place among the Meiteis in Manipur is a unique feature in their history. The Meiteis did not continue in following Nimandi[172] and Ramandi[173] cults, rather they rejected them. They, however, accepted Chaityana Vaishnavism because of Vaishnavite Sankritanas being a form of worship of Krishna and Radha through hymns of praise and dramatization of scenes from their lives and from their sporting in the gardens of Vrindavan.[174] As a result Meitei classical music and dance drama became well known to outsiders.

5.2. Existence of Indigenous Cults

Even though Sankirtanas brought some sort of unification to the soul of Meitei culture the opposition to the Hindu faith by the indigenous cult was so strong that a compromise had been made so that a Meitei Vaishnava could worship the indigenous gods and goddesses. The traditional Meitei worship style was

---

170 Reconciliation or fusion of differing systems of belief, as in philosophy or religion, especially when success is partial or the result is heterogeneous. " Syncretism," http://www.answers.com/topic/syncretism (23 Feb 2013).

171 Sukhdev Singh Chib, *North-Eastern India: Caste, Tribes & Culture of India,* vol. 8 (New Delhi: Ess Ess Publications, 1984), 89.

172 Nimandi Vaishnavism of Madhavacharya Sect which was sometimes known as Nimandi taking the name from the preceptor Nimbaka Acharya. R.P. Athparia & S.S. Data Choudhury, "Socio-Religious Transformation among the People of Manipur," in *Religion in North-East in India*, edited by Soumen Sen (New Delhi: Uppal Publishing House, 1993), 34.

173 Ramandi was originated from Rama cult, R.P. Athparia & S.S. Data Choudhury, "Socio-Religious Transformation," 34.

174 R. Constantine, *Manipur Maid of the Mountains* (New Delhi: Lancers Publishers, 1981), 41.

continued in various forms.[175] They continued to worship Soraren, Pakhangba, Sanamahi, Ima Laimaren and 365 *Umanglais*.[176] In relation to this Gangmumei Kabui writes:[177]

> A religious syncretism had occurred and a fine synthesis had been affected. At the same time, the indigenous Meitei gods and goddesses were identified with that of the Hindu gods and goddesses. Thus Soraren, King of heaven was identified with Indra, Nongpok Ningthou with Shiva, Panthoiba with Durga or Parvati, Wangbaren, the water god with Varuna, etc. Legends about the exploits of Arjuna, and his fight with Brabuvahana had been created. Thus, Manipuri Vaishnavism is not purely a brand implanted from Bengal but adopted to suit the local tastes and ideas which show vitality and the accommodating qualities of Hinduism.

Although there had been no systematic and aggressive attempt to destroy all the traditional *lais,* certain of them had been purified, and Hinduism clearly had been given royal patronage. The old religion, however, was not yet finally dead.[178] The religious synthesis may be regarded as having three aspects:[179]

1) The *lais,* who did not have any great significance, seem to have been allowed to pass into forgetfulness.
2) The facility of the Hindu gods to assimilate and to become identified with traditional deities.
3) The traditional *lai* came to be worshiped according to Hindu ritual; for example, in the substitution of bloodless offering for animal sacrifices.

There was a greater emphasis on integration of both of them. Meitei *lai* was integrated into the Hindu system and the Hindu gods into Meitei culture. Regarding the integration Parratt also mentions, "The Vaishnavism practiced in Manipur became a peculiarly Manipuri Vaishnavism in form, adopting aspects of Meitei culture and being modified by it."[180] So this integrated factor had brought mutual settlement of differences in religious aspects and created a sense of belonging among the Meiteis in Manipur valley. Indeed this sense of belonging to Vaishnavism is one of the rejective factors for the Meiteis.

---

[175] R.P. Athparia & S.S. Data Choudhury, "Socio-Religious Transformation," 34.

[176] Kh. Ratan Kumar, *Lai Haraoba of Manipur: Indigenous Festival of the Meitei: A Socio-Historical Perspective* (Imphal: Smt. Ph. Pratima Devi, 2001), 49-51.

[177] Gangmumei Kabui, "Socio-Religious," 93.

[178] L. Bhagyachandra Singh, *A Critical Study of the Religious Philosophy of the Meeteis Before the Advent of Vaishnavism in Manipur* (Imphal: L. Jayantakumar Singh, 1991), 165.

[179] Gangmumei Kabui, "Socio-Religious," 93-94.

[180] Saroj Nalini Parratt, *The Religion of Manipur,* 169.

6. The Success of Vaishnavism in Manipur

From the above it is clear there were various reasons for the success of Vaishnavism in Manipur. Its development is to be understood in terms of the prevailing intellectual and social climates. The crucial factors are discussed below.

6.1. Royal Benefaction

Vaishnavism spread rapidly all over Manipur under the patronage of such powerful monarchs as Garibniwaj, Chourajit, Gambhir Singh, Nara Singh, Chandrakirti etc. They neutralized the antipathy of the people by assuming the title of Lainingthou (King of gods), and posed as an incarnation of Vishnu for the restoration of dharma.[181] Their Vaishnavite leaning added to their glory and divinity which is best expressed by the constant association of the image of Vishnu with King. Manipur suffered from repeated Burmese invasions and the political situation was extremely bad. Able and noble Kings like Jayasimba and Gambhir could restore the social order after overcoming the Burmese. Those Kings were greatly respected by the people as the rescuers of their race. Many people were attracted to the Vaishnava fold by their pleading and good examples hence they could convert many into their path.[182]

The support of the Kings for Vaishnavism was partly due to the desire to obtain the help of the Goswamis[183] of Bengal. They realized that the search for political help must be circumscribed by the religious considerations. For King Jayasimha this policy was not a sudden affair. He established his relationship with the East India Company through Haridas Gosai. The Goswamis of Bengal helped him in many ways. This, at once, evoked his admiration for Vaishnavism. After coming to Manipur the King with his subjects accepted the Vaishnavism of Chaitanya. Similarly the Goswamis of Murshidabad helped King Chandrakirti and his mother in securing his accession to the throne. It was for this reason that he had deep reverence for the Bengal Gosais as his gurus.[184]

Not only the Kings, but the nobles also took an important part in the propagation of this cult in Manipur. It is mentioned in the chronicle that they spent a large sum of money in the erection and consecration of temples and

---

[181] W. Yumjao Singh, *An Early History of Manipur*, 112-13.

[182] T. C. Hodson, *The Meitheis,* 84-85.

[183] Goswamis are renounced teachers in the religious traditions of India. The title "goswami" comes from two words: "go," meaning senses, and "swami," meaning master. Thus goswamis are meant to be masters of the senses. Those who can use the title "goswami" are usually those who have taken the sannyasa vows, belonging to the order of Hindu life in which they renounce all family, material and social ties, take a vow of celibacy and live only to teach the ways of God. "Goswamis," http://www.answers.com/-topic/goswami (23 Feb 2013).

[184] L. Ibungohal Singh, *Meaning of Mayang* (Imphal: Manipur Sahitya Parishad, 1962), 17.

installation of images. Some donated liberal charities and fed the Brahmins and the Vaishnavas.[185]

6.2. Religious Liberalism and Adaptability

Another factor in the success of Vaishnavism in Manipur is religious liberalism and adaptability. The Vaishnavism in its travel from Bengal to Manipur borrowed many local elements and associated itself with pre-Vaishnavite gods. It was the policy of most of the Meitei Kings to unite the conflicting interests of ancient Meitei religion and Vaishnavism. There was mutual compromise and in this process the primitive gods were amalgamated with Hindu gods. The Kings issued injunctions, equating Kwak-tanba festival with Durgapuja festival, the Heikru Hidongba festival with the boat festival of Radha and Krishna. Varuni festival was merged with the remembrance day of Nommai Petanga. Some ancient rites and ceremonies were incorporated into the Vaishnava faith. Sanamahi was made a devotee of Krishna—Nongpok Ningthou and Nongpok Panthoibi were identified with Siva[186] and Durga[187] respectively.[188]

In addition, the successful acceptance of Vaishnavism by the Meiteis is also due to the fact that pre-Vaishnavite religious life was characterized by dance, drama and music. Among the Meiteis it was usual to engage in dance as a means of true worship. This is in tune with Chaitanya's *sankirtan* which is a simple mode of musical worship of Radha and Krishna through hymns of praise and enactment of scenes of the divine spot. This sankirtan was far more effective than sermon. On the whole, very few Vaishnavas delivered sermons. Chaitanya method of group singing in private homes added fresh, active and vital links of communication to the masses. The narration and hearing of religious parables, interaction and debates at crucial sessions represented indispensable aids to the propagation of Vaishnavism. Such functions lasted for several days, weeks and even months. As noted earlier, the Vaishnavite texts figured prominently in the discourses, and were attended to by varying numbers of people.[189]

Kings, nobles and the masses lived a spartan life. They spent their money in organizing sankritan and other related religious ceremonies. Sometimes for many days the Kings kept their gates open to the poor and thousands used to throng

---

[185] L. Ibungohal Singh, *Meaning of Mayang,* 19.

[186] The destroyer; one of the three major divinities in the later Hindu pantheon. WordWeb, 2012 ed, version 6.75, s.v; "Siva."

[187] Hindu goddess of war; a malevolent aspect of Devi. WordWeb, 2012 ed, version 6.75, s.v; "Durga."

[188] M. Kirti Singh, *Religious Development in Manipur in the 18th & 19th Centuries* (Imphal: Manipur State Kala Akademi, 1980), 177.

[189] S.N. Sharma, *The Neo-Viasnavite Movement and the Satra Institutions of Assam* (Gauhati: Department of Publication, Gauhati University, 1966), 22-24.

at the palace. They sat to eat in long rows without any distinction of caste[190] or creed. Uninvited persons were welcome to the *kirtan*.[191] Food was extensively distributed among them from midday till evening, batch after batch. The tidings of the royal *kirtan* spread far and wide. Apart from the royal feast there were also other feasts at the individual houses. Such generous works were a great help in the propagation of Vaishnavism.[192]

6.3. Receptiveness of the People Particularly Brahmins

As we have discussed earlier, many Brahmins came to Manipur in various periods and from various places. One of the reasons for their coming into Manipur was due to the persecution by Muslims in various parts of India, which compelled them to seek refuge. Having taken refuge in Manipur, they began to develop social and religious festivities apart from the old religious ones. As they conducted most of the religious rites and rituals, they were able to witness Vaishnavite religious ceremonies conducted in most of the localities in Manipur valley and in due course of time Meiteis were attracted to it. As mentioned earlier, Brahmins had some voice in the society. They made efforts in explaining to the Kings and people, the importance of Hindu rites and philosophy of Vaishnavism. They invented stories tracing the descent of the Kings from the illustrious Kshatriya princes of the Epics. They superimposed the gotra[193] system upon the Meiteis.

Brahmins were known to have dedicated themselves to literary and philosophical pursuits. They cultivated this both in mind and body. They illustrated their points of arguments with analogies and incidents drawn from Vaishnavism and early Meitei traditional religion. They were able to discover the similarity between the Meitei folk songs of Lai haraoba[194] and the *Vipralambha*

---

[190] (Hinduism) a hereditary social class among Hindus; stratified according to ritual purity. Indu Bhushan, "Caste," in *Encyclopedia of Oriental Philosophy and Religion: Hinduism,* vol. I, edited by N. K. Singh and A. P. Mishra (New Delhi: Global Vision Publishing House, 2005), 131-32.

[191] Even though the term 'Kirtan' has been explained in brief earlier—we may also refer to E. C. Dimock for further explanation. E. C. Dimock, "Kirtana," in *Abingdon Dictionary of Living Religions,* edited by Keith Crim, Roger A. Bullard Larry D. Shinn (Nashville: Abingdon Press, 1981), 408-10.

[192] Lairenmayum Ibungohal Singh and N. Khelchandra Singh, ed., *Cheitharol Kumbaba*, 127, 51, 329, 69.

[193] Gotra is the Sanskrit term for a much older system of tribal clans. The Sanskrit term "Gotra" was initially used by the Vedic people for the identification of the lineages. Generally, these lineages mean patrilineal descent from the sages or *rishi*s in Brahmins, warriors and administrators in Kshatriyas and ancestral trade men in Vaisyas. "Gotra," http://www.britannica.com/search?query=Gotra (23 Feb 2013).

[194] Lai Haraoba is an ancient Manipuri fertility rite or pleasing of god, celebrating cosmic union between male and female principles. In later days, it was enlarged to incorporate cosmological and ideological categories of the Meitei nation, assuming an intense and complicated ritual theatre structure. The celebration of Lai Haraoba is still being observed by Meiteis. "Lai Haraoba,' http://www.indianetzone. -com/31/lai_haraoba_indian_ritual.htm (20 Mar 2013).

songs (feelings of separation). The pure erotic love is one of the crucial features of Gaudiya Vaishnavism. Before the introduction of Vaishnavism, the dual incarnations of Nongpok Ningthou (northern King) and Nongpok Panthoibi and of Khamba and Thoibi set the examples of unalloyed love in Manipur. This was compared with that of Radha and Krishna.[195]

Another aspect in the rapid growth of popular support for Vaishnavism over these centuries is the concept of Krishna as a god of the common people. As a result of discourses on Vaishnavism, the cult of Krishna impressed them more than Siva, Sanamahi and Phakhangba.[196]

6.4. External Influence Intelligently Channelized through the Ruling House

The Chronicle makes frequent references to the immigrant Brahmins who came to Manipur. Mendicants, yogis, pilgrims and missionaries belonging to different sects used to come. Manipur was flooded by scriptures and idols. It is significant that the descendants of Advaita, Nityananda and Nidhirama Achariya defended the Chaitanya School strongly. Some induced the Kings to follow the doctrine of ahimsa and bhakti. It was because of their efforts that Manipur has remained the stronghold of Vaishnavism since 18th century.

Further, the names of people and places were named after the Gaudiya Vaishnava names and terms thereof, remaining as memories testifying the contact of Manipur with other parts of India. The root meanings of Sri, Singh, Devi, and Sharma imply that they are Vaishnava Hindus. It shows the love of the people for their faith. Gauranga, Gaura, Chaitanya, Nimai, Visvambhara, Nityai, Haridas, Narottam, Radha, Radhe, Krishna, Gopal, Rama etc., have become common names in Manipur. In addition to this, Meiteis were also named after Nabadwip, Nadiya, Bhubneswar, Vrindavana ksetra etc., which are the holy places with Vaishnavite associations. This shows them not only as followers of Vaishnavism but as preservers of it.[197]

6.5. Influence of the Varna Order

Another crucial aspect of the success of Vaishnavism is connected with the varna[198] order which was introduced in Manipur. The ruling family and the majority of

---

[195] L. Ibungohal Singh, *An Introduction to Manipur*, 31.

[196] L. Ibungohal Singh, *An Introduction to Manipur*, 32.

[197] J. Shakespeare, "The Religion of Manipur," *Transactions of the Folk-Lore Society*, xxiv/iv (December, 1913): 412-16.

[198] There are four varnas in Hinduism namely Brahmin, kshatriya, Vaishya and shudra. Influence of varna helped in building Hinduism among the Meiteis. "The Caste System," http://www.vepachedu.org/-castemore.-htm. (23 Feb 2013). cf. WordWeb, 2012 ed, version 6.75, s.v; "varna." cf. Irving Hexham, "Varnas," in *Concise Dictionary of Religion* (Illinois: InterVarsity Press, 1993), 226.

the Meiteis call themselves Kshatriya. The Kings proclaimed themselves as the upholders of Varnasrama system. The Brahmins performed priestly functions. The people were urged to perform the duties in conformity with the varna order. The merchants and traders were the worshippers of Visnu and other deities of Vaishnavism. Actuated by the desire for religious merit they constructed many temples in several villages. They placed idols in these temples. The Kings and some of the well-to-do families made a gift of land to the Brahmins. Suitable areas of land were allotted for the worship of gods and erection of *mandapas* (social gathering place). It was due to their religious leanings that every village has a temple.[199]

Something should be said about the activities of the sudras.[200] It is to be noted that lower orders, the Lois, (scheduled caste Meiteis), Phunganai (servant), Tengkhul (servant of the King employed as a class of gardener), and Kei (servant of the King employed as a class in charge of granary) served the King and not the three higher classes, as found in the Smrti systems of the Hindus. They are not identical with the sudras in other parts of India. They professed Vaishnavism with the consent of Kings. The spread of Vaishnavism was in tune with the loose form of varna order as found in Manipur. The members of the higher varnas thought that they can earn spiritual merit by religious works; and the members of the lower varnas could hope that their condition could be better in the next world by following the social order imposed upon them by a Brahminical society.[201] In this manner the influence of the varna order helped in the growth of Vaishnavism in Manipur valley.

7. Impact of Sanskritization

Sanskritization[202] among the Meiteis in Manipur valley had an indelible impact on contemporary society, traditional religion and culture, based on the doctrine of animism, indigenous language and literature, art and architecture, coins and inscriptions, sculpture and iconography etc. Sanskritization in Manipur is not a homogeneous growth of religious thought, rather it represents religious and cultural integration and synthesis of old and new faiths. This really appears to be a distinct phase in the socio-religious history of Manipur. The introduction of Hinduism went a long way in transforming the structure of society and old religious beliefs and practices. A new cultural and artistic tradition was

[199] M. Kirti Singh, "The Social Implication of Vaishnava Movement in Manipur,' in *Magazine, G.P. Women College* (Imphal: G.P. Women College, 1969), 17-18.

[200] The lowest of the four varnas: the servants and workers of low status. WordWeb, 2012 ed, version 6.75, s.v; "Sudra."

[201] T. C. Hodson, *The Meitheis,* 84-85. According to Hodson, none of the ordinary definitions of caste applied to the social order of the Meiteis.

[202] The term Sanskritization here means the conversion of Meiteis into Vaishnavism or in a broader sense; it means the conversion of Meiteis into Hinduism.

constructed. It also led to the enrichment of the language and literature. As a result of the cultural fellowship and mutual contacts of the Meiteis with the Aryan Hindus in the ancient times and with the Brahmins coming from outside and Vaishnava missionaries of different schools during both the medieval and the modern periods, a new composite civilization flourished in the valley of Manipur.

To examine the cumulative effects of Sanskritization on Meitei society, religion and culture in a true historical perspective, it is necessary to focus on the crucial changes which took place in the course of the Sanskritization of a considerable section of population, because the changes concerned proved to be indirectly very helpful in the rise and growth of Vaishnavism. As stated earlier, one of the characteristic features of the history of Sanskritization in Manipur is the co-existence of animism and Vaishnavism. The modification of traditional social customs, rites and rituals, assimilation of many primitive cults and animistic beliefs into Hinduism and identification of the traditional gods and goddesses with the divinities of Hindu pantheon are some of the crucial fundamental features of Sanskritization, which flourished in Manipur in general between the second half of the 15th and the early part of the 19th centuries.

M.N. Srinivas rightly points out that Sanskritization had a great impact on the contemporary society. Within a comparative framework, that the lower castes Sanskritize (i.e., they adopt upper caste practices) so as to move up in the social/caste hierarchy.[203] So also among Meiteis, Sanskritization had a tremendous impact on their existing society. The traditional social customs and rites were greatly modified after the adoption of Vaishnavism. It was after the advent of Hinduism that the rite of initiation began. The sacred thread ceremony became popular and it was adopted by both Brahmins and Kshatriyas. The rites of birth, marriage and death were also performed in conformity with Hindu practices. In this regard, T.C. Hodson has rightly pointed out that the birth ceremony in Manipuri society is in line with the Vaishnava Hindu tradition.[204] Marriage ceremonies were performed both according to Hindu and traditional rites. As a result of Hindu influence, two important forms of marriage known as Brahma and Gandharva,[205] as prescribed in the Hindu scriptures, were added to the other traditional forms of marriage. Further, the restriction imposed on marriage between the families within the same *gotra* (clan) was evidently the result of the impact of Hinduism. Marriage within the same caste, sanctity of *gotra* or *sagei*

[203] M.N. Srinivas, *Social Change in Modern India*. 157-58.

[204] T. C. Hodson, *The Meitheis,* 112.

[205] In Hinduism the gandharvas (*gandharva*) are male nature spirits, husbands of the Apsaras. They have superb musical skills. They guarded the soma and made beautiful music for the gods in their palaces. A gandharva means a singer in the court of Gods. In Hindu law, a Gandharva marriage is one contracted by mutual consent and without formal rituals. "Gandharvas," http://www.answers.com/topic/gandharva (23 Feb 2013).

and the freedom granted to Brahmins in the society was also the inheritance of Sanskritization.

Another area of influence is the method of disposing of a dead body. It was greatly influenced by the Brahminic methods in their society. But at the same time the continuance of the traditional customs and the importance of the role played by the Maibas (traditional priest) cannot be denied.[206] The Hindu method of cremation was compulsorily adopted during the time of Garibniwaj in place of burial, which was the traditional practice in the pre-Hindu period. The purification ceremony, which is still in practice, was also a Sanskritized method. It was adopted both by Brahmins,[207] Kshatriyas[208] and other Hindus.[209]

One of the explicit impacts of Sanskritization of Meiteis was the popularity of Brahmins in their society.[210] The traditional rites and rituals and ceremonies and festivals were controlled, governed, guided and regulated by the Brahmins.[211] Blood sacrifice was a common practice in the pre-Hindu period, and there is no doubt about the prevalence of the practice of the animal sacrifice before the adoption of Vaishnavism. But with the acceptance of it, the ban was imposed on blood sacrifice. From the chronicle as well the oral tradition, it is quite evident that the human and animal sacrifices for worshipping traditional *lais* (gods) were also prevalent before the coming of Hinduism. But such practices were modified after receiving the touch of Hinduism. Subsequently, in the 18th century, restrictions were also imposed on the eating of meat and consumption of wine. [212] As stated earlier, before the time of King Garibniwaj the influence of Hinduism on Meitei society was not very strong, particularly during the early medieval period.

One of the remarkable changes witnessed in the course of Sanskritization, which was going on between 15th and 19th centuries, was that most of the immigrant Brahmins became part and parcel of Meitei society. After their settlement in different parts of Manipur the basic structure of the traditional society underwent changes. They were allotted various *sagei* (clan), which they still bear today. Their marriage relations with the Meitei women completed the process of their assimilation in the society. Later on, the settlements of the descendants of the

---

[206] T. C. Hodson, *The Meitheis,* 116.

[207] The highest of the four varnas: the priestly or sacerdotal category. WordWeb, 2012 ed, version 6.75, s.v; "Brahmins."

[208] A member of the royal or warrior Hindu caste. WordWeb, 2012 ed, version 6.75, s.v; "Kshatriya."

[209] Some of these traditional practices will be discussed deeper in the following chapter.

[210] Rev. Lalrinliana Colney worked as an evangelist for twelve years among the Sanskritized Meiteis in Manipur Valley. Interview with Lalrinliana Colney, Manipur Valley Missionary, Mizoram Presbyterian, Imphal West, 27 November, 2012.

[211] T. C. Hodson, *The Meitheis,* 117. cited in. Interview with Lalrinliana Colney, Manipur Valley Missionary.

[212] T. C. Hodson, *The Meitheis,* 119.

Brahmins further resulted in a change in the ethnic composition of the society, but at the same time, it created genetic problems as well.

Another important consequence of the impact of Hindu culture on Meitei society during the medieval period was the adoption of Hindu ceremonies and festivals and identification of local deities with Hindu deities, before the time of Charairongba. One of the aspects worth mentioning about the impact on society and religion is the adoption of Hindu rituals and festivals. There are evidences of Hindu influence on the Meitei festivals.[213] It is believed that all together seven festivals were introduced into Manipur directly under the influence of Vaishnavism. Three of these are Holi, Janmastami and Ratha Yatra and directly connected with Krishna, whose worship became very popular after the advent of Chaitanya Vaishnavism in the State. The other festivals are Baruni (the north Indian Ganga Saptami) dedicated to Siva and Durga Puja, Saraswati Puja and Diwali, all of which became popular after the adoption of Hindu customs and practices.[214]

With the coming of Vaishnavism, traditional religious systems also underwent transformation. After the Meiteis were brought within the fold of Brahminical Hinduism, their traditional gods and goddesses were identified with the deities of Hindu pantheon. Hinduism not only led to the absorption of the people within the newly emerging Hindu society but also to the transition from the old faith of the so called pre-Hindu period to the new faith of the Hindu era.

A syncretism of the old pre-Hindu Meitei religious rites and rituals, beliefs and practices etc. with the Hindu Brahminical religious rituals and mythology took place. The old popular deities of Meiteis like Panthoibi and Sanamahi and other animistic deities were worshipped along with Hindu deities. For example, Mei has been identified with Brahma, Ishing with Vishnu, Nungshit with Siva, Shorarel with Indra, Marjing with Kubera, Khoriphaba with Varuna, Wangbaral with Yama, Irum with Agni and Taoroinai with Anata. The Maibas and Maibis (priest and priestess) were harmonized with Brahminical ones.[215] J. Shakespeare, a noted authority, also argues that though the progress of Hinduism in Manipur was slow it was achieved by a compromise with ancient faith.[216] T. C. Hodson, a popular authority on the subject, dealt with it in the following words:[217]

> Here we have the stately fabric of Hinduism with its elastic case of accommodation. We have the fresh healthy indigenous system of

[213] As a Christian Missionary, Rev. Lalthoruol Sanate worked for fourteen years among the Sanskritized Meiteis in Manipur Valley. Interview with Lalthoruol Sanate, Manipur Valley Missionary, Evangelical Church of India, Imphal East, 18 July, 2012.

[214] W. Yumjao Singh, *An Early History of Manipur*, 41-42.

[215] W. Yumjao Singh, *An Early History of Manipur*, 43-48.

[216] J. Shakespeare, "The Religion of Manipur," 414-16.

[217] T. C. Hodson, *The Meitheis,* 95-96.

> animism, and as a result of the commingling of these forces and this point a medley of religious benefits in which every phase of human imagination finds its place .... The old order of things has not passed away by any means and the Maiba, the doctor and priest of the animistic system still finds a livelihood despite the competition on the one hand of the Brahmins, and the Hospital Assistant on the other.

Hence, Hinduism and traditional practices went on side by side among the Meiteis in Manipur valley. As mentioned earlier, it is worthwhile to reflect again in brief the notable changes which were witnessed during the reigns of Charairongba, Garibniwaj and other successors. During the reign of Charairongba along with the worship of Hindu deities like Vishnu,[218] Durga and Sakti,[219] the worship of the great traditional goddess Panthoibi also continued. It is significant to note that after the process of Sanskritization began, the goddess Panthoibi was identified with Kali. As a matter of fact, Hinduism coexisted with the traditional gods and goddesses, which can best be proved by the fact that the temples dedicated to both the traditional and Hindu gods were erected almost at the same time during his reign.[220]

But Sanskritization did not always flow smoothly among the Meiteis. Later on with the accession of Garibniwaj to the throne of Manipur, a new era of Hindu renaissance and reformation, as well as revolt, started. The declaration of Hinduism as the State religion produced mixed results. As a result of the forcible Sanskritization of a considerable section of Meitei population the feeling of resentment grew. In his bid to impose Hinduism the King destroyed the images of many traditional gods and goddesses and many scriptures dealing with the animistic time. Royal support was extended to the worship of Hindu gods and goddesses. With the revival of the Chaitanya school of Vaishnavism, Hinduism made further progress. In order to establish the supremacy of Hindu gods, many lais (traditional gods) were destroyed and burnt down.

With the appointment of the guru as preceptor to the King the influence of the traditional priests and priestesses gradually began to decline. This sometime resulted in conflict between the representatives of the ancient faith and those of the new, both on political and religious grounds.[221] On the whole the attitude of the King (Garibniwaj) to traditional religion was extremely hostile. It is true that Vaishnavism did not receive the wide support from the followers of the

---

[218] The sustainer; a Hindu divinity worshipped as the preserver of worlds. WordWeb, 2012 ed, version 6.75, s.v; "Vishnu."

[219] The female or generative principle; wife of Siva and a benevolent form of Devi. WordWeb, 2012 ed, version 6.75, s.v; "Sakti."

[220] Lairenmayum Ibungohal Singh and N. Khelchandra Singh, ed., *Cheitharol Kumbaba*, 59-60.

[221] T. C. Hodson, *The Meitheis,* 94.

old religion. However, it would not be correct to say that the King completely destroyed the traditional religion. This is borne out by the fact that some of the traditional gods were placed under the supervision and control of the Brahmins. This was tactically done for increasing the importance of Brahmins and reducing the significance of Maiba and Maibi in Meitei society. Thus, we find that Hinduism and traditional faith sometimes coexisted and sometimes opposed each other. On the other hand, both syncretism and synthesis of the two different religious orders, as well as the conflict between the two faiths moved in a cyclic order in course of Sanskritization, which was going on in full swing during the time of King Garibniwaj. The image of this King appears to be both as a protector and destroyer of the old faith, and a guardian of the new faith. The domination of one over the other or the subordination of one to the other appears to be a regular phenomenon in the religious history of Manipur. However, the reign of Garibniwaj marked a departure to a great extent from the earlier trend, and ultimately saw the dominance of Hinduism over the animistic cult.

Socio-religious condition of Meitei society underwent in a new shape during the time of King Chingthang Khomba, (1759-1762).[222] He not only confirmed the Chaitanya Vaishnavism as the State religion but also introduced certain changes in the religious life of the people in Manipur. His period was a period of compromise between Hinduism and traditional faith. From the native chronicle it appears that the worship of the popular house-hold deity, Sanamahi, was never neglected during his time. With the creation of the image of this deity the Sanamahi cult retained its popularity.[223]

Lord Avebury rightly remarks by saying that, "In both countries, Burma and Manipur, however the older religious ideas still survive beneath the surface of the philosophical system borrowed from India, which are reflected to a large extent in the lives, sentiments and beliefs of the people."[224] Further during the time of Chingthang Khomba the traditional mode of worship of the Meitei god was Sanskritized. The worship of both traditional and Hindu deities is beautifully illustrated in the chronicle. According to it, we find that the images of Govindaji, as well as the image of Sanamahi and that of other Meitei gods were treated equally. The King, the queen, the common people, the Brahmins, the followers of Ramanandi cult and the followers of traditional faith enjoyed the royal patronage together.[225]

---

[222] Chingthang Khomba, 56th King of Manipur, reigned for three years. He is also known by various names, i.e., Bhagychandra, Karta Maharaj and Nungmang Khomba. N. Tombi Singh, *Manipur and the Mainstream,* 48.

[223] Lairenmayum Ibungohal Singh and N. Khelchandra Singh, ed., *Cheitharol Kumbaba*, 118, 40.

[224] Lord Avebury, *The Origin of Civilization and the Primitive Condition of Man* (London: Longmans Green Co., 1911), 24.

[225] Lairenmayum Ibungohal Singh and N. Khelchandra Singh, ed., *Cheitharol Kumbaba*, 127, 33.

As a result of the acceptance of the Chaitanya Vaishnavism the songs, music and dance were greatly affected along with the Rasa dance known as Rasa-lila (Rasa dance) based on the famous traditional dance lai haraoba. The devotional songs based on bhakti cult were composed for the singing of Kirtan in Vaishnavite style. Thus, the cultural pattern of Manipur during his time was greatly Sanskritized. After coming under the influence of Chaitanya Vaishnavism along with newly introduced Rasa dance, the old dances assisted and guided by Meitei dance teachers, Pandits and Maiba and Maibis, never lost their popularity. Music, dancing and fine arts received encouragement during his time along with the Rasa dance based on Radha-Krishna cult of Vaishnavism. The religious folk-dance was also transformed. The older ritualistic dance like lia haraoba was the basis on which the charming Rasa or Radha-Krishna dance-plays have been built up.

The Rasa dance of Manipur was also introduced in Bengal by those Meiteis, who were in Sylhet. Later it was taken by Rabindranath Tagore in his school at Santiniketan and further spread to other parts of India. Bengali and North Indian Hindu-dresses were adopted by the Meiteis. Thus, we find that by and large, the religious synthesis was maintained. Two faiths—traditional and Hinduism flourished side by side during this time as well.

Linguistic changes and literary progress are the other two important aspects. It is believed that the Meiteis obtained an alphabet probably during the time of King Kiyamba. But on the other hand 1700 A.D. has also been suggested as the date for it. Our concern here is not on the origin but how and why the script has been replaced. In the olden time, the knowledge of this script was confined to the priests only and it never spread among the masses. Quite a good number of old manuscripts including the works on Manipur history and culture were written in this script. But after the acceptance of Vaishnavism, the Bengali script was introduced in place of the archaic script, and this new script came to be used for different purposes. This happened during the reign of King Garibniwaj.

The newly introduced Bengali script had great bearings on coins, inscriptions and literature. Under the influence of Vaishnava form of Hinduism, the history of coins took a different turn. All the descendants of King Charairongba, down to the last independent King Kulachandra, issued coins bearing either the Devanagari or the Bengali script. The use of Nagari and Bengali scripts and the Sanskrit words in the bell metal, gold and silver coins from the time of King Garibniwaj onwards bear a testimony to the impact of Hinduism on the designs, patterns and styles of the coins etc. The use of the initial letters of the names of the issuing Kings, for example, "JE SHRI GARIBNIWAJA MEKHLESHWAR GOMTI RANI SSE" and "SHRI GAMBHEERA SIMHA NRIPAVARASYA CHANDRABDA," the use of the Hindu deities worshipped, for example, "JE SHRI RAM, JAY RAM," "SHRI SHRI GOVINDA," "SHRIMADRADHA GOVINDA," etc., as depicted on the different coins issued between 1709 and 1834 A.D. reflect a strong Hindu influence on the socio-religious and socio-cultural aspects of the Meiteis in Manipur valley.[226] Thus, introduction of Hinduism marked the beginning of a new age in the history of Manipuri coinage.

Further, the impact of Sanskritization can also be seen on the inscriptions. We find the use of "Shree" and "Raam" for the first time in the "Ningel Inscription" of King Garibniwaj, who was a great disciple of Vaishnavism. The use of this word in both the archaic Meitei script and the Bengali script in the inscription issued since the time of Garibniwaj is additional evidence of the influence of Vaishnavism.[227] Thus, both the numismatic and epigraphic evidence proves the use of the new Bengali script which came into use after the declaration of Hinduism as the State religion during the time of Garibniwaj.

Vaishnavism had also brought a great change in the area of literature among the Meiteis in Manipur. This change was again witnessed particularly during the time of Garibniwaj. A new trend followed, so far as the art of writing is concerned. The attention of the local writers was diverted towards producing those kinds of literature which could focus mainly on Hindu religion and culture. The primary objective behind this motivation was to create awareness among the people about the richness of the Hindu culture and consciousness for preserving and promoting the newly introduced Vaishnava form of Hinduism. The early Meitei literature prior to the middle of the 18th century A.D. popularly known as Chronicle were written mostly in the old Meitei language and archaic script.[228] But after the introduction of Bengali script under the influence of Hinduism the history of literature took a different turn.

The Rig-Veda, the Ramayana, the Mahabharata, Srimad Bhagavat Purana, other texts on Brahminical Hinduism like Bhagavata Gita, Manusamhita, Geeta Govinda, Govinda Lila Amritam etc. were translated into Meiteilon with parallel original Sanskrit text. The rich Meitei literature proved to be a powerful force for the propagation and popularization of the Hindu religion and culture.[229] Here it must be mentioned that particularly the Vaishnavite literature translated into Meiteilon proved to be very helpful in promoting the further growth of Hinduism.

The Bengali version of Kritivasi's Ramayana was adopted by Meiteis. The Adi, the Virata and Asvamesha, Parvans of the Mahabharata were also translated into Meiteilon. The old myths and legends of the Meiteis were also linked up inextricably with Brahminical legends. The ancient mode of prayer and worship

---

[226] P. Gunindra Singh, *Manipur Numismatic*, 30-33; cited in., "Coins of Manipur," *Bulletin of Mutua Museum*, no. 1 (October, 1980): 43-44.

[227] M. Bahadur, P. Gunindra Singh, *Epigraphical Records of Manipur*, vol. 1. (Imphal: Mutua Museum, 1986), 9-12.

[228] Appendi 6. Meitei archaic scripts (alphabets) which were destroyed by King Garibniwaj are shown here. "Manipuri Alphabet," http://www.omniglot.com/writing/manipuri.htm (21 Feb 2013).

[229] M. Bahadur, P. Gunindra Singh, *Epigraphical Records of Manipur*, 12.

as described in some of the native Chronicle was also changed into Vaishnava form of worship as described in Vaishnava literature.[230]

A further impact of Vaishnavism was on art. The artistic history of Manipur was also affected under the influence of Brahminic religion. A new Hindu style was adopted in the field of architecture, sculpture and iconography. The change in the architectural style can particularly be seen in the Hindu temples whose construction began from the time of King Kiyamba in the 15th century. It has already been noted that the Vishnu temple at Bishnupur built during the time of this King for the spread of Vishnu cult in Manipur was very similar to the temples built in various parts of India during the 7th and 9th centuries. The architectural style of the Krishna temple and various other temples built during the time of King Charairongba was very similar to the Bengal school of architecture ascribed to the 17 and 18th centuries. The temple of Hanuman built by King Garibniwaj also bears similarity to Bengali hut-type temple of the contemporary period.[231] Hence, it may be positively observed that the architectural styles of the temples in Manipur were greatly influenced by Hindu religious teachings.

In short, Sanskritization of Meiteis in Manipur had a strong impact on existing society, traditional religion and culture, based on the doctrine of animism, indigenous language and literature, art and architecture, coins and inscriptions, sculpture and iconography etc. This Sanskritization is not a homogeneous growth of religious thought; rather it represents religious and cultural integration and synthesis of traditional faith practice and Hinduism.

8. Concluding Remarks

As we have seen in this chapter, the origin of Hinduism in Manipur is not a recent phenomenon but centuries old. The Hinduism in Meitei society has been deeply planted during this long era. The spread of Hinduism was done by many Brahmins in various periods. One of the reasons for being in the iron grip of Vaishnavism in this place was the continual influence of the immigrant Brahmins. The royal patronage of Meitei Kings and religious syncretism have had helped a lot in the growth as well. It was because of these that Manipur has remained the stronghold of Vaishnavism since 18th century. Hence, most of the Meitei Hindus continue to resist the introduction of other religions in their society including Christianity.

We may recall the question raised at the beginning of this chapter as to how and why the Sanskritization of Meiteis in Manipur valley is taken as the principal cause for the rejection of Christianity among this community. Essentially, we have already discussed the question being asked in detail based on the origin of Hinduism; the influence and the spread of Hinduism; various stages of Hinduism; the rise of Hinduism as the State religion; further development and

---

[230] M. Bahadur, P. Gunindra Singh, *Epigraphical Records of Manipur*, 14.

[231] P. Gunindra Singh, *Manipur Numismatic*, 33-35.

the synthesis of Hinduism in Manipur. Nevertheless, to answer the question being asked explicitly, we shall now consider in brief the crucial points that have been identified. The Sanskritization of Meiteis in Manipur valley is taken as the principal cause for the rejection of Christianity among this community because:

1) The origin of Hinduism is not a recent phenomenon but centuries old. The Hinduism in Meitei society has been deeply planted there, hence Meitei Hindus continue to resist the introduction of other religions in their society.
2) The influence and the spread of Hinduism was done by many Brahmins in various occasions and periods. So one of the reasons for being the stronghold of Vaishnavism in Manipur was the continual influence of the immigrant Brahmins. It was because of their efforts that the State has remained the stronghold of Vaishnavism since 18th century. This religious phenomenon continues to exist even today.
3) Another aspect is the growth of Hinduism. The growth of Hinduism among the Meiteis in Manipur valley went through various stages under the royal patronage of various Kings. During this long journey many changes took place, including transforming the traditional society, religion and culture, manners and customs, language and literature, art and architecture, etc. In other words, the Hinduism in Manipur is neither infant nor immature but a fully adult and matured one. The religion is fully secured and protected by its followers; hence other religions are unable to penetrate successfully among the Meiteis.
4) Finally, there is the royal patronage and the religious syncretism. The royal patronage of Meitei Kings and the religious syncretism have helped a lot in the growth of Vaishnavism as well. The Vaishnavism in Manipur borrowed many local elements and associated itself with pre-Vaishnavite gods. It was the policy of most of the Meitei Kings to unite the conflicting interests of ancient Meitei religion and Vaishnavism. There was mutual compromise, which can be observed in the following: synthesis of the Meitei religion with its gods and goddesses and traditions; its myths and rituals, its legends and traditions; its social custom and practices and its priests and ceremonials and of Brahminical Hinduism with its special emphasis on the worship of Krishna. Meiteis not only have made significant contribution to the Hindu culture through its Vaishnavism, its dance and music, its art and culture and its literature but continue to hold Vaishnavism as the formal religion of their State. As a result, a sense of belonging to Hinduism is devoutly and steadfastly held and Meiteis continue to resist other religions.

Among all the scholars who have written history of Manipur, the observation a British scholar, J. Shakespeare, may be taken as the most valuable one. He has precisely stated that the use of the term Hinduism for Meiteis in Manipur can be justified by the devotion of the people to Krishna, the importance of the Brahmins in the society and enthusiasm of the people to protect the Hindu culture and religion.[232] Therefore, because of all these factors, the Sanskritization of Meiteis in Manipur is ascertained as the principal cause for the rejection of Christianity among this community. Keeping this principal cause in mind, we shall now move to deal with another and major cause for the rejection of Christianity among Meiteis in Manipur valley.

232 J. Shakespeare, "The Religion of Manipur," 451.

Chapter 4

Revivification of Traditional Religion
A Major Cause for Rejection of Christianity

Introduction

The current chapter is a historical study of the revivification of traditional religion amongst the Meiteis and how this appears to be a major cause for rejection of Christianity among this ethnic group. As set out in the preceding chapter, the Sanskritization in Manipur valley had affected the racial and cultural identity and self-consciousness of the Meiteis.[1] The adoption of Bengali School of Vaishnavism and replacement of ancient Meitei scripts by Bengali scripts had facilitated the development of alien impact upon the Meiteis. This synthetic feature has been in existence among the Meiteis for centuries. In opposition to this, the revival movement started during the reign of King Churachand in a Meitei village in Cachar of Assam. The key leader of the movement was Naorem Pullo,[2] commonly called Laininghal Naoria,[3] and it was under his initiative and leadership the revivification movement took place.

To better follow this revival, the current chapter is divided into two parts. In the first part, we shall be looking at some of the traditional values and beliefs which were in practice by the Meiteis before the revival movement began. The beginning of the revival movement, confrontation, reasons, objectives and achievements are some of the important areas which will be dealt with in the second part. The chapter will then conclude with an evaluation and concluding remarks.

---

[1] Appendix- I, Naorem Sanajaoba, "From the Cradle of Pithecanthropus," in *Manipur: Past and Present,* vol. I, edited by Naorem Sanajaoba (Delhi: Mittal Publications, 1988), i-ii.

[2] The names Naorem Pullo and Laininghal Naoria will be used interchangeably.

[3] R. Constantine, *Manipur Maid of the Mountains* (New Delhi: Lancers Publishers, 1981), 73-74.

1. Traditional Values and Beliefs

Before we begin looking at the revival movement, it is important for us to briefly note the traditional values and beliefs of Meiteis which were in practice by their forefathers. As stated earlier the Meiteis had their own religion, script and practices before their forceful conversion into Vaishnavism.[4] They were followers of an exclusive system of religious beliefs and practices,[5] some of which cultic practices and traditional values are detailed below for our further understanding.[6]

1.1. Creation Mythology

In the pre-Hinduism period, Sanamahi was the most important god of the Meiteis. According to the mythology of this community, Asheeba (another name of Sanamahi) created the sky with all its cosmic and celestial bodies and the Earth with all things—both animate and inanimate. Last of all, he created humans, looking at the shadow of his father, Yaibirel Sidaba (Yaibirel = Supreme Soul, Sidaba = Immortal). He did all this on the advice of his father. His younger brother Pakhangba[7] was made the temporal King of the State while he (Sanamahi) was made the spiritual King of mankind. He was told to stay in the house of humans and protect the life and property of human beings. His mother Leimarel Sidabi (Leima = supreme queen, Sidabi = immortal), the universal mother, was also asked to stay together in the house of humans with him. So, all the Meiteis worshipped Sanamahi as a household god inside the house at the south-western corner where he was supposed to stay.[8] He was worshipped even by the King as a god for all the people. The worship of Sanamahi by a prince with a special ritual was regarded as a sure preliminary to an attempt by the worshipper at the throne, and reserved for the King alone. In the prehistoric time, during the reign of King Kangba, the system of belief and ritual of Sanamahi was known as *Areppa Laining* (Areppa = determined, *Laining* = worship).[9]

---

[4] Konsam Manikchand, "The Evolution of the Meitei State: A Confederacy through the Last Two Millennia," in *Manipur: Past and Present,* vol. I., edited by Naorem Sanajaoba (Delhi: Mittal Publications, 1988), 145-146.

[5] Sukhdev Singh Chib, *North-Eastern India: Caste, Tribes & Culture of India,* vol. 8 (New Delhi: Ess Ess Publications, 1984), 89.

[6] Earlier, in chapter 2, under the heading Anthropological Background, we have discussed the origin of Meitei, the early Meitei state and traditional and cultural values but we have not dealt with some other of these cultic practices and traditional values, nor in sufficient detail. Therefore, we provide more detail that will be helpful in our understanding of revivification.

[7] In the olden days for centuries the Meiteis used to worship 'Pakhangba' the divine ruler of the Meiteis. He had two forms: a human form during the day time and a snake form in the night time, S.S. Shashi, "Manipur: Historical and Cultural Background," in *Tribes of Assam and Manipur,* edited by S.S. Shashi (New Delhi: Anmol Publications Pvt. Ltd., 1995), 201.

[8] O. Bhogeshwar, *Ningthourol Sheireng* (Imphal: O. Bhogeshwar, 1967), 2.

[9] Rajen & Ibohal, *Sakok Lamlel* (Imphal: Rajen, 1973), 4.

It was only during the reign of King Khagemba (1597-1652 A.D.) that the image of Sanamahi was moulded with bell metal for the first time. Another important *Imung lai* (household deity) was Ima Leimarel Sidabi. She was supposed to stay in the northern side of the house opposite to the *Phung-ga* (traditional fire place). She was regarded as the Universal mother and represented by a big earthen pot with water. The third important place of worship inside the house was *Phung-ga Lairu* (*Lai* = god, *ru* or *aruba* = important—important god of *Phung-ga*). This place was just at the western side of the fire place which was in the middle of the house. This was the place where in the early period of social evolution of the Meiteis the dead bodies of their forefathers were probably buried.[10] So, this place was regarded as the place of *Apokpa* (ancestor). This place was so respected by the members of the family that even a small child was not allowed to step over it.[11]

There were four gods who were regarded as the guardians of four important directions:[12]

1) Thanjing, the guardian of the South-West;
2) Marjing, guardian of the North-East;
3) Wangbarel, guardian of the South-East; and
4) Koubru, guardian of the North-West.

In every religious ceremony these four gods were invoked by the *Maiba* and *Maibi* (priest and priestess) to prevent the evil spirits from damaging the ceremony. They were regarded as the incarnations of the four gods who had guarded the earth while it was being created by Sanamahi. They were also worshipped as *Umang lai* (*Umang* = forest. *lai* = god) by the people of the local area.[13]

1.2. Tree Cults

Tree cults can be understood in Meiteilon as *Umang lai*. This concept may have been derived from the *lai* who was associated with trees or forests.[14] According to Meitei tradition, there are 365 *Umang lais*[15] including those associated with

[10] This inference is drawn from the following practices: (I) For the Ancestor worship, the invitation offerings are buried in a small hole dug at the *Phunga Lairu.* (2) *Andro Lois* (a group of Meitei who had not been converted into Hinduism) carry back to the house all the bones which are not burnt to ashes and bury them in a pot to the south west of the *Phunga* (Hearth) (3) Offerings are made at this place in connection with a marriage ceremony in the Meitei community to know whether the ancestors are in favour of the marriage or not. A. Minaketan, *Meitei Lairol* (Imphal: A. Minaketan, 1951), 7-8.

[11] Th. Bheigachandra ex-chairman of Yaipha Lamjing Kanglup, Khundrakpam, Imphal East, Manipur, letter to the author, 22nd November 2010.

[12] N. Kullachandra, *The Meitei Lai Haraoba* (Imphal: Rajo Maibi, 1953), 4.

[13] Jyotirmoy Roy, *History of Manipur* (Calcutta: K.L. Mukhopandhyay, 1958), 177.

[14] Sukhdev Singh Chib, *North-Eastern India: Caste,* 89.

[15] Appendix 2, 365 *Umang lais* are listed with names one after the other under the subheading, "Names of *Umang lai.*" Kh. Ratan Kumar, *Lai Haraoba of Manipur: Indigenous Festival of the Meitei:*

families, with *yeks* (clans) and with community as a whole. So a tree such as *tairen* (Cedrela toona, a cedar) is still used by *maiba* for cultic purposes. *Lais* could be divided into three categories on the basis of their jurisdiction: 1) *Umang lai* of one *Sagei* (a group of families having the same surname), 2) *Umang lai* of a village or villages and 3) *Umang lai* as guardians of four directions.[16] So, the tree cult had been an important part of Meitei culture in pre-Hinduism period.

1.3. Names of *Umang lai*

Ratan, a Meitei scholar, remarks that there were 365 *Umang lais,* precisely the number of days in a year in the Western calendar.[17] These 365 *Umang lais* can be divided into three categories on the basis of their jurisdiction.[18] The *Umang lai Haraoba* is a very ancient dance that pleases the *Umang lai.* In the *Haraoba,* it was compulsory on the part of the elders and youths to participate in one way or another.[19] The customary law relating to *Lai Harnoba* was so strict that when it took place in a particular village, during the festival no member of the village was allowed to leave the village and no outsider was allowed to enter the village. In case an outsider came to the village, he/she had to stay outside till the end of the *Haraoba.* The religious festival of the community was performed for the prosperity of the people within the jurisdiction of the deity. In this public worship, the legend of the creation of the Universe was expressed in song and dance under the guidance of *Maibas* and *Maibis.* It was performed once a year. Every Meitei village was within the jurisdiction of one *Umang lai* or another.[20] In addition there were also a number of *Lam lai* (*Lam* means outdoor or land or place). Their places of worship were at the tops of the hills.

1.4. Animism

T.C. Hodson believes 'animism' to be the ancient beliefs of the Meitei and states that "we are justified in holding them to be still animists." The worship of ancestors by the early Meitei was also indicated by Hodson who writes, "If the definition of ancestor worship is strictly narrowed, we have in Manipur, among the Meiteis

---

A Socio-Historical Perspective (Imphal: Smt. Ph. Pratima Devi, 2001), 52-62.

[16] Kh. Ratan Kumar, *Lai Haraoba of Manipur,* 49-52.

[17] Names of *Umang lai* have been given in Appendix 2, therefore we are not repeating them here.

[18] *Umang lai haraoba* (Pleasing of Umang lai) was a community festival. Sairem Nilabir, "The Revivalist Movement of Sanamahism," in *Manipur Past and Present: The Ordeals and Heritage of a Civilization,* vol. 2, edited by Naorem Sanajaoba (New Delhi: Mittal Publications, 1991), 110. Sukhdev Singh Chib, *North-Eastern India,* 96.

[19] Jyotirmoy Roy, *History of Manipur,* 184.

[20] N. Manihar, Ex-member Chingkei Laiharaoba Committee, Phaknung, Imphal East, Manipur, letter to the author, 28th September 2010.

only, the form of ancestor-worship which is practiced by all Meiteis."[21] About the traditional Meitei religion, J. Shakespeare states thus: [22]

> The worship of the *Umang lais*, or forest god, and other lesser supernatural beings, such as the *Sa-roi-nga-roi*, evil spirits, which are always on the lookout to injure human beings; the *Hellois*, beautiful female forms which lure foolish men into waste places and then disappear, leaving their victims bereft of reason, and *Hingchabis* or witch. Originally there were only nine of these forest gods and seven goddesses, but these have now increased to 365, and the Pundits claim that from their books they can trace the pedigree of every one of these 365 divinities back to one or other of the original nine gods or seven goddesses.

The Meiteis worshipped *Umang lais*. They were so called, because generally the place of worship of this *lai* was in a grove which was regarded as sacred.[23] No one was allowed to cut down the trees. If somebody violated this rule, it was believed that the person would suffer from sickness or death. *Umang lai* does not mean the god of forest. As their dwelling places were outside the houses, they were worshipped as *lam lais* (*lam* = outdoor, *lai*=god).[24]

1.5. Cultic Significance of Stones

The cultic significance of stones among the Meiteis is significant. We can still find some of the crucial stones in Manipur valley.[25] Some of them are at a place called Nungjengmacha. There is the tongue of Pakhangba transformed into a stone having supernatural power. At the Khoibaching there is the Nongshaba in the shape of a round stone. This is said to be only for the King. At Thayonglok there is a stone conch of Mahadiv. In the Chinga hill there is a precious stone with the sun and the moon on the top, where manuscripts of the genealogy of the five Meitei religious leaders are written.[26] Even today, when people see any unusual stone in an isolated place, they consider it as a supernatural stone.[27]

1.6. Blood Sacrifice

In the pre-Hindu period blood sacrifice was commonly practiced on important occasions. Some of the animals that the Meiteis commonly used for sacrifice were

---

[21] T. C. Hodson, *The Meitheis* (Delhi: B.R. Publishing Corporation, 1975), 95 & 97.

[22] J. Shakespeare, "The Religion of Manipur," *Transactions of the Folk-Lore Society*, XXIV/ IV (December, 1913): 421.

[23] Sukhdev Singh Chib, *North-Eastern India: Caste,* 89.

[24] Kh. Ratan Kumar, *Lai Haraoba of Manipur,* 53.

[25] Kh. Ratan Kumar, *Lai Haraoba of Manipur,* 130.

[26] Sairem Nilabir, "The Revivalist Movement," 110.

[27] B. K. Ahluwalia, *Social Change in Manipur* (Delhi: Cultural Publishing House, 1984), 139.

buffalo, mithun, pig, and cock. Concerning this, S. N. Parratt observes a buffalo or mithun used to be sacrificed on the occasion of the *Lai haraoba* of the god, which took place one to three years after the building of a *Laisang*.[28] There was a similar practice among the other tribal ethnic groups in Manipur. This practice has been stopped among most of the tribal groups with the coming of Christianity.[29] However, there are some practices which are still continued by the Meiteis today.

1.7. *Apokpa Khurumba*

Meitei was a community who worshipped and venerated their deceased forefathers as gods with an elaborate system of rituals. *Apokpa Khurumba* (Apokpa = ancestor, Khurumba = bowing down or worship) was performed by the Meiteis in order:[30]

a) to get a long life;
2) to have a child by a woman who was barren; and
3) to increase property of the poor.

There were three kinds of *Apokpa Khurumbas*:[31]

1) *Yek pokpa Khurumba* (*Yek* = clan, worship of clan ancestor);
2) *Sagei pokpa khurumba* (*Sagei* = a group of families having the same surname, worship of family surname ancestor); and
3) *lmung Pokpa Khurumba* (*Imung* = family, worship of family ancestor).

For ancestor worship, each of the seven *yeks* of the Meiteis had specific varieties of flowers with specific colours, water from specific areas, fire taken by different methods, *Sareng* (a kind of fish) of different colours, dao of different shapes etc.[32] *Apokpa Khurumba* was not a mere show of respect to their ancestors; the Meiteis believed in the immortality of the soul. They believed that it was only the body that perished. They believed that even after death their forefathers looked after the welfare of their children and that with proper ritual, they could be asked for blessings.[33]

In addition to the above mentioned gods and goddesses, they also worshipped Pakhangba, Nongsaba and a number of goddesses like Panthoibi (goddess of love and courage), Iraileima (goddess of water), and Phauoibi (goddess of paddy).

---

[28] Saroj N. *Parratt, The Religion of Manipur: Beliefs, Rituals and Historical Development* (Calcutta: Firma KLM Private Limited 1980), 119.

[29] Mang Khongchai, Lecturer, Trulok Theological Seminary, Dewlahland Imphal West, Manipur, letter to the author, 13th February 2011.

[30] N. Kullachandra, *Apokpa Tounirol* (Imphal: N. Kullachandra, 1937), 5.

[31] Sairem Nilabir, "The Revivalist Movement," 110.

[32] Sairem Nilabir, "The Revivalist Movement," 111.

[33] Kh. Ratan Kumar, *Lai Haraoba of Manipur,* 47-49.

These goddesses were regarded as the incarnations of Ima Leimarel Sidabi (immortal mother deity).

1.8. Perception of Salvation

Lainingthau Sanamahi (*Lai* = god, *ningthou* = King, sana or Sanna = spreading, mahi = quality) looked at the shadow of his father, Sidaha Mapu (Sidaba=immortal, Mapu = Master or Owner) and created humans.[34] The humans lived very happily without suffering from sickness and death, but they ignored worship of his/her creator, so Sidaha Mapu sent down diseases and death on them. At this point Sanamahi came forward and requested his father to save humans from sorrows and sufferings. Sidaha Mapu felt pity on him and said, "I am you and you are me, humans can be free from suffering only through the worship of you." He asked Sanamahi and Leimarel Sidabi to incarnate as *Maiba* (Priest) and *Maibi* (Priestess) and to show them the way to salvation.[35]

According to Meitei scripture, to unite together with *Yaibirel Sidaba* or *Sidaba Mapu*, after death is Salvation. The soul of each person emerges from *Yaibirel Sidaba* (Immortal Supreme Soul) and comes down on the earth through the Sun, the Moon, and Stars. Then it enters into one's father and last of all, the mother. The soul stays there for 10 months and then emerges from the womb of the mother on earth as a human being. After death the soul should be sent back along the same path through which it comes down. Sending up of the soul to heaven is done by a *Maiba* with proper ritual. When the soul unites with *Yaibirel Sidaba*, the Supreme Soul, there is Salvation.[36]

The Meiteis had an enlarged system of rituals for birth, marriage and death, which are considered the major terminal points of Meitei life. They include those dicussed in the following sections.

1.9. Birth Ceremonials

As far as the Meitei traditional birth ceremony is concerned, there are two significant ceremonials:[37]

1) *Kokthokchamthokpa* (Kokthok or Kokthokpa = cleaning or shaving; chamthokpa = washing) and
2) *Ipanthaba* or *Yupanthaba* (feeding of water or rice beer).

The first one was performed after five months of pregnancy to retain the strength and courage of the mother during pregnancy and child birth. The shadow which was regarded as the sixth soul by the Meiteis was invoked not to

[34] R. Constantine, *Manipur Maid of the Mountains*, 38.

[35] Sairem Nilabir, "The Revivalist Movement," 111.

[36] O. Bhogeshwar, *Ningthourol Sheireng*, 3-4.

[37] Sairem Nilabir, "The Revivalist Movement," 112.

leave the body. This was carried out by a *Maiba* with the second ritual *Ipanthaba* or *Yupanthaba*[38] and was held on the completion of five days after the birth of the child.[39] So, naturally it was performed in the morning of the sixth day for the prosperity of the child. In this ceremonial the *Maibi* fed the child with uncooked food and water. The mother's love for her child was also ceremonially experienced.[40]

A further ceremony relating to the feeding of the child was *Chak-Umba* (*chak* = cooked rice, *Umha* = eating slowly). When the child was about six months old, this ceremony was performed to feed the child cooked food for the first time. He/She was given five mouthfuls of food. The first mouthful was for knowing Sidaba Mapu (universal father), the second for knowing Ima Leimarel Sidabi (immortal mother deity), the third for attracting the five souls, the fourth for knowing his father and mother and the fifth, for increasing his/her knowledge and wisdom.[41]

1.10. Marriage Ceremonial

Marriage Ceremonial was another social formal practice among the Meiteis in Pre-Vaishnavism. There were four stages before the actual marriage ceremony took place, they are:[42]

1) *Hainaba* = approach by the parents of the boy to the girl's family;
2) *Yathangthaba* = giving of consent to the marriage by the girl's family. This was done only when the boy's parents came at the girl's residence for that purpose;
3) *Waroipot puba* = taking of food, fruits and flowers to the family of the girl to mark the final agreement to the marriage;
4) *Heijing pot puba* = taking of fruits and other food items for the *apok asha,* deceased forefathers of the girl's family who were regarded as deities of the family.

---

[38] This traditional ritual is still retained by the *loi* Meiteis in Andro, Khurkhul, Phayeng & Sekmai in Manipur. Concerning this Bino Devi comments thus: "*Ipanthaba* or *Yupanthaba*—for the purification of the household and the sub-clan, *Maiba* and *Maibi* are professional who generally conduct this ritual, takes a utensil filled with water in one hand and a 'tairen leaf,' on the other hand. With the twig of 'tairen,' which has leafs the *Maibi* sprinkles the water from the utensil over the person and around the house." L. Bino Devi, *Lois of Manipur: Andro, Khurkhul, Phayeng & Sekmai* (New Delhi: Mittal Publication, 2002), 35-36.

[39] Sairem Nilabir, "The Revivalist Movement," 112.

[40] O. Bhogeshwar, *Ningthourol Sheireng,* 6.

[41] K.B. Singh, *Traces of Pre-Hinduism in Meitei Society Folklore,* vol. 5 (Imphal East: Meitei Lup Publications, 1964), 201-206.

[42] Sairem Nilabir, "The Revivalist Movement," 112.

Along with the above stated four stages there were three important *lais* connected to the marriage ceremony. They are: [43]

1) *Imung lai* (household god and goddess),
2) *Sagei lai* (deities or the sub-clan to which the family of the girl belonged) and
3) *Lam-lai* (the Umang Lai and other outdoor deities) of the locality.

On the day of the marriage, offerings were brought by the groom's parents for the gods and goddesses of the bride. Food and drink were distributed to all the friends and relatives who came to the ceremony. Two Meitei *ngamus* (one variety of fish) were released in the water to know the future of the bride and the groom. The ceremony would end only when the bride and the groom exchanged food in each other's mouths in front of Sanamahi, the household god of the bride, and bowed down before him for their prosperity in the future. Marriage was performed at the residence of the bride.[44]

1.11. Status of Women

The women in ancient Meitei society were held in a very high social status.[45] There was equality between men and women, with women even enjoying higher status than the men. Women were the head of the families. The society was matriarchal as was evident from the fact that the worshipping of Goddesses was started from ancient period in Manipur.[46] The reduced status of mainland Indian women during the Mughal period did not affect the status of women in Manipur. The position of women in a subordinate status was only legitimized with the coming of Vaishnavism in Manipur.[47]

An example of this importance of the woman is that, in the *Umang lai Haraoba*, the *Maibis* are considered to be more important than the *Maibas*. It is also considered that the origin of the female *Maibi* was earlier than that of her male counterpart.[48] Saroj N. Parratt further writes:[49]

> The *Maibi* plays a more important role in the festivals and the *Lai* (god) is thought to take more pleasure in female ritual functionaries. Furthermore women are more likely to become possessed. More

---

[43] K. B. Singh, *Traces of Pre-Hinduism in Meitei Society*, 205-206.

[44] K. B. Singh, *Traces of Pre-Hinduism in Meitei Society*, 205-207.

[45] The role and the status of Meitei women has been highlighted earlier however this section focuses mainly on the religious aspect. cf. L. Bino Devi, *Lois of Manipur*, 32-36.

[46] Oinam Bhogeswar Singh, *Ningthourol Lambuba* (Imphal: Oinam Bhogeswar Singh, 1967), 92.

[47] Ksh. Bimola Devi, "Manipuri Women-A Study," in *Manipur: Past and Present*, vol. I., edited by Naorem Sanajaoba (Delhi: Mittal Publications, 1988), 160.

[48] Saroj N. *Parratt, The Religion of Manipur*, 96.

[49] Saroj N. *Parratt, The Religion of Manipur*, 97.

significantly, when a man becomes possessed by the *Lai,* he will wear the clothes of the female *Maibi*, and may be spoken of as a male *Maibi.*

A woman becomes a *Maibi* either by being chosen at the *Lai Haraoba* or by being directly possessed by the *lai*. The best *Maibis* are those who are possessed by *Lai* at an early age such as six to seven years. But older women of 50 or 60 years old also may become *Maibis*. Possession by *Lai* leads to abnormal behaviour. In the festivals, she usually dances in a wild manner and frequently falls into a trance. The dress of the *Maibi*[50] is quite different from others. The *Phanek* and the chaddar are all white and an additional waist wrapper (also white) is worn on top of the *Phanek*. A long-sleeved white blouse is worn and flowers are usually placed in the hair and behind the ears.[51]

1.12. Disposal of the Dead

Meitei community before the coming of Vaishnavism followed four types of disposal of the dead: 1) Disposal in water, 2) Disposal in open air, 3) Burial and 4) Burning. It seems that the first kind of disposal of dead was in practice in the very early period of the social evolution of this community, before the beginning of ancestor worship. The most common practice was by burial.[52] The ritual was carried out in the midst of the sound of drums and gongs and wailing and crying of the friends and relatives of the dead. The ceremony was performed by a *Maiba.* They believed that if the ceremony had not been performed with proper ritual, the spirit of the deceased would do harm to the family. After the completion of one year, a ceremony known as *Phiroi* (first death anniversary) was performed. This was the final ceremony for the dead. There were special rituals and ceremonies for the death of an infant and also in the case of an unnatural death.[53]

2. Revivification Movement

We can see that the religious practices of the Meiteis can be divided into three periods—the traditional religious practices, then Vaishnavism, then the revival movement. Much of the success of the revival movement sprang from the fact many Meiteis still followed some practices of their traditional religion even during the Vaishnavism period, so efforts to launch the revival movement fell on fertile ground.

We will now look into this movement, which was started during the colonial period, and has been undergoing various changes in its nature and dimensions

---

[50] Professor Gajrani has vividly described the dress of *Maibi* in his book thus, "The *Maibi* dress themselves very distinctively. It is all white. A *Phanek* (long skirt) over which is worn an additional waist wrapper below the hips, a white blouse mostly with full sleeves, an *Inaphi* (shawl) is also worn. S. Gajrani, *History, Religion & Culture of India,* vol. 6. (Delhi: Isha Books, 2004), 151.

[51] Ksh. Bimola Devi, "Manipuri Women: A Study," 166.

[52] Rajen & Ibohal, *Sakok Lamlel,* 7-9.

[53] Saroj N. Parratt, *The Religion of Manipur*, 119.

ever since. It originated as anti-Hinduism, anti-Brahmins and then finally turned out to be anti-Indian in nature as it strives towards the restoration of the Kangla[54] to its historical glory and the demand for recognition of Meitei language in the eighth schedule of the Indian Constitution.[55] Thus, a key issue arises as to why the anti-Hindu movement was so strong during the colonial period and continues today. To understand the movement better, we must appreciate it has undergone various changes shaped by different socio-political systems and organizational structures of the movement since its beginnings. Unless we study those changes, we will not be able to understand the movement fully

2.1. The Movement

Meiteis are firmly rooted into their traditional belief in spite of the fact that Vaishnavism, when it became the State religion, tried to completely uproot their traditional belief by imposing on every Meitei the obligation to follow it. Despite this obligation, it did not succeed in penetrating fully the existing religious beliefs of the Meiteis. Consequently, the Sanamahi faith found fertile ground and strong roots among them, based on their traditional beliefs, and now this revival movement is getting stronger among the Meiteis in Manipur valley. Therefore, this can be regarded as a major cause for the rejection of Christianity among this group of people. In order to understand this more fully, we shall now consider the historical aspects of the movement.

2.1.1. Characteristics, Development and Concept of the Movement

We have seen in the preceding chapter the pervasive force of Hindu culture and its influences on the Meiteis. Every village has at least one Hindu temple with a big community hall called *Mandapa.* A Brahmin family looks after the temple, run by the charity of the people. Not only is this place an important centre for Vaishnavite festivals but also most of the ceremonies of marriage and death are performed in this place. However, despite this, there are many clear signs among the Meiteis of their adherence to their traditional beliefs. Every Meitei house keeps a basil plant called *Tulsipung* in the middle of courtyard as a symbol of their adherence to the Vaishnavite faith but instead of the basil plant, some Meiteis put a particular plant called *Tairel,* which is another sign of adherence to their old pre-

[54] 'Kangla, located at the present day Imphal, is the most important Historical and Archeological site of Manipur. The kingdom of Manipur was established and developed at 'Kangla'. Being a site of political and religious significance, 'Kangla' has grown into a formidable fortress city through the centuries. It is from this capital that the "Ningthouja" clan gradually wielded enough political and military power and grew-up to be the most dominant clan in Manipur. Pangambam Bharat Singh, *Kangla: The National Heritage of Manipur* (Imphal: Pangambam Bharat Singh, 2008), ii-iv. cf. Pandit N. Khelchandra Singh, "Tracing Origin of Kangla in Pre-Pakhangba Or Khaba Era," http://books.e-pao.net/Heritage_Manipur/ (1 April 2013).

[55] Gangmumei Kabui, "Socio-Religious Reform Movement," in *History of Modern Manipur, 1826-1949*, edited by Lal Dena (New Delhi: Orbit Publishers, 1991), 102.

Hindu faith of Sanamahism.[56] It is a symbol of resistance to the increasing force of Hinduism that had been witnessed during colonial period.

Another gesture towards the old faith is in the wearing of the pottu mark (*chandan.*) All Meitei males and females wear this tilak mark *on* their forehead on every religious occasion.[57] But the Sanamahi and Hindu tilaks are quite different, and so the wearing indicates to which religious group the wearer belongs. Hindu Meiteis use pink colour *Chandan* and start with an elongated quadrilateral mark on the bridge of the nose. This is connected by two parallel lines reaching up to the forehead. On the other hand, the Sanamahi Meiteis use black colour *Chandua* which is stamped on the forehead in a single round shape.

A further sign of their adherence to their old faith is their refusal to allot space within their houses to the Hindu deities, as required by the Vaishnavite culture. Instead, in every Meitei house, three propitious places are dedicated to three important deities of their ancient faith.[58] Thus, it is clear that while the Meiteis may follow the Hindu religion on the surface, deep down their loyalty and integrity belong to their ancient faith, and it is this deep-rooted belief which enables them to reject other religious beliefs and practices including Christianity. At present this belief has grown up as a strong force to resist and replace the alien culture and religion of Hinduism, despite its centuries-old association with the Meiteian[59] culture. But obviously such a strong force would also lead to a rejection of other faiths as well, including Christianity.

As seen in the preceding chapter, the process of two and half centuries of Sanskritization was a landmark in the social and cultural transformation of Meiteis in Manipur valley. Development of religious and cultural identity and self-consciousness were the most significant landmarks of this era. Adoption of the Bengali school of Vaishnavism and replacement of ancient Meitei script with Bengali script facilitated the promotion of cultural features of Bengali Hindus over Meiteis. However, the process of Sanskritization never totally penetrated into the ancient faith of the Meiteis as their ancient faith had been fully internalized in the minds of all. The influence of Vaishnavism was found only in the domain of culture in the form of the observance of rites, rituals and festivals but never

---

[56] The ancient Meitei religion is based on a vast body of knowledge written in the ancient archaic Meitei script (the script of Meitei is not popular among the masses as it was replaced with Bengali script after the burning of the Meitei scriptures by the Hindu missionaries in 18th Century). As only few persons, called *Pandit,* after the influence of Hinduism, can read, this knowledge is confined only to them.

[57] Kunj Bihari Singh, "Manipur Vaishnavism: A Sociological Interpretation," in *Themes in Indian Sociology 3: Sociology in India,* edited by Rowena Robinson (New Delhi: Sage Publications India Pvt. Ltd., 2004), 130.

[58] Meiteis consider every house as the most sacred temple of the three deities, i.e., Sanamahi, Leimarel and Phungga Lairu. These deities are honoured with lamps every evening for the prosperity of the family.

[59] Of or relating to or characteristic of Meiteis or their language or culture.

eliminated the native faith completely. Though many Meiteis followed the advice of the Brahmins in the performance of rites and rituals,[60] they never forget the Meitei *Maiba* and *Maibi* whose advice is supreme in ancient Meitei religious life. Thus, in the conflict of these two forces, one backed by the Maharaja and the other backed by the council of Meitei scholars (*Maichous*), the Meiteis faced a serious problem of confusion of loyalties. Thus today, when a Meitei talks about his/her belief, it is the belief of the ancient Meitei deities, yet despite this, he/she is still deeply influenced by Hindu culture. Therefore today Meitei society can be seen as a field of conflict and compromise between two religious forces,[61] rather than a syncretization of the two.

Apart from the Sanskritization, the Burmese invasion[62] and British colonialism[63] have spread wide and the people are aware of such outside influences. While opening up more and more to the outside world, the society is returning to its roots. The understanding of their culture and belief system encourages them to believe that such a return to the past could help them preserve their identity that is constantly threatened by the influence of more dominant cultures. This particular effort of reviving past glory is also part of their attempt to reduce the strain induced by various forces that threaten the native culture of Meiteis. However, the richness and uniqueness of their culture that is retained in the *Lai-Haraoba* festival inspire them to hope that the past could provide the solution to the problem that they are facing today.

This pride makes the Meiteis very emotional and sentimental about the pressures that their culture faces today. Thus, these feelings encourage them to imagine a socio-political space in which there is no protection for them to preserve their culture. Therefore, today, Meiteis have started adhering strictly to the belief and practices of their traditional religion and at the same time they have also started claiming their religious sites and territory, which can be seen as a spatial strategy for the establishment of a nation. They not only follow their traditions, but also mobilize people in large numbers to participate and promote their pre-Hindu culture and traditions. They are also reclaiming various religious sites and land, which were the original abodes of the traditional Meitei deities but occupied later by the Brahmins.

---

[60] Kunj Bihari Singh, "Manipur Vaishnavism: A Sociological Interpretation," 130.

[61] Here, 'Sanamahism' refers to the particular religious belief and practices, which the Meiteis had before their forceful conversion into Hinduism. Apart from the Sanamahi deity, Meiteis also believe in various deities like ancestors, village deities, household deities and other spirits, which are believed to be the guardians of various places, lake, rivers etc. Therefore, it is difficult to use a proper term which can explain the religious phenomenon of the Meiteis. However, without going deeper, the particular beliefs and practices that they had before the advent of Hinduism in Manipur is generally termed as Sanamahi in the present work.

[62] We have already discussed the Burmese invasion in the preceding chapter, therefore, we are not going to elaborate again here.

[63] We shall be looking at the British colonialism in Manipur in the succeeding chapter.

2.1.2. Beginning of the Movement

The revival movement can be traced to the establishment of Meitei *Apokpa Marup* (association in the name of a Meitei ancestral deity), an association formed by a Meitei, named Naoriya Phullo in Cachar district of Assam in 1930 for the revival of Meitei tradition, religion and script.[64] He founded this group in order to investigate the ancient religion and culture of the Meiteis. After forming this association, its members started excluding the Brahmins from their religious rites, rituals and festivals. Instead they employed *Piba* (eldest living male of a clan) to fulfill the functions of their socio-religious organization. The adherents of this movement are variously known as Sanamahi *Chatpa,* Meitei *Marup,* Sanamahi *Laining,*[65] etc., of which Sanamahi-*Chatpa* and Sanamahi *Laining* became well-known. But organizationally they prefer to call themselves as Apokpa *Marup* in Cachar and Meitei *Marup* in Manipur. Because of Phullo's great contribution in the revival of the Meitei socio-religious life, all the organizations concerning this new movement all over the region of the North-eastern India today pay him respect with the title 'Laininghal Naoriya'. It was through his own efforts that the Meiteis could revive their script and organize their own religious festivals and cultural practices without the Brahminical functionaries.[66]

Naoriya Phullo was born at Jhariban Laishram village of Cachar district in Assam in 1888.[67] During his childhood he was popularly called 'Phundrei' by his villagers because of his good health and figure.[68] His childhood experiences in the Bengali-dominated areas in Cachar made him initiate the revival movement. It was during his high school life that Naoriya Phullo experienced humiliation and embarrassment from his Bengali classmates. They used to make fun of him

[64] Meiteis are spread in Burma and many other parts of North-Eastern area like Cachar and Guwahati of Assam; a few districts in Tripura etc. The repeated Burmese invasion had uprooted the social and economic life of people. Thousands of people fled to Cachar and many were taken prisoners and deported to Ava. It is recorded that about 3 lakh Meitei prisoners were taken to Ava. Gangmumei Kabui, "Social and Religious Reform Movement in Manipur in 19th and 20th Century," in *Bulletin of the Division of History* (Imphal: Centre of Post-Graduate Studies, J.N.U.,1974), 54.

[65] Sanamahi *Chatpa* = following Sanamahi, Meitei *Marup* = Meitei group, Sanamahi *Laining* = worshipping Sanamahi.

[66] Gangmumei Kabui, "Social and Religious Reform Movement in Manipur," 56-57, 75.

[67] The 124th birth anniversary of Laininghan Naoriya Phullo was observed by Apokpa Marup at Naorem Chapru Kha Community Hall, Imphal. The observance was attended by agriculture director L Palendro, art and culture deputy director W Mera, agriculture chief engineer K Manoranjan, ZCC Keishamthong vice-president Paozarung Thamei, ZCC Mahabali vice-president Kamei Dun Kamson, H Puren of Apokpa Marup as the dignitaries. "Naoria Phullo remembered," *Imphal Free Press* (Imphal), 22 August 2011. cf. "Naoriya Phullo's birth anniversary celebrated," *The Sangai Express* (Imphal) 1 September 2010.

[68] K.B. Singh, "Social Stratification and Mobility in Manipur," in *North East India: A Sociological Study*, edited by S.M. Dubey (Delhi: Concept Publishing Company, 1978), 62-64.

by saying, "*nize aksarnai, nir vashar sahitya nai,*" which roughly means "you have no alphabet; you have no book in your language."[69] During Hindu festivals some of his Bengali friends would ask him, "Don't you have your own religion and deities?"[70] These humiliations and embarrassments prompted him to think seriously about the Meiteis' language, script, culture, tradition and religion. Being just a school student he could not do anything at that point of time. However, he never stopped thinking over the issue of Meitei language, script and religion. Most of the time, he thought seriously about the socio-religious' life of the Meiteis in Cachar.[71]

As already mentioned in the preceding chapter, Meitei adopted Bengali script as the medium of instruction in both social and religious institutions after it was strictly imposed by the Meitei King. The trend was further consolidated by the British policy when they employed the Bengalis in the colonial administration in Assam and Manipur. The Meitei socio-cultural life in Cachar was also highly influenced by the Bengali Hindu culture. While they were at home they wore the Meitei clothes and lived in Meitei traditional fashion. However, when they went out of the home, the men folk wore dhoti and women wore sari and used red tilak on their forehead, which made them no different from the Bengali Hindus.[72] However, the racial and ethnic factors marked the difference between the Meiteis and the Bengalis. These racial factors denied and prevented them from being considered as Hindus.[73]

This cultural confusion of the racial and religious identities brought a serious crisis in the socio-cultural identity of the Meiteis in Cachar district of Assam. A particular remark from his Bengali friends compelled Naoriya Phullo to realize his identity and to start working for the development of their traditional Meitei religion and culture. After he completed his education he became a school teacher

[69] *"Langjeel": A Special Issue on the 91st Birth Anniversary of Lainingbal Naoriya; Lainingbal Phulo and Our Clan* (Imphal: Malem Yaiphasang, 1988), 5-6.

[70] These questions are the point of reference of the origin of the Sanamahi movement taken by the leaders till today. Thus, the absence of the script, language and religion and enthusiasm to revive the lost script and religion is the turning point of the Sanamahi movement. Re-inventing the identity of the pre-Hindu Meiteis and use of the same as a legitimate source of the establishment of a new socio-political system is the main basis of the present Sanamahi movement. These are frequently pronounced in most of the occasions of the Sanamahi movement. *"Langjeel": A Special Issue*, 6.

[71] Sairem Nilabir, "The Revivalist Movement," 116.

[72] Still this influence is in the public sphere. However, Meiteis retain their ethnic identity in the private sphere. Thus this dichotomy between the private and public life especially in the culture and tradition makes a dilemma among the Meiteis in Cachar. However, the Sanamahi movement is providing an alternative means to resolve the crisis.

[73] When the Meiteis in Cachar performed their religious rites and rituals followed by the *Sanskirtans* of the devotional songs of the Hindu, the Bengalis insulted the Meitei saying that the medium of the devotional songs used Bengali language. K.B. Singh, "Social Stratification and Mobility in Manipur," 64-65.

at the age of twenty-six. During this period he studied important social, cultural and religious books including Veda, Vedanta, Upanishad, and the Gita, so that he could critique Hinduism and Brahminical order. In 1916 he left the post of school teacher and became a clerk at Silchar D.C. office. Thereafter he joined the police service as a Sub-inspector.[74]

It was in 1925-26, while he was posted in Rangia and Amingao that he met some Meiteis from Manipur who took a serious interest in reviving the Meitei culture and tradition. Because his mind was haunted by the memory of the insults that he had faced during his school days, he developed a determined aim to make some efforts for the revival of the Meitei culture and religious belief and practices. He therefore retired voluntarily from his service in 1930 at the age of forty-one and formed the association of Meitei Apokpa *Marup* at Laishram Leikai of Cachar district, Assam. He also did research work on Meitei history, culture, and religion. For this purpose he visited various religious places of the ancient Meitei religion and civilization in Manipur. Then he started mobilizing people in his village and published many important articles related to the ancient tradition and culture of the Meiteis. Many of his articles were later on published in a book entitled *Eigi Wareng,* which is a criticism of Brahmin and Hinduism. He also wrote many other books on different subjects of Meitei traditional culture, belief and practices.[75] Many of these writings also contain poems, hymns and philosophy. Some of the hymns are extremely powerful and influenced thousands of people. The version of one of the poems in his book, *Tengbanba Amasung Lainingthou Laipao* is given below—

> *"Houre Houro Parikhoi*
> *Mapugi Paobu Lakle Ebungosing*
> *Houro Houro Parikhoi*
> *Poklen Pokpa Ya-olle*
> *Tungna Mang Oirakle*
> *Pangdharuba Singli Hourakle."*[76]

The loose translation of the above poem is—

> Awake, awake sons,
> Descending is the message of Lord, lads,

---

[74] M. Kirti Singh, *Religion and Culture of Manipur* (Delhi: Manas Publications, 1988), 49. cited in. Sairem Nilabir, "The Revivalist Movement," 115-17.

[75] Of those books mention can be made of: *Eigi Wareng* (critics of Hinduism and Brahminical ideology); Meitei *Hourakpham Wari* (an account of the origin of Meiteis), Meitei *Esei* (Meitei religious song); *Tengbanba Amasung Lainingthou Laipao* (Verses on the Almighty God); *Singtha Cheilharol* (a book on the Meitei rites and rituals); *Thayin-Nongyin* (a book on Meitei socio-religious Philosophy); *Ahal Yathang* (advice of the elders); etc.

[76] Laininghal Naoriya, *Tengbanba Amusung Lainingthou Laipao, Creator and God's Message* (Cachar: Moirengjamba Munal, 1946), 1.

Awake, awake sons,
Woken up is the ancestor of the ancestors,
Now back becomes front
Returning is the wind gone by,
Rejuvenated is the nerve numbed.

Naoriya Phullo had high regards for his motherland Manipur, which is expressed in some of the poems written by him. The following poetic version contains his love for motherland and language.

"Koubru Chingna Lemphuni
Kanglanadi Khoidhouni
Loktak Sana Tengotni
Meitei *Thawai Oibani.*

.... Meiteilon-*na Sak-chage* Meiteilon-*na Sonjage*
Eswar Haiba Mingkheido Apokpani Haijage.

.... *Phaarabasu Emani Thirabasu Emani*
Ematabu Nungsini Ematabu Thougalni."[77]

The translation reads—

Koubru Mountain is the tip of the head,
Kangla the navel
Loklak, the golden bowl
Are Meitei's soul.

.... Desire, sing in Meiteilon, chanting in Meiteilon,
Desire, to call god my father.

.... Whether good or ugly, you are mother,
Will love and worship Mother only You.

The Sanamahi movement originated as the criticism of the Brahminical ideology in the Meitei socio-religious life.[78] Phullo along with some close friends struggled hard for the revival of the Meitei socio-religious life. They also asked the Meiteis in Cachar to denounce and discard the Hinduism and Brahmins in their socio-religious life. Because of his new activities, he was ostracized by the orthodox Meitei Hindus in Cachar from the Hindu Meitei community and was identified

[77] Laininghal Naoriya. *Meitei Seireng (Meitei Poem)*, 18-21.

[78] M. Kirti Singh, *Religion and Culture of Manipur*, 117.

as *Amangba* (polluted). However, he never lost his passion for the development of Meitei socio-religious life. He also went from place to place in most parts of North East India and spread his idea about the revival of Meitei identity and culture. Ultimately, after leading the movement for one decade Phullo died on June 30, 1941.[79] After his death his followers in Cachar and Manipur valley made many efforts to develop the traditional Meitei religion, culture, language and script.[80]

2.1.3. Beginning of the Movement in Manipur

Naoriya Phullo in his trips to different religious places in Manipur met various individuals and influenced them with his thought and enthusiasm to revive the Meitei traditional religion, culture and script. Many of the Meiteis were also already disappointed with the Hinduism due to the excessive behaviour of the Brahmins after the revival of the Brahmasabha during the colonial period.[81] The news of the Meitei revival also had already reached Manipur valley in 1934. Naoriya Phullo's idea about the revival of the Meitei culture, religion and language had greatly influenced three Meiteis, viz. T. Bokul, P. Surachand and P. Ibomcha from Imphal.[82] In order to spread the revival movement in Manipur these three men went to Cachar in 1935, on the day of Krishna Janma festival to meet Naoriya Phullo. There they met Naoriya Phullo and listened to his ideas about the importance of the revival and preservation of the Meitei tradition, culture, religion and script. On listening to his talk these three Meiteis decided to return to Manipur and mobilize the people to join the movement. When they came back to Manipur after one year and nine months, they constituted one organizing committee consisting of seven members, namely: T. Bokul, P. Surachand, P. Ibomcha, A. Nungshirei, A Lilasing, L. lboton and T. Yaima.[83] These people started mobilizing people in and around Thabalkhong areas of Imphal West to discard Hinduism and follow only the Meitei religion.[84]

---

[79] *"Langjeel,"* (August 1979): Leaflet, An Issue on the 91st Birth Anniversary of Laininghal Naoria.

[80] In Meiteilon Public ostracism is known as *inthokpa,* which is the most powerful instrument of social control among the Meiteis. This practice though is not familiar today in the urban areas, it is prevailing in the villages. For denouncing Hinduism and mobilizing people to discard Brahmins, Naoriya Phullo and his three brothers and four brothers-in-law were ostracized from the socio-religious functions of the Hindu Meiteis in Cachar. *"Langjeel,"* (August 1979).

[81] N. Bisheswar, *The Last Expression on My Death Bed* (Imphal: Pax Publication, 1986), 6.

[82] Gangmumei Kabui, "Socio-Religious Reform Movement," 102.

[83] Sairem Nilabir, "The Revivalist Movement," 117.

[84] Sairem Nilabir, "The Revivalist Movement," 119.

However, during 2nd World war, the activities of this movement were stopped for about two years.[85] As soon as normal life had been restored in 1944 they started organizing meetings and formulated strategies to organize the Meitei socio-cultural functions without Brahmins. On its first meeting on 2nd September 1944, eleven persons participated and decided to meet every Sunday to discuss the formalities related to the rites, rituals and ceremonies of the Sanamahi revival movement. Since Meiteis were forced to abandon their traditional faith practice Sanamahi and compelled to follow Vaishnavism for about 250 years,[86] it was a major problem for these people to conduct the traditional Meitei rites and rituals related to birth, marriage and death in the same manner they had done in the past. In order to conduct the said rites and rituals they formed different subcommittees to formulate the structure and formalities to be adopted by the Sanamahi Meiteis. Following this strategy two persons: L. Iboton (formerly a musician of the Hindu Sankirtan[87]) and K. Nabachandra (formerly also a singer of the Hindu Sankirtan) took the responsibility for the preparation of the devotional songs of the Meitei socio-religious life.[88] After preparing all these formalities finally they formed an organization called Meitei *Marup* on 14th May 1945 at Thambalkhong Leikai in Imphal. It had 18 members and T. Bokul and N. Manikchand became the president and secretary of the organization respectively. These members also went to different places in Manipur and mobilized people to restore the traditional Meitei religion.[89]

On the day of the formation of the Meitei *Marup* organization they also hoisted the "Seven-Colour Flag" as the symbol of unity among the seven clans (*Yek-Salais* of the Meiteis).[90] While hoisting the flag by the president they also raised

---

[85] Manipur was one of the major battle fields of the 2nd World war. On 10th May 1942, for the first time, Imphal was bombarded. Many people in Imphal area left their home and took shelter in distant villages of the rural and hill regions. Only in 1944 valley people came back when peace was restored. N. Lokendro Singh, *The Unquiet Valley* (New Delhi: Mittal Publications, 1998), 163-68.

[86] As this has already been discussed in the preceding chapter, we shall not go further concerning the forceful conversion of Meiteis into Hinduism.

[87] *Kirtan* (Sanskrit: "to repeat"; also Sankirtan) is call-and-response chanting performed in devotional traditions. A person performing *kirtan* is known as a *kirtankar*. *Kirtan* practice involves chanting hymns or mantras to the accompaniment of instruments such as harmonium, drum, and *karatal* hand cymbals. It is a major practice in Vaishnava devotional worship, "Definition of Sankirtan," http://dictionary.baby-lon.com/sankirtan/ (19 Feb 2013).

[88] Iboton and Nabachandra were active members of the Sankirtan team before they became the followers of Sanamahism.

[89] Meitei *Marup Hourakpagi Wari* (Story of the Origin of Meitei Marup) (Imphal: Meitei Marup, 1993), 15.

[90] Meitei Marup Hourakpagi Wari, 16.

slogan. This shows the basic goal of the Meitei *Marup* toward the establishment of a nation. The main slogan that was raised on that day is as follows.[91]

Slogan	Refrain
Lainingthou Sanamahi-*na*	*Yaiphare*
Apokpa-*na*	*Yaiphare*
Eema Leipak-*na*	*Yaiphare*
Naoriya Phullo-*na*	*Yaiphare*

The loose translation of the above slogan and refrain is –

Slogan	Refrain
Sanamahi, the 'Supreme God'	The Great
Ancestor	The Great
Motherland	The Great
Naoriya Phullo	The Great

The Sanamahi movement took definite shape in Manipur when P. Surachand became the President of the Meitei *Marup* in 1945. Under his presidentship, the Meitei *Marup* was established in Manipur with its own written constitution. It passed a number of resolutions which included, among others, to substitute Sanskrit terms and names by pure Meitei terms and names, to adopt Meitei hymns in religious rites, rituals and ceremonies, and to abandon Hindu festivals. The leaders of the movement who were the disciples of Naoriya Phullo also carried on the ideology of Phullo through his books, journals, meetings of polemical character. They planned to replace the Hindu ways and to bring confidence to the Meitei masses. Some of the Meiteis who were uncomfortable with the roles and attitude of Brahmins discarded the use of *lugul* (sacred thread) and *urik* (tulsi beads).[92]

The Meitei *Marup* organization in Manipur was not an independent organization of the Apokpa *Marup* in Cachar. It was formed as the branch of the Apokpa *Marup* in Cachar. Indeed, there was a strong relationship between the

[91] Meitei Marup Hourakpagi Wari, 18.

[92] M. Kirti Singh, *Religion and Culture of Manipur*, 52.

organizations in Manipur and Cachar. In this regard T. Bokul, the then president of the Meitei *Marup* remarked thus.[93]

> In Cachar Laininghal Naoriya formed Apokpa *Marup* and organized a strong movement for the revival of Meitei nationality, Meitei religion and Meitei culture ... Meitei *Marup* as a branch of Apokpa *Marup* was born on 14th May 1945 in Meitei Leipak (Meitei land).

This relationship between the Meiteis in Manipur and Cachar is still maintained by the leadership of both the sides.[94]

2.1.4. Confrontation of the Movement

The Sanamahi movement, starting from its beginning, faced various confrontations. The leaders of the movement had public debate with the leaders of the Hindu religion during the formative stage. In 1946-47 a number of debates were organized in which strong arguments took place between Hindu Meitei scholars and the Sanamahi protagonists led by T. Bokul. The leaders of the Sanamahi protagonists overpowered the Hindu scholars. In order to marginalize the group of the Sanamahi protagonists, in 1947, the institution of the Brahma Sabha[95] took up different repressive measures against the Sanamahi leaders.[96]

Ksh. Bimola Devi rightly puts the monopoly of the Brahma Sabha thus, "The Brahma Sabha was the apex body of the Meitei society regulating the dos and don'ts of the religious norms and practice of Hindu Vaishnavism in Manipur." [97] On 31st October, 1947 the institution of the Brahma Sabha backed by the King of Manipur ostracized the movement leaders for denouncing Vaishnavism and Brahmins. The head of the Brahma Sabha issued an order to ostracize 38 leaders and followers of the Sanamahi movement on the ground that they denounced Hinduism without any respect for the Vedas and Brahmins.[98] The Brahma Sabha

---

[93] Sairem Nilabir, "The Revivalist Movement," 117.

[94] Religious occasions such as Sanamahi Chenghongba, Mera Chaoren Houba, Emoinu Erat Thouni etc.—both the Meitei groups use to share each other and participate in the rituals. "*Mera Chaoren Houba*," *Manipur Mail* (Imphal) 26 September 2011.

[95] Brahma Sabha was founded by the Hindu reformer Rammohun Roy (1772-1833) in August 1828. After a period of much groping his religious views took some definite shape by 1828 when in August of that year he established the Brahma Sabha (later Brahma Samaj) or Society of God. Although, this newborn society had the cordial claim to be regarded as a universal religion, it became and remained a sect of Hinduism. The religious tenets of the new creed were embodied in the Trust Deed of the Brahma Samaj. Manilal Chhotalal Parekh, *The Brahma Samaj: A Short History* (Michigan: Oriental Christ House, 1929), 25-26.

[96] Sairem Nilabir, "The Revivalist Movement," 118.

[97] Ksh. Bimola Devi, "Society and Politics in Manipur," in *Society, Politics and Development in North East India*, edited by Asok Chakraborty and Satyabrata Chakraborty (New Delhi: Concept Publishing Company, 2008), 101.

[98] Sairem Nilabir, "The Revivalist Movement," 118.

also proclaimed their names and asked every Hindu Meitei not to invite them to any of their socio-religious functions. The Brahma Sabha also informed all the Hindu Meitei not to mingle with them and if any one of them was invited, the host would be immediately declared as *amangba*.[99] This harassment did prove effective: for fear of the Brahma Sabha's warning, none of the Sanamahi Meiteis were invited to any functions, and if any of them happened to come as invitee all the Hindu Meitei-invitees would leave the place of the ceremony immediately.[100]

On hearing the reports of the ostracism of the 38 members of the Sanamahi movement from the Meitei socio-religious functions, more than 20 orthodox Hindus at Thambalkhong, Imphal warned two leaders of the Meitei, Marup P. Surachand and P. Ibomcha to leave the village.[101] However, the problem was resolved through the intervention of the State. Thus, the leaders of the Sanamahi movement faced various challenges designed to humiliate and harass them by the orthodox Hindus.

But these were not the only problems and challenge the Sanamahi movement faced in the beginning; there were also social issues. One of the main problems was when a Sanamahi follower died, his or her body was not allowed to be cremated according to the Meitei custom and the funeral had to proceed without any help from the Hindu Meiteis. Hijam Irabot, who was the leader of reformist movement, protested against the injustice and exploitation of the people in the name of religion and in defiance of both the King and Brahmasabha, Irabot performed the funeral ceremony of the people who were outcaste. The members of the Meitei *Marup* were also not given any co-operation in the form of labour during harvesting and other agricultural activities, which was essential for any villager among the Meiteis. Any marriage between the Hindu Meiteis and Sanamahi Meiteis was also highly controversial.[102] Thus, there developed a new socio-religious association of the Sanamahi Meiteis, which was parallel to those of the Hindu Meiteis. The development of such new socio-religious association of the Meitei *Marup* or Sanamahi movement is the beginning of the divide between the Meiteis into two religious groups.

The politics of ostracism and victimization of the Sanamahi Meiteis on the socio-religious ground has indirectly helped the development of the Sanamahi movement especially after 1947 when democratic government of Independent

[99] The term '*amangba*' in Meiteilon is associated with the doctrine of untouchability in Hinduism. An *amangba* person means an untouchable person or outcaste.

[100] Sairem Nilabir, "The Revivalist Movement," 118.

[101] Sairem Nilabir, *Lainingthou Sanamahi Amasung Sanamahi Laining Hinggat Echou* (*Sanamahi the almighty and the Restoring weave of Sanamahism*) (Imphal: Sairem Nilabir 2002), 147.

[102] In those days the orthodox Meiteis considered the Sanamahi Meiteis as untouchable. This attitude led many Meitei Hindus not to marry their children to those of any Sanamahi family. If a boy and girl happened to love each other, the objection is surely from the Hindu Meiteis but not from Sanamahi Meiteis.

Manipur was established finally. This superiority of the Brahmins also geared up the Sanamahi movement to an extremist form towards the 'de-Sanskritization' of Meitei culture and the establishment of a Meitei State in the later part of the movement.

2.1.5. Reasons for the Movement—One Beginning, Two Separate Roads

Although the movement started as a means to develop and protect the Meitei culture, both in its point of origin in Cachar and later in Manipur, it later took two divergent roads; the movement in Cachar was a reversion against the Bengali-dominated culture established there, while the movement in Manipur was rather, eventually, a socio-political effort to protect the distinctive culture. In the case of the revival movement among the Meiteis in Cachar, the acculturation pressure due to the interaction with culturally more dominant Bengali communities produced a state of resentment and confusion, which led the Meiteis to resist or reject the former. But the origin of this movement among the Meiteis in Manipur valley was attached to the feeling of safeguarding their distinct culture and belief that had been constantly threatened by 'Sanskritization', and 'colonialism'.

To understand the situation better, and why Christianity is regarded as an "alien religion" which is not acceptable to the Meiteis of Manipur, it is useful to consider the reasons behind the split between the two groups.

Many people believed that the Sanamahi movement among the Meiteis was the consequence of Indian domination after Manipur was forced to merge with the Indian Union on 21st September 1949.[103] However, it is too naive and historically wrong to assume this is the reason. Rather, it is because the movement was started during the colonial period outside Manipur and way back to Manipur of late 1930s. The reason for the movement in Cachar was primarily due to Meiteis' humiliating experience in Bengali-dominated Cachar, while in both those places in those days the aim was to revive and adopt the Meitei culture, tradition, belief and script. However, it also may not be wrong to say that it is at least partly the result of Manipur's merger with India that has ensured the continuation of the movement till today.

As mentioned earlier there were different factors responsible for the emergence of the Sanamahi Movement among the Meiteis in Cachar and in Manipur. Generally revival movements occurred among the smaller communities in contact with the dominant culture. In case of the revival movement among

[103] The disagreement over the merger of Manipur with the Indian Union is still going on. Most of the Meiteis argue that the princely State of Manipur was forcibly merged with the Indian Union in 1949. The strategies and circumstance in which the King of Manipur signed the agreement were doubted to be democratic. All the insurgent groups in the valley also strongly challenge the merger of Manipur with the Indian Union. N. Lokendro Singh, *The Unquiet Valley*, 229-30; A Bimol Akoijam & Th. Tarunkumar, "Armed Forces Special Powers Act 1958: Disguised War & Its Subversions," *Eastern Quarterly*, 3/1 (January—March, 2005): 12-13.

the Meiteis in Cachar, the main reason was the culture clash between the Meiteis and the Bengali communities, while in Manipur it was the feeling of safeguarding their distinct culture against 'Sanskritization', and 'colonialism'.

This tendency among the Meiteis has been clearly highlighted in a dramatic play called *The Pebet.*[104] In the play we see three kinds of characters—a Cat, a mother *Pebet* and her children. The play portrays the Hindu indoctrination of the Meiteis by the immigrant Brahmins in the 18th Century. In this play the real fear of the mother *Pebet* is not that her children will be killed and eaten by the Cat but rather they will be absorbed into 'cat's culture.'[105]

Today, Meiteis of Manipur feel that their culture, tradition, religion, polity and territory have been threatened by various exogenous factors of 'Hinduism', 'British colonialism', and later on by the merger of Manipur into the Indian Union. In the initial stage the Sanamahi movement appeared to be a purely socio-religious movement, but now it has assumed various other political goals of the Meiteis. It is, therefore, a claim for a political space defined by a particular identity and history, which is also free from the influence of outsiders. However, the Sanamahi movement among the Meiteis in Cachar originated and is continued without an imagined political space defined by a particular history, culture, and identity. In this case, it is a particular effort of some sections of the people to challenge the domination of the Bengalis in their socio-cultural identity, and to create a socio-cultural space for the Meiteis outside Manipur. This space so far does not assume any political power in the present day socio-political system of the Assam.

Concerning the reason for the movement led by the Meiteis in Cachar, Sajal Nag rightly remarked, "the rejection, socio-religious ostracization and disapproval of the Meithei (Meitei) Hindus by the Bengali caste-Hindus made the Meithei (Meitei) community reject Hinduism and go back to their former animist religion known as Sanamahi."[106] The Meiteis in Cachar district are surrounded by the Bengali Hindus. The adoption of the Bengali dresses, language and script by the Meiteis promoted the domination of the Bengalis in the socio-cultural identity of the Meiteis. The Meiteis came to have two identities. In the private spheres, especially at home, they wore the Meitei dress and spoke Meitei language. However, whenever they went out, they immediately adopted their Bengali identity. Thus, the public life of the Meiteis was completely influenced by the Bengali identities,

[104] It is the depiction of a popular Meitei folktale narrated by grandparents to their grandchildren. *Pebet* is a very rare small bird, which could be an extinct species. In the story mother *Pebet* guards her children by circumventing the grasping attention of the Cat (the cat is Vaishnavite in the directors' tactics). Mother *Pebet* flatters and boosts her ego till her children are ready to protect themselves. Once they are grown up, she resists the cat that captures the youngest among her children. In the play the cat is clearly portraying the role of Vaishnavite Brahmins to indoctrinate the Meiteis in the Hindu way of life. Rustom Bharucha, "Politics of Indigenous Theatre: Kanhailal in Manipur," *Economic and Political Weekly,* vol. 26/11 (March, 1991): 749.

[105] Rustom Bharucha, "Politics of Indigenous Theatre: Kanhailal in Manipur," 749-50.

[106] Sajal Nag, *Contesting Marginality* (New Delhi: Manohar, 2002), 100.

language, script, culture, festivals, etc. This private-public predicament of the Meiteis was the basis of the origin of the Sanamahi movement in Cachar. The harsh economic problems of the Meitei peasantry, along with the religious and cultural arrogance of the Bengali high caste Hindus in Cachar, made the life of the Meiteis difficult.[107] Such minorities often blame the more dominant communities for the grievances of their socio-economic backwardness. These circumstances naturally prompted the Meiteis to establish a distinct Meitei identity, which could challenge the dominant identity of the Bengalis in Cachar.

However, in Manipur valley the reason for starting the Sanamahi movement was the search for a socio-political space, which could safeguard the Meitei's distinct identity and also ensure equality for all the ethnic communities of the region. Thus, the main ground for the rise of the Sanamahi movement there was that their past historical experiences threatened the uniqueness of culture, polity, territory and ethnic harmony among various groups. The Meiteis felt that the socio-political status they enjoyed in the past was lost due to the epochs of the Burmese occupation of Manipur (1819–1826),[108] the British colonialism in Manipur,[109] and the merger of Manipur with India.[110] Manipur had been an independent kingdom from 33 A.D.; this ended with British colonialism in 1891 and the merger of Independent Manipur again in 1949 with the Indian Union.[111] Even after the merger, Manipur remained as Part-C State of dominant India till 1972, and Manipur statehood was granted only in 1972 after a long agitation.[112] All these political developments in Manipur's history stirred many youths to seek to establish a political space defined by their historical and cultural identity. As a result, today the Sanamahi movement is supported by many young men and women.

2.1.6. Nature and Objectives of the Movement

It is not easy to provide a precise statement of the nature and objectives of the movement, due to the many changes that have taken place during the past 80 years of its existence. Originally it seemed to be a socio-religious revival movement. However, later the aims shifted toward different dimensions shaping the socio-political destination of the Meiteis. Now the movement—about the revival of their tradition, religion, culture, language, and scripts—has various other goals like ethnic and territorial integrity of Manipur. In the first stage the movement started

---

[107] Sajal Nag, *Contesting Marginality*, 121.

[108] Naorem Joykumar Singh, *Colonialism to Democracy: A History of Manipur, 1819-1972* (Delhi: Sprectrum Publications, 2002), 2-4.

[109] Naorem Joykumar Singh, *Colonialism to Democracy*, 82 ff.

[110] Naorem Joykumar Singh, *Colonialism to Democracy*, 174 ff.

[111] L. Iboongohal Singh, *Introduction to Manipur*, 3rd edition (Imphal: Ibochaoba Singh, 1987), 228-30.

[112] Naorem Joykumar Singh, *Colonialism to Democracy*, 196 ff.

as anti-Bengali, anti-Brahmin and later on became anti-Hindu.[113] In Manipur the nature of the movement is more about the anti-Brahmin as the Hindu social system is dominated by the Brahminic community who migrated from Bengal and other places in today's mainland India during the period of Sanskritization.[114] However, the leaders of the movement denied this view and stressed that they are not against any other religion and community. They hold that in Manipur the Sanamahi deity is worshipped not only by the Meitei community but also by other communities like Brahmins, Tribals, and Muslims. Therefore, they further maintained that they are not against any community in the region. By upholding this ideology, they subsequently changed the name of the movement from Meitei *Marup* to 'Sanamahi movement', in order to broaden the horizon of the participants. The movement also strongly rejected the identification of Meiteis with the Kshatriya varna[115] and denied having any link with the Indo-Aryan heritage claimed by the early promoters of Hinduism. Thus, the movement was started as a purely socio-religious movement, but it changed its dimension according to the change of the socio-political system.

The assembly of the Manipur Sanamahi movement's organization in 1945 passed a number of resolutions and some of the important ones among them are as follows:[116]

1) It is to denounce the alien culture and religion.
2) It is to revive the cultural heritage of the Meiteis.
3) It is to do research in the ancient history and other literatures of the Meitei.
4) It is to revive the Meitei scripts.
5) It is to worship and chant religious hymns in the mother tongue.
6) It is to strengthen the unity between the hill and valley people and to live together as brothers and sisters.
7) It is to strengthen the bond of unity among the Meiteis who are living inside and outside the territory of Manipur.
8) And it is to let the world know that a community known as Meitei has been in existence with their old distinct cultural and religious identity in the North-Eastern part of India.

---

[113] Some writers do not agree to characterize this movement as anti-Hindu and anti-Brahmins. However, they contradict themselves when they say that the leaders are asking the Meitei to 'renounce' Hinduism and follow Sanamahi religion. Sairem Nilabir, "The Revivalist Movement," 117.

[114] The migration of Brahmins has already been dealt with in the preceding chapter.

[115] (Hinduism) the name for the original social division of Vedic people into four groups (which are subdivided into thousands of jatis), a Hindu caste or distinctive social group of which there are thousands throughout India; a special characteristic is often the exclusive occupation of its male members (such as barber or potter).

[116] *Meitei Marup Hourakpagi Wari,* 17. cited in. Sairem Nilabir, "The Revivalist Movement," 119.

What the Sanamahi followers emphasize most at present is its effort to bring inter-ethnic harmony among the various ethnic groups in the State. Most of the people are actively trying to bring a closer relationship between the hill and the valley people. The movement is against or is a reaction to the two and a half century old process of Sanskritization. It is to revive the Sanamahi cult and other important deities, which are the deities of the indigenous religion of the Meiteis and other indigenous communities. However, the sentiment of the movement is indicative more of a political trend rather than a regeneration of the Meitei religious belief. It is also manifested in many occasions when they turned their interest to the demand for the recognition of Meitei script in the eighth schedule of the Indian constitution rather than in the revival of script and religious philosophy of the Meitei religious life, and also when they demand the restoration of the Kangla[117] as the important religious place of the Meiteis.[118]

A number of educated Meiteis have also denied calling the present revival movement Sanamahi revivalism.[119] They believe that Manipur has been following a culture of religious syncretism where the Brahmins and the Meiteis worship Meitei gods and goddesses and Hindu gods and goddesses. The two religious systems in certain forms have been in co-existence.[120] On the one hand, some of the Sanamahi religious groups especially the members of Lainingthou Sanamahi Temple Board assert that they have discarded all Hindu customs and followed purely Meitei system.[121] The primary goal of the Sanamahi movement is to restore the pre-Hindu Meitei scripts, custom, culture and religious beliefs and practices. In other words, it aims at the de-Sanskritization of Meitei socio-cultural identity and history. This process of the de-Sanskritization of the Meitei identity also has several socio-political implications in the present context of Manipur.

---

[117] Pangambam Bharat Singh, Kangla: The National Heritage of Manipur, ii-iv.

[118] Sushanta Talukdar, "Rediscovering a Heritage," *Frontline,* 22/18, (August-September, 2005): 67.

[119] Some of the moderate groups do not agree that the movement is anti-Hindu and anti Brahmins, because generally religious groups in Manipur whether Hindu, Islam or other animistic sects, worship Sanamahi. Though they tried to revive the culture of Sanamahism, they are never against Brahmins or any other religion, they claimed.

[120] The religious syncretism has been dealt in the preceding chapter.

[121] The "Laininglhou Sanamnhi Temple Board" was formed in 1976 when some groups of people, mostly youths, demanded to install the idol of the Sanamahi from a Brahmin to its original abode at 'Tolong Yumpham' inside the First Manipur Rifle Compound. It is a body of persons who are well versed in Meitei religious belief and practices. However, the Brahmins, though they have the same knowledge, cannot be members of this group. In order to function smoothly, the nominees of the government also formed a twelve-member committee. They help the religious authorities in various other functions of the temple in its maintenance.

2.1.7. Change of Name

Sanamahi movement has undergone various changes and development in its organizational structure, issues, strategies, and nature during its existence. After Phullo's death, his followers in the Manipur valley changed the name of the Apokpa *Marup* or Meitei *Marup* to Sanamahi movement (named after a Meitei household deity) in 1945 when Pukhrambam Surchand became the president of this new organization.[122] However, people still perceived this organization as Meitei *Marup* organization, because the organization not only provides the emphasis on the Sanamahi deity but also equal importance is given to all the traditional deities of the Meiteis. So, some of the members still call their organization the Meitei *Marup*.

The alteration of the name of the movement from the Apokpa *Marup* or Meitei *Marup* to the Sanamahi movement has its political implications as far as its activities in the latter part of the movement are concerned. As Manipur is inhabited by many ethnic groups like the Meiteis, Kukis, Nagas, Pangals (Muslims),[123] and other sub-tribes, this movement has made many efforts to maintain the territorial integrity and ethnic harmony in the region. As we have seen in the previous chapter, till the beginning of the 18th Century there was a process of assimilation of the hill tribes with the Meitei population. However, by the beginning of the 18th Century due to the notion of purity and pollution associated with the Hindu caste system, social distance between Hindu Meiteis and non-Hindus like Kukis and Nagas were widened, especially when the latter became Christians. Now the hill tribes have started many movements to establish a separate political territory like *Nagalim* for Nagas,[124] and a separate homeland for the Kukis[125] so on and so forth. To remove this alienated feeling and allow all groups to live together harmoniously, the Meiteis need to ensure a society, which is free from the values of purity and pollution. The Meiteis also argue that the deity of Sanamahi is worshipped not only by the Meiteis but also by many communities in the region. Therefore, they gave the movement the name of Sanamahi.

2.2. Achievements

It is necessary at this point to go into detail to demonstrate some of the achievements of the movement, in each case showing its determination to take back sacred sites and deities which had been taken over and converted to Hindu use in the move to

[122] Sairem Nilabir, "The Revivalist Movement," 119.

[123] Muslims of Manipur are historically called Pangal which derives from "Pang"; it may have derived from "Bangal", from where they migrated in the early seventh century. Salam Irene, *The Muslims of Manipur* (New Delhi: Gyan Books Pvt. Ltd., 2010), 22-23.

[124] Phanjoubam Tarapot, *Bleeding Manipur* (New Delhi: Har-Anand Publications Pvt. Ltd., 2005), 18-19.

[125] Phanjoubam Tarapot, *Bleeding Manipur*, 19-20.

Vaishnavism. This is essential to the basic premise of this thesis that the strength of the revival movement among the ordinary people is such that conversion in large numbers to any other religion, including Christianity, is unlikely.

The revival movement from its inception has been involving in various issues, through which it has become a major factor for social change among the Meiteis in Manipur. During the period from 1975 to 1980 there was a new wave in the revival Movement, organized and launched by educated youths. Their main target was to restore and revive the traditional *Lais* and *Lai-phams*[126] from the hands of the Brahmins and Sanskritised Meiteis.[127] It is their decisive devotion that has enabled them to restore and revive those traditional *Lais* and *Lai-phams* and now this revival movement is growing stronger among Meiteis. As stated above, this decisive devotion is a major cause for the rejection of Christianity among this group of people. As far as the revival of *Lais* and *Lai-phams* is concerned, it is important to look at some of the achievements.

2.2.1. Restoration of Lainingthou Sanamahi

A detailed account of the events leading to the ultimate restoration of an ancient Meitei idol to its original temple is included here to emphasise the major part the activities of the Sanamahi movement, in finally obtaining the restoration of the idol, played in the propagation of the Meitei traditional religion and culture in Manipur. The revival movement in Manipur was not so rigorous till 1975. The movement was confined within a few sections of the people especially among the old people who adhered to the Sanamahi religion strictly. Conversely, from 1975 the movement became very intensive among the masses when some youths belonging to 'Pan Manipuri Youth League' (PMYL) organization supported the movement. It was in 1975 that some people who adhered to the Meitei Sanamahi *Laining* gathered and started various kinds of agitation demanding the restoration of Lainingthou Sanamahi idol[128] at Tolong Yumpham or Haying Khongbal (inside the First Manipur Rifles Compound), in Imphal. PMYL took a very active role in organizing the people by holding demonstrations and processions. The idol of Lainingthou Sanamahi was with a Brahmin named Laihaothabam Suryamani Sharma at Keisamthong Moirangningthou Leirak, in Imphal west.[129]

---

[126] *Lais* means deities and *Lai-phams* or *Lai-maphams* means places of deities. These terms can also be understood as holy place or places.

[127] R. K. Saha, "An Ethnic Movement in Manipur Valley," in *Tribal Movements in India,* vol. I, edited by K. S. Singh (New Delhi: Ramesh Jain Manohar Publications, 1982), 106-111.

[128] The Meiteis did not have the practice of idolatry in the ancient time. However, the worship of the idol in the temple called *Laishang* or *Phura* appeared after the coming of Hinduism. The appearance of this form of worshipping traditional deities was influenced by Hinduism. The practice of this culture followed by Sanamahi Meiteis indicates that they are still imitating the Hindu form of worship.

[129] Government of Manipur, *Extraordinary Gazetteer,* no. 149. (Constitution of the Lainingthou Sanamahi Temple Board), 1976, 12.

As mentioned in the preceding chapter, all the important deities of the Meiteis were looked after by the Brahmins after removing the traditional functionaries of the *Maiba* and *Maibi.* This Brahmin was worshipping this deity similarly to the way the Hindus worship (with *Tulsi* leaves in his own temple). A group of Sanamahi followers started claiming that the image of the Sanamahi be returned to its original abode and worshipped publicly by the people according to the Meitei traditional religious rites. They also argued that the Sanamahi should not be worshipped by the Brahmins in the Hindu fashion with *Tulsi* leaves, which is a taboo in the Meitei religion.[130] They also demanded the restoration of the image to its original abode before the *Mera Chaoren Houba,*[131] which usually started from 1st to 5th day of *Mera* (September-October). This festival also forms an important part of Meitei traditional religion.

In order to remove the image from the custody of Brahmins some people formed an organization called Uttra Sanglen in 1975. Consequently, a large group of people including King Okendra, the symbolic King of Manipur, went to the house of the said Brahmin and requested him to release the image for public worship on the eve of *Mera Chaoren Houba* festival.[132] In this connection, more than 157 persons including 13 women were arrested by the police. However, they were released at night on the same day.[133] In the same year, again they went to take the image but were arrested under section 144 of I.P.C. The arrest of these people led to the formation of another bigger or stronger organization called 'Lainingthou Sanamahi Thougal Kanglup'. In view of the increasing tension between the Meiteis and Brahmins on this contentious issue, a curfew was imposed in the Imphal district on 24th September, 1976 in order to stop any untoward incident. However, on the same day, hundreds of people assembled and moved toward the temple of the Brahmin to take the image to restore it to its original place. In this event the police shot dead two young men, Oinam Chaoba of Oinam village and

---

[130] The difference between the Sanamahi Meiteis and Hindu Meiteis is the use of *Tairen* and *Tulsi.* The religion of a Meitei also can be identified with the plant— *Tairen* and *Tulsi* that has been put in the middle of the courtyard. These two plants have been used by the Brahmins and *Maibas/ Maibis* respectively for sprinkling holy water in the religious functions of the Hindu and Sanamahi.

[131] *Mera Chaoren Houba* is an important traditional religious celebration of the Meiteis. The Governor of Manipur and the Chief Minister greeted the people of Manipur on this occasion. In his message the Governor Gurubachan Jagat said the traditional festival of *Mera Chaoren Houba,* which is celebrated in Manipur every year, aims to preserve and promote unity and integrity among all communities of the State. The celebration will help in deepening the age-old tradition of co-existence in the pluralistic society of Manipur. The Chief Minister in his message urged the people to make utmost efforts to rejuvenate the affection, brotherhood and friendship among all the indigenous people of Manipur. "Greetings from Governor, CM on *Mera Chaoren Houba,*" *Hueiyen Lanpao* (Imphal) 27 September 2011.

[132] Meitei Pumnamakhi Lainingthou Sanamahi (Sanamahi as the god of all Meiteis) (Imphal: Lainingthou Sanamahi Thougal Kanglup, 1976), 4-5.

[133] Sairem Nilabir, "The Revivalist Movement," 120.

Heisnam Kumar of Heingang village.[134] Moreover, many of the members of the Lainingthou Sanamahi Thougal Kanglup were also arrested by the police, and jailed for more than 20 days. In order to fulfill the sentiment of the public as well as to find solution, the government of Manipur passed a bill on 6th December 1976 known as Lainingthou Sanamahi Temple Bill and the Governor granted his consent on 1st March 1977. Nevertheless, the bill did not become an act for a long time due to the socio-religious instability among the Meiteis.[135]

Yensembam Gulamjat Meitei,[136] the then president of the Lainingthou Sanamahi Thougal Kanglup, submitted a memorandum to the Chief Minister on 16th March 1977 urging the formation of a Temple Board and a judicial inquiry on the death of the two young men. It was on 18th April, 1977 that the Government of Manipur circulated a notification saying that the Sanamahi Temple Act 1976 would immediately come into effect from 19th April, 1977. Accordingly, a Board known as the Lainingthou Sanamahi Temple Board was formed to look after the affair of the temple and its management. The Board consisted of eleven members who were nominated by the Government of Manipur. Finally, on the night of 11th October 1977, the image of the Sanamahi was brought back from the temple of the Brahmin to its original abode at Tolong Yumpham.[137] On 13th October 1977, the then Chief Minister, Yangmaso Shaiza, announced in front of the public gathering in the new compound of the temple thus:[138]

> From today onwards the people of Manipur could bow down and worship the god freely as a public god. He also declared that the taking of the image from the Brahmin was a measure carried out by the Government on time and very sensitively.

Since the year 1977, the Government of Manipur declared *Mera Chaoren Houba* as a general holiday in Manipur and that was a historic declaration for the people. As far as the contribution of the Lainingthou Sanamahi Temple Board is concerned, one can without any doubts say that the temple Board contributed much in reviving the Meitei religion and culture. They have published pamphlets,

---

[134] "Resistance," *An English Weekly* 24/9 (October, 1976): 3.

[135] Government of Manipur, *Extraordinary Gazetteer*, no. 213. (Constitution of the Lainingthou Sanamahi Temple Board), 1977, 94.

[136] Yensembam Gulamjat of Heiranggoithong was the Second vice president of the Lainingthou Sanamahi Temple Board.

[137] Government of Manipur, *Extraordinary Gazetteer*, no. 213, 96. cf. This special issue was published on the 10th Anniversary day of the installation of the image of Sanamahi. Lainingthou Sanamahi Board, *Lainingthou Sanamahina Haying Khongbal Tolong Yumphamda Lengsillakpa, (coming of Lainingthou Sanamahina at Tolong)*, (Imphal: Lainingthou Sanamahi Board, 1987), 7.

[138] Because of his contribution in the restoration of the image of Sanamahi deity, still people in the Sanamahi temple at Imphal portray the photograph of late Yangmaso Shaiza on many important occasions of the Sanamahi ceremonies. Sairem Nilabir, "The Revivalist Movement," 120.

booklets and leaflets regarding Meitei religion, culture and tradition. In the Constitution of this Board the need for reviving and promoting Meitei traditional religion, culture, etc., are clearly stressed. The aim and objective of the Board is to preserve the religion, culture and the identity of the Meiteis.[139] The Board also tried to translate different posts and positions of the Board in the Meitei language. For instance, the President is called *Luchingba,* the Vice President is called *Ngamthang Luchingba,* General Secretary is called *Thouburel,* and Finance Secretary is called *Selungba.* Certain rules and regulations are also laid down for the people who come to worship the image. People who are not properly dressed in the Meitei traditional way are not allowed to enter the temple.[140] Thus, the Sanamahi movement, which started as a small sect in the beginning, became an important socio-religious institution when they formed Lainingthou Sanamahi Temple Board in 1976.[141] Now there are various other local organizations, which co-operatively work with Lainingthou Sanamahi Temple Board in popularizing the traditional culture and religion of the Meiteis in various places.

2.2.2. Nongkhrang *Parei Hanba*

(Nongkhrang = a kind of tree, *Parei* = binding, *Hanba* = Unwinding or undoing); According to the Puyas, the meaning of Nongkhrang *Parei Hanba* was to free one from the binding of an oath. In the year 1729, during the reign of King Garib Niwaz, on the 5th day of *Wakching* (December-January), Meiteis were forced to adopt Hinduism.[142] He ordered them to dive in the water of Lilong River (a confluence of two important rivers of Manipur which is about 8 km to the south of Imphal) with branches of Nongkhrang in hand. It was a serious kind of oath-taking that they would not renounce Hinduism. In the reign of Bhagyachandra (1759-98), another second oath-taking of the above nature was also carried out, not to renounce Hindu-Gouriya Vaishnavism.[143]

In order to free the Meitei community from the binding of the oath, a special function was organized by a group of followers of Sanamahism on October 6, 1974, on the full moon day of *Phairel* (February-March). In that function Okendrajit, the King of Manipur read out a written statement which should be followed by Pandit *Loisang* (office of the Palace scholars). Some *Maibas* and devotees dived in the water of Lilong River with ritual to free from the binding of the oath which had been imposed on their forefathers some two hundred and fifty

[139] Government of Manipur, *Extraordinary Gazetteer*, no. 213, 97-99.

[140] Here are a few rules set by Lainingthou Sanamahi Temple Board. Every devotee should take bath before entering temple. Male should wear white dhoti (a long loincloth), white shirt or yellow silk shirt, white turban (for those who are functionaries of the temple), white shawl but not other colours. (As written on the notice Board of the Lainingthou Sanamahi Temple Board).

[141] "Sanamahi," *Prajantrantra* (Imphal), 12 October 1976, 1.

[142] Kh. Ratan Kumar, *Lai Haraoba of Manipur,* 16.

[143] Pandi Chandrasing, *Nongkhang Pareihanba* (Imphal: Sanamahians, 1968), 7.

years ago. They did so representing the entire Meitei community. After this ritual, the Meiteis were given freedom to accept their long lost traditional religion which is free from casteism.[144] The Chairman of the Meitei National Front (MNF) justified the above activities of taking over the *lais* and the *laiphams* on the ground that India is a secular State and every minority community has the right to protect its own culture and religion.[145]

2.2.3. Revivification of Nongpok Ningthou and Panthoibi

The Nongnaiching hill is an important home of the Meiteis. It is the abode of Nongpok Ningthou and Panthoibi, the legendary hero and heroine of the Meitei mythology, and one of the most important titular deities of the Meiteis. It is also the traditional custom of the Meiteis to climb the hill and worship the deity on *Cheiraoba,*[146] the New Year day of the Meiteis. Before climbing the hill to seek the blessings from Nongpok Ningthou, the devotees take a bath in the Chingoi River, which is at the foot of the hill. This practice of taking a bath in the Chingoi River is known as Chingoi *Iruppa* (immersing in the holy water of *Chingoi* River).[147]

Nevertheless, during the reign of King Chandrakriti (1850-1886), the Chingoi *Iruppa* was transformed into a Hindu festival of *Varuni Kaba,* the worshipping of Lord Shiva while Brahmins were employed after the construction of the temple at the top of the hill. A major project for the development of Hindu pilgrimage was also done in late 1940s. But in 1951, a group called the Sanamahi Cult started worshipping Meitei deities at the Nongmaiching instead of Hindu deity Siva. And in 1978, the devotees of the Sanamahi revivalism took over the *Laipham* (abode of the Nongpok Ningthou). The *Ching-Tam Lai Marup* (the hill and valley religious association) performed the ritual, with the support of the Meitei National Front, an organization currently spearheading the revival of Meitei culture, religion and script. From that day onwards the Nongmaiching Hill was under full control of the Meitei Sanamahi movement, and no one from the Shri Gobindaji Temple Board was allowed to interfere with the worship of

---

[144] S. N. Parratt, The Religion of Manipur, 120.

[145] H. Tiken, President Meitei National Frond (MNF) Wangkhei, Imphal West, Manipur, letter to the author, 17th September 2010.

[146] The local inhabitants of Manipur follow strict religious rituals and traditional cultures of the region during the celebration of *Cheiraoba.* A grand feast, comprising of several local delicacies, is prepared to observe the special occasion. Representing the religious fervor of the place, the native population worships their local deities and seeks divine blessing and eternal happiness on the special festive occasion of *Cheiraoba.* An integral part of the cultural ancestry and religious heritage of Manipur, the local inhabitants still follow the age-old custom of climbing the nearby mountain ranges of the area with the belief that this would help them to reach the zenith of success in their daily affairs. "*Cheiraoba,*" http://www.mapsofindia.com/manipur/society-and-culture/cheiraoba.html (19 Feb 2013).

[147] Pandi Chandrasing, "Chingoi Iruppa," *Meetyeng* 21 (October-December, 1979): 5-6.

the Nongpok Ningthou and Panthoibi.[148] Accordingly, the Hill of Nongpok Ningthou is also under the control of Sanamahi Meiteis now.

2.2.4. Commemoration Day for Burning of the Puyas

The Puyas[149] were the ancient religious books written in traditional Meitei script. During the reign of Garib Niwas (1709–1748),[150] more than 120 books on different subjects were burnt to ashes on the advice of his religious Guru Santa Das Gosai.[151] In order to commemorate this event, the devotees of the traditional religion observed the first condolence day at Mongba Hanba Umang in the small hours of the morning of the 23rd day of *Wakching* (December-January), 1978. On that night, a number of youths came along with pieces of firewood and made a funeral pyre in the Mongba Hanba Umang (Present Mahaballi Grove). About 500 books which had been written for Sanskritization of the Meitei society were burnt on the Pyre. The seven-colour flag of the Meitei nationality was lowered to half mast. Two images of two persons, who had burnt the ancient Meitei Puyas were also burnt down. This was done secretly.[152]

On January 21, 1979 the second condolence day was observed openly in front of Kangla *Utra* (inside the old Palace Compound), Imphal. The then Speaker of Manipur Legislative Assembly was the Chief Guest. A procession was taken, led by the volunteers of the MNF in black dress. Images of King Garib Niwaz and Santa Das Gosai were made and burnt down. A number of holy books of Vaishnavism including the Meiteilon versions of the Mahabharata and the Bhagavad-Gita were burnt on a funeral pyre.[153] Since that year, the condolence day for burning Puyas had been observed openly under the leadership of the MNF[154] to show that Hinduism had been imposed on the Meiteis by force and that it had not been spread with love and service.[155]

---

[148] Lairenmayum Ibungohal Singh and N. Khelchandra Singh, *Cheitharol Kumbaba* (*The Chronicles*) (Imphal: Manipur Sahitya Parishad 1967), 641, 652 and 676.

[149] Blazing of the Puyas has been cited in the preceding chapter nevertheless we shall be looking here in brief in the context of the achievement done by followers of the revivification movement.

[150] Ravindra Pratap Singh, *Geography of Manipur* (New Delhi: National Book Trust, 1982), 3.

[151] Ng. Kangjia Mangang, *Revival of a Closed Account: A Brief History of Kanglei Script and the Birth of Phoon (Zero) in the World of Arithmetic and Astrology* (Imphal West: Sanamahi Laining Amasung Punsiron Khupham, 1969), 13.

[152] "Resistance," An English Weekly, 4.

[153] "Simanta Patrika," *The Manipur Daily* (Imphal), 23 January 1979, 1.

[154] V.I.K. Sarin, *India's North-East in Flames* (New Dellhi: Vikas Publishing House PVT LTD, 1980), 117.

[155] The burning of *Puya* (ancient Manipuri texts) in front of Kangla Uttra by the then King Pamheiba at the behest of Hindu missionary leader Shanti Das Gosai on the 17th day of Manipuri month of *Mera* in the year 1732 was observed today as the *Puwarigi Amamba Numit* (black day) by All Clubs, Organizations, Associations and Meira Paibi Lup (ACOAM)-Lup, Kangleipak, at GM

2.2.5. Revival of *Kongba Maru Laipham*

The mountain of Koubru in the north of Imphal is believed to be the place where the first human settlement was made in Manipur. It was taken over by the Brahmins as an important abode of the Hindu deity, Lord Shiva.[156] The pool on the top of the hill was renamed as Sarasvati Kunda, Radha Kunda, Lakshmi Kunda, etc.[157] However the devotees of the Sanamahi revival movement restored the place as the important abode of the Meiteis on 22th March, 1979. Now the management of the abode is under the control of the Kongba Maru *Laipham Thoupu Kanglup* (committee of the management of the Kongba Maru *Laipham*). Regarding the takeover of the management, an agreement was signed between the individuals, who were in charge of the management, and the Kongba Maru *Laipham Thoupu Kanglup* in the office of the Saikhul S.D.C. under civil case no. Misc. 3 of 1979 on April 22, 1979.[158] Hence, the religious sites that had been taken over by the Hindus were restored by the Sanamahi followers.

2.2.6. Revival of the *Mongba Hanba Umanglai*

As far as sacred places are concerned, the Mongba Hanba *Umanglai* was the most sacred place of the Meiteis in the valley.[159] Because of this, it is a place where all the important images of the Meitei traditional deities were destroyed and buried during the reign of King Garib Niwaz. After that a Hanuman image carved out of a stone was installed at this place in 1729, and since then it has been worshipped as an important place of the Hindu religion generally known as Mahabali.[160] The revival movement, in order to restore the habitat to its original religious use, formed an association known as Mongba Hanba *Umanglai Kanba Lup* (committee of Mongba Hanba *Umanglai*) to preserve and worship the Mongba Hanba as a holy place of Meiteis. This committee also published and distributed a number of leaflets urging people to support the committee to save and promote the Meiteis' worship of forest grove. However, the Brahmin families who had been occupying the place since 18th Century resisted the demand of the restoration of Mongba Hanba to the Meiteis. In 1979, a number of devotees of Sanamahi marched to restore the abode as the original place of the Meitei religion. On that day more than ten persons were arrested including the President of the Meitei

---

Hall, Imphal. "Burning of *Puya* Commemorated as Black Day by ACOAM," *Imphal Free Press*, 26 October 2010. cf. Apendix-3 of preceding chapter.

[156] The destroyer; one of the three major divinities in the later Hindu pantheon.

[157] Lairenmayum Ibungohal Singh and N. Khelchandra Singh, *Cheitharol Kumbaba*, 660-661.

[158] Sairem Nilabir, "The Revivalist Movement," 121.

[159] Jamini Devi, *Cultural History of Manipur: Sija Laioibi and the Maharas* (New Delhi: Mittal Publications, 2010), 43.

[160] "Ireipak Machasingda Pijaba Paojel," *Meitei National Front* (Feb. 1979): 7-9.

National Front, although they were released on the same day.[161] Today this place is a contested site between the followers of Sanamahi and Vaishnavism.

2.2.7. Panthoibi Instead of Durga

During the reign of King Chandrakirti in Manipur, the worship of Durga[162] was very popular in Manipur. Hindu Meiteis formed committee(s) for worshipping Durga during Durga *Puja* festival. These committees closely cooperated with the Brahmins in their localities and observed the festival in the community hall attached to the Brahmin temple. This festival in Manipur is observed for five days from the first to the fifth day of the Mera (September-October) every year. It also forms one of the most important festivals among the Vaishnava Meiteis.[163] It is believed that the Meitei Hindu scholars popularized this festival through the identification of the goddess, Durga with the Meitei goddess, Panthoibi.[164] However many Meiteis who follow the traditional Sanamahi religion formed a committee called the Panthoibi Erat Thouni (Panthoibi worship group) for worshipping Panthoibi in place of the Hindu deity, Durga. Whenever there is the Durga *Puja* festival we now find the Panthoihi Eratpa (worshipping of Panthoibi) too.[165] It seems that the particular festival of the Panthoibi Eratpa was introduced by the Meitei Sanamahi religious groups in order to counter the Hindu religious festival.[166] It is recorded that since 1960, there has been an increase in the number of the committees for the worshipping of Panthoibi in place of Durga *Puja* festival.[167] However, common people are not so much aware of the trend of the competition between the two groups; particularly as in public the sites do not have much difference, as many of the devotees visit both the places to offer flowers, fruits and coins.

---

[161] Sairem Nilabir, "The Revivalist Movement," 122.

[162] Hindu goddess of war; a malevolent aspect of Devi.

[163] E. Nilakanta Singh, *Fragments of Manipur Culture* (New Delhi: Omsons Publications, 1993), 35.

[164] S.S. Shashi, "Manipur: Historical and Cultural Background," 206.

[165] Sairem Nilabir, "The Reavivalist Movement," 123.

[166] The legendary woman Panthoibi rebelled against this sort of submissive situation and denial of independent choice. She rebelled against her father and all the norms of patriarchy in Manipuri society. She became a voluntary actor and stood out even as the rallying point for other seekers of independence among counterparts. Once she would put her foot down and make a determined choice, no amount of coaxing or persuasion could deter or waive her from her trajectory. She would go through all the trials and tribulations of a rebel to ultimately emerge as a Goddess. M. Chandra, *Panthoibi Khongun (Footsteps of Panthoibi)* (Imphal: Sahitya Parishad Manipur, 1999), 41.

[167] Mangibabu Meitei, Panthoibi Erat Thouni Secretary, Chingarel Tejpur, Imphal East, Manipur, letter to the author, 11 June 2011.

2.2.8. Revival of Hiyangthang Lairembi Abode

The fresh consciousness of the Meitei identity also prompted the movement to reinstate the Meitei deity called Hiyangthang Lairembi, who had to cede her place to the Hindu goddess Durga during the forceful conversion into Vaishnavism. A new committee known as Ereima Thougal Lup (Ereima worship committee) made many efforts to replace this Hindu goddess with the Meitei goddess known as Hiyangthang Lairembi. Hiyangthang Lairenbi,[168] worshipped at Hiyangthang, a hillock located in the southern outskirt of Imphal, was one of the most important female deities of the Meitei tradition. Hiyangthang (Hiyang = the boat; thang = port) was named after the harbour where the Sidaba Mapu docked his boat while coming down by boat from the Koubru mountain during the period the valley was covered with water.[169] With the conversion of Meiteis into Vaishnavism and in accordance with the wish of the Hindu missionary, the identity of the deity was changed to Kamakhya Devi, a Hindu goddess. Though Kamakhya was worshipped once a year during Durga *Puja* festival, it constitutes one of the most important and biggest festivals of the Vaishnava Meiteis during the Durga *Puja*.[170] At present this place is overcrowded with the devotees of the Kamakhya on the eve of the festival. From early morning devotees rush to the place to offer flowers, fruits and coins, and to beg blessings.[171] The influence of the Sanamahi on this festival is much less compared to the influence of Vaishnavism.

Nevertheless, followers of Sanamahi claimed it to be a rightful place for the Meiteis where the deity of Lairenbi or Ereima is to be worshipped every year on the occasion of the traditional Meitei New Year[172] day, with the help of *Maiba* and *Maibi*.[173] In September, 1979, the Hiyangthang Ereima *Thougal Lup* (committee

[168] Hiyangthang Lairenbi is also known as Ereima—both the names are used synonymously.

[169] This is a common folklore which is still believed by many Meiteis that once upon a time the whole valley was covered with water. And the Koubru came down from his abode by boat and docked it (hiyang) at the place. Since then the place is known as Hiyangthang.

[170] Sairem Nilabir, "The Revivalist Movement," 121.

[171] The deity of Kamakhya has been very popular among the Hindu people in the neighbouring state of Assam. In the beginning of the Vaishnavism in Manipur, the deity was identified as Durga and still people perform Durga Puja every year in this place and the most popular place in Manipur.

[172] The Meitei New Year (*Sajibu Nongma Panba Cheiraoba*), a traditional celebration is an integral part of Meiteis. To celebrate, people clean and decorate their houses and make a sumptuous variety of dishes to feast upon after offering food to the deity on this day. This is the first date of the Meitei Lunar calendar. After the feast, as a part of the rituals, people climb the nearest hill tops or the "Cheiraoching" in the belief that it would excel them to greater heights in their worldly life. It is observed during the month of March/April. This year the New Year was celebrated with gaiety and enthusiasm across Manipur on 4th April. Pratibha Patil, the President of India conveyed her wishes to people of Manipur on this auspicious occasion. "Meitei New Year Brings in Hope for Peace and Unity," *The Times of India* (Guwahati), 4 April 2011, 5.

[173] *Maiba* and *Maibi* are the traditional Meitei priest and priestess—they were very powerful and instrumental in the socio-religious life of the Meiteis before their forceful conversion into Vaishnavism.

of Hiyangthang Ereima) organized a movement to restore the abode to its original heritage. The committee also appealed to the people to begin to worship the traditional Meitei goddess from 22th September, 1979 onwards, instead of the Hindu deity, Kamakhya. A 'Planning Cell' consisting of seven members including Ch. Akaba, the president of the MNF was constituted. An agreement was made between the president of MNF and the Secretary of the 'Lai Committee', which was in charge of the abode. Under that agreement the devotees were allowed to worship any goddess whether it is Durga or Ereima according to their choice.[174] As a result a temple of the Ereima was also built at the foothill of the abode. The worship of the deity of Ereima in the form of pre-Hindu worship is still carried out on every Sunday in the premises by followers of the Sanamahism, but it is held outside the Kamakhya temple.

2.2.9. Revival of Traditional Script and Common Festivals

The ideological shift of the movement from socio-religious ground to the politics of language is another landmark in the achievement of the movement. By 1980s, the Sanamahi movement took a different shape when it turned its attention from not just the revival of Meitei script but also to the demand for the recognition of Meitei language in the Constitution of India.[175] However by 1990s there has been a change in the direction being taken by the movement. During this period, the Sanamahi movement started organizing various socio-cultural festivals, in a major effort to bring ethnic harmony among the various ethnic groups.[176] This changing direction of the movement may be due to the result of the emergence of various ethnic conflicts: Kuki-Naga conflicts,[177] Meitei-Pangal (Muslim) conflict,[178] resulting in the loss of thousands of lives in 1990s in Manipur.

---

[174] Sairem Nilabir, "The Revivalist Movement," 122.

[175] Kailash S. Aggarwal, "Monistic Pluralism: Language Ideology in a Language Movement," in *Linguistic Structure and Language Dynamics in South Asia: Papers from the Proceedings of SALA XVIII Roundtable*, edited by Anvita Abbi, R. S. Gupta and Ayesha Kidwari (Delhi: Motilal Banarsidass Publishing Private Limited, 2011), 260.

[176] Sairem Nilabir, "The Revivalist Movement," 123.

[177] Lal Dena, "AMCO's Peace Efforts During the Kuki-Naga Conflict, 1992–1994," *Kuki International Forum.* http://kukiforum.com/2010/04/amcos-peace-efforts-during-the-kuki-naga-conflict-19921994-2/. (19 Feb 2013) For further information on the effect of the clash: "Sex Trade Thrives in Conflict-Ridden Manipur," (12 June 2007). http://www.indiatogether.org/2007/jun/wom-sxmanipur.htm (19 Feb 2013).

[178] The following source also gives the outcome of the Meitei-Pangal (Muslim) conflict. "Sex Trade Thrives in Conflict-Ridden Manipur," (12 June 2007). http://www.indiatogether.org/2007/jun/wom-sxmanipur.htm (19 Feb 2013).

Therefore, the Sanamahi movement started using various socio-religious platforms like *Lai-Haraoba,*[179] *Mera-Hou Chongba, Ching Tam Potlanba,*[180] etc. to bring peace and harmony among the ethnic groups. The reason behind the shift from Meitei script and language movement to the organizing of such common festivals is possibly due to the Meiteis' policies to pacify the people of other communities who had been alienated by the Meitei language movement. These ethnic groups whose mother tongue is not Meiteilon felt a strong sense of alienation when Meiteis demanded the recognition of Meiteilon in the Eighth Schedule of the Indian Constitution in 1992 and to use the same as the medium of instruction in schools. So by 1990s the demand for autonomy of the Nagas and Kukis became very strong, which not only threatened Manipur's age-old cultural and territorial integrity but also resulted in a series of ethnic clashes in the State. Thus, the Sanamahi movement shifted from language politics to the politics of cultural and territorial integrity of Manipur, which is clearly manifested in the Meiteis' interest in the revival and popularizing of some festivals having common origin with hill and valley people in Manipur. Concerning this particular area of study, we can see that Meitei Sanamahi movement has dual roles—first, the role of exclusivist identity, frequently spelled out more vocally in the language recognition movement, and second, the role of unity and integrity manifested in the promotion of traditional festivals, which provide space for identity of other ethnic groups.

Evaluation and Conclusion

The institutionalization of the Sanamahi movement enables the leaders and the followers to carry and translate the ideology into action; they are able to mobilize people to participate on a large scale. The establishment of Meitei Apokpa *Marup* and Meitei *Marup* in Cachar and Manipur respectively is part of the effort of leaders to provide proper direction to the Sanamahi movement with definite principles. Their main effort is to revive and preserve the socio-religious identity of Meiteis by abandoning all the elements that are of Hindus; this is clearly manifested in their action when the leader, Naoriya Phullo started strongly opposing the observance of Hindu festivals, use of Sanskrit and Bengali language and employment of Brahmins in socio-religious ceremonies of the Meiteis. He also preached the exposition of pure Meitei belief and Meitei way of life so that Meitei racial identity would not be threatened by a more dominant identity.

---

[179] Sophia Chanu, "Lai-Haraoba," *Indian Folk Life* 1/1 (July, 2001): 19-20.

[180] *"Mera Houchongba"* one of the few festivals in the state not related with religious rites in any form was celebrated today to bring all ethnic communities together on a common platform leaving behind all the odds confronting the state. Likewise, *"Ching Tam Potlanba"* meaning exchange of gifts between the people of hills and valley is another crucial observance in bringing peace and harmony among the various ethnic groups. It is a historic festival which symbolises the age-old brotherhood among the indigenous people of Manipur. "*Mera Houchongba,*" *The Sangai Express* (Imphal), 3 October 2009. cf. "*Mera Houchongba,*" *Imphal Free Press* (Imphal), 28 September 2011.

According to the movement, the best means of gaining liberation from the yoke of Brahminic domination is to worship the genuine Meitei deities, and sing hymns written in the Meitei language instead of in Bengali and Sanskrit.

As well as propagating anti-Hindu and anti-Brahminic ideology, Naoriya Phullo had also tried to challenge publicly the leaders of the Hindu organization through public debate which was arranged between the followers of Sanamahism and Hinduism. In that debate Naoriya Phullo defeated Pandit Atompapu Sharma. Through these strategies the leaders of the Apokpa *Marup* movement drew the attention and the active participation of the people in large numbers.[181] Phullo was a critic of Hinduism and its culture. His attack on Vaishnava Meiteis—Kings like Gariba Niwaz, Bhagyachandra and Hindu missionaries like Santi Das Gosai—awoke the people' minds to a strong resolve to throw off the Hindu elements, which mainly originated from the Brahminic domination in Meitei socio-religious life.

For Naoriya Phullo, Meiteis' culture and religion, which he called 'Meiteism' or 'Sanamahism', is not the offshoot of the tribal culture or some accepted theories propounded by the European anthropologists like McCulloch, Pemberton, T.C. Hodson and Grierson.[182] Phullo's theory was that the Meiteis were the descendants of Lainingthon Sorare and their religion was the worshipping of Poklen Pokpa Shatlen Shatpa along with the host of pre-Hindu Meitei deities. For his tireless effort and contribution to the revival of Meitei religious life, his followers gave him the title of *Taibang Phaoba Naoriya Ahan* thereby meaning "elderly man who takes human birth". His ideology was to establish a distinct Meitei identity, which is neither of tribal origin nor the Vedic origin. He and his followers were also against the *Maibas* and *Maibis* who are required functionaries for conducting the rites and ceremonies related to various cultures of *Umanglais*. According to the interpretation of the Apokpa *Marup, Maibas* and *Maibis* are the products of the kingship. They also alleged that they (*Maibas* and *Maibis*) use Sanskrit hymns and songs and as such they are not allowed to perform any rites and rituals of the Apokpa culture. Therefore, the Apokpa *Marup,* according to Kriti Singh, can be called 'Counter Reformation' as it upholds the total primitive belief of the

[181] The King of Manipur was in constant touch with the Meiteis outside Manipur such as Burma. Hojai, Cachar, Lamka in Assam, Nabadwip in West Bengal. Dhaka. Sylhet in Bangladesh, and Vrindavan and Mathura in U.P. M. Kirti Singh, *Religion and Culture of Manipur*, 33.

[182] The British ethnographers and political agents in Manipur held the view that Meiteis are the descendents of the surrounding hill tribes of Manipur. They drew out this view from some observable facts that there are similarities between the customs of hill tribes in Manipur and the customs that the Meiteis retain till today. Particularly the appearance of tribal identity in some core rituals of the Meiteis like *Lai-Haraoba* and *Phambal Kaba* is an indication of their common origin that the British claimed. The origin of Meiteis has been dealt with in chapter two under the heading 'Anthropological Background'.

Meiteis.[183] The teachings of the Brahmins were straightaway rejected and devotion to a doctrine evolved by Apokpa *Marup* was declared essential for salvation.

Consequently, there is a difference between the ideologies of the leaders in the valley of Manipur and in the Cachar district in Assam. The Meiteis in Manipur feel the importance of maintaining a social harmony not only between the Meiteis and Hill tribes but also between various ethnic communities in the region. Therefore, many of the followers of Sanamahi culture in Manipur valley did not accept the ideology of Naoriyo Phullo. They claimed that the Sanamahi was the common religion of both the Meiteis and hill tribes. Therefore, the leaders in Manipur valley after the death of Naoriya Phullo changed the name of the movement from the Apokpa *Marup* to Sanamahi *Laining* movement or Sanamahi movement. This name change indicates the ideological shift of the leaders from an exclusivist identity—so called Meitei identity—to a broader identity of Manipur.

It is clear from this study that the Sanamahi movement in Manipur and Cachar originated and developed from two different socio-political contexts. The Sanamahi movement in Cachar was due to the result of the socio-cultural domination of the Meiteis by the Bengalis. However, the Sanamahi movement in Manipur though started as an anti-Brahmin and anti-Hindu movement changed its direction according to the change of the socio-political system in the area. The main basis of the Sanamahi movement in Manipur is to remove the Brahminic influence in the Meitei socio-religious life as well as to establish a space exclusively enjoyed by the Meitei and other indigenous communities. The contest over the name of the land, 'Manipur', also indicates the major goal of the Sanamahi movement at present. The installation of traditional Meitei deities instead of Hindu deities also indicates that Meiteis want to replace the Hindu identity by their pre-Hindu identity. It is also their effort to link a physical place, such as religious sites, monuments, hills, rivers, etc. with an imagined mental space to produce another real space of power. The claim of various sites at hill and valley by the Sanamahi followers as important religious abodes is also their particular effort to establish a space exclusively enjoyed by a particular group. This claim also necessitated redefining land, sites and territory with a specific identity. The redefining of the land Manipur as 'Kangleipak' is a spatial aspect of the Sanamahi movement, which seeks to redefine and re-identify a territorial space with an identity of the past. It is their re-articulation of an imagined space toward the real space as a legitimate socio-political space of the Meiteis and every ethnic group in the State.

It is the theme of this study that the revival movement focuses on three key areas: 1) Denouncing alien elements (anything that does not have an origin connected to Meitei and Manipur—Hinduism and its Brahminic manipulation in Meitei society are taken as a key alien element). 2) Reviving traditional values

[183] Kirti Singh, *Religion and Culture of Manipur*, 52-53.

i.e., religion, culture, language, script etc. and 3) Preserving those traditional values.

It is clear from the evidence adduced in this study that denouncing alien elements, reviving traditional values and preserving those traditional values are the key concerns of this movement, and these restorative activities were taken up in order to safeguard their traditional religion, culture, language, script etc. The followers of the revival movement of Sanamahism spread awareness that Meiteis have had enough socio-religious and socio-cultural discrimination under the yoke of Hinduism and its Brahminic exploitation. Therefore they strongly reject other religious teachings including Christianity, for they believe that allowing or accepting the teachings of any other religion than traditional revival values of Meiteis would hamper the hard-earned revival process. Hence, this factor is put forward as the major cause for the rejection of Christianity among the Meiteis in Manipur valley.

Chapter 5

British Colonialism in Manipur
Minor Cause for Rejection of Christianity

Introduction

The principal and the major causes for the rejection of Christianity have been dealt with in the preceding chapters. Keeping these in mind, this thesis will finally consider the minor cause for the rejection of Christianity among the Meiteis in Manipur valley—the period of British colonialism in Manipur. This will be done under three headings—1) a brief historical account on the early connection of Manipur with the British; 2) the beginning of direct British rule and its effects; 3) the outbreak of *Nupi Lan*. The chapter will end with some concluding remarks.

To briefly recapitulate[1] on the history of the coming of Christianity to Manipur, the Christian missionary William Pettigrew came to Manipur under the patronage of a British official, A. Porteous. It was a matter that colonial rule and Christian missionary zeal combined, as in many other situations, to bring good government and Christianity, in theory, to a so far untouched region. However in Manipur this did not happen. It was during the political unrest that led to the massacre of seven British officials that Pettigrew decided to commit to go to Manipur as a missionary among the Meiteis. But Pettigrew's vision of evangelization of Meiteis did not take place. As has been detailed previously, Pettigrew came to an area fiercely Hindu in its religion, which led the population to be strongly against any move to convert. But added to this was the Meiteian reaction to British colonial rule, which was not well received by the local population.

[1] Christianity in Manipur has been dealt with elaborately in chapter three. Therefore, we are not going to deal with it here again. But we are recalling some crucial thoughts of it for our deliberation for this current chapter.

1. Early Connection with British

The invasion of Manipur by Burma[2] in the years 1755 and 1758 compelled the king of Manipur to seek external support and finally it led to the establishment of a colonial power in Manipur. In the middle of the 18th century, when Burma, her traditional rival, became a strong military power under the able leadership of Alaungpaya, Manipur remained as a weak country,[3] mainly because of her unhealthy political condition prevailing at that time among the royal princes of Manipur. Such a deteriorating political condition was a great opportunity for a traditional enemy like Burma. In the meantime, Ajit Shah a royal prince, tried to get help from the British East India Company[4] against Jai Singh, alias Chingthangkhomba, the king of Manipur. To remove such an undesirable political development, the king of Manipur proposed the establishment of a friendly relationship between Manipur and East India Company. Accordingly, he sent his counsel Haridass Gossai, with a letter to Verelst, the British Chief Agent at Chittagong in 1762, in which the king gave his reasons why his uncle Ajit Shah was dethroned and expelled from the country, and sought a friendly alliance with the British East India Company. The British authority was happy to receive the proposal of a friendly alliance from Manipur for two reasons i.e., political and commercial,[5] and was quick to accept the King's proposal; it even agreed to extend full co-operation to Jai Singh against the possible threat from the Burmese.[6]

The political motivation for this move on the part of the Company was that they thought that such a proposal would give them a good chance to take revenge against Burma, which had destroyed the British factory at Negrais in lower Burma, at the instigation of the French. They further anticipated that this alliance would enable the company to obtain reparation from Burma for the repeated ill-treatment of the factory at Negrais. Apart from this, since Manipur was situated in a very sensitive area politically, the British authority regarded it as strategically important. Therefore they felt that the alliance with Manipur would generate intensive diplomatic activity on the political chessboard of the north-

---

[2] The ruling military junta changed its name from Burma to Myanmar in 1989, a year after thousands were killed in the suppression of a popular uprising. Later the capital Rangoon also became Yangon. "Burma." http://thesou- ndofhope.org/countries/burma/ (20 Feb 2013). However for our research work, we will use both the names according to the background.

[3] Alaungpaya also spelled Alaunghpaya (24th September 1714 to 11th May 1760) was king of Burma from 1752 to 1760, and the founder of the Konbaung Dynasty. By his death in 1760, the former chief of a small village in Upper Burma had reunified all of Burma, subdued Manipur. He also founded Yangon in 1755. "Alaungpaya Dynasty," Encyclopedia Britannica, http://www.britannica.com/EBchecked/topic/12381/Ala-ungpaya-Dynasty (20 Feb 2013).

[4] Hereafter it is referred to as East India Company.

[5] Anil Chandra Banerjee, ed., *The Eastern Frontier of British India, 1784-1826* (Calcutta: A Mukherjee & Co, 2005), 27.

[6] Anil Chandra Banerjee, ed., *The Eastern Frontier of British India*, 54-55.

eastern frontier[7] which could be advantageous to themselves. Their opinion was that the mere possession of Cachar would not make an effective barrier against the advance of Burma; only the valley of Manipur would be able to put up a strong positive resistance to Burma. Mr. Vansittart, the Governor General, also had asserted that the authority should not lose such a favourable opportunity to put pressure on Burma.[8]

The proposal also interested the British for its potential commercial possibilities. The authorities argued that the alliance with Manipur would pave the way for having a trade relationship with other countries particularly China. They believed that this alliance would enable the British merchants to come into direct contact with China and would prove extremely useful in the expansion of her trade and commerce with Burma and north-eastern frontiers. Even before gaining power in the north-east region, the British had already interested themselves in the commercial possibilities of that frontier.[9] With regard to the policy of the British, R.C. Majumdar observes thus:[10]

> It would be idle to pretend that such a risky and costly expedition was undertaken only to divert the military resources of the enemy from the British borders. The real reason was undoubtedly the establishment of secure footing in south Burma which possessed good harbours and afforded facilities of a rich trade.

Lord William Bentinck, the Governor-General of India, also wrote about the importance of Manipur in his minute of March 25, 1838. He mentioned that the establishment of a Manipur dynasty seems to have been a scheme peculiarly favoured by the late Agent Mr. Scott as set out in his observations thus:[11]

> Well founded prospect of defense of our frontier in that direction by the interposition of a race of people known to entertain a rooted antipathy to the only enemy against whose aggression it was necessary to guard the fertility of a country of which a highly coloured description had been given.

Keeping this view in consideration, the British authority accepted the proposal of friendship alliance, and a treaty was concluded on the 14th September 1762. Haridas Gossai signed the treaty on behalf of the king of Manipur and

---

[7] Nirode K. Barooah, *David Scott in North-East India, 1802-1831: A Study in British Paternalism* (New Delhi: Munshiram Manoharlal, 1970), 77.

[8] Nirode K. Barooah, *David Scott in North-East India*, 85.

[9] Anil Chandra Banerjee, ed., *The Eastern Frontier of British,* 10-12.

[10] R.C. Majumdar, ed, *The History and Culture of the Indian People: British Paramountcy and Indian Renaissance* (Bombay: Bharatiya Vidya Bhavan, 1970), 49.

[11] Alexander Mackenzie, *History of the Relation of the Government with the Hill Tribes of the North-East Frontier Bengal* (Calcutta: Home Office Department Press, 1884), 150.

Henry Verelst, Chief of Chittagong was his counterpart on behalf of the East India Company.[12] Thus, the relationship between Manipur and British which was established for the first time in that year was one of the most important landmarks in the history of Manipur.

As a response to the terms of the treaty, East India Company sent a large body of troops in 1763 under the command of Mr. Verelst. Unfortunately bad weather caused a diplomatic breakdown which was never healed. When the troops reached Khaspur, the capital of Cachar, they were compelled to halt there because of nonstop heavy rain. The rain was so heavy and continuous that they were obliged to return to Chittagong via Jai Nagar.

After this all communication between Manipur and the British completely ceased. However, though the terms of the treaty were not properly implemented, this agreement made a spring board for the extension of the British imperialist policy throughout all the various areas of the north-eastern region of India.[13]

1.1. Further Contact with British

Then after a long gap of more than half a century, communication between Manipur and British was again restored in the year 1819 when the Burmese forces occupied Manipur and began to create a threat to the border areas of the British Indian Empire.[14] Thus, the occupation of Manipur by Burmese forces compelled Manipur to seek help from the British and to reopen the communication with them since it had ceased completely in 1763. Indeed the period from 1819-1826 was one of the most important periods in the history of this tiny kingdom. There were a series of internecine quarrels among the princes of the kingdom. Due to the unstable political situation, the Burmese forces easily overpowered the king of Manipur and ruled the country for seven years. This period is known in the history of this State as the "*Chahi Taret Khuntakpa*" (Seven Years' Devastation).[15]

The military activities of the Burmese forces in north-east India created an alarming situation along the border areas under British control and it led to the outbreak of war between the British and Burma. This development presented a great opportunity for the princes of Manipur. However, though they had a strong desire to liberate Manipur from the hands of Burma they were not in a position to do so because of their weakness. Taking the opportunity presented by this development they decided to seek help from the British and for the execution of their plan they put the responsibility on Gambhir Singh, an intelligent and capable prince of Manipur.[16] He approached the British authorities to extend

[12] Alexander Mackenzie, *History of the Relation of the Government*, 151-52.

[13] Anil Chandra Banerjee, ed., *The Eastern Frontier of British*, 48-50.

[14] Anil Chandra Banerjee, ed., *The Eastern Frontier of British*, 287.

[15] Kh. Sarojini Devi, *British Political Agency in Manipur, 1835-1947* (Imphal: Linthoi Publications, 2005), 8-9.

[16] Anil Chandra Banerjee, ed., *The Eastern Frontier of British*, 57, 350-352.

their co-operation for the liberation of Manipur. The British authorities also warmly welcomed the request from the princes of Manipur as they strongly felt that if they could get help from the local people they would be able to defeat the Burmese easily. Therefore, the British authority agreed to give military training to the Manipur soldiers. Thus, with the help of the British, Gambhir Singh established a military force of 500 men. This force was known as 'Manipur Levy' and they were trained by two British Officers; they were Lt. Pemberton and Cpt. Grant. Thus, with the help of the British, Gambhir Singh defeated the Burmese forces in Manipur and they were further chased by the Manipur army up to the Ningthi or Chindwin river.[17] The war came to an end by the Treaty of Yandaboo, signed on the 24th February, 1826.[18]

As expected, Gambhir Singh became the king of Manipur and thus after this war the relationship between Manipur and the British was developed in a very cordial and harmonious way and in order to strengthen the relationship again an office of the British Political Agency was established in Manipur in 1835. The duties of the Political Agents were to preserve the friendly relation between Manipur and the British and to be a medium of communication between these two authorities. George Gordon was the first Political Agent[19] in Manipur. After the establishment of this office the Political Agent rendered help not only in the strengthening of their relationship but also helped in the consolidation of the position of the king in the administration of the State. Thus, the relationship between Manipur and the British was maintained without any disturbances and misunderstanding until Manipur was occupied by the British in the year 1891.[20]

2. Beginning of Direct British Rule

For Meiteis, the year 1891 is an unforgettable year in the history of the kingdom of Manipur. It marked the close of an important era and the beginning of a new chapter. Since that time, Manipur, which had long maintained her sovereignty, entered a period of domination under the British Empire. The task to decide the future status of Manipur was entirely left in the hands of the British imperialists.[21]

---

[17] Kh. Sarojini Devi, *British Political Agency in Manipur, 1835-1947,* 9-10.

[18] Appendix – 1. Anil Chandra Banerjee, ed., *The Eastern Frontier of British,* 405. cited in. Kh. Sarojini Devi, *British Political Agency in Manipur, 1835-1947,* 106. cited in. "Treaty of Yandaboo, February 24, 1826", http://www.upr-info.org/IMG/pdf/COHR_IND_UPR_S1_2008 anx_ Annex_X_Treaty_of_Yandab -oo_1826.pdf (16 Feb 2013).

[19] Appendix – 2, Captain Gordon was the first British political agent in Manipur. The names of the British officers who served as political agents in Manipur are listed in the given appendix. Kh. Sarojini Devi, *British Political Agency in Manipur, 1835-1947,* 93-94. cited in. Pandit N. Khelchandra Singh, "British Officers Who Served As Political Agents in Manipur: Table No. 2 -2," http://books.epao.net/Heritage_Ma-nipur/epShow Chapter.asp?src=kangla/agents (17 Feb 2013).

[20] Kh. Sarojini Devi, *British Political Agency in Manipur, 1835-1947,* 10-11.

[21] Rashi Meitei, History Lecturer, Sawombung Higher Secondary, Imphal East, Manipur, letter to the author, 23 March, 2012.

Lord Landsdowne, the viceroy, in his telegraph of 5th June, 1891 to the Secretary of State maintained that, "Manipur is a subordinate native State. We rendered it independent of Burma. We have recognized succession in Manipur, and have asserted suzerainty in many ways; Manipur ruling family has repeatedly acknowledged their position of dependence."[22]

2.1. Outbreak of Palace Revolt

The outbreak of palace revolt in 1890 gave a very good opportunity to the British to interfere in the domestic affairs of Manipur.[23] This was the time when Surchandra Singh, the eldest son of the late king Chandrakriti Singh became king of Manipur. The late king had eight sons from six queens. Eight sons were (l) Surchandra (2) Kullachandra (3) Tikendrajit (4) Pakkasana (5) Angousana (6) Zillangamba (7) Keshwajit (8) Gopalsana.[24]

After the death of King Chandrakriti, his eldest son Surchandra became the ruler of Manipur and Kullachandra became the Jubaraj (Crown Prince). But soon the brothers were divided into two groups—king Surchandra, Pakkasana, Keshwajit and Gopalsana on the one side and Kullachandra, Tikendrajit, Angousana and Zillangamba on the other side.[25]

On the 21st September 1890 an open revolt broke out. Without giving any resistance, King Surchandra Singh along with his younger brothers fled into the residency of the British Political Agent and finally he resigned the throne in favour of his rebellious brother. He left Manipur for Vrindaban[26] in Central Province. Before leaving Imphal, Surchandra Singh handed over all the clothes of the king, the sword, belt and other ceremonial objects to Tikendrajit. Then Kullachandra became the king of Manipur and Tikendrajit became the Jubaraj. Meanwhile, Surachandra Singh, instead of going to Vrindaban, went direct to Calcutta, where he submitted an application to the British authorities complaining that he was forcibly removed by his stepbrother from the throne of Manipur and requesting

---

[22] Robert Reid, *History of Frontier Areas Bordering on Assam, 1883-1941* (New Delhi: Eastern Publishing House, 1983), 60.

[23] Rashi Meitei, History Lecturer.

[24] Kh. Sarojini Devi, *British Political Agency in Manipur, 1835-1947,* 32-33.

[25] Gangmumei Kabui, "The Anglo-Manipur War of 1891," in *History of Modern Manipur, 1826-1949,* second edition, edited by Lal Dena (New Delhi: Orbit Publishers & Distributors, 1991), 49-50.

[26] Vrindaban which is considered to be an important holy place by the Vaishnavite Meiteis is situated on the bank of the holy river Yamuna. The name 'Vrindavan' is derived from 'Vrinda' another name from the basil (sacred Tulsi plant for Hindus) where Lord Krishna as a child and in adolescence used to play and graze his cows along with other shepherd boys and girls. It is here that he performed many of his *leelas* or games to enlighten the people about his divinity. "Vrindavan's Geographic Features," http://www.radhava-llabh.com/vrindavan.html (20 Feb 2013).

the British authorities to restore him again as the king of Manipur.[27] Further he also complained the action and behaviour of Grimwood, the Political Agent in Manipur, towards him. Thus, the quarrel among the princes of Manipur and the submission made by Surchandra to the British authorities for his personal benefit created a very good opportunity for direct interference in the internal affairs of the kingdom.[28]

2.2. Interference of the British

After a prolonged deliberation, the British decided a policy according to which Kullachandra Singh would be recognized as the King of Manipur and former king Surchandra Singh would not be restored to his position again. Secondly, the entire affairs of the kingdom both internal and external should be carried on in accordance with the advice of the office of the Political Agency in Manipur. Lastly, the British Government considered Tikendrajit Singh as the key cause of the Manipur upheaval and so they decided that he should be deported from Manipur immediately. At the same time, the British Government decided to keep a small army of 200 soldiers inside the campus of the residency. Then they asked J.W. Quinton, the Chief Commissioner of Assam, to go to Manipur with instructions to implement the decision of the government.[29] Regarding the decision of the British Government; R. C. Majumdar remarks:[30]

> The decision to say the least of it is very curious. It accepted the revolution as a fait accompli and condoned the person who got the greatest benefit out of it, but banished another who was not known to have taken any part in it, but who they held without any positive evidence as its chief instigator.

Quinton arrived at Imphal on 22nd March 1891 and immediately asked for a durbar with the princes of Manipur.[31] However, Quinton failed to arrest Tikendrajit Singh. So in the early hours of the morning of 24th March, at about 3: 30 a.m. the British forces suddenly attacked the house of Tikendrajit. Violent fighting took place between the Meitei troops and the British forces.[32] As a result, Lt. Brackenbury was mortally wounded, three Gurkhas were killed, and Lt. Luggard and forteen others were also wounded. Quinton had no alternative but to sign an armistice which was agreed to on both sides and thereby Meitei armies

---

[27] N. Joykumar Singh, *Social Movement in Manipur*, second ed. (New Delhi: Mittal Publications, 2005), 24-25.

[28] Gangmumei Kabui, "The Anglo-Manipur War of 1891," 51.

[29] N. Joykumar Singh, *Social Movement in Manipur*, 25.

[30] R.C. Majumdar, ed. *History and Culture of the Indian People*, 717.

[31] N. Khelchandra Singh, *Battle of Khongjom* (Imphal: N. Khelchandra Singh, 1983), 29.

[32] Robert Reid, *History of Frontier Areas Bordering on Assam, 1883-1941*, 145.

stopped fighting.[33] Finally the British requested a cease-fire.[34] The Commissioner wrote to king Kullachandra, "On what condition will you cease fire on us and give time to communicate with the viceroy, and repair the telegraph…."[35] In reply to his petition king Kullachandra wrote:[36]

> …received your letter, I have never any intentions to fight with you. As your troops attacked the palace, my men had to fight in self defence. There is none in my palace who can read and understand English. But as I received your letter immediately after the ceasefire, I take it that you want to discuss for peace. If your soldiers give up arms, I shall conclude with you in a moment.

As a result of negotiation initiated by the Chief Commissioner, the king agreed and a durbar was arranged between the king and the Chief Commissioner. But in the meeting no solution was agreed to due to the policies of the British. At that time, a large number of indigenous people also were assembled outside the durbar hall to hear the outcome of the meeting. The meeting ended without any positive result.[37] When the British officers were coming out from the durbar hall, the people who assembled there chased them; Grimwood was speared to death by Kajao Singh and Lt. Simpson was wounded by sword. To save the situation all the remaining British officers including Quinton was again put inside the durbar hall but later on they were also executed by the royal executioners.[38]

The news of the death of five British officers was received with shock by the British government. The Viceroy Lord Lansdowne immediately sent a large army to Manipur from three different directions.[39] General Collet was the Supreme Commander of these forces. The Kohima column was led by him; the Tammu column was led by Brigadier General T. Graham. Then an unequal war was fought between Manipur and the British and finally on 27th April, 1891 at about 7 a.m. Manipur was completely occupied by the British.[40] All the princes of Manipur and some high officials who were the leaders of this war were also arrested. In

---

[33] Kh. Sarojini Devi, *British Political Agency in Manipur, 1835-1947*, 37.

[34] Gangmumei Kabui, "The Anglo-Manipur War of 1891," 52-53. cited in. N. Khelchandra Singh, *Battle of Khongjom*, 29-30.

[35] Robert Reid, *History of Frontier Areas Bordering on Assam, 1883-1941*, 146.

[36] R.C. Majumdar, ed. *History and Culture of the Indian People*, 725.

[37] Kh. Sarojini Devi, *British Political Agency in Manipur, 1835-1947,* 38.

[38] N. Joykumar Singh, *Social Movement in Manipur*, 25-26. cited in. Kh. Sarojini Devi, *British Political Agency in Manipur, 1835-1947,* 38.

[39] The three different directions were: i) the British column coming via Kohima, Nagaland; ii) the British column coming via Cachar (Silchar), Assam; iii) and the British column coming viaTammu, Burma. Kh. Sarojini Devi, *British Political Agency in Manipur, 1835-1947,* 39.

[40] Gangmumei Kabui, "The Anglo-Manipur War of 1891," 56, 62. cited in. Kh. Sarojini Devi, *British Political Agency in Manipur, 1835-1947,* 40.

order to try their cases, a special military tribunal was established by the British authorities consisting of three persons, Lt. Col. St. John Michel as President; Major R.K. Ridgeway, Commandant of the 44 Gurkha Rifle and A.W. Davis, Deputy Commissioner of Naga Hills as members. The British authorities accused the princes of Manipur and officials on three basic charges. They were: 1) waging war against the Queen Empress of India; 2) abetment of murder of British officers 3) and murder.[41]

2.3. Trial and Execution

The cases of the princes were considered by the Governor-General-in-Council. The princes were permitted to submit their petitions in writing only. Their legal advisor Manmohan Ghosh, a Barrister of Calcutta High Court, submitted his argument in writing. Sir A.E. Miller, the law member of the Council defended the government action. The Council rejected Tikendrajit's appeal. The trial of Tikendrajit aroused a great sensation in India. The British press demanded revenge; the bureaucrats wanted to hang the princes.[42] Captain Hearsey describes the contemporary British attitude and opinion when he writes:[43]

> The tone of the government organs, such as the English Man of Calcutta, the Pioneer and the Morning Post of Allahabad, especially the latter, has been, towards the accused princes of Manipur, spiteful and vindictive in the extreme, and this feeling, in a very great measure, has been shared by the government officials; these organs have been incessant throughout the whole course of the trials; it has to say, been a cry of hang first and try afterwards. Lansdowne the Viceroy of India was also revengeful and determined to carry out the death sentence. Queen Victoria herself intervened on behalf of Tikendrajit. She telegraphed to the Viceroy on 12 August saying that the lawyer of Tikendrajit, "appeal to me for commutation. Is it possible to do this?" Queen Victoria wanted to save the life of Tikendrajit. But Viceroy replied the same day rejecting the Queen's proposal saying that commutation of the death sentence would be a grave public misfortune.

After hearing all the allegations made by the British against the royal princes of Manipur and some noblemen, the tribunal gave a final judgment on the following lines i.e., king Kullachandra, Prince Zillangamba and Angousana were sentenced to life imprisonment and Tikendrajit, Thangal General. Kajao,

---

[41] N. Joykumar Singh, *Social Movement in Manipur*, 26.

[42] Kh. Sarojini Devi, *British Political Agency in Manipur, 1835-1947,* 41-42. cited in. Gangmumei Kabui, "The Anglo-Manipur War of 1891," 68.

[43] Gangmumei Kabui, "The Anglo-Manipur War of 1891," 69.

Niranjan Subedar and Charai Thangal were given the death sentence.[44] And Tikendrajit and Thangal were hanged on the 13th August, 1891.[45] With the loss of her sovereignty on the 27th April, 1891, Manipur became a colonial dependency of the British.[46] The Gurkha Regiments who succeeded in the battle still celebrate their victories, but they remember the battle as one of the hardest battles they had ever fought in their victorious history as soldiers of Her Imperial Majesty. For the colonial forces it was one shining account of imperial expansion with courage and bravery, while from the point of view of the people of Manipur it was a heroic sacrifice for the cause of freedom. Hence the day, 13th August, 1891, is now observed as 'Patriotic Day' by Meiteis.[47]

2.4. Annexation of Manipur

The occupation of Manipur was followed by the introduction of colonial rule in Manipur. However, there were a lot of discussions among the top officials of the British authority on the question of whether the Manipur State should have been annexed completely or not.[48] Ward, the new Chief Commissioner of Assam was in favour of the complete annexation. In support of his argument he pointed out three important reasons. He says:[49]

1. In view of the recent events at Manipur I think that we should be not only justified in annexing that State but that it is imperative for the maintenance of our prestige, as a lesson and a warning to other Native States in India, and without any regard whatever to the financial consideration that we should do.
2. I have little doubt that the whole of the hill populations being one third of the total population of the State, would welcome an annexation. In the case of the hill tribes, I think there are obvious reasons why they

[44] Appendix - 3. "The Anglo Manipur War 1891 and its Consequences," Manipur State Archive (1990) http://-archivesmanipur.nic.in/whoswho.htm#THE%20ANGLO. (16 Feb 2013). cited in. Gangmumei Kab-ui, "The Anglo-Manipur War of 1891," 68.

[45] For colonial forces it was one shining account of imperial expansion with courage and bravery, while from the point of view of the people of Manipur it was a heroic sacrifice for the cause of freedom. Different Meitei organizations, NGOs and educational institutes are now observing August 13 as 'Patriots' Day'. It shows their strong feeling against the oppressive rule of British government. Appendix - 4, "Patriot's Day observed across the State," *Sangai Express* (Imphal), 14 August, 2012, 1.

[46] Gangmumei Kabui, "The Anglo-Manipur War of 1891," 57-61. cited in. N. Joykumar Singh, *Social Movement in Manipur*, 26.

[47] Appendix - 5. "Clarion Call for Wide Observation of Patriots' Day on August 13," *Imphal Free Press* (Imphal) 11 August, 2011, 1. Manipur government observed the Patriots' Day celebration at the Manipur Tikendrajit House, in New Delhi. "Manipur Government Observes Patriots' Day in New Delhi," *Manipur Mail* (Imphal), 14 August, 2011, 1.

[48] Rashi Meitei, History Lecturer.

[49] R.C. Majumdar, ed. *History and Culture of the Indian People*, 67.

should do so. Under the circumstances, unless we took upon ourselves thirty years ago of protecting the people of the State against oppression, and against the necessary consequences of misrule and periodical revolution. I consider it to be a moral duty imposed upon us to annex.

3. Lastly, I have no doubt, looking at the matter solely from a financial point of view that there are no grounds whatever for thinking that annexation will result in financial loss to Government.

But Lord Lansdowne expressed a different opinion. According to him the Manipur rebellion was the work of one man and not a deliberate attempt to shake off the British yoke. He further mentioned that as a result of that rebellion against the lawful ruler whom the British recognized and as a result of waging war against Queen Victoria, the State as a whole had been guilty of rebellion and might have to forfeit its right to exist as a State. But as far as the question of annexation was concerned, Lord Lansdowne categorically stated thus, "I am in principle strongly opposed to needless annexation, and I would have scrupulous regard for the independence of Native State in subordinate alliance with us so long as they remain loyal, and do nothing to forfeit their right to our protection."[50] After a lot of discussion, the British authorities finally decided not to annex Manipur, but instead to establish a native rule under a king on suitable grounds as an act of mercy.[51] The view of the British authority was incorporated in a proclamation dated the 21st August, 1891 which was notified later on the 18th September, 1891. The proclamation was as follows:[52]

- Whereas the State of Manipur has recently been in armed rebellion against the authority of Her Majesty the Queen Empress of India.
- It is hereby notified that the Manipur State has been liable to the penalty of annexation and now at the disposal of the Crown.
- It is further notified that Her Majesty, the Queen Empress of India, has been pleased to forgo Her right to annex to Her Indian Dominion the territories of the Manipur State; and has graciously asserted to the re-establishment of Native rule under such conditions as the Governor-General in council may consider desirable, and with person of such rule as the Governor-General in council may select.
- The Governor-General in council will make known hereafter the name of the person selected the rule of the State and the conditions under which he will be invested with powers.

---

50 Government of India, Department of Foreign and External, *Foreign Department Proceedings*, nos. 127-47 October 1891, 145-48. cited in. Government of India, Department of Foreign and External, *Foreign Department Secret* (E), no. 133, October, 1891, 162.

51 Memoranda on the Indian States, 1931.

52 Robert Reid, *History of Frontier Areas Bordering on Assam, 1883-1941,* 70-71.

- Subsequently for the establishment of an indigenous rule, the British authority selected Churachand Singh a minor boy of hardly five years old and great-grandson of King Nara Singh as the king of Manipur.[53] On the 18th September, 1891 H.M. Durand, Secretary to the Government of India notified the appointment of Churachand Singh as the king of Manipur, in the Gazette of India. The British authority stated that the Chiefship of Manipur State would descend in the direct line of primogeniture, provided that in each case the succession was approved by the Government of India.[54] Further it was also mentioned that the Manipur State, as a kind of punishment for waging a war against the Queen Empress of India, had to pay an annual tribute of Rs. 50,000/-. In addition the Manipur State was imposed a fine of Rs. 2, 50, 000/- for the attack on the British subjects and which was to be paid in installment basis within five years. Apart from this the British authority would have the right to interfere in the day to day internal administration of the State.[55]

With these conditions the British authority declared Churachand Singh, five years old and great-grandson of King Nara Singh, as the ruler of Manipur and he was also conferred the title of king with an eleven gun salute. Then simultaneously, by an order No. 1878-E. dated 21st September 1891, Major Maxwell was appointed as the Political Agent in Manipur and Superintendent of the State. The order further stated that during the rule of minor King Churachand Singh, the whole administrative responsibilities of the State would be in the hands of the Political Agent. On the 29th April, 1892, Maxwell, on behalf of the British Government, installed King Churachand Singh on the throne of Manipur.[56] Robert Reid rightly observed that "From 1891 Manipur entered a new phase of its history characterized on the terms of the closed control by the British Government until power was made over to the young king and his durbar in 1907 by direct administration by British officers."[57]

---

[53] Meiteis have had a great respect of king Nara Singh because it was he who restored the kingdom of Manipur from the hands of Burma and there was remarkable prosperity during his reign as well. British authority in order to impress the native people for their newly colonized kingdom as well as to rule over, selected Churachand Singh a great-grandson of King Nara Singh as the king. It was indeed a strategic selection. "Maharaja Nara Singh's Death Anniversary Held," *The Sangai Express* (Imphal), 11 April, 2012, 2.

[54] Government of India, *Gazette,* part - I: 22 August, 1891, 485. cited in. Government of India, Department of Foreign and External, *Foreign Department Resolution and Proclamation*, (E), no. 1700, August, 1891. 372.

[55] R.C. Majumdar, ed, *The History and Culture of the Indian People*, 1034.

[56] Government of India, Department of Home and Social Welfare, *Annual Administrative Reports of Political Agency*, 1892-93, 9.

[57] Robert Reid, *History of Frontier Areas Bordering on Assam, 1883-1941*, 73.

2.5. Narcissistic Policy of British

A colonial policy was the general principle followed by a colonizing power to regulate the relationship between her and her dependency. A colonial policy would have clear cut objectives for the attainment of which administrative machinery was created to work in the colony.[58] The British established a native rule with Churachand Singh as the king. The decision of the establishment of native rule has been precisely described as an act for the convenience of the British government.[59] Indeed the period of King Churachand Singh can be divided into two parts. The first part was from 1891 to 1907 and the second part was from 1907 to 1941. The first part was a very significant period in the colonial history of Manipur because it was a period of regency administration during which the British authorities established several changes in the administrative system of the State. These changes, in fact, greatly affected the traditional practices of the State.[60] It is a well known fact that the colonial and imperialistic policy of the British emphasized mainly the economic and judicial aspects of the particular State. Their main concern was to bring a rapid transformation of traditional Manipuri economy into a colonial economy whose nature and structure were determined by the needs of the British economy.[61] Therefore to implement this main objective they disrupted the traditional structure of the existing economic systems. However, the British would never become an integral part of the social life of the colonial State. They would always remain as a foreigner in the land and exploit the resources and carry away the natural wealth of the land as a tribute.[62] Regarding the colonial policy of the British, Tara Chand further remarked that:[63]

> There can happen no greater misfortune to a country than to be conquered and ruled by an alien race. In cases where the conqueror settled down in the conquered land, makes it his home and brings his parties, and conqueror and the conquered live together and evolve common ways of living and mutual understanding, even though they might retain some of their original ways and costumes. But when the conqueror remains attached to their homeland and stays as alien

[58] Lal Dena, "Manipur Under Paramountcy of the British Crown: Some Admonition of Colonial Rule 1891-1919," *Bengal Past and Present*, vol. xcviii/1, serial no. 187 (July-Dec., 1979): 107.

[59] Thambal Singh, Retired History Lecturer, Soibam Leikai, Imphal West, Manipur, letter to the author, 17 January, 2012. cited in. Lal Dena, "Manipur Under Paramountcy of the British Crown, 107.

[60] N. Joykumar Singh, *Social Movement in Manipur*, 29.

[61] N. Joykumar Singh, *Social Movement in Manipur*, 30.

[62] Tara Chand, *History of the Freedom Movement in India*, vol iii (New Delhi: Publications Division, 1972), 288.

[63] Tara Chand, *History of the Freedom Movement in India*, 289.

> sojourners in the conquered country in order to govern and exploit, then in that case the conquest is an evil, whether the rulers are civilized or savage.

This was precisely the case in Manipur. Even today people still think that Manipur could not possibly face any bigger misfortune than the British colonialism of 1891. The British remained attached to their homeland and stayed as alien sojourners in Manipur in order to rule and exploit the people and land.[64]

2.6. Obliteration of *Lallup* System

The first measure of the British authority was abolition of the '*Lallup* system.' According to this system every male subject between 16 years and 60 years of age was required to work for the State for 10 days out of 40 days.[65] But if a person failed to carry out his *lallup* duties, he must give a substitute in place of himself or he must pay a fine.[66] This *lallup* system was an integral part of the culture of the people of Manipur in the context of the period; it was not possible to do social welfare and developmental work without the man power.[67] With the help of *lallup*, the kings could carry out a lot of developmental works such as construction of roads, canals and bridges.[68] Major Maxwell himself admitted the importance of this system particularly in a small and economically backward country like Manipur. But he felt that the amount of the payment made by a person who could not perform the *lallup* was very low. In the early times the amount was not much but in later days it rose to six or seven rupees. Maxwell writes:[69]

> When a husband was unable to perform his *lallup* due to sickness the substitute was purchased by the wife's industry, and again the idle husband was relieved, when practicable, by the same means. Again the groans of the *lallup* coolies reached my ears, and in consequence of the *lallup* disappointment has been expressed by the subjects of the State at our rule.

This was the time when Manipur was going through a transitional period. Taking the advantage of internal political crisis, Maxwell abolished the *lallup*

---

[64] R.K. Tamphasana Devi, History Lecturer, G.P. Women College, Imphal West, Manipur, letter to the author, 21 January, 2012.

[65] The duration 40 days is associated with the ancient Meitei religious ceremony. R.K. Tamphasana Devi. History Lecturer.

[66] Robert Reid, *History of Frontier Areas Bordering on Assam, 1883-1941*, 73.

[67] R.K. Tamphasana Devi, History Lecturer.

[68] J. Roy, *History of Manipur* (Calcutta: East-light Book House, 1973), 28.

[69] Robert Reid, *History of Frontier Areas Bordering on Assam, 1883-1941*, 74.

system on 29th April, 1892, the day of the installation of minor Churachand Singh as the king of Manipur.[70]

The main propose of having *lallup* was feudal service. This was wrongly described as a forced labour by the political agent. The service might be in the form of military duties or developmental or economic work.[71] As an acknowledgement of the service to the king and society, those who rendered *lallup* were exempted from paying revenue. Historically, this *lallup* was started by king Loyamba in 1110 A.D. This king in his famous edicts known as 'Loyamba Shilyen' divided Manipur valley into six administrative units known as *lup* or *pana*.[72] Each *pana* sent a team of workers who were to work for the State. Each team was called *lallup* (meaning war organization, *lal* means war, *lup* means organization).[73] The *lallup* played a vital role in protecting the land and people of Manipur. During the peaceful time, *lallup* contributed in the developmental and economic life of the kingdom. Hence, the role of *lallup* was an integral part of the culture of the people of Manipur.[74] James Johnstone's observations concerning *lallup* are worth mentioning:[75]

> *Lallup* extended to every class in the community. Women were naturally exempt, but among men, the blacksmith, goldsmith, carpenters etc. pursued their different crafts in the Rajas' worship for the stated time, while the bulk of the population, in fact executed great public works for the benefit of the State. The system was a good one when not carried to excess; it pressed heavily on nobody.

Ethel St. Clair Grimwood also agreed with Johnstone but after British conquest of Manipur, Maxwell, the political agent condemned and abolished the traditional *lallup* system which was an essential pillar for the Meitei socio-political and socio-economic society.[76]

---

70 Robert Reid, *History of Frontier Areas Bordering on Assam, 1883-1941,* 75. cited in. R.K. Tamphasana Devi, History Lecturer.

71 Kh. Sarojini Devi, *British Political Agency in Manipur, 1835-1947,* 53.

72 Sanamani Yambem, "The Lallup System of Manipur: Transformation from Conscript Warrior to Conscript Labour," in *Social Science and Social Concern*, edited by S.B. Chakrabarti (Delhi: Mittal Publications, 1988), 76.

73 Gangmumei Kabui, "Socio-Religious Reform Movement," in *History of Modern Manipur, 1826-1949,* second edition, edited by Lal Dena (New Delhi: Orbit Publishers & Distributors, 1991), 98.

74 Gangmumei Kabui, "Socio-Religious Reform Movement," 98. The vitality of the *lallup* in Meitei society has also been pointed out by Tamphasana. R.K. Tamphasana Devi, History Lecturer.

75 Sir James Johnstone, *My Experiences in Manipur and the Naga Hills* (London: S. Low, Marston and Company Limited, 1896), 23.

76 The author Ethel St. Clair Grimwood is the wife of Mr. Frank St Clair Grimwood who was the Political Agent in Manipur in 1891. In this book she writes about the Experience that she had ***in*** Manipur. Ethel St. Clair Grimwood**,** *My Three Years in Manipur: And Escape from the Recent Mutiny*

2.7. Enforcement of Heavy Taxation

The British authorities introduced changes in the revenue administration of the State as well. Thus, they introduced the institution of house tax system.[77] The tax was fixed at Rs. 2/-per house per annum in the valley and Rs. 3/- per house per annum in the hill areas. Maxwell estimated that this would produce a sum or Rs, 50,000/- (fifty thousand) annually and this amount would be of great help in his work.[78] Another load given to the people of Manipur was revenue tax system and the rate was fixed at Rs. 5/-(five) per *pari* (2.50 acre). Thus, this new system conferred on the State tenants a permanent inheritable and transferable right of occupancy so long as they paid the revenue demanded from them by the State. In 1892, Maxwell distributed *pattas* to the landholders and he also asked the eight secretaries to make a survey of the cultivable land area of the State.[79]

In this connection, it has been rightly observed that with the help of these new changes in the land administration, the previous traditional system of the king's share was replaced by the new system of fixed money payment, assessed on land.[80] In the year 1894-95 the area of land under *patta* was 27, 331 *paries* or 68,327 acres and the work of the collection of revenue was entrusted to the clerks of the State office. But the payment of revenue was not regular and so the revenue received was still short and a large number of areas were left in arrears. So, in order to discharge their policy for the collection of revenue, Maxwell divided the entire Manipur valley areas into four *pannahas* or divisions. They were Ahallup *pannahas*, Naharup *pannahas*, Khabam *pannahas* and Laifam *pannahas*. He also appointed a '*Lakpa*' or manager for each *pannaha* and 10% of the total collection of the revenue of the concerned *pannaha* was given to the *lakpa* as remuneration as well as for the maintenance.[81] Thus, with this new system, the demand of the land revenue was increased from Rs. 170,000/-, including the house tax in 1892-93 to Rs. 273,507/- in 1906-07; its total percentage was 76. 57% in 1892-93 to 98.24% in 1906-1907.[82]

Apart from the land revenue the British authority also began to acquire the revenue from other sources, like foreigner tax, fishery tax, salt tax, forest tax, tea-seed tax, law and justice tax, jail tax and so on. In addition to this they also collected revenue from the foreigners who were neither a government servant nor

---

(London: Richard Bentley and Son, 1891), 45. cited in. Sir James Johnstone, *My Experiences in Manipur and the Naga Hills,* 113-114. cited in. R.K. Tamphasana Devi, History Lecturer.

[77] V. Vungzamoi, History Lecturer, G.P. Women College, Imphal West, Manipur, letter to the author, 23 January, 2012.

[78] J. Shakespear, *Manipur under British Management 1891-1907* (Shillong: n.p. 1907), 37.

[79] J. Shakespear, *Manipur under British Management 1891-1907,* 38.

[80] Lal Dena, *British Policy Towards Manipur, 1891-1919* (Imphal: n.p., 1984), 15.

[81] J. Shakespear, *Manipur under British Management, 1891-1907,* 11.

[82] *Foreign Department Proceedings,* no. 66, 1903, 6. cited in. Kh. Sarojini Devi, *British Political Agency in Manipur, 1835-1947,* 51-52.

a merchant of the Sadar Bazar.[83] The tax was fixed at Rs. 5/- (five) per head and in 1906-1907 the State received a revenue from foreigners to the tune of Rs. 8,964/-. The collection of revenue from fisheries also was increased from Rs. 8,859/- in 1891-92 to Rs. 35,283 in 1906-1907. From the department of law and justice, the collected revenue was Rs. 893/- in 1892-93 but it was increased to Rs.14, 705/- in 1906-07. From jail, the revenue was increased from Rs. 435/- in 1902-03 to Rs. 2,879/- in 1906-07.[84] Thus during the regency period, the British authority imposed a heavy financial load on the people of Manipur.[85]

2.8. Control of Judicial System

Another notable expansion of the colonial administration was the control of the judicial system of the State.[86] The colonial policy on the system of indirect rule generally emphasized the judicial aspect of native authority, encouraged greater formality in native courts and insisted on close supervision by administrative officials. The British authority perhaps thought that the modification of the judicial system of the native court would strengthen their administrative position. So in order to bring a successful colonial administration, they first modified the judicial aspects.[87] Such an administrative policy of the British, particularly in the context of Manipur has been rightly observed by Lal Dena "as an act for the cathartic changes in the native's administrative structure."[88]

According to the Meitei traditional judicial system, the King's court was the highest court of appeal in Manipur[89] and the other courts were i) *Pacha* court, ii) Military court and iii) *Cheirap* court. Apart from these, there were also other lower courts for each *pannaha* or division. It was known as Panchayat Court or village council Court and it had the power to try all the civil suits in which the subject matter in dispute did not exceed Rs. 50/-(fifty) and some minor degrees of criminal offences; such types of courts were also established in town areas and it was known as Town Panchayat. For Muslims also a separate court was established at Lilong[90] and it was known as Mohammadan Panchayat Court and it dealt only with all the cases and disputes among the Muslim people of the State. The

---

[83] V. Vungzamoi, History Lecturer.

[84] *Foreign Department Proceedings,* no. 66, 1903, 7.

[85] V. Vungzamoi, History Lecturer.

[86] Rajendro Singh, History Lecturer, Modern College, Imphal East, Manipur, letter to the author, 7 February, 2012.

[87] Government of India, Department of Foreign and External, *Foreign Department External* (A), nos 18-23, August 1907, 1. cited in. Lal Dena, *British Policy Towards Manipur, 1891-1919*, 11.

[88] Lal Dena, *British Policy Towards Manipur, 1891-1919*, 12.

[89] Lal Dena, *British Policy Towards Manipur, 1891-1919,* 12. cited in. Rajendro Singh, History Lecturer.

[90] Lilong is a town and a Panchayat in Thoubal district of Manipur, the area is predominately settled by Muslims.

other three higher courts also got their own area of jurisdiction. The *Pacha* court dealt with all the cases of women of the State, the military court dealt with all the cases involving the soldiers and the *Cheirap* court was the second highest court of appeal next to the king's court.[91]

In the pre-colonial period the above stated Meitei indigenous courts were fully functional and able to settle all related crimes, cases, problems in the State.[92] Nevertheless the political agent realized the fact that those indigenous judicial courts would not give them political power to subjugate the Meiteis. Thus, in order to fulfill their colonial policy the British authority established colonial courts in Manipur.[93] Diminishing the centuries-old practices of the native Meitei courts, Maxwell says that "these local courts have not been working long enough to enable me to form a judgment whether they satisfy the public but the Town Panchayat has so far carried on business with considerable promptness."[94]

In this way the regency administrator justified establishing the court of the Political Agent, the court of the Assistant Political Agent, the court of the Superintendent of the State, the court of the Assistant to the Superintendent of the State. The court of the Political Agent and the court of the Assistant Political Agent heard all the appeals or tried all the civil and criminal cases in which British subjects were concerned or in which one of the parties was a British subject.[95] The main intention of the British was that the people of the State should feel the existence of the British authority through their involvement in judicial system. At the same time they wanted to show to the natives that their judgment is superior to the native system.[96]

According to this new arrangement the position of the Political Agent and Superintendent of the State, so far as the law and justice were concerned, was equivalent to that of a district magistrate and the Court of Session. However, the Chief Commissioner of Assam could exercise the power of Court of Session and Higher court as far as the criminal and civil proceedings were concerned within the limit of the Manipur State.[97] Thus, the changes which were established

---

[91] *Foreign Department External* (A), nos 18-23, August 1907, 2. cited in. Lal Dena, *British Policy Towards Manipur, 1891-1919,* 13.

[92] Lal Dena, *British Policy Towards Manipur, 1891-1919*, 15. cited in. Rajendro Singh, History Lecturer.

[93] V. Vungzamoi, History Lecturer.

[94] *Administrative Report of the Manipur Political Agency*, 1892-93, 9.

[95] *Administrative Report of the Manipur Political Agency,* 1892-93, 9.

[96] F. S. Furnivall, *Colonial Policy and Practice: A Comparative Study of Burma and Netherlands India* (Cambridge: Cambridge University Press, 1948), 285. Rajendro also gave similar reference about the involvement of the British authority in the judicial system. Rajendro Singh, History Lecturer.

[97] Government of India, Department of Foreign and External, *Foreign Department Proceedings*, (E) no. 18, September 1962. 4.

in the law and justice administration of Manipur had tremendously increased the importance and status of the British authority over the State. On the other hand, this deliberate policy of the British brought the independence of law of the native ancient kingdom to an end. J. Shakespear precisely observed that this new system would enable the Superintendent to exercise sufficient power to prevent the courts abusing their control.[98]

2.9. Civil and Military Supremacy

The administrative policy of the British in Manipur was further tightened by the mobilization of the civil and military forces. The transformation of these forces added to the British strength to stabilize their position among the common people.[99] As stated earlier, in the pre-colonial period, Manipur had its own system of civil police force and it played a positive and constructive role in safeguarding the property and life of the State. However the British authorities introduced their own policy in the area of civil and military organizations as well.[100] As a first measure, the British authority established a system of Rural Police force by appointing one *Chawkidar* for every 100 (hundred) houses with a salary of Rs. 2/- (two) per month and half a *pari* of free land along with 12 (twelve) pots of paddy from the village.[101] These village *Chawkidars* were also empowered by the British to try all the minor cases of disputes between families and other minor crimes which happened in their jurisdiction. In 1893—94 the British authority organized the civil police forces in a more systematic way by appointing one Sub-inspector, one Head Constable and eleven Constables,[102] this number later being increased by 30.

But establishing a military police force proved a more difficult task, with problems developing among the local soldiers, when their loyalties to their own people proved much stronger than their loyalty to the British authorities. Originally the force was to protect frontier areas from the neighbouring areas and to prevent internecine war between the tribal people in the hill areas. With this objective, in 1892-93 the Political Agent in Manipur raised up a military force consisting of 14 native officers, 49 non-commissioned officers and 400 military personnel.[103] But later mass desertions by the Manipur soldiers in 1894-95 led to men from other areas being enlisted and paid a salary. Thus with this new arrangement British authorities reorganized and strengthened their military

[98] J. Shakespear, *Manipur under British Management 1891-1907,* 1.

[99] Priya Devi, History Lecturer, Modern College, Imphal East, Manipur, letter to the author, 8 February, 2012.

[100] J. Shakespear, *Manipur under British Management 1891-1907,* 3.

[101] Government of India, Department of Home and Social Welfare, *Administrative Report of the Manipur Political Agency,* 1907-08, 2.

[102] *Administrative Report of the Manipur Political Agency,* 1907-08, 3.

[103] J. Shakespear, *Manipur under British Management 1891-1907,* 4.

forces. However further mass resignations followed in 1897-98, leading to a further review of policy regarding the military forces in Manipur. The authorities argued that a localized force might become intimate with the people and this might shake their loyalty to the British Government.[104] This argument gained ground; it was felt the replacement of the regular troops by a military police would be detrimental to the British interest. Then on 16th May 1907, a letter was written to the Chief Commissioner, which, while it was apparently concerned with concerns of loyalty among the members of the police force, really spelt out the basic continuing problem in Manipur—the people's dislike/distrust of the British administration. Maxwell's letter read—[105]

> "The arguments in favour of retaining a barrack of regular troops at Manipur are that the people of the country are not well disposed towards the British Government, that the minor Raja is of weak character and that disturbances are not unlikely to arise from intrigues regarding the succession, that a police force would be more likely than regular troops to join hands with the people against the government or with one section and that there is more danger of disloyalty in a police force than in a regiment of regulars."

The Chief Commissioner of Assam finally decided that it would be safer to put regular troops for at least ten years in Manipur, and this was what ultimately happened. It was justified by the argument that it was to deter/prevent the possible armed uprising against the British authorities.[106] It is clear that the main motive of the British behind this policy was simply to strengthen their political power in Manipur.[107] Such a military policy of the British was rightly identified by Lal Dena as "the task of placing the administration of the State on a firm footing could not be isolated from that of the mobilization of the military forces which was a necessary condition of an imperial power."[108]

The British action was also to demonstrate their superiority over the people of this area; they compelled the native people to disarm and asked them to surrender their weapons.[109] In the first year of the colonial administration, the British authorities collected about 400 fire arms.[110] At the same time the British authorities also imposed various oppressive measures against the people

[104] Government of India, Department of Foreign and External, *Foreign Department External* (A), no. 25, July 1904, 3.

[105] *Foreign Department External* (A), no. 25, July 1904, 4.

[106] *Foreign Department External* (A), no. 25, July 1904, 5.

[107] Priya Devi, History Lecturer.

[108] Lal Dena, *British Policy Towards Manipur, 1891-1919,* 17.

[109] Priya Devi, History Lecturer.

[110] Government of India, Department of Home and Social Welfare, *Administrative Report of the Manipur Political Agency,* 1891-92, 3.

as punishment for rebellion. The Meitei army which participated in the last war was sent to Khuzama,[111] Nagaland to carry back rations required for the British troops.[112]

All the actions, both civil and military, introduced by the British, in the period 1891-1907, aimed at strengthening their authority and colonial administrative policies over the people in Manipur.[113] But all these repressive actions of the colonial administration were treated by the native people as a great insult to them, being imposed by an alien ruler.[114] Hence, the bitterness against the British, which has lasted to the present day, and helps to explains the rejection, even to the present day, of such "alien" things as what they saw as the British religion—Christianity.

2.10. Monopoly over the State Durbar

The assumption of overall political power over the Meitei was another regressive step in the history of the British colonial rule in Manipur. This was particularly so when the colonial administration claimed a monopoly of the Manipur State Durbar.[115] This was brought about at the same time as the British assumed administrative authority over King Churachand Singh on the 15th May, 1907. Certainly, the reconstitution of the Manipur State Durbar was a very significant development in the colonial history of Manipur because it reflected the de-facto position of the British Political Agent in Manipur over the administrative position of the State.[116] According to the new arrangement the king himself was the President of the Durbar and he was assisted by an English I.C.S. Officer as the Vice-President. Besides this, there were another six native members who were also entrusted with different portfolios and then members were appointed by the government of India on the recommendation of the king of Manipur and they could be removed by an order of the government. The education, medical and armed State police portfolios were given to the Vice-president. Other portfolios like judiciary, works, civil, police and jail were entrusted to the ordinary members.[117] However, after this new arrangement the influence of the Political Agent over the

[111] Khuzama is an Angami Naga village which is about 72 miles from Kohima, the present capital of Nagaland.

[112] Government of India, Department of Foreign and External, *Foreign Department Progression*, nos. 1-19. October, 1893, 35.

[113] R.K. Tamphasana Devi, History Lecturer.

[114] R.K. Tamphasana Devi, History Lecturer.

[115] Rajendro Singh, History Lecturer.

[116] Kh. Sarojini Devi, *British Political Agency in Manipur, 1835-1947*, 62.

[117] Government of India, Department of Foreign and External, *Foreign Department Progression*, nos. 18-23, August, 1907, 1-2.

affairs of the Durbar was so great that he had the power of access to every affair of the Durbar. It is mentioned that:[118]

> Should the king, the Vice-president... the members in-charge of the department concerned not approve of the order passed, he may have the matter referred to the Political Agent who may request the Durbar to reconsider the matter. If the Durbar adheres to its former orders the Political Agent may refer the matter to the government of India for orders. In such cases action shall be stayed after the first reference till final order is passed.

Another egoistic and divisive policy of the British was that the entire administration of the hill areas was left in the hand of the Vice-President who was also an English Officer.[119] As a result of this, a strained relationship was developed between the people of the valley and the hills.[120] In the early days, the king of Manipur directly dealt with all the affairs of the people of the hills and hence there was cordial relationship between the valley and the hills.[121] But regrettably with the coming of alien power and with its new administrative system this intimacy was lost.[122] Thus, it reflected seriously on the future administration and social relationship of the State. Since then a serious lack of understanding developed and growing dichotomy was created between the people of the hills and the valley.[123]

3. Outbreak of Opposition to Economic Control—*Nupi Lan*

The establishment of British colonial power was not without opposition from the people of Manipur. *Nupi Lan*–which means women's war in Meiteilon—occurred in 1939 and is one of the important movements in the history of Manipuri women.[124] But even before that the Meitei had rebelled against their alien overlords. Their dissatisfaction was first expressed in 1904, within a short span of thirteen years from the occupation by the British. This movement was also launched by the women of Manipur as a protest against the injustices of the colonial authorities. This protest achieved nothing except to fuel the simmering resentment of the people. There were two notable further movements against the

---

[118] *Foreign Department Progression*, nos. 18-23, August, 1907, 3.

[119] *Foreign Department Progression*, nos. 18-23, August, 1907, 5.

[120] Priya Devi, History Lecturer.

[121] Hokey Kaikho, Former General Secretary, Manipur Baptist Convention, Imphal West, Manipur, letter to the author, 18 November, 2010.

[122] Th. Kumar Meitei, Former Executive Secretary, Meitei Baptist Association, Lungthabal, Imphal East, Manipur, letter to the author, 4 October, 2011.

[123] Hokey Kaikho, Former General Secretary.

[124] Kh. Sarojini Devi, *British Political Agency in Manipur, 1835-1947*, 61.

colonial rule, one in 1917-19 and another in 1930-32, and resentment finally boiled over into action in 1939 in the *Nupi Lan.*[125]

The *Nupi Lan* took place in 1939 at Khwairamband[126]—a bazaar which was founded by a Meitei king named Khagemba in 1580 A.D. and which is also known as *Ima Keithel or Ima* market.[127] This agitation is widely considered to be the turning point in the emergence of political awareness and self consciousness among the Meiteis in Manipur.[128] It was the first successful attempt to voice their grievances against British suppression. The colonial authority regarded the outbreak of this movement as the most important event of the year 1939.[129]

But in spite of these protests, the colonial rulers did not make any attempt to introduce any positive changes for the welfare of the common people. Instead of making any positive improvement in the administrative system, they further added more hardship on the common people by introducing complicated social evils like *Mangba-Sengba* (clean and unclean) by exploiting their traditional village economy. Ultimately, it produced a serious effect in the body politic of the State.[130]

The economic exploitation by outside traders under the control of the colonial authority destroyed all prospects of economic development of the State. Therefore, such a type of monopoly over the entire social, political and economic system of the State, created by the feudal rule with the leadership of the imperial force, created a serious threat to the normal life of the common people.[131] The *Nupi Lan* of 1939 represented a spontaneous outbreak of the suppressed energy of the oppressed people, and was a movement launched by the Meitei women of Manipur. As has been noted in previous chapters, Meitei women always played a high-profile role in the socio-economic life of the

---

[125] Th. Binarani Devi, "Women's Movement in Conflict Situation in Manipur," in *Society, Politics and Development in North East India,* edited by Asok Chakraborty and Satyabrata Chakraborty (New Delhi: Concept Publishing Company, 2008), 111-13.

[126] Khwairamband has been the main commercial centre of Manipur since the time of king Khagemba in 1580 A.D. Khagemba was the founder of this centre. "*Nupi Lan,* 1939," *Lamyanba* 5/51(December 1973): 6.

[127] "*Nupi Lan*, 1939," *Lamyanba* , 7.

[128] Besides the *Nupi Lan* two other major movements too took place against the discriminatory policy of the British authority in Manipur. They were the 'Kuki Rebellion of 1917-1919' and the Zeliangrong Movement of 1930-1932'. However, we have limited our focus within the *Nupi Lan* as it is directly associated with the Meitei community which is the focal point of our research work. Therefore, it is an expression of main focus of our research work; it does not imply a lack of acknowledgement of those movements; nor does it involve a brush-off of the movement against the British colonial policy in Manipur.

[129] Government of India, Department of Home and Social Welfare, *Administrative Report of Manipur*, 1939-1940, 1.

[130] "*Nupi Lan*, 1939," *Lamyanba,* 8-9.

[131] E. W. Dun, *Gazetteer of Manipur* (Delhi: Vivek Publishing House, 1981), 62.

State,[132] enjoying maximum independence and a high status. In fact this high status accorded to the womenfolk is regarded with pride as one of the greatest qualities of Manipur culture.[133] While they were seldom given political and administrative responsibilities, the internal and external trade of the State was managed by them. Their centre of activities was at '*Ima Keithel*', a major market place, located in the heart of Imphal city. The whole market was managed by them only. In addition the market place served as an important venue for social and political interaction among them.[134]

Meitei society is an agrarian society, and in any agrarian economy, including the Meiteis, rice plays a major role. The most important trade industry of the Meitei women was the rice trading business. The involvement of women in this trade was enormous. They participated in this trade right from the beginning of the transplantation of rice up to the selling of the final product.[135] In the pre-colonial period there emerged a strong belief for having a self sufficiency in the Meitei economy, and every household became a great centre of production. The responsibility for this economic activity was entirely on the shoulders of the womenfolk. This was one of the reasons why they gained maximum power in this field and why it was respected by the society.[136] But after Manipur was colonized in 1891, the whole system was changed. British authorities began exploiting the traditional economy of the State in order to accumulate resources for themselves.[137] The main aim of colonial conquest was to satisfy the desire of the British to secure for themselves the most advantageous strategic economic position.[138]

In order to implement their desire successfully, they utilized the services of the big traders from outside the State. Then they began to import goods from outside and also began to control rice trading business of the people within the State.[139] This biased economic trend degraded the importance of the Meitei womenfolk. Soon outside traders began to capture the monopoly of buying and selling which previously was under the management of the Meitei womenfolk. However in spite of the challenges and hardship womenfolk faced, their morale

---

132 R. K. Tamphasana Devi, History Lecturer.

133 S. P. Sen, *Social and Religious Reform Movement in the Nineteenth and Twentieth Century* (Calcutta: International Book Trust, 1979), 410.

134 S. P. Sen, *Social and Religious Reform Movement,* 411.

135 Kh. Sarojini Devi, *British Political Agency in Manipur, 1835-1947*, 61-62.

136 *Lamdamsida Nupigi Ihou (Women's Movement of the Land)* (Imphal: The Manipur Chanura Leisem Marup, 1981), 1.

137 R. K. Tamphasana Devi, History Lecturer.

138 Georgy Rudenko, *Colonialism and Neo-Colonialism* (Moscow: Novosti Press Agency Publishing House, 1970), 17.

139 E. W. Dun, *Gazetteer of Manipur,* 63.

was very high and they were always ready to fight for justice.[140] One of the best examples of this was an outbreak in 1904 of resistance against the request by the British authorities for the Meitei to rebuild a house. The house of two officials had been destroyed by fire, and the then Political Agent in Manipur, Lt. Col. Maxwell, asked the people of Imphal area to rebuild it at their own cost. The Meitei refused, and it was the Meitei women who led the resistance against the request. This was successful, and eventually the British authority was compelled to rebuild the house at their own cost.[141] A further resistance, again led by Meitei women, occurred in 1925, being launched against the increase of the 'water tax' rate. Thus, the Meitei womenfolk set an example by rising up in protest against perceived acts of injustice of the colonial authority.[142]

The most significant positive result of the women's activities was that it rendered great assistance to the growth of socio-political and socio-economic consciousness among the indigenous people in Manipur.[143] The eruption of the '*Nupi Lan*' as already pointed out, was directly related to the political, social and economic conditions of the State which developed after the introduction of the colonial administration system.[144] The new administrative policy introduced by the British after the 1891 war had brought tremendous changes in every aspect of the life of the Meitei people of the State of Manipur,[145] seriously disturbing their until-now normal life.

Conclusion

It is clear from the previous chapters that Meiteis had reason to consider the period under British rule as dark years in the colonial history of Manipur.[146] Obviously the main intention of the British was clearly to get an advantageous economic position from their colony. Therefore, in order to achieve their aspiration they adopted various administrative and economic measures. Colonial officers were fully convinced that the Meitei people, due to their conventional character, always kept their loyalty to the king and the family which enjoyed the highest status in the social hierarchy of the country. So, because of this understanding, British might have had an idea to give respect

140 "Manipur Itihasta Nupi Lan", (Nupi Lan in the History of Manipur) Lamyanba 5/52 (January 1974): 4.

141 Government of India, Department of Foreign and External, *Foreign Department Secretary* (E), nos. 872-84, March 1905, 204-9. cited in. Kh. Sarojini Devi, *British Political Agency in Manipur, 1835-1947*, 62.

142 "*Nupi Lan*, 1939," *Lamyanba*, 9-11.

143 Th. Binarani Devi, "Women's Movement in Conflict Situation in Manipur," 114.

144 Memma Devi, President, Manipur Keithel Nupi Marup, Imphal, Manipur, letter to the author, 16 June, 2012.

145 Kh. Sarojini Devi, *British Political Agency in Manipur, 1835-1947*, 62.

146 "*Manipur Itihasta Nupi Lan*", (*Nupi Lan in the History of Manipur*), 7.

to the feelings of the people of the State. Hence, colonial authority appointed a minor prince of hardly five years old as the ruler of Manipur i.e., from 1891 to 1907. During this time, the whole responsibility of the administrative affairs of the State was taken over by the British. During this span of sixteen years, the British manipulated to the maximum every administrative area and brought a new shape of administration. But the administration was not based on the interest and benefit of the indigenous people but that of the colonizers. Hence, to achieve their objectives they adopted various oppressive measures against the Meitei people in Manipur.

Thus, the occupation of Manipur by the British brought a series of calculated changes in the State. After the introduction of the new administrative system, the entire administrative shape was changed and traditional village economy was changed to colonial economy. Traditional judicial system of the State was overshadowed by the colonial judicial system. Apart from this, the British authorities, in order to demonstrate their colonial authority, perpetrated unbearable torture on the common people of the State. The policy of the disarmament of the population of the State and other repressive measures carried out by the colonial government against the people, as a mark of punishment for rebellion, was taken by the people of Manipur as an insult to them. They strongly felt that it was offensive to their self respect.[147] The reaction of the people to these administrative changes followed closely—the first anti-imperialist activities broke out in the year 1904. Though the movement was suppressed it gave a good lesson to the British administration.

As mentioned earlier, Meiteis continue to have ill feeling towards Christianity because Christianity was introduced by English missionary, William Pettigrew, soon after Manipur was colonized by British in 1894. To make it worse, Pettigrew entered Manipur with full patronage from Mr. A. Porteous.[148] British colonial power and Christian missions in Manipur were linked together.[149] Even though the Christian missions acted in a spiritual and sympathetic manner, however the exploitative nature of the British power has overshadowed the work contributed by Pettigrew and his Christian followers.[150] As a result of the colonial activities, Meiteis still have ill feelings towards the British and their religion Christianity dating from the colonial period in Manipur.[151] The resentment against the British,

---

[147] "*Manipur Itihasta Nupi Lan*", (*Nupi Lan in the History of Manipur*), 5.

[148] Lal Dena, *Christian Missions and Colonialism*, 31. Rev. Debendra Meitei has also cited that Pettigrew entered Manipur with full patronage from Mr. A. Porteous. Debendra Meitei, Former Executive Secretary, Meitei Baptist Association, Kakching, Manipur, letter to the author, 28 April 2012.

[149] Lal Dena, *Christian Missions and Colonialism*, xii.

[150] Th. Kumar Singh, The First Meitei Executive Secretary, Meitei Baptist Association, Langthabal, Manipur, letter to the author, 15 April 2012.

[151] Debendra Meitei, Former Executive Secretary, Meitei Baptist Association.

which has lasted to the present day, helps to explain the rejection of such "alien" things as Christianity which they saw as the British religion. Therefore this factor is ascertained as a minor cause for the rejection of Christianity among the Meiteis in Manipur valley.

Retrospection and Conclusion

Given the amount of research that has been done into the Meiteis of Manipur valley, their culture and, most particularly, their religious beliefs, it may appear unusual that the writer has chosen to add to it. However the writer is concerned in this study with an aspect which has to date been totally ignored—why has one particular religion—Christianity—been so unsuccessful in gaining followers in the valley? It is this lack of success which the writer is pursuing. Any new religion introduced into a specific culture can expect to make slow progress in the initial stages, but the situation in Manipur valley is different—Christianity has run into a "stone wall". What this book reveals is that there is a rejection of Christianity which goes far deeper than the usual reluctance to consider something new—this rejection by the general Meiteis is more deeply rooted; there are reasons for rejection, on historical, religious and cultural grounds. Indeed, it is likely that patriotism plays a part in the rejection. Christianity came to Manipur in 1894. Yet in this century, out of approximately 1.3 million Meiteis in Manipur valley alone, there are around only 5000 believers, even after more than a century of missionary endeavor.

The book has dealt in detail with the coming of Christianity by William Pettigrew, how he was detained in Cachar, Assam for three years before he was allowed to come to Manipur, and his attempts to preach the Gospel to the Meiteis and the hill tribes. It traces his activities, his departure, and the efforts of his loyal followers in the 1960s to carry on his work.

The book then examined the events experienced by the Meiteis in the centuries before Pettigrew's arrival, and the events in the period since his departure, and has offered three important reasons for the failure of Christianity to penetrate the region. These are: the adoption of a particular form of Hinduism, the subsequent determined efforts to revive the Meitei's traditional religion, and the effects of British colonialism, which appear to have triggered an almost aggressive and even patriotic reaction against anything British or connected to the British—such as a "British" religion—Christianity. The book has examined in detail these three reasons under the headings Sanskritization, Revival of Sanamahism (the Meiteis' traditional religion), and British Rule.

The writer limited his study among Christians to the Baptist works based on Meitei Baptist Association (MBA),[1] which covers the period from 1982 to 2008. This is because the MBA is the primary Meitei-led and Meitei-staffed mission organization, established in 1982, in order to resume the missionary work among the Meiteis. Despite its efforts, it is still unable to do a fruitful ministry. The rejection of Christianity among the majority Meiteis in Manipur valley continues. The researcher's choice in this is an expression of historical connection; it does not imply a lack of acknowledgement of those Meitei churches associated with other denominations in Manipur valley; which also have been neglected by the majority Meiteis, or does it involve a disregard for the history of Christianity among the Meiteis in Manipur valley. The MBA has strong historical ties to Manipur Valley. Baptist mission was the first Christian mission established in Manipur through the activities of William Pettigrew, who after his arrival joined the American Baptist Missionary Union and took over the Manipur field. MBA was established with the help of Baptist churches which were planted by William Pettigrew and his followers under the American Baptist Missionary Union. MBA is primarily Meitei-led and Meitei-staffed Baptist mission organization that functions exclusively amongst the Meiteis in Manipur valley. And MBA is the only Meitei Christian organization directly affiliated to the Manipur Baptist Convention (MBC), which is one of the conventions of the Council of Baptist Churches in North-East India (CBCNEI). CBCNEI is the biggest Baptist body in India.

Nevertheless, despite the limitation to one denomination, the researcher argues this research will have implications upon all the Meiteis, including those Meiteis in Assam, Tripura, Burma and other parts of the World. Given the results of his study, the researcher believes this research work is breaking new ground in its efforts to suggest the causes to the "stone wall" problem.

The writer believes a study of the causes for rejection of Christianity among the Meiteis in Manipur valley is crucial at this point of time as the rejection of Christianity in this community is increasingly obvious. It is strange that given its history in Manipur, Christianity is now supposed to be an alien one to the majority of Meiteis, but they continue to hold wrong conceptions, based on the three reasons given above.

Oddly enough, the majority of the Meiteis think that Christianity is for tribal people (i.e., Nagas and Kukis) as they are the ones who have been mostly Christianized. Yet the historical reality is that during the time of King Surachandra Singh, William Pettigrew arrived in Imphal on the 6th February 1894 to start Mission work through education, and he started his work amongst the Meiteis.[2]

[1] The Meitei Baptist Association is situated at Wangjing of Thoubal district, which is one of the districts in Manipur valley.

[2] L. Leiren Singh, "Reverend William Pettigrew and Modern Education in Manipur," in *Rev. William Pettigrew: A Pioneer Missionary of Manipur* (Imphal: Fraternal Green Cross, 1996), 7. cf.

The gospel of Jesus Christ was not first preached to the Nagas or Kukis but to the Meiteis. So, the writer hopes this study will also enable the majority of Meiteis to understand the historical reality, and thereby a positive attitude towards Meitei Christians and Christianity could be developed.

This work will also help towards creating a platform for a possible dialogue between minority Meitei Christians and majority Meiteis. Due to lack of historical facts and findings, there is great hatred towards Christianity and Christians among the dominant Meiteis in Manipur valley. And this study will further help to initiate a wider inter-religious dialogue among the followers of the various religions in the valley—Christianity, Hinduism, Sanamahism, and Buddhism. The socio-political, socio-religious and socio-economic conditions of present day Manipur are in a chaotic situation, and at this juncture, to have a common platform for inter-religious dialogue would be meaningful and helpful.

But there is another and urgent reason for finding common ground among the religions in Manipur. Rejection has brought persecution to the minority Meitei Christians. Concerning this Kh. Chaoba Singh, state secretary, All India Christian Council (AICC) remarks:[3]

> Manipur repeats the burning of Churches in valley after five years. Two churches reported burnt down and one attempted to destroy in Imphal West District of Manipur. A new communal force is suspected to be behind the serial attacks on Churches. There is report of an uprising Hindutva like communal force in Manipur, which has started targeting Meitei Christian minorities. To save from communal riots like Gujarat 2002 and Kandhamal, all civil society must resist and oppose the uprising neo communal force in Manipur.

Mr. Sam Paul of AICC writes about some of the incidents that recently took place in Manipur valley.[4]

> Now, we are very much concerned that Meitei Christians are in panic of recent series of attacks by some fanatic groups belonging to the fundamentalists, promoting the divisive Hindutva philosophy. On 11 May 2009, a Baptist church at Phumlou, and a catholic church at Phayeng, Imphal West district were set on fire by some unknown fanatics.

Lal Dena, "Christian Proselytism 1894-1949," in *History of Modern Manipur, 1826-1949*, edited by Lal Dena (New Delhi: Orbit Publishers & Distributors, 1991), 105.

3 Kh. Chaoba Singh, State Secretary, All India Christian Council, Imphal, Manipur, letter to the author, May 12, 2009.

4 Sam Paul, National Secretary-Public Affairs, The All India Christian Council, Secunderabad, Andra Pradesh, letter to the author, May 14, 2009.

> On May 10, 2009 an unknown person suspected to be a member of a newly formed group, allegedly backed by an outlaw outfit has warned Church members to stop Church building construction in Lamshang in Imphal West district.
>
> From these series of attacks on Meitei Christians, there is a growing fear that an organized attack on Christians to intimidate, frighten and harass by the fanatic groups seems to be emerging. They are targeting to destroy the peace and harmony among all religious groups by attacking minority Meitei Christians.

Given the lack of research into the problem of rejection of Christianity in Manipur, the writer hopes the study will also enable Meitei Christians to understand the historical events which have resulted in the rejection of Christianity among this group of people and to suggest ways in which they may be able to find an acceptable strategy in their missionary venture.

A brief overview of the three reasons argued as the cause for rejection of Christianity will show how deeply rooted that rejection is in culture, history and religion.

Sanskritization of Meiteis developed over several centuries, until in the 18th century it became the official religion of the Meiteis through the Hindu version of Vaishnavism. It had a great socio-religious and socio-political impact. The impact of Vaishnavism was considerable upon the Meiteis since the religion was followed first by the kings, the *pibas*[5] and the nobles. It gained ground among the common people because it was enforced on them. Soon after becoming an official religion in Manipur, Vaishnavism enlisted the full support of the priests and the common people as is evidenced from the history of temples, land-grants, and endowments towards the establishment of religious centres.[6]

It was not a "pure" Hindu version, but a syncretized version in which traditional Meitei religious beliefs were combined. The Vaishnavism in Manipur borrowed many local elements and associated itself with pre-Vaishnavite gods. It was the policy of most of the Meitei Kings to unite the conflicting interests of ancient Meitei religion and Vaishnavism. There was mutual compromise, which can be observed in the following—synthesis of the Meitei religion with its gods and goddesses and traditions; its myths and rituals, its legends and traditions; its social custom and practices and its priest and ceremonials and of Brahminical Hinduism with its special emphasis on the worship of Krishna. Meiteis not only have made significant contribution to the Hindu culture through its Vaishnavism, its dance and music, its art and culture and its literature but also continue to hold Vaishnavism as the formal religion of their State. There is a rigid obedience

---

[5] The male chiefs of the clans- traditionally, *pibas* were highly regarded.

[6] L. Bimol Singh, "Meitei Christian Identity: Problems and Prospects," *The Sathri Journal: Journal of Contextual Theology,* 3/1(May, 2009): 56.

to their religion which makes it difficult for any other "foreign" religion (like Christianity) to make headway.

The second impediment to an acceptance of Christianity in Manipur is, oddly enough in the light of the above, another religion—Sanamahism. But Sanamahism is something special—it is a revival of the traditional, pre-Hindu religion of the Meiteis, which was over a long period syncretized with Vaishnavism, as indicated above. It began to appear during the 20th century, and soon gained a firm foothold among the Meiteis. But it was not a totally religious movement, but an attempt to revive ancient Meitei culture in all its forms, right down to teaching the ancient script in schools.

The movement focuses on three key areas—denouncing alien elements (anything that does not have origin with Meitei and Manipur—Hinduism is taken as a key alien element); reviving traditional values i.e., religion, culture, language, script, and preserving those traditional values—an attempt to re-establish a sense of true Meitei identity. No doubt all the restorative activities were taken up in order to safeguard their traditional religion, culture, language and script. The followers of the revival movement started to spread awareness that Meiteis had had enough socio-religious and socio-cultural discrimination of their culture under the yoke of Hinduism. Followers of Sanamahism are pressing all the Meiteis to give up Hinduism and follow Sanamahism.[7] As part of this, they strongly reject other religious teachings including Christianity for they believe that allowing or accepting the teachings of any other religion rather than traditional revival values of Meiteis would hamper the hard earned revival process.[8]

The final important reason for rejection of Christianity is the extremely deep-rooted anger, even today, against the British for their treatment of the Meiteis during the period of colonial rule, as is shown by the answers to the researcher's questionnaires. Conquest of the northeast of India proceeded along political and commercial lines, revolts and rebellions were put down harshly; the hanging of Meitei heroic martyrs after a mock trial has never been forgotten (the stand taken by the martyrs continue to be a source of inspiration).

The *Nupi lan* or the 'war of women' in Manipur in 1904 is equally honoured; memories of exploitation, torture and death of the people of Manipur are burned deep into the Meitei psyche. Because of all these, people of Manipur still have ill feelings towards the British and also towards their religion. To the Meiteis, Christianity came with the British (Pettigrew entered Manipur with the blessing

---

[7] Sairem Nilabir, "The Revivalist Movement of Sanamahism," in *Manipur Past and Present: The Ordeals and Heritage of a Civilization*, vol. 2, edited by Naorem Sanajaoba (New Delhi: Mittal Publications, 1991), 118.

[8] The followers of the revivification movement do not oppose Christianity being practiced by other ethnic groups in Manipur. Their main concern is for Meiteis and its society. W. Kaboklei,General Secretary, Ima-lup, Laipham Khunnao, Imphal West, Manipur, letter to the author, 4 February, 2010.

of a British official present at the time), therefore Christianity is "the British religion" and not acceptable.

These, then, are the reasons the writer presents as a barrier to the spread of Christianity in Manipur today—longstanding Hinduism, a revival of Meitei self-identity, and an anger against the trials and tribulations of the British colonial era. However these findings are not merely a static recording of "reasons why…"; they come at a time when rejection of Christianity has turned into persecution of the loyal little minority. Unless the Meiteis in general, and even the Christian Meiteis, can come to understand the background to this rejection, and can move through and beyond it to some form of acceptance of each other's position, there will, from what the writer has discovered, never be peace in the valley.

The writer hopes his book could, by establishing a better understanding of the historical reasons for rejection, form the basis of a dialogue between the people of the valley that would go some way towards finding a more peaceful future for them all.

Appendix – 1

(- of Chapter-1)

Manipur Map

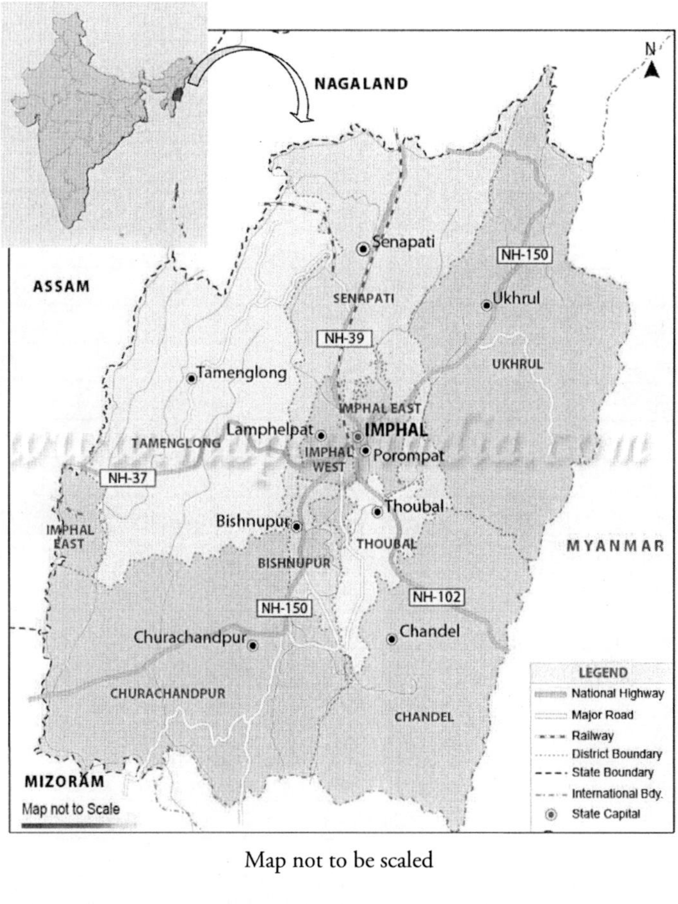

Map not to be scaled

Source-Appendix 1: "Manipur Map," *Maps of India.Com* (12 Jan 2012): http://www.mapsofindia.-com/maps/manipur/

Appendix – 1
(- of Chapter-2)

The Ahom Dynasty

Ruler	Period	Ruler	Period
1. Sukapha	1228–1268	21. Supungmung	1663–1669
2. Suteupha	1268–1281	22. Sunyatpha	1669–1673
3. Subinpha	1281–1293	23. Suklampha	1673–1675
4. Sukhaangphaa	1293–1332	24. Suhung	1675
5. Sukhrangpha	1332–1364	25. Gobar	1675
6. Sutupha	1364–1376	26. Sujinpha	1675–1677
Interregnum	1376–1380	27. Sudaipha	1677–1679
7. Tyao Khamti	1380–1389	28. Sulikpha	1679–1681
Interregnum	1389–1397	29. Supatpha	1681–1696
8. Sudangpha	1397–1407	30.Sukhrungpha	1696–1714
9. Sujangpha	1407–1422	31. Sutanphaa	1714–1744
10. Suphakpha	1422–1439	32. Sunenpha	1744–1751
11. Susenpha	1439–1488	33. Surampha	1751–1769
12. Suhenpha	1488–1493	34. Sunyeopha	1769–1780
13. Supimpha	1493–1497	35. Suhitpangpha	1780–1795
14. Suhungmung	1497–1539	36. Suklingpha	1795–1810
15.Suklenmung	1539–1552	37. Sudinpha	1810–1818
16. Sukhamphaa	1552–1603	38.Purandar Singha	1818–1819
17. Susenghpha	1603–1641	Burmese Rule	1819-1824
18.Surampha	1641–1644		
19. Sutyinpha	1644–1648		
20. Sutamla	1648–1663		

Source-Appendix 1: "Ahom Dynasty," http://www.absoluteastronomy.com/topics/Ahom-_ Dynasty (24 Feb 2013).

Appendix – 2

(- of Chapter-2)

The Treaty of Yandaboo

King Bagyidaw (d. October 1846), king of Myanmar (Myanmar) from 1819 to 1837. The seventh monarch of the Konbaung, or Alaungpaya, dynasty, he was defeated in the First Anglo-Myanmar War (1824-26). As a result of his defeat, the provinces of Arakan and Tenasserim were lost to the British. Bagyidaw was the grandson of King Bodawpaya, who had narrowly avoided war with the British over the frontier between Bengal and Arakan. Bagyidaw was an ineffectual king, but his general, Maha Bandula, influenced him to follow Bodawpaya's policy of aggressive expansion in northeastern India. He conquered Assam and Manipur, making them Myanmar tributaries. The border with British India thus extended from Arakan on the Bay of Bengal northward to the foot of the Himalayan Mountains. The British, angered over Myanmar border raids in pursuit of rebel forces, launched a war on March 5, 1824. Bagyidaw's armies were driven out of Assam, Arakan, and Manipur. British forces occupied southern Myanmar and advanced toward the capital, Amarapura (near present-day Mandalay). On Feb. 24, 1826, Bagyidaw's government signed the Treaty of Yandabo; its terms included surrendering of Tenasserim and Arakan to the British, payment of an indemnity equivalent to Pound 1,000,000 (10,000,000 Kyat silver coins), and renunciation of all Myanmar claims in Assam and Manipur, which became British protectorates. During the remaining years of his reign, Bagyidaw attempted to mitigate the harsh terms of the treaty. In 1826 the king negotiated a commercial treaty with the British envoy, John Crawfurd, but refused to establish formal diplomatic relations unless he could deal on an equal basis with the British sovereign, rather than through the East India Company at Calcutta. Bagyidaw failed to persuade the British to give Tenasserim back to Myanmar, but a deputation that he sent to Calcutta in 1830 successfully reasserted the Myanmar claim to the Kale-Kabaw Valley, which had been occupied by the Manipuris. After 1831 Bagyidaw became increasingly susceptible to attacks of mental instability, and in 1837 he was succeeded by his brother, Prince Tharrawaddy Min.

Source-Appendix-2: "King Bagyidaw." http://www.journeysmyanmar.com/historical_-timeline.htm (24 Feb 2013).

Appendix – 3
(- of Chapter-2)

A Brief Historical Background of the Baptist Missionary Society

The Baptist Missionary Society was founded in 1792 by William Carey (1761-1834). As a youth, Carey had developed an interest in missionary work in the South Seas through reading the accounts of Captain Cook's 1769-1770 voyages to that region. This interest was accentuated when Carey read Jonathan Edwards' book *Life of Brainerd*. In 1792, Carey himself authored a paper, "*An Inquiry into the Obligations of Christians to use Means for the Conversion of the Heathen*." His two sermons in that year, one before the Baptist Association at Nottingham and the other before the Baptist Association at Kettering, were impassioned pleas for missions, and these are generally credited with spurring the interest in others which resulted in the founding of the Baptist Missionary Society on October 2, 1792.

The original intent of the Society was to foster mission work in the South Seas, but this was given up when a definite burden was felt for the heathen of India. In March 1793 William Carey sailed with John Thomas (1757-1792) and they landed in Calcutta in November of that year. Work was concentrated in the areas of Bible translation, preaching, teaching, and the founding of schools. It was not until 1800, however, that Carey baptized the first Hindu convert. In 1810 the India work was organized into five missions, and by 1813 the Society could report sixty-three workers, native and European, involved in twenty mission stations. Two other men heavily involved in organizing the India work were Joshua Marshman (1768-1837) and William Ward (1769-1823).

A mission begun in Sierra Leone in 1795 proved to be abortive. Work was not resumed in West Africa until 1842, when stations were founded both on the Spanish island of Fernando Po, and in Cameroon. Spanish authorities halted the Fernando Po mission in 1858. The Cameroon work continued until 1887, when German colonization there paved the way for the Basle Missionary Society to take over that mission. In 1878, the Baptist Missionary Society entered the Congo and Angola. Missionaries were forced to withdraw from both areas in 1961.

A mission was begun on Ceylon in 1812. In 1813 the West Indies work was begun in Jamaica, followed by mission stations in British Honduras (1822), the Bahamas (1833), Trinidad and the Dominican Republic (both 1843), and Haiti (1845). A mission was founded in France in 1834; other European stations later included Norway and Italy. Attempts to place missionaries in China were not successful at first, but work was established there by 1877. The Society extended itself into Japan in 1879 and into Palestine in 1880. With the Communist takeover in China in 1949, the Society withdrew from there and sought to continue its mission to the Chinese people via Hong Kong. In 1853, work was begun in Brazil. The Society also participated with other mission boards in Nepal and Sierra Leone missions.

Bible translation and publishing were important functions of the Society. By William Carey's death in 1834, it had already translated the entire Bible into forty languages and dialects. Joshua Marshman translated the Bible into Chinese and prepared a Chinese grammar and dictionary. In addition, many sacred texts of the Chinese and Hindus were translated into English. The Society's publishing arm, the Carey Press, was in 1847 amalgamated with the Kingsgate Press of the Baptist Union of Great Britain and Ireland to form the Carey Kingsgate Press Limited.

Source-Appendix-3: "Record of the **Baptist Missionary Society** –Collection 223," *Billy Graham Centrre Archives.* http://www.wheaton.edu/bgc/archives/-GUIDES/223.htm (24 **Feb 2013).**

Appendix – 4
(- of Chapter-2)

Accord of Yandaboo,
February 24, 1826

ARTICLE I

There shall be perpetual peace and friendship between the Honourable Company on the one part, and His Majesty the King of Ava on the other.

ARTICLE 2

His Majesty the King of Ava renounces all claims upon, and will abstain from all future interferences with the principality of Assam and its dependencies, and also with the contiguous petty States of Cachar and Jyntea.

With regard to Munnipore, it is stipulated that, should Gumbheer Singh desire to return to that country, he shall be recognized by the King of Ava as Rajah thereof.

(Signed Archibald Campbell) (L.S.)

Largeen Meonja,
(Woonghee) (Signed) T. C. Robertson
Captain Royal Navy (L.S.)

(Seal of the lotoo) (Signed) Hy. D. Chads
Captain Royal Navy (L.S.).

Shwagum Woon
Atawoon

Source-Appendix-4: "Accord of Yandaboo, February 24, 1826," in *Manipur: Past and Present,* vol. I, edited by Naorem Sanajaoba (Delhi: Mittal Publications, 1988), 471.

Appendix – 5
(- of Chapter-2)

Agreement Regarding Compensation For The Kubo Valley, 1834

Major Grant and Captain Pemberton, under instructions from the Right Honourable the Govemor-General-in-Council, having made over the Kubo Valley to the Burmese Commissioners deputed from Ava, are authorized to state:

1. That it is the intention of the Supreme Government to grant a monthly stipend of five hundred Sicca Rupees to the Rajah of Munnipore, to commence from the nineth day of January One Thousand Eight Hundred and Thirty-four, the date at which the transfer of Kubo took place, as shown in the Agreement mutually signed by the British and Burmese Commissioners.
2. It is to be distinctly understood that should any circumstances hereafter arise by which the portion of territory lately made over to Ava again reverts to Munnipore, the allowance now granted by the British Government will cease from the date of such reversion.

(Sd/-)
F.J. Grant, Major

(Sd/-)
R. Boileu Pemberton; Captain

Langhthabal Munnipore,
January 25, 1834

Source-Appendix-5: "Agreement Regarding Compensation for the Kubo Valley, 1834," in *Manipur: Past and Present,* vol. I, edited by Naorem Sanajaoba (Delhi: Mittal Publications, 1988), 468.

Appendix – 6
(- of Chapter-2)

Arthington Aborigines Mission

Arthington Aborigines Mission was a private mission society of English millionaire named Robert Arthington of Leeds, England. Robert Arthington was born in Leeds on May 20, 1823, the only son of Robert and Maria Arthington, who were leading figures in the Leeds meeting of the Society of Friends. In 1848 Arthington followed the example of his mother and two of his three sisters in leaving the Society of Friends and eventually found his spiritual home at South Parade Baptist Church in Leeds. Robert Arthington owned a brewery but had abandoned his business after adopting strict temperance principles in 1846. Nevertheless, on his death in 1864, he left a fortune of £200,000 to his son. Robert junior never set up his own business, but a combination of prudent investment, notably in British and American railways, and a notoriously parsimonious lifestyle augmented his fortune to an extent of which he himself was unaware until the final months of his life.

In 1885, Robert Arthington wrote to the Assam Baptist Mission stating his desire to open a work among any evangelized tribes in and around Assam or elsewhere in India. Robert is said to have commissioned about thirteen Missionaries in 1890 and one of those missionaries happened to be the first Christian missionary of Manipur, William Pettigrew. Pettigrew joined the Arthington Aborigines Mission in 1890 and was commissioned to go to India in the same year. He was then just a young man of twenty one. He along with three other missionaries and a doctor arrived at Kolkata, Bangal by the end of 1890 and were warmly received by Rev, and Mrs, St Dalmas.

Source-Appendix-6: Brian Stanley, "Robert Arthington," in *Biographical Dictionary of Christian Mission*, Gerald H. Anderson ed. (Michigan/Cambridge: William B. Eerdmans Publishing Company, 1999), 30. cited in. Elungkiebe Zeliang, *A History of the Manipur Baptist Convention* (Imphal: Manipur Baptist Convention, 2005), 19-20.

Appendix – 7
(- of Chapter-2)

Scanned Record of Baptism and Marriage of Mr. Angom Porom Singh

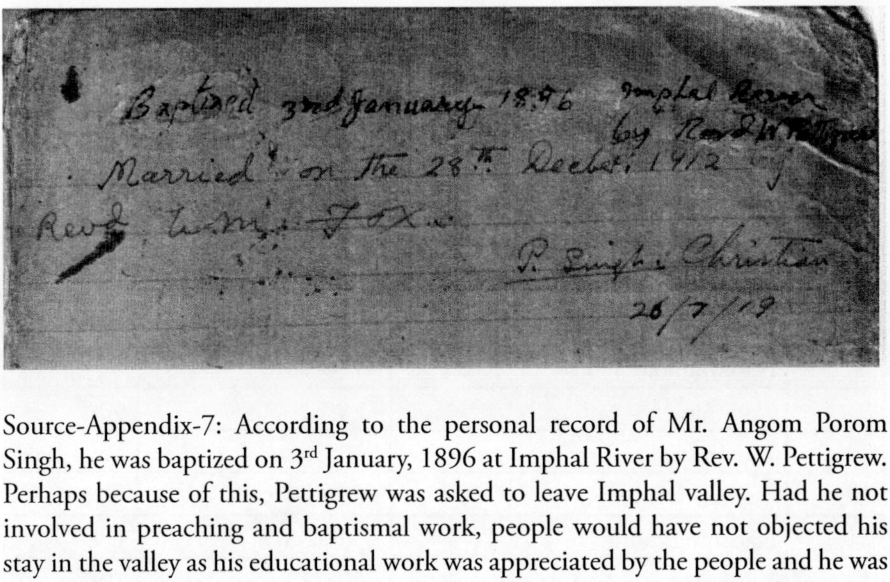
Baptized 3rd January 1896 Imphal River by Revd W. Pettigrew
Married on the 28th Decbr. 1912 by Revd W. M. Fox.
P. Singh Christian
26/7/19

Source-Appendix-7: According to the personal record of Mr. Angom Porom Singh, he was baptized on 3rd January, 1896 at Imphal River by Rev. W. Pettigrew. Perhaps because of this, Pettigrew was asked to leave Imphal valley. Had he not involved in preaching and baptismal work, people would have not objected his stay in the valley as his educational work was appreciated by the people and he was a well-liked teacher. Therefore, many Christians particularly among the Meiteis believe that Mr. Porom Singh must have been the first person baptized by William Pettigrew in Manipur.

Moses Singh, Former Mission and Evangelism Secretary, MBA, letter to the author, 24 March 2011. Moses Singh is a grandson of Mr. Angom Porom Singh.

Appendix – 1
(- of Chapter-3)

Kings of Manipur

Sl. No.	Names	Period of reign A.D.	Number of years
1.	Nongda Lairen Pakhangba	33-154	121
2.	Khuiyoi Tompok	154-264	110
3.	Taothingmang	264-364	100
4.	Khui Ningonba	364-379	15
5.	Pengsiba	379-394	15
6.	Kaokhangba	394-411	17
7.	Naokhamba	411-428	17
8.	Naophangba	428-518	90
9.	Sameirang	518-568	50
10.	Urakonthouba	568-658	90
11.	Naothingkhong	663-763	100
12.	Khongtekcha	763-773	10
13.	Keirencha	784-799	15
14.	Yaraba	799-821	22
15,	Ayangba	821-910	89
16.	Ningthoucheng	910-949	39
17.	Chenglie-Ipan-Lanthaba	949-969	20
18.	Keiphaba Yanglon	969-984	15
19.	Irengba	984-1074	90
20.	Loiumba	1074-1112	48

Sl. No.	Names	Period of reign A.D.	Number of years
21.	Loitongba	1122-1150	28
22.	Atom Yoiremba	1150-1163	13
23.	Iyanthaba	1163-1195	32
24.	Thayanthaba	1195-1231	36
25.	Chingthang Lanthaba	1231-1242	11
26.	Thingbai Shelhongba	1242-1247	5
27.	Puranthaba	1247-1263	16
28.	Khumomba	1263-1278	15
29.	Moiramba	1278-1302	24
30.	Thangbi Lanthaba	1302-1324	22
31.	Kongyamba	1324-1335	11
32.	Telheiba	1335-1355	20
33.	Tonaba	1355-1359	4
34.	Tabungba	1339-1394	35
35.	Lairenba	1394-1399	5
36.	Punsiba	1404-1432	28
37.	Ningthoukhomba	1432-1467	35
38.	Kiyamba	1467-1508	41
39.	Koiremba	1508-1512	4
40.	Lamkhyamba	1512-1523	11
41.	Nonginphaba	1523-1524	1
42.	Kabomba	1524-1542	18
43.	Tangjamba	1542-1545	3
44.	Chalamba	1545-1562	17
45.	Mugyamba	1562-1597	35
46.	Khagemba	1597-1652	55
47.	Khunjaoba	1652-1666	14
48.	Paikhomba	1666-1697	31
49.	Charairongba	1697-1709	12
50.	Garibniwaj	1709-1748	39
51.	Chitshai	1748-1752	4
52.	Bharatsai	1752-1753	1

Sl. No.	Names	Period of reign A.D.	Number of years
53.	Maramba	1753-1759	6
54.	Chingthangkhomba (Bhagychandra)	1759-1762	3
55.	Maramba	1762-1763	1
56.	Chingthangkhomba	1763-1798	35
57.	Labanyachandra	1798-1801	3
58.	Madhuchandra	1801-1803	2
59.	Chourjit	1803-1813	10
60.	Marjit	1813-1819	6
61.	Takuningthou (Herachandra)	1819	1
62.	Yumjaotaba	1820	1
63.	Gambhir Singh	1821	6 months
64.	Jai Singh	1822	1
65.	Jadu Singh (Nongpok Chinslenkhomba)	1823	1
66.	Raghab Singh	1823-1824	1
67.	Nongchup Lamgaingamba (Bhadrasing)	1824	1
68.	Gambhir Singh (Chinglen Nongdrenkhomba)	1825-1834	9
69.	Chandrakirti (Ningthempishak)	1834-1844	10
70.	Nara Singh	1844-1850	6
71.	Debendra Singh	1850-	3 months
72.	Chandrakirti (K.C.S.I.)	1850-1886	36
73.	Shurchandra	1886-1890	4
74.	Kulachandra	1890-1891	1
75.	Churachand Singh	1891-1941	50
76.	Bodhchandra Singh	1941-1955	14

Appendix – 2

(- of Chapter-3)

The Vishnu Temple at Bishnupur, Manipur was built during the reign of King Kiyamba (1467-1508 A.D.)

The original name of Bishnupur was Lumlangdong (now Lamangdong). History recorded the facts of its origin. As soon as Kiyamba ascended throne of Manipur in 1467 A.D, he conquered Kiyang, which was a Shan kingdom in the Kabow Valley. Then he assumed the name of Kiyamba which means the conqueror of Kiyang. There always had been a good relation between the Pongs and the Meities. During the reign of Kiyamba there was a good relation between Kiyamba and the Pong King Khe-Khomba. In fact it was the good foreign policy of King Kiyamba that he was able to have a good relation with the neighbouring countries.

King Kiyamba built Vishnu temple, a temple of brick at Bishnupur which has now become a protected historical monument under the Ministry of H.R.D (Archeology), Government of India. It is now standing as a symbol of the remains of ancient times. And the statue got by Kiyamba from the Pong king is very important since it gives us the idea of the religious beliefs of those days and the very name that it had given.

Source-Appendix-2: "Bishnupur: The Land of the Dancing Deer," http://bishnupur.-nic.in/history.htm. (21 Feb 2013).

Appendix – 3
(- of Chapter-3)

Puya Meithaba Observed

IMPHAL, Oct 25: Rally of local priests, traditional martial arts artistes, exhortation speeches and observing two minutes silence marked the Puya Meithaba (burning of Puya) observance held today at Gandhi Memorial (GM) Hall.

Even though the main observance programme was held at GM Hall, the rally proceeded to Kangla where events that led to burning of ancient chronicles were re-enacted in front of the Kangla Uttra. The observance is organized for the past many years in remembrance of a particular event called, "Puya Meithaba" which took place in the year 1732 on the 17th day of Mera (September-October) in the Meitei calendar.

It is said that due to the influence of a Bengali scholar namely Shantidasa Gosai, king Garibniwaj (Pamheiba), ruler of the then Independent Manipur (known as Kangleipak) ordered consigning of the Puya into flame. Puya is regarded by the Meiteis as a sacred and important compilation of historical events, tradition, culture and most importantly principle of human kind. Therefore, burning of such crucial book is being assumed as one of the darkest chapters in the history of Manipur.

Today's observance organized by All Clubs Organization and Meira Paibi Lup, Kangleipak was led by titular king Leishemba Sanajaoba with a number of scholars, cultural troupes of various communities and eminent personalities taking part in it. Martial artistes displayed indigenous martial arts while the priests performed rituals invoking blessing of the almighty.

The participants then returned to GM Hall where various speakers were unanimous in stating that burning of the Puya is the chief factor for present day Manipur unable to make significant progress towards socio-economic and political emancipation. They were of the opinion that destruction caused to the ancient chronicle at the behest of the Bengali scholar was part of a larger agenda of religious warfare.

Source-Appendix-3: "Puya Meithaba Observed," The Sangai Express (Imphal), 26 October 2010.

Burning of Puya Commemorated as Black Day by ACOAM

IMPHAL, Oct 25: The burning of Puya (ancient Manipuri texts) in front of Kangla Uttra by the then King Pamheiba at the behest of Hindu missionary leader Shantidasa Gosai on the 17th day of Manipuri month of Mera in the year 1732 was observed today as the Puwarigi Amamba Numit (black day) by All Clubs, Organizations, Associations and Meira Paibi Lup (ACOAM)-Lup, Kangleipak, at GM Hall, Imphal.

The observance function was graced by the titular King of Manipur, Leishemba Sanajaoba as the chief guest and Indrakumar Ningomba, president of ACOAM Lup, as the president. Speaking at the occasion, Leishemba Sanajaoba said that the state of Manipur has been disintegrated ever since the burning of Puya that took place in 1732. The Manipuris have almost lost their way in this new world. The Seven Years' Devastation, British colonialism, merger with the Indian Union and disunity between hill and valley people are some of the bad consequences of burning of Puya, he noted. He further stated that the Puya was not just a text on the religion or culture of Manipuri society but it was a valuable text based on the universal truths. The true identity of Manipuris lies in the valuable words of Puya and hence the present generation should render utmost help and support to unearth the lost relics of the state such as Puya which would serve as the guiding light to many people, Sanajaoba enjoined. The titular king also appealed to the people of Manipur to have unity and fraternity amongst themselves for a peaceful and progressive society.

The secretary of ACOAM Lup, Indrajit Tourangbam stated that the burning of Puya has been observed as a black day in the history of Manipur as the loss of such valuable ancient text has made the people of Manipur timid and cowardly. The people of Manipur seem to have lost their true identity after the burning of Puya, he added. N. Birchandra said that the burning of Puya by the then king Pamheiba for the sake of preaching Hinduism in Manipur had almost destroyed the whole social setup of Manipuri society. The people should try to find out the lost text of Puya for the welfare of the Manipuri people, he appealed.

The observance was also attended by the leaders of various social organizations of the state including IPSA, NIPCO, FREINDS, KSA, Kangleichal and others. The Western Art, Social and Cultural Progressive Association (WASCPA), New Cachar Road, also observed the Puya Meithaba Numit at the auditorium of Science Museum, Takyelpat, with MLA Sapam Kunjakeshwar as the chief guest. The 278th year celebration in memory of "Puya Meithaba." was also held at the office of "The NE Sports & Arts", New Delhi with Ksh Raghumani Singh, chairman, Sangai Educational Society, Th. Somorendro, publisher and joint editor, The NE Sports & Arts, and social worker Loitongbam Rajesh Singh as the chief guest, president and guest of honour respectively.

Source-Appendix-3: "Burning of Puya Commemorated as Black Day by ACOAM," Imphal Free Press, 26 October 2010.

Puya Destruction Remembered on Black Day

IMPHAL, Jan 18: As in the previous years, the Meitei National Front (MNF) observed today as 'Black Day'. The function held in commemoration of the day on which puyas were consigned to flames in front of Kangla Uttra was attended by a number of people belonging to different indigenous groups. After taking out a public procession from Hapta Kangjeibung till Kangjeibung and again returning to the starting point, cultural dances of different ethnic groups were presented besides holding a meeting.

Giving the key-note address, MNF vice-president Thokchom Wangamba Meitei noted that the unfortunate event of burning puyas pulled apart different ethnic groups and sowed seeds of distrust among them. Former Minister RV Mingthing said that the day of burning puyas was the day when all people were hurt deeply. Observing that puyas were the guide of this land, he lamented that Manipuris since then have become a Nation without any guide. He also called upon all to make up this deficiency. During the observance, the Maichou Ningshing Mana was conferred on Naoriya Amusana. The Chingmi Tammi Nungshi Khudol Mana was awarded to Lhouvum Shatkho.

Today's observance was graced by titular king Sanajaoba as chief guest. Other presidium members were Ch Wangambi Leima of MNF, former Minister RV Mingthing, former IGP Abdul Rehman, Motbung Village Authority advisor L Lhouvum Shatkho, Khongbal Khamenlok Area Development Committee president L Katui, Naoriya Amusana of Hailakandi Laishram Khul, Assam, MNF advisor Moirangthem Naodalenkhomba, Kangla Fort Board member Sairem Nilbir, MNF advisor Tokpam Thawailemba, Deputy Director of Manipur State Archives Dr K Sushila, president of the United Manipuri Muslim Women Development Organization Anwari Nurjahan, Maram Centre chief K Tarumba, former chief of Icham Kom Keirap Luthatsomy Kom, chief of Purumchumbam Chothe Kom Y Maipakchao Chothe, advisor of the Moreh Meitei Lai Thougal Kanglup Yensenbam Toungamba, headman of Sadhu Koireng Ngirel Koireng, Purum Likli chief Renalchomy Purum, social worker Sathang Haokip from Churachandpur, Henboi Misao of Women and Child Development, former chief of Thangal Surung K Abung Thangal, Longa Koireng chief S Sothel Koireng, Oriental College lecturer Dr TB, script writer Chana Lukhoi , president of Malem Leishemkol Kangla TM Rajen Ayangba and advisor of Umang LaiThougal Lup Jiri Lairembi Leikai Hamom Dhani Meitei.

Source-Appendix-3: "Puya Destruction Remembered on Black Day," The Sangai Express (Imphal), 19 January 2009.

Puya Meithaba Date Fixed

Imphal, Oct 8: A seminar held at Kangla Hall here today resolved that it was on Sunday, the 17th day of Mera in 1732 that the Manipuri puyas have been destroyed by setting on fire in front of Kangla Uttra by religious missionary Shantidasa Gossai and then king of Manipur Pamheiba. Organized under the aegis of ACOAM-Lup Kangleipak, the seminar held with the main objective of determining the exact date of destroying the Manipuri puyas further resolved that 17th day of Mera would be observed as Puya Meithaba Numit (burning of puyas) every year.

Source-Appendix-3: "Puya Meithaba date fixed," The Sangai Express (Imphal), 9 October 2008.

Appendix – 4
(- of Chapter-3)

Burmese (Ava) Wars

There were a number of significant wars during this era between the Meiteis, the Burmese. Meidingu Marjit (1813–1819) with the help of Ava invaded Kangleipak (Manipur) in 1813 and defeated his brother-Chaurajit. He then ascended the throne in 1813 and ruled for six years.

Chahi Taret Khuntakpa, the Seven Years Devastation (1819–26)

Meitrabak (Manipur) had never before faced such a national catastrophe brought about by the Burmese conquest. The new ava king, Bagidaw, invited Marjit to attend his coronation ceremony and to pay homage to him. Marjit refused to attend the coronation, which offended the Burmese king. The Burmese king sent a large force under the command of General Maha Bandula to humble Marjit. Marjit was defeated and he fled to Cachar. Thus, Meitrabak was brought under the Ava rule for Seven Years (1819–1826) which is known as Chahi Taret Kuntakpa in the history of Meitrabak. The flight of Marjit from Meitrabak and Ava conquest in 1819 marks the end of mediaeval period in the history of Meitrabak.

Meitrabak Princes in Cachar

In the early nineteenth century, the Meitrabak princes after being dislodged from Meitrabak made Cachar a springboard for the reconquest of Meitrabak. In 1819, three brothers occupied Cachar and drove out Govind Chandra to Sylhet. The kingdom of Cachar which was divided between Govinda Chandra and Chaurajit in 1818, was repartitioned after the flight of Govind Chandra among the three Meitrabak princes. Chaurajit got the eastern portion of Cachar bordering Meitrabak which was ruled from Sonai. Gambhir Singh was given the land west of Tillain hill and his headquarters was at Gumrah, Marjit Singh ruled Hailakandi from Jhapirbond.

Meidingngu Gambhir Singh (1826–1834)

With the strong 500 Meitei Levy and with the help of British East India Company, Gambhir Singh expelled the Ava / Burmese from Meitrabak beyond the Ningthi Turel (Chindwin River). He ruled the country from Langthabal Capital. He died on 9 January 1834 and was succeeded by his infant son Chandrakirti / Ningthem Pishak (1834–1844).

Source-Appedndix-4: "History of Manipur," http://www.answers.com/topic/history-of-manipur#Anglo-Burmese_Advents (21 Feb 2013).

Appendix – 5
(- of Chapter-3)

The Umang Lai

The term "Umang Lai" is used generally to cover all the categories of Manipuri gods, although it has a narrower meaning when it applied specifically with sacred groves. Etymologically the term Umang Lai means Forest or Wood deity (Umang=forest, Lai=god), but in many cases deities termed Umang Lai's have no connection with trees whatsoever. Umang Lais can be classified broadly into four categories:

1) **Ancestral Gods:** Ancestors or Gods that were believed to have had a human existence at past. Examples are Pakhangba, Nompok Panthoibi etc.
2) **Gods associated with Salai:** Gods associated with particular Salai (clan). For example, Thangjing is the god of the Moirangs, Okmaren as for the Khumans etc.
3) **Domestic Deities:** The Yumjai Lai's or clan gods associated with particular clan or family groups (Sagei). Traditionally there are 445 Sagei's, each of which has its own Lai's. Household deities like Sanamahi, Leimaren and Phungga falls into this category.
4) **Tutelary Deities:** Guardian spirit connected with particular place or areas. For example, Marjing is the guardian of North-East.

Source-Appendix-4: Khomdon Singh Lisam, Encyclopaedia of Manipur, vol. 3 (Delhi: Kalpaz Publications, 2011), 335-37.

Appendix – 6
(- of Chapter-3)

Meitei Alphabet

As a part of the revival movement, since the early 1980s the Meitei scripts have been taught in schools in Manipur.

Notable features: This is a syllabic alphabet in which consonants all have an inherent vowel /a/.Other vowels are written as independent letters, or by using a variety of diacritical marks which are written above, below, before or after the consonant they belong to.

Each letter is named after a part of the human body. Meiteilon is one of the official languages of the Indian state of Manipur in north-east India and has about 1.6 million speakers. It is a member of the Tibeto-Burman branch of the Sino-Tibetan language family and is also spoken in Bangladesh and Myanmar.

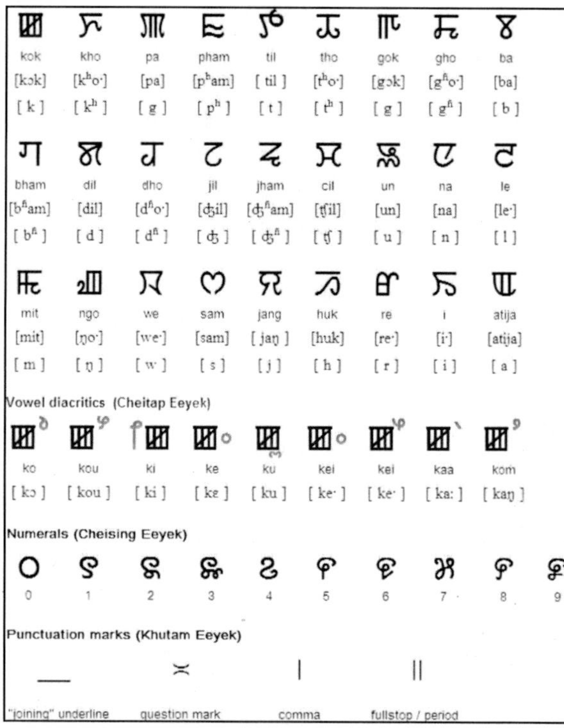

Source-Appendix-6: "Manipuri Alphabet," http://www.omniglot.com/writing/manipuri.ht-m (21 Feb 2013).

Appendix – 1
(- of Chapter-4)

Origin of the Meiteis

R. Boileau Pemberton traced the origin of the Meiteis to the great Tatars—rejecting the Hindu origin claimed by the Hindunized Meiteis of the present day, it may safely conclude them to be descendants of a Tatar colony, which probably emigrated from the north-west borders of China during the sanguinary conflicts of supremacy, which took place between the different members of the Chinese and Tatar dynasties, in the 13th and 14th centuries; at which time, there was an extensive kingdom called Pong, occupying the country between the frontiers of Yunan, and the hills separating the Kubo valley from Manipur (Report on the Eastern Frontier of British India, 1835). Eminent Manipuri historians Professor Gangmumei Kabui and Pandit Ningthoukhongjam Khelchandra endorse the view that the Pongs (Shans with their capital at Mogaung) entered Manipur in 698 A. D. (cf. Cheitharol Kumbaba, the Manipuri Royal Chronicle). Pandit N. Khelchandra suspects that 'Khunlai', the younger brother of Khunlung, the first Pong king might have been a Meitei. It is widely accepted that Shamlung, the younger brother of king Sukanpha settled in Meiteileipak for ten years; the evidence of Shamlung's arrival are indicated by names of places, fruits which bear the name of 'Pong' even today.

A reputed Meitei archaeologist, Okram Kumar Singh, comments on the migration of the South East Asians: it seems highly probable that a group of people from the regions of South China equipped with fully ground and polished stone tools and corded tripod wares entered into Manipur following the courses of Irrawady river and its tributaries' (Archaeology in Manipur, Series-I, Napachik: A Stone Age Site in the Manipur Valley, 1983). Sunitikumar Chatterjee also noted that from 2,000 B.C. onwards, Sino-Tibetan speakers from China pushed South and West and infiltrated into India. A Meitei school floats a proposition that a particular Meitei era had been evolved one and half millennia before the Christian era. A Meitei historian W. Ibohal Singh observes 'Reference is made that counting of age by era system started by Mariya Phambalcha (Maliya Fambalcha) from 1396 B.C" (On fixing date of Cheiraoba, 1980). Although, the Meitei era, 'Mariya Phambalcha' has not yet been accorded public or official recognition, it points towards the remote antiquity of the Manipuri civilization.

The Thai school of Meitei origin is increasingly drawing adequate attention, although the early Meitei Kingdom was several centuries older than Siam or the present day Thailand, founded in the 13th century by Rama Khamheng. It was possible that the Thai population movement which started in the pre-Christian era had reached Manipur before the Thai branches scattered in many places like Laos, Cambodia, Central Burma or other parts of the South East Asia. The trade route also operated between the West and China via Manipur. John F. Cady points out, 'A well-defined overland trade route to India via the Mekong, Salween and Irrawady river gorges was opened in 120 A.D.' (South East Asia: Its historical development, 1964). Centuries before the destruction of Nan Chao in 1253 A.D. by Mongols and subsequently after the destruction, the Thais moved and migrated towards the south following Irrawady, Chindwin and then to Assam (See D.J.M. Tate, the Making of Modern South East Asia, Vol. I, 1977). John Cady writes that following the destruction of Nan Chao, the Thais moved towards south in 700 A.D. and the Pyu capital, Halingyi fell to the Nan Chao Shans in 850 A.D. Nan Chao, the original homeland of the Thais (Shans) in China started disintegration following the Christian era. It was possible that the first wave or subsequent Nan Chao waves could have joined the trade route so as to eventually reach the Manipuri land. This wave could have even constituted one of the seven principalities or merged with the Manipuri autochthones thereby creating a new primitive ethnos.

The Thai proposition is strengthened by the evidence of the population movement of the Mon and Thai peoples to the South-Western side of Burma which merges with the present Shan belt of Burma (E.H.G. Dobby, South East Asia, pp. 191-95). By strange coincidence, some of the places or rivers in Southern Indo-China bear names very similar to the Meitei names; further investigations may reveal the etymological riddle. Dobby refers to 'Myittha' route. Etymologically, 'Myittha' and even 'Man-Thai' are very close to the word 'Meitei', which is pronounced very often by the foreigners as 'Meethei' or 'Maithai'. Charles A. Fisher refers to 'Myittha' river in this note: 'One important new mining development remains to be mentioned, namely that of the Sub-bituminous coal deposits at Kalewa, near the confluence of the Chindwin and Myittha rivers, some 500 miles from Rangoon'. The names like 'Luwang', 'Kha' which is the Laotian equivalent of one million Mois in Indo-China, 'Mon', 'Thai' and 'Myittha' bear close resemblance to the names of early principalities of Manipur.

Source—Appendix-1: Naorem Sanajaoba, "From the Cradle of Pithecanthropus," in *Manipur: Past and Present,* vol. I., edited by Naorem Sanajaoba (Delhi: Mittal Publications, 1988), i-ii.

Appendix – 2
(- of Chapter-4)

365 *Umang lais* are:

1. Moirang Thangjing
2. Heingang Marjing
3. Sugnu Wangbrel
4. Awang Sekmai Koubru
5. Yaiskul Nongsaba
6. Sugnu Lokningthou
7. Sugnu Sanamahi
8. Thanga Chingningthou
9. Koirengei Pakhangba
10. Maibam Lokpaching Loyarakpa
11. Top Chingtha Lanamung
12. Yairipok Nongpok Panthoibi
13. Kodompokpi Sorarel
14. Yurembam Unam Sorarel
15. Yambem Yairi Ningthou
16. Tairenpokpi Koubru
17. Phaknung Chingkhei Guru
18. Awang Yumnam KhUnou Puthiba
19. Khurai Puthiba
20. Wangu Wangbrel
21. Ningel Nongpok Ningthou
22. Chandrakhong Yenkhurakpa
23. Andro Panam Ningthou
24. Andro Pureiromba
25. Tangjeng Lokningthou
26. Nungu Lokningthou
27. Phayeng Koubru

28. Nachou Sorarel
29. Kha-Potsangbam Pungaba
30. Ningthoukhong Oknarel
31. Eething Thangjing
32. Oinam Nongsaba
33. Haobijam Chairel-Iakpa
34. Laishram Eereima
35. Moirangthem Thangjillg
36. Tongbram Lairema
37. Salam Sorarel, Sanahal
38. Heisnam Chingningthou
39. Ngangkha Lawai Thangjing
40. Maibam Tampak Lainingthou
41. l.aisangbam Nongsaba
42. Philem Khoriphaba
43. l.aiphrakpam Khana-chaoba
44. Khoyangbam Ayangleima
45. Phairelbam Loklaoleima
46. Ahanthem Sanamahi
47. Mairembam Leikoi Ningthou
48. Khuman Maharaba
49. Hemam Pakhangba
50. Konjengbam Sorarel
51. Kiyam Vi Ningthou
52. Thong-ngam Thongnang Ninghtou
53. Kum-phi San-thong Nongthou
54. Sagang Santhong Ningthou
55. Kodompokpi Khoriphaba
56. Patsoi Khunjao Pakhangba
57. Pat-soi Khunou Nong..;ka-bi
58. Sa-chep Ching-Khoi Puri-Pu-ra-ba
59. U-khong-sang Nongpok
60. U-yal A-rong-Ning-thou
61. Khoirom Nongpok Ningthou
62. Khaman Pakhangba
63. Oinam Tang-Iei-ha-da-Ee-rei-ma
64. Oinam Laipham Eereima
65. Oinam Thingel Eereima
66. Lamdeng Laikhurembi
67. Lambal Koubru
68. Changangei Khuromba
69. Sorokhaibam Phou-oi-bi

70. Wangkhei Laishram Fereima
71. Wangjing Ningthou
72. Lairen Sajik Koubru
73. Tentha Eekop Ningthou
74. Thoudam Eerong Leima
75. Khurai Konsam Leikai Ching-jroi-bi
76. Lamsang Eesing Chaiba
77. Utlou Panthoibi
78. Kiyam-kei Pakhangba
79. Ching-nga Makha Soram Yumjao Lairem-ma
80. Malom Khun-jaoba
81. Thoubal Sabal Tongba Thouban Ningthou
82. Haoga Sorarel
83. Kontha Marjing
84. Phumlou Keiroi Koubru
85. Phumlou Siphai Koubru
86. Hao-reibi Pakhangba
87. Sarangthem Lairemma
88. Leisangthem Lairemma
89. Heikrujam Loiyarakpa
90. Leimapokpam Siphai Thangjing
91. Leimapokpam Khunpham Sebu Leima
92. Aa-ra-pati Pureiromba
93. Awang Potsangbam Koubru
94. Angom Yumjao Leima
95. Langpok Ningthou
96. Kangabam Yumjao Leima
97. Potsangbam Thou-ri-phi Koubru
98. Keisampat Yumjao Leima
99. Taobungkhok Loi-ya-rak-pa
100. Pishum Huidrom Yumjao Leima
101. Kairang Marjing
102. Loitang Khunou Koubru
103. Haorang Sabal Koubru
104. Haorang Keirel Koubru
105. Moitangpok Korouhanba
106. Lamlai Pureiromba
107. Yurem-bam Huidon Pokpi
108. Wangoi Sanamahi
109. Wangoi Wangbrel
110. Patsoi Taomang Naothingkhong
111. Patsoi Nongabi

112. Chinga Makha Eerom Yumjao Leima
113. San-jen-bam Koubru
114. Lamangdong Yangoi Ningthou
115. Kwa-si-phai Pakhangba
116. Thiyam Konjin Phunan Ningthou
117. Kakching Khullen Khamlangba
118. Kakching Khullen Naohal
119. Kakching Khullen Eerum Ningthou
120. Kakching Khullen Sekmai Ninghtou
121. Kakching Khoriphaba
122. Wairi Khamlangba
123. A-ra-pati Eereima
124. Eerengpal Eerum Ningthou
125. Paonam Eeshing Chaiba
126. Thoubal Yangoi Ningthou
127. Kanga-mung Khujoi Loi-ya-rakpa
128. Ngairangbam Loiyarakpa
129. Waithou Puthiba
130. Khundrakpam Marjing
131. Tmgri Marjing
132. Sapam Salai Khongjom Ningthou
133. Shalungpham Eekop Ningthou
134. Thoubal Nong-gang-khong Thoubal Ningthou
135. Ke-kru Nongpok Panthoibi
136. Chabung Company Wangbrel
137. Eeram Siphai Nga-ngou;-rakpa
138. Mutum Phi-phou Eerong Leima
139. Kakwa Naorem Panthoibi
140. Iroisemba Thongamacha
141. Naran Konjin Koubru
142. Mayang Imphal Khuman Pqkpa
143. Lairenjam Lairem-ma
144. Thangbi-jrou Thangba
145. Meitram Shebu Leima
146. Shagol Tongba Pakhangba
147. Keinou Khul-leima
148. Thongam Mon-dum Khul-leima
149. Sa-mram Khong-jom Ningthou
150. Lourembam Lai-rem-ma
151. Konjengbam Lai-rem-ma
152. Top Langmai Leima
153. Thongam Punganba

154. Tharoijam Yumjao Leima
155. Uripok Yurembam Huidom Pokpi
156. Elangbam Pang-ganba
157. Mayang Yao-reibi
158. Mayang Langjing Mamang Koubru
159. Mayang Langjing Maning Koubru
160. Lang-mei-thet Panthoibi
161. Khumbong Panthoibi
162. Awang-Khunou Koubru
163. Phoi-jing Chaning Leima
164. Taothong Koubru
165. Uripok Khamlangba
166. Akham Khamlangba
167. Uripok Lai-Khu-rembi
168. Elangbam Khangpokpi Pungamba
169. Luker Khoimom Lairemma
170. Lamboikhul Eereima
171. Gobindagram Puthiba
172. Khonghampat Luwangpokpa
173. Khonghampat Koubru
174. Pamam Khul Loyarakpa
175. Ngariyanbam Koubru
176. Nambol Khoriphaba
177. Phougakchao Phou-oi-bi
178. Kha Thounaojam Panthoibi
179. Uchek-kol Moriba
180. Nambol Konkham Loiyarakpa
181. Khundrakpam Pang-ganba .
182. Meinam Lairem-'ma
183. Achanbigei Marjing
184. Kang-nga-mung Maisnam Loiyarakpa
185. Keirao Langdum Keirao Lakpa
186. Wahengbam Yumjao Leima
187. Tekcham Eekop Ningthou
188. Langmeidomg Pakhangba
189. Eengourok Nongpok Ningthou
190. Heinoupok Loiyarakpa
191. Chinga Makha Meisnam Luwangpokpa
192. Pukhao Ahallup Eereima
193. Khurai Lai Awangba
194. Wangbal Eekop Ningthou
195. Hiyangthang Lairemma

196. Huirem Chingbal Leima
197. Naharup Pureiromba
198. Pungdongbam Panthoibi
199. Nung-goi Puthiba
200. Sagolband Pakhangba
201. Lamding Wangjing Ningthou
202. Chingtham Khongjom Ningthou
203. Ningthoukhong Thang-narel
204. Yumnam Yumjao Lairembi
205. Sagolmang Eeteima
206. Patpal Eerum Ningthou
207. Ning-ngu Laimanai
208. Charangpat Mamang Arong Ningthou
209. Khangabok Eekop Ningthou
210. Peng-gi Arong Ningthou
211. Moirang Punshi Lairemma
212. Pourabi Puthiba
213. Khwai Lainingthouhanba
214. Loktonbam Arai Leima
215. Nakalbam Chingol Ningthou
216. Khurai Mamang Yangoi Ningthou
217. Khurai Angouba
218. Khurai Puthiba
219. Soubol Lairemma
220. Top Langmai Leima
221. Sekta Laiyingthou Achengba
222. Khangkhui
223. Khurai Ningthem Pokpa
224. Angom Pokpa (Leithong)
225. Atom Khuman Pakhangba Ningthou Pokpa
226. Lamdeng Thurnkhong Lairemma
227. Lamdeng Poireiton Laikhurembi Leima Leinaotabi
228. Luwang Guru Sangol
229. Khagi Maibi Yumpham
230. Thinungei Loyarakpa
231. Thinungei Ramji Ningthou
232. Eethai Phou-oi-bi
233. Thangtek Yangoi Ningthou
234. Ngairangbam Khunou Loiyarakpa
235. Kha Yumnam Khunou Loiyarakpa
236. Khurai Soubon Lairemma
237. Uchekon Panthoibi

238. Konthoujam Lairemma
239. Takhel Nongpok Ningthou
240. Pukhao Laipham Ireima
241. Khongjom Ningthou
242. Ahallup Marjing
243. Thongak Lairemma Langol
244. Irengbam Khoriphaba
245. Langol Kameng Koubru
246. Kongpal Langmai Leima
247. Wakharakpa
248. Pangei Marjing
249. Lamabam Irongleima
250. Keirao Lakpa
251. Khekman Wangbren
252. Khekman Pakhangba
253. Khekman Leikairakpa
254. Wangkheirakpa Yumjao Lairemma
255. Shagolmang Ireima
256. Meinam Lairemma
257. Langmeidong Pakhangba
258. Elangbam Pang-ganba
259. Meijrao Lakpa
260. Lairenjam Lairemma
261. K yamgei Khagemba
262. Kyamgei Mungyamba Pakhangba
263. Salungpham Nongpok Ningthou
264. Kabowakching Loyarakpa
265. Ningthoubung Puraba
266. Kangamung Siphai Loiyalakpa
267. Pangal Siphai Nungthel-Ieima
268. Hiyanglam Panganba
269. Phouden Pakhangba
270. Phouden Nongpok Ningthou
271. Heinoukhongnembi Laishram Lairemma
272. Nongchup Sanjenbam Koubru
273. Shamuroulakpa
274. Shamuroulakpa Khwai Ningthou
275. Shamuroulakpa Leitang Ningthou
276. Morok Ingkhol Koubru
277. Keinou Ahongshangbam Lairemma
278. Keinou Thongthak Koubru
279. Ngaikhong Yangoi Ningthou

280. Karam Nongsaba
281. Waheng Khumal Pakhangba
282. Shagoltongba Suraisam Khagemba
283. Soubam Mawao Leima
284. Khaidem Nganuleima
285. Maibakhul Marjing
286. Maklang Nungthil Leima
287. Heiyen Ikop Ningthou
288. Hangun Kalikha
289. Tera Khunou Ikop Ningthou
290. Tentha Khunou Ikop Ningthou
291. Sinam Kom Lainingthou
292. Kabo Wakching Nongabi
293. Keibi Ireima
294. Langol Ningthou
295. Tarung Leima
296. Phubala Pakhangba
297. Pechi Arong Ningthou Ikop Ningthou
298. Thangmeiband Kangabam Naothingkhong
299. Khurai Lai Khurembi
300. Charangpat Mayai Nongpok
301. Laphupat Kalika
302. Thanmapokpi Thangjing
303. Sairem Khul Koubm
304. Khabi Lairembi
305. Waroi Ching Malang Humoiba
306. Yaingang Pokpi Haoreima Sambubi
307. Nongpok Kameng Khamlangba
308. Kakmayai Panthoibi
309. Thongam Mondum Nungang Maharaba
310. Kwarokching Tarang Saraba
311. Ningol Phou-oi-bi Lokchao Thanungba
312. Chandrakhong Nongpok, Sawang Lal-lam Phoriba
313. Koirengei Pakhangba Khuman Pokpa
314. Kongmam Konglouton Loukhiba
315. Koubm Inammung, Chandeba, Khongdeba
316. Kaodmkna Koubm
317. Khurkhul Ichum Lairemma
318. Sekmai Wangbren
319. Phayeng Sawang Soraren
320. Leimram Koubm
321. Thongjao Mayangamba

322. Nung Santhong, Pan Santhong Nung-Yungbi
323. Chothe Thangwai Pakhangba
324. Ngakchou Pokpi Yangoi Ningthou
325. Ishok Chingphu Ningthou
326. Kha Loulembam Panthoibi
327. Thiyam Laikon Pakhangba
328. Sansenbam Panthoibi
329. Pukhrambam Panthoibi
330. Thounaojam Panthoibi
331. Awang Jiri Kabok-Khong Lairemma
332. Kha Potsangbam Panganba
333. Naorem Panthoibi
334. Pombikhok Louningthou
335. Kondong Lairemma
336. Chairen Khunbu Leima Khunmabi Panthoibi Tangkhul Huithok Pakhangba.
337. Nongmaijing Noingpok Apanba Khalongnachingba Laipham
338. Kanto Khullel Koubru

Source—Appendix-2: Kh. Ratan Kumar, *Lai Haraoba of Manipur: Indigenous Festival of the Meitei: A Socio-Historical Perspective* (Imphal: Smt. Ph. Pratima Devi, 2001), 52-62

Appendix – 1

(- of Chapter-5)

TREATY OF YANDABOO
February 24, 1826

Article No. 1.

There shall be perpetual peace and friendship between the Honourable Company on the one part of His Majesty the King of Ava of the other.

Article No. 2.

His Majesty the King of Ava renounces all claims upon, and will abstain from all future interferences with the principality of Assam and its dependencies, and also with the contiguous petty States of Cachar and Jyntea.

With regard to Munnipore, it is stipulated that, should Gumbheer Singh desire to return to that country, he shall be recognized by the King of Ava as Rajah thereof. (Signed Archibald Campbell) (L.S.)

Largeen Meonja,
(Woonghee) (Signed) T.C. Robertson
Captain Royal Navy (L.S.)

(Seal of the lotoo) (Signed) Hy. D. Chads
Captain Royal Navy (L.S.).

Shwagum Woon

Atawoon

Source—Appendix-1: "Treaty of Yandaboo, February 24, 1826", http://www.upr-info.org/IMG/pdf/COHR_IND_UPR_S1_2008anx_Annex_X_Treaty_of_Yandaboo_1826.pdf (16 Feb 2013).

Appendix – 2
(- of Chapter-5)

List of the British officers who served as political agents in Manipur

Sl. No.	Tenure	Political Agents
1.	1835-1844	Capt. Gordon
2.	1844-1862	Major W. McCulloch
3.	1862-1863	Dr. Dillon
4.	1863-1867	Major W. McCulloch
5.	1867-1875	Dr. R. Brown
6.	1875-1877	G. H. Damant
7.	1877-1886	Sir James Johnstone
8.	1886 (for six weeks)	Major Trotter
9.	1888-1891	Mr. St. C. Grimwood
10.	27th April—30th Nov., 1891	Major H. St. P. Maxwell
11.	1st Dec.,1891-1893	Lt. Col. H. St. P. Maxwell
12.	1893-1895	A. Porteous
13.	1895-1896	Lt. Col. H. St. P. Maxwell
14.	1896-1898	Capt. H. W. G. Cole
15.	1898-1899	A. Porteous
16.	1899-1902	Lt. Col. H. St. P. Maxwell
17.	1902-1904	Major Alber E. Woods
18.	1904-1905	Lt. Col. H. St. P. Maxwell
19.	1905-1908	Col J. Shakespeare
20.	1908-1909	A. W. Davies
21.	1909-1914	Col. J. Shakespeare

22.	1914-1917	Lt. Co. H. W. G. Cole
23.	1917-1918	J. C. Higgins
24.	1918-1920	W. A. Crosgrave
25.	1920-1922	L. O. Clarke
26.	1922	C. Gimson
27.	1922-1924	L. O. Clarke
28.	1924-1928	J. C. Higgins
29.	March 12-Nov. 29,1928	C. G. Crawford
30.	1928-1933	J. C. Higgins
31.	1933-1946	C. Gimson
32.	1946-1947	G. P. Stewart
33.	1947 (till 15th August)	J. F. Pearson

Source—Appendix–2: Kh. Sarojini Devi, *British Political Agency in Manipur 1835-1947* (Imphal: Linthoi Publications, 2005), 93-94.

Appendix - 3

(- of Chapter-5)

Names of the Native Freedom Fighters

The five patriotic Manipuri who were hanged by the Britishers on the charge of waging war against the Empress are:

1) Jubraj Tikendrajit – hanged on 13th August 1891
2) General Thangal – hanged on 13th August 1891
3) Niranjan Subedar – hanged on 8th June 1891
4) Kajao Singh, Jamandar – hanged on 25th May 1891
5) Chirai Naga of Mayangkh – hanged on 13th October 1891

While Jubraj Tikendrajit and General Thangal above were publicly hanged at Pheida Pung (present B.T. Park), the rest of the freedom fighters were hanged inside the jail.

Beside those five heroes who were hanged many more persons were also accused and punished for waging war against the Empress.

Name of convicts who were transported for life

1) Kullachandra Dhaja Singh, (Ex-Regent)
2) Prince Angao Singh, Senapati
3) Lokendrajit Birjit Singh, Wangkheirakpa
4) Samu Singh Colonel alias Luwang Ningthou
5) Chongtham Nilamani Singh, Ayapurel Major
6) Chongtham Mia Singh, Major
7) Uru Singh, Usurba
8) Chauba Hada, Machahal
9) Ghun Singh, Kongdram
10) Kumba Singh, Laisraba
11) Dhaja Singh, Mayengba
12) Nam Singh, Nepra, Machahal
13) Trilok Singh, Nongtholba Satwal

14) Dhon Singh, Sagolsemba
15) Ghun Singh, Indujamba Jamadar
16) Ningthouba Singh, Chingshuba
17) Thaoba Singh, Phanjao Jamadar
18) Tonjao Singh, Mangsatba Jamadar
19) Chaobatol Singh, Heigrujamba Subadar
20) Paradhumba Singh, alias Ashangba kut
21) Chowkami Naga of Mayangkhang
22) Gowho Naga of Mayangkhang

Source—Appendix – 3: "The Anglo Manipur War 1891 and its Consequences," Manipur State Archive (1990) http://-archivesmanipur.nic.in/whoswho.htm#THE%2-0ANGLO. (16 Feb 2013). cited in. Gangmumei Kabui, "The Anglo-Manipur War of 1891," in *History of Modern Manipur 1826-1949*, 2nd edition, edited by Lal Dena (New Delhi: Orbit Publishers & Distributors, 1991), 68.

Appendix - 4

(- of Chapter-5)

Patriots' Day observed across the State

IMPHAL, Aug 13: Different organizations, NGOs and educational institutes have observed Patriot's Day in separate functions across the State. All Manipur Elementary School Teachers' Association organized the day at Modhu Girls Junior High School. Apunba Poramlen Marup, Manipur, International Modernized Academy, Manipur People's Democratic Front, Social Volunteers Association, Manipur Pradesh Trinamool Congress, Manipur University, All Manipur Recognized Private Schools' Welfare Association, CI College Students' Union, Modern College Students' Union also observed the day. Empowerment of Community for Human Education and Multitude Advancement and Action and Implementation for Development organized a painting competition for children in connection with Patriot's Day celebration. Manipuri Literary Society organized a kavi sammelan in connection with the day. National Identity Protection Committee organized Patriot's Day at Yaingangpokpi. Manipur Pradesh Congress Committee organized the day at Congress Bhavan. All Manipur Students' Union, Imphal East District Committee also observed the day at CC Higher Secondary School. United People's Front Moirang Zonal Council, DM College of Arts Students' Union, All Manipur Tammi Chingmi Apunba Nupi Lup, Singjamei, Lilong United Clubs' Organization, Ereipak Ennat Chanura Loinasillon Imphal Public Higher Secondary School, Kangla Local Association Manipur State Bharat Scouts and Guides, All Manipur Women's Social Reformation and Development Samaj, Lilong Haoreibi College Students' Union, All Mayai Lambi Clubs' Organisation, August Observation Committee, Wangjing-Lamding, Social Amity, Integrity and Prosperity Organization, All Manipur Nupi Marup, Nongchup Imphal Meira Paibee Apunba Lup also observed Patriot's Day. Apunba Meira Paibee Apunba Lup, Hojai also observed the day at Hojai. Nupi Samaj Churachandpur district and Churachandpur United Club Organisation also separately observed the occasion. The Nupi Samaj's observance was held at Praja

Mandop Leikai while that of CUCO was held at Forest Gate Tuibuong. Various social workers, tribal chiefs and prominent figures from various walks of life attended the day's observation respectively.

Source—Appendix-4: "Patriot's Day observed across the State," *Sangai Express* (Imphal), 14 August, 2012, 1.

Appendix - 5

(- of Chapter-5)

Clarion call for wide observation of Patriots` Day on August 13

IMPHAL, August 11: Various organizations including student bodies and political parties have called on for wide observation of the Patriot's Day commemorating the victims of August 13, 1891 Anglo Manipur war. A statement issued by the Democratic Students' Alliance of Manipur (DESAM) has appealed to all sections of the society for mass observation of 'Patriot's Day' and to pay befitting floral tributes to the martyrs who laid down their lives in safeguarding the sovereignty of Manipur and to make the sacrifices more meaningful. The statement further urged the authority concerned to include the grim reminder (Anglo-Manipur war 1891) of the Manipur history in school syllabus of primary to university level to elaborately enlighten the younger generation on the historic event.

The All Manipur Students' Union has informed that altogether 201 schools of the State will observe the Patriot's Day. On the other hand, the Manipur State council-Communist Party of India has also informed that it would observe the Patriot's Day, August 13 at the Irawat Bhawan of Manipur, Imphal. It said the CPI will pay befitting floral tribute at the portrait of the two late leaders Thangal General and Bir Tikendrajit. At the same time, the Manipur Peoples' Party in a statement has informed that it will observe the day at its head office located near the Polo ground. The general secretary of the party in a statement has appealed to various sections of the society to widely observe the day and pay befitting floral tribute to the martyrs who made extreme sacrifices for Manipur.

Source—Appendix-5: "Clarion Call for Wide Observation of Patriots' Day on August 13," *Imphal Free Press* (Imphal) 11August, 2011, 1.

Manipur government observes patriots' day in New Delhi

NEW DELHI, August 13. Manipur government observed the Patriots' Day celebration at the Manipur Tikendrajit House, Bir Tikendrajit Marg, Chanakyapuri here this morning. Three photographs of Paona Brajabasi, Bir Tikendrajit and Thangal General were decorated at the base of the statue of Bir Tikendrajit where a large number of Manipuris from National Capital Region paid their homage to the great patriots of Manipur who fought against the mighty Britishers and sacrificed their lives for the cause of their motherland.

The sitting Lok Sabha member Dr. Thokchom Meinya led the VVIPs and public while paying floral tributes to the great patriots. Two minutes silence was observed as a mark of respect to the departed souls. Manipur Legislative Assembly member from Yaiskul Constituency Elangbam Suraj and former Manipur Chief Minister R. K. Dorendra were among those dignitaries who paid floral tributes to the martyrs.

The 13th August is a red-letter day in the history of Manipur as on this fateful day in 1891, the two great patriots, namely Bir Tikendrajit, the prince of Manipur and General Thangal were hanged in broad daylight by the British in the presence of thousands of men and women at Pheidapung, Imphal Outer Pologround, as these heroes had defended the freedom of Manipur against the British.

Source—Appendix-5: "Manipur Government Observes Patriots' Day in New Delhi," *Manipur Mail* (Imphal), 14 August, 2011, 1.

Bibliography

Primary Sources

"Ireipak Machasingda Pijaba Paojel / Messages Given to the People." *Meitei National Frond (*Feb. 1979): 5-12. (Meiteilon).

Kullachandra, N. *Apokpa Tounirol / Worship Manual of Apokpa*. Imphal: N. Kullachandra, 1937. (Meiteilon).

Kumar, Thiyam. *Manipurgi Christian Lamyanba / The Christian Pioneer of Manipur*. Khurai Lamlong: MBA, 2008. (Meiteilon).

____________. *Meitei Baptist Association.* Wabagai: A. Lakhop & S. Beikul, 1993.

Meitei *Pumnamakhi Lainingthou Sanamahi* (*Sanamahi as the god of all Meiteis*). Imphal: Lainingthou Sanamahi Thougal Kanglup, 1976. (Meiteilon).

Pettigrew, William. *Forty Years of Mission in Manipur: Mission Report of Rev. William Pettigrew.* Compiled by Jonah M. Solo & K. Mahangthei. Imphal: Christian Literature Centre, Imphal, n.d.

Pettigrew, William. "Manipur State 1932-1981." *The Baptist Missionary Review* 3/2 (November, 1932): 432-63.

____________. *Mission Reports and Letters: 1891-1932.* Compiled by Champhang Jajo. Guwahati: Phila Jajo, n.d.

____________. *Ukhrul Mission School.* Rangoon: American Baptist Mission Press, 1922.

Interviews

Chanu, Th. Bimola. Secretary of Yaiskul Meira Paibi, Imphal West. Interview, 22 May, 2012.

Colney, Lalrinliana. Valley Missionary of Mizoram Presbyterian, Imphal West. Interview, 27 November, 2012.

Gangte, S. Principal of MBC Higher Secondary School Chingmeirong, Imphal. Interview, 8 May 2010.

Haokip, P. Chaplain of Kangpokpi Mission Hospital. Interview, 10 May 2010.

Meitei, L. Chingkheingamba. General Secretary of Kangleipak Yaipha Lup Khurai, Imphal. Interview, 21 May, 2012.

Sanate, Lalthoruol. Valley Missionary of Evangelical Church of India, Imphal East. Interview, 18 July, 2012.

Singh, Y. Yaima. Lecturer of BM College, Imphal East. Interview, 23 May, 2012.

Personal Correspondences

Bheigachandra, Th. Former chairman of Yaipha Lamjing Kanglup, Khundrakpam, Imphal East. Letter to the author, 22 November 2010.

Devi, Priya. Lecturer of the Modern College, Imphal East. Letter to the author, 8 February, 2012.

Devi, R.K. Tamphasana. Lecturer of the G.P. Women College, Imphal West. Letter to the author, 21 January, 2012.

Devi, Th. Shushila. Women Secretary of the Meitei Baptist Association, Wangjing. Letter to the author, 21 September, 2010.

Kaboklei, W. General Secretary of the Ima-lup, Laipham Khunnao, Imphal West. Letter to the author, 4 February, 2010.

Kaikho, Hokey. Former General Secretary of the Manipur Baptist Convention, Imphal West, Manipur. Letter to the author, 18 November, 2010.

Khongchai, Mang. Lecturer of the Trulok Theological Seminary, Dewlahland Imphal West, Manipur. Letter to the author, 13 February 2011.

Kumar, Th. The First Executive Secretary of the Meitei Baptist Association, Wangjing. Letter to the author, 23 January, 2010.

Makangwo, Hormi. Former Mission and Evangelism Secretary of the Meitei Baptist Association, Wangjing. Letter to the author, 14 March 2010.

Manihar, N. Former member of the Chingkei Laiharaoba Committee, Phaknung, Imphal East. Letter to the author, 28th September 2010.

Masangthei, T. Retired Missionary of the Council of Baptist Churches in North East India, Panbazar, Guwahati. Letter to the author, 29 January 2010.

Meitei, Mangibabu. Secretary of the Panthoibi Erat Thouni Chingarel Tejpur, Imphal East. Letter to the author, 11 June 2011.

Meitei, Rashi. Lecturer of the Sawombung Higher Secondary, Imphal East. Letter to the author, 23 March, 2012.

Meitei, Th. Kumar. Former Executive Secretary of the Meitei Baptist Association, Lungthabal, Imphal. Letter to the author, 4 October, 2011.

Paul, Sam. National Secretary-Public Affairs of the All India Christian Council, Secunderabad, Andra Pradesh. Letter to the author, May 14, 2009.

Risom, Ngaranmi. Former Mission and Evangelism Secretary of the Manipur Baptist Convention, Imphal. Letter to the author, May 2008.

Singh, A. Thaningjao. Former President of the Meitei Baptist Association, Wangjing. Letter to the author, 25 February 2010.

Singh, Angom Moses. Former Mission and Evangelism Secretary of the MBA. Letter to the author, 24 March 2011.

Singh, Angom Moses. Mission Coordinator of the Manipur Baptist Convention, Imphal. Letter to the author, 26 March 2010.

Singh, Chaoba. Mission and Evangelism Secretary of the Meitei Baptist Association, Wangjing. Letter to the author, 9 January 2010.

Singh, Kh. Chaoba. State Secretary of the All India Christian Council, Imphal. Letter to the author, May 12, 2009.

Singh, N. Debendra. Former Executive Secretary of the Meitei Baptist Association, Wangjing. Letter to the author, 28 April 2012.

Singh, N. Debendra. Former Executive Secretary, Meitei Baptist Association, Wangjing. Letter to the author, 17 January 2010.

Singh, Paonam Bihari. Early Meitei Christian and Deacon of the Wangjing Centre Baptist Church, Wangjing. Letter to the author, 13 February 2010.

Singh, Ph. Dhaneswor. Executive Secretary of the Meitei Baptist Association, Wangjing. Letter to the author, 11 September, 2010.

Singh, Rajendro. Lecturer of the Modern College, Imphal East. Letter to the author, 7 February, 2012.

Singh, Roman. Deacon of the Phaknung Baptist Church, Imphal East. Letter to the author, 27 September, 2010.

Singh, Th. Kumar. Former Executive Secretary of the Meitei Baptist Association, Wangjing. Letter to the author, 15 April 2012.

Singh, Th. Kumar. Former Field Secretary, Meitei Baptist Association, Wangjing. Letter to the author, 8 March 2010.

Singh, Thambal. Retired Principal of the Sawombung Higher Secondary, Imphal East. Letter to the author, 17 January, 2012.

Thoihenba, L. General Secretary of the Meitei Thang-Ta Lup, Kurai, Imphal East. Letter to the author, 11 January, 2010.

Tiken, H. President of the Meitei National Frond, Wangkhei, Imphal West. Letter to the author, 17th September 2010.

Vungzamoi, V. Lecturer of the G.P. Women College, Imphal West. Letter to the author, 23 January, 2012.

Government Documents and Records

Government of India. Department of Foreign and External. *Foreign Department External.* (A). Nos 18-23, August 1907.

Government of India. Department of Foreign and External. *Foreign Department External.* (A). No. 25, July 1904.

Government of India. Department of Foreign and External. *Foreign Department Proceedings*. Nos. 127-147, October 1891.

Government of India. Department of Foreign and External. *Foreign Department Proceedings*. (E). No. 18, September 1962.

Government of India. Department of Foreign and External. *Foreign Department Progression*. Nos. 18-23, August, 1907.

Government of India. Department of Foreign and External. *Foreign Department Progression*. No. 1-19, October, 1893.

Government of India. Department of Foreign and External. *Foreign Department Resolution and Proclamation*. (E). No. 1700, August, 1891.

Government of India. Department of Foreign and External. *Foreign Department Secret*. (E). No. 133, October, 1891.

Government of India. Department of Foreign and External. *Foreign Department Secretary*. (E). Nos. 872-84, March 1905.

Government of India. Department of Home and Social Welfare. *Administrative Report of Manipur*, 1939-1940.

Government of India. Department of Home and Social Welfare. *Administrative Report of the Manipur Political Agency*, 1891-1892

Government of India. Department of Home and Social Welfare. *Administrative Report of the Manipur Political* Agency, 1907-1908.

Government of India. Department of Home and Social Welfare. *Annual Administrative Reports of Political Agency*, 1892-1893.

Government of India. *Gazette*. Part-I, 22 August, 1891.

Government of Manipur. *Extraordinary Gazetteer*. No. 149. (Constitution of the Lainingthou Sanamahi Temple Board), 1976.

Government of Manipur. *Extraordinary Gazetteer*. No. 213. (Constitution of the Lainingthou Sanamahi Temple Board), 1977.

Government of Manipur. *Proceeding of the Manipur State Durbar*. (R). No. 4, 1917.

Secondary Sources

Unpublished Dissertations

Jamir, Temsu. "Christianity and Tribal Ecumenism in the North East India with Special Reference to Nagaland." Master of Theology Dissertation, Senate of Serampore College, 2004.

Singh, K. B. "The Meiteis of Manipur." PhD Dissertation, Bombay University, 1962.

Singh, N. Debendra. *A Study on the Introduction and Growth of Christianity among the Meiteis of Manipur*. Bachelor of Divinity Dissertation, Senate of Serampore College, 1992.

Unpublished Diary

Maxwell, H. *Unpublished Diary*. Political Agent in Manipur, Record of the Government of Manipur, 1895.

Articles in Newspapers

Hueiyen Lanpao (Imphal), 27 September 2011.
Imphal Free Press (Imphal), 26 October 2010.
Imphal Free Press (Imphal), 26 October 2010.
Imphal Free Press (Imphal), 22 August 2011.
Imphal Free Press (Imphal), 28 September 2011.
Imphal Free Press (Imphal), 11 August, 2011.
Manipur Mail (Imphal), 14 August 2011.
Manipur Mail (Imphal), 14 August 2011.
Manipur Mail (Imphal), 26 September 2011.
Prajantrantra (Imphal), 12 October 1976.
The Hindu (Chennai), 18 April 2011.
The Manipur Daily (Imphal), 23 January 1979.
The Sangai Express (Imphal), 1 September 2010.
The Sangai Express (Imphal), 11 April 2012.
The Sangai Express (Imphal), 14 August 2012.
The Sangai Express (Imphal), 19 January 2009.
The Sangai Express (Imphal), 26 October 2010.
The Sangai Express (Imphal), 3 October 2009.
The Sangai Express (Imphal), 9 October 2008.
The Times of India (Guwahati), 4 April 2011.

Articles in Periodicals (Author-wise)

Akoijam, A. Bimol & Th. Tarunkumar. "Armed Forces Special Powers Act 1958: Disguised War & Its Subversions." *Eastern Quarterly* 3/1 (January-March, 2005): 11-27.

Barpujari, S. K. "Early Christian Missions in the Naga Hills: An Assessment of their Activities." *Journal of Indian History* 48 (April, 1970): 421-35.

Bharucha, Rustom. "Politics of Indigenous Theatre: Kanhailal in Manipur." *Economic and Political Weekly* 26/11 (March, 1991): 73-9.

Chandrasing, Pandi. "Chingoi Iruppa." *Meetyeng* 21 (October-December, 1979): 1-7.

Chanu, Sophia. "Lai-Haraoba." *Indian Folk Life* 1/1 (July, 2001): 18-31.

Chatterji, Sunil Kumar. "Kirata-Jana-Krti: The Indo-Mongoloids, their Contribution to the History and Culture of India." *Journal of the Asiatic Society of Bengal* 16/2 (June, 1950): 142-62.

Damant, G. H. "Notes on Manipuri Grammar." *Journal of the Asiatic Society of Bengal* XLIV/1. No. II (June, 1875): 173-181.

Dena, Lal. "Manipur Under Paramountcy of the British Crown: Some Admonition of Colonial Rule, 1891-1919." *Bengal Past and Present* XCVIII/1. No. 187 (July-December, 1979): 105-28.

Dikshitar, V.R.R. "Aryanisation of East India." *IHQ* XXI (December, 1945): 28-35

Downs, F. S. "Early Christian Contacts with North-East India." *Indian Church History Review* 5/1 (June, 1971): 64-75.

Downs, F. S. "The Establishment of the American Baptist Mission in Assam, 1836-1841." *Indian Church History Review* 5/1 (June, 1972): 70-78.

Hodgson, B. H. "On the Indo-Chinese Borders and their Connection with the Himalayans and Tibetans." *Journal of the Asiatic Society of Bengal* XXII/1 (June, 1875): 1-25.

Shakespeare, J. "The Religion of Manipur." *Transactions of the Folk-Lore Society* XXIV/IV (December, 1913): 409-455.

Singh, H. Ranbir. "Vaishnavism in Manipur: It's Advent." *Manipur Sahitya Parishad* 2/1 (April, 1985): 1-10.

Singh, L. Bimol. "Meitei Christian Identity: Problems and Prospects." *The SATHRI Journal: Journal of Contextual Theology* 3/1 (May, 2009): 39-66.

Singh, W. Yomjao. "Report on the Archaeological Studies in Manipur." *Manipur Bulletin* 2/1 (January-June, 1935): 1-16.

Talukdar, Sushanta. "Rediscovering a Heritage." *Frontline* 22/18 (August-September, 2005): 65-73.

Articles in Periodicals (Caption-wise)

"Coins of Manipur." *Bulletin of Mutua Museum* No. 1 (October, 1980): 43-54.

"Ireipak Machasingda Pijaba Paojel." *Meitei National Front* (February, 1979): 1-12.

"Langjeel." *Celebration committee of Laininghal Naoria* (August, 1979): 1-4.

"Manipur Itihasta Nupi Lan." *Lamyanba* 5/52 (January, 1974): 4-9.

"*Nupi Lan*, 1939." *Lamyanba* 5/51(December, 1973): 1-8.

"Resistance." *An English Weekly* 24/9 (October, 1976): 3-7.

"Sculpture of Manipur." *Bulletin of Mutua Museum* No. 2 (December, 1982): 23-36.

Component Parts in Other Edited Volumes

Acharyya, N. N. "Manipur in the Eye of Foreign Historians." In *Manipur: Past and Present.* Vol. I. Edited by Naorem Sanajaoba. Delhi: Mittal Publications, 1988.

Aggarwal, Kailash S. "Monistic Pluralism: Language Ideology in a Language Movement." In *Linguistic Structure and Language Dynamics in South Asia: Papers from the Proceedings of SALA XVIII Roundtable*. Edited by Anvita Abbi, R. S. Gupta and Ayesha Kidwari. Delhi: Motilal Banarsidass Publishing Private Limited, 2011.

Ali, Abdul. "Note on the Early History of Manipur." In *Bengal Past and Present*. Vol. XXVI. Part 2. No. 52. Calcutta: Calcutta Historical Society, 1923.

Athparia, R. P. & S. S. Data Choudhury. "Socio-Religious Transformation among the People of Manipur." In *Religion in North-East in India*. Edited by Soumen Sen. New Delhi: Uppal Publishing House, 1993.

Bagchi, Tilak and K. Jonathan. "Ethnicity and Inter-Tribal Relation in the Hills of Manipur." In *State, Development and Identity in South Asia: A Search for Alternative Paradigms*. Edited by R. Vashum & Prakash Louis. New Delhi: Indian Social Institute, 2002.

Budhi, Chongtham. "The Ethnonym Meitei." In *Manipur: Past and Present*. Vol. I. Edited by Naorem Sanajaoba. Delhi: Mittal Publications, 1988.

Das, J. N. "Rights Over Land among Tribes of North-East India." In *Tribal Situation in North-East India: Tribal Studies of India*. Series T. 170. Edited by Sarthak Sengupta. New Delhi: Inter-India Publications, 1994.

Dena, Lal. "Christian Proselytism, 1894-1949." In *History of Modern Manipur, 1826-1949*. Edited by Lal Dena. New Delhi: Orbit Publishers & Distributors, 1991.

Devi, J. Bimal & Dilip K. Lahiri. "Manipur: Palace Politics and Administration." In *Proceedings of North East India History Association*. Fourth Session. Shillong: North-Eastern Hills University, 1983.

Devi, Ksh. Bimola. "Manipuri Women: A Study." In *Manipur: Past and Present*. Vol. I. Edited by Naorem Sanajaoba. Delhi: Mittal Publications, 1988.

Devi, Ksh. Bimola. "Society and Politics in Manipur." In *Society, Politics and Development in North East India*. Edited by Asok Chakraborty and Satyabrata Chakraborty. New Delhi: Concept Publishing Company, 2008.

Devi, Th. Binarani. "Women's Movement in Conflict Situation in Manipur." In *Society, Politics and Development in North East India*. Edited by Asok Chakraborty and Satyabrata Chakraborty. New Delhi: Concept Publishing Company, 2008.

Dubey, S. M. "Inter-Ethnic Alliance, Tribal Movements and Integration in Northeast India." In *Tribal Movements in India*. Vol. 1. Edited by K. S. Singh. New Delhi: Manohar Publications, 1982.

Haokip, Peter. "A Response to Dr. Thomas C. Joshua: Christian Impact and Conflict Resolution in Manipur." In *Impact of Christianity on North East India*. Edited by J. Puthenpurakal. Shillong: Vendrame Institute Publications, 1996.

Ibochuba, K. "Anglo-Manipuri Relations (1762-1947)." In *Manipur: Past and Present.* Vol. I. Edited by Naorem Sanajaoba. Delhi: Mittal Publications, 1988.

Kabui, Gangmumei. "Glimpses of Land and People of Ancient Manipur." In *Manipur: Past and Present.* Vol. I. Edited by Naorem Sanajaoba. Delhi: Mittal Publications, 1988.

Kabui, Gangmumei. "Social and Religious Reform Movement in Manipur in 19th and 20th Century." In *Bulletin of the Division of History.* Imphal: Centre of Post-Graduate Studies, J.N.U., 1974.

Kabui, Gangmumei. "Socio-Religious Reform Movement." In *History of Modern Manipur, 1826-1949.* 2nd Edition. Edited by Lal Dena. New Delhi: Orbit Publishers & Distributors, 1991.

Kabui, Gangmumei. "The Anglo-Manipur War of 1891." In *History of Modern Manipur, 1826-1949.* 2nd Edition. Edited by Lal Dena. New Delhi: Orbit Publishers & Distributors, 1991.

Khayi, Sina. "Contribution of Mrs. Alice Pettigrew in the Field of Women's Education in Manipur: 1896-1933." In *Rev. William Pettigrew: A Pioneer Missionary of Manipur.* Edited by Lal Dena. Imphal: Fraternal Green Cross, 1996.

Manikchand, Konsam. "The Evolution of the Meitei State: A Confederacy through the Last Two Millennia." In *Manipur: Past and Present.* Vol. I. Edited by Naorem Sanajaoba. Delhi: Mittal Publications, 1988.

Nilabir, Sairem. "The Revivalist Movement of Sanamahism." In *Manipur: Past and Present: The Ordeals and Heritage of a Civilization.* Vol. 2. Edited by Naorem Sanajaoba. Delhi: Mittal Publications, 1991.

Priyobrata, Maharajkumar. "Reminiscences of the First and Last Chief Minister: Under Manipur State Constitution." In *Manipur: Past and Present.* Vol. I. Edited by Naorem Sanajaoba. Delhi: Mittal Publications, 1988.

Ranjit, R. K. "Emergent Ethnic Processes in Manipur." In *Manipur: Past and Present.* Vol. I. Edited by Naorem Sanajaoba. Delhi: Mittal Publications, 1988.

Ratha, S. N. "Migration into Assam – The Past History, the Present Realities and Future Implications." In *Ethnic Groups Cultural Continuities and Social Change in North East India.* Edited by Indira Barua, Sarthak Sengupta and Deepanjana Dutta Das. Delhi: Mittal Publications, 2002.

Saha, R. K. "An Ethnic Movement in Manipur Valley." In *Tribal Movements in* India. Vol. I. Edited by K. S. Singh. New Delhi: Manohar Publications, 1982.

Sanahal, R. K. "Vaishnava Religious Movement in Manipur." In *Souvenir of Manipur Rajya Hindu Sammelan.* Imphal: Manipur Rajya Hindu Sammelan, 1981.

Sanajaoba, Naorem. "From the Cradle of Pithecanthropus." In *Manipur: Past and Present.* Vol. 1. Edited by Naorem Sanajaoba. Delhi: Mittal Publications, 1988.

Sanajaoba, Naorem. "The Roots: South East Asian Personality." In *Manipur: Past and Present.* Vol. I. Edited by Naorem Sanajaoba. Delhi: Mittal Publications, 1988.

Shashi, S. S. "Manipur: Historical and Cultural Background." In *Tribes of Assam and Manipur.* Edited by S. S. Shashi. New Delhi: Anmol Publications Pvt. Ltd., 1995.

Shyamkishor, S. "Observations on the Value-System of the Traditional Meitei Society." In *Manipur: Past and Present.* Vol. 2. Edited by Naorem Sanajaoba. Delhi: Mittal Publications, 1991.

Singh, K. B. "Social Stratification and Mobility in Manipur." In *North East India: A Sociological Study.* Edited by S. M. Dubey. Delhi: Concept Publishing Company, 1978.

Singh, Ksh. Shyamkanhai. "Hill Administration under the Manipur Constitution." In *Proceedings of North East India History Association.* Fourth Session. Shillong: North-Eastern Hill University, 1983.

Singh, Kunj Bihari. "Manipur Vaishnavism: A Sociological Interpretation." In *Themes in Indian Sociology 3: Sociology in India.* Edited by Rowena Robinson. New Delhi: Sage Publications India Pvt. Ltd., 2004.

Singh, L. Leiren. "Reverend William Pettigrew and Modern Education in Manipur." In *Rev. William Pettigrew: A Pioneer Missionary of Manipur.* Imphal: Fraternal Green Cross, 1996.

Singh, M. Kirti. "The Social Implication of Vaishnava Movement in Manipur." In *Magazine, G.P. Women College.* Imphal: G.P. Women College, 1969.

Souvenir: Meitei Baptist Association Silver Jubilee Celebration, 1982-2008. Khurai Lomlong Keithel: MBA, 2008.

Stanley, Brian. "Robert Arthington." In *Biographical Dictionary of Christian Mission.* Edited by Gerald H. Anderson. Michigan/Cambridge: William B. Eerdmans Publishing Company, 1999.

Yambem, Sanamani. "The Lallup System of Manipur: Transformation from Conscript Warrior to Conscript Labour." In *Social Science and Social Concern.* Edited by S. B. Chakrabarti. Delhi: Mittal Publications, 1988.

Books

Ahluwalia, B. K. *Social Change in Manipur.* Delhi: Cultural Publishing House, 1984.

Aier, I. T. Apok & I. Bendangangshi. *The Religion of the Ao Nagas.* Guwahati: Bendangangshi, 1997.

Albaugh, Dana M. *Between Two Countries: A Study of Four Baptist Fields-Assam, South India, Bengal-Orissa and South China.* Philadelphia: The Judson Press, 1935.

Allen, B. C. *Assam District Gazetteers: Naga Hills and Manipur.* Vol. IX. Calcutta: Baptist Mission Press, 1905.

Avebury, Lord. *The Origin of Civilization and the Primitive Condition of Man.* London: Longmans Green Co., 1911.

Bagchi, Prabodh Chandra. *India and China: A Thousand Years of Cultural Relations.* New York: The Philosophical Library, 1951.

Bahadur, M. & P. Gunindra Singh, *Epigraphical Records of Manipur.* Vol. 1. Imphal: Mutua Museum, 1986.

Banerjee, Anil Chandra. *The Eastern Frontier of British India, 1784-1826.* Calcutta: A. Mukerjee & Co., 1946.

____________. Ed. *The Eastern Frontier of British India, 1784-1826.* Calcutta: A Mukherjee & Co, 2005.

Barooah, Nirode K. *David Scott in North-East India, 1802-1831: A Study in British Paternalism.* New Delhi: Munshiram Manoharlal, 1970.

____________. *David Scott in the North-East India, 1802-1831: A Study in British Paternalism.* New Delhi: Munshiram Manoharlal, 1970.

Basanta, N. *Socio-Economic Change in Manipur, 1891-1947.* Imphal: N. Basanta, 1998.

Bendangangshi, I. *Glimpses of Naga History.* Mokokchung: Naga Patriots from Soyim, 1993.

Bhandarkar, R. G. *Viashnavism, Saivism and Minor Religious Systems.* Reprinted. New Delhi: Asian Educational Service, 1965.

Bhattacharyya, Padmanath Vidyavinod. *Mr. Gait's History of Assam: A Critical Study.* Allahabad: The Indian Press, 1908.

Bhogeshwar, O. *Ningthourol Lambuba.* Imphal: O. Bhogeswar, 1967.

____________. *Ningthourol Sheireng.* Imphal: O. Bhogeshwar, 1967.

Bhuyan, Surya Kumar. *Early British Relation with Assam.* Shillong: Department of Historical and Antiquarian Studies in Assam, 1948.

____________. *Studies in the History of Assam.* Gauhati: Srimati Laksheswari, 1965.

Bisheswar, N. *The Last Expression on My Death Bed.* Imphal: Pax Publication, 1986.

Brara, N. Vijaylakshmi. *Politics, Society and Cosmology in India's North East.* Oxford: Oxford University Press, 1998.

Brown, R. *Statistical Account of Manipur.* Reprinted. Delhi: Sanskaran Prakashan, 1975.

Carey, S. Pearce. *William Carey.* London: Hodder and Stoughton Limited, n.d.

Carey, William. *The Garo Jungle Book*. Reprinted. Tura: Tura Book Room, 1993.

Champhang, Jajo. *Christian Life in a Tribal Context: In Manipur*. Ukhrul. J. Champhang, 1919.

____________. *The Indigenisation and Contextualisation of Christian Life in a Tribal Context: In Manipur State of North-East India*. Ukhrul: Jajo C., 1990.

Chand, Tara. *History of the Freedom Movement in India*. Vol III. New Delhi: Publications Division, 1972.

Chandra, M. *Panthoibi Khongun (Footsteps of Panthoibi)*. Imphal: Sahitya Parishad Manipur, 1999.

Chandrasing, Pandi. *Nongkhang Pareihanba*. Imphal: Sanamahians, 1968.

Chib, Sukhdev Singh. *North-Eastern India: Caste, Tribes & Culture of India*. Vol. 8. New Delhi: Ess Ess Publications, 1984.

Clark, Mary Mead. *A Corner in India*. Philadelphia: American Baptist Publication Society, 1907.

Constantine, R. *Manipur Maid of the Mountains*. New Delhi: Lancers Publishers, 1981.

De, S. K. *Early History of the Vaisnava Faith and Movement in Bengal*. Calcutta: General Printers and Publishers, 1942.

Dena, Lal. *British Policy Towards Manipur, 1891-1919*. Imphal: n.p., 1984.

____________. *Christian Missions and Colonialism: A Study of Missionary Movement in Northeast India with Particular Reference to Manipur and Lushai Hills, 1894-1947*. Shillong: Vendrame Institute, 1988.

____________. *Cultural History of Manipur: Sija Laioibi and the Maharas*. Delhi: Mittal Publications, 2010.

Devi, Jamini. *Education in Manipur*. Imphal: Rai Pravina Brothers, 1989.

Devi, Kh. Sarojini. *British Political Agency in Manipur, 1835-1947*. Imphal: Linthoi Publications, 2005.

Devi, L. Bino. *Lois of Manipur: Andro, Khurkhul, Phayeng & Sekmai*. Delhi: Mittal Publication, 2002.

Dihingia, Hemeswar. *Assam's Struggles Against British Rule: 1826-1863*. New Delhi: Asian Publication Services, 1980.

Doniger, Windy. *The Hindus: An Alternative History*. New Delhi: Penguin/Viking, 2009.

Downs, Frederick S. *History of Christianity in India: North East India in the Nineteenth and Twentieth Centuries*. Vol. V. Part 5. Bangalore: The Church History Association of India, 1992.

____________. *The Mighty Works of God: A Brief History of the Council of Baptist Churches in North East India: The Mission Period, 1836-1950*. Gauhati: Christian Literature Centre, 1971.

Dun, E.W. *The Gazetteer of Manipur*. Delhi: Vivek Publishing House, 1957.

Eliot, Charles. *Hinduism and Buddhism: An Historical Sketch*. Vol. 3. London: Edward Arnold, 1957, 1st print 1921.

Furnivall, F. S. *Colonial Policy and Practice: A Comparative Study of Burma and Netherlands India*. Cambridge: Cambridge University Press, 1948.

Gait, Edward. *A History of Assam*. Calcutta: Thacker Spink & Co, 1926.

Gajrani, S. *History, Religion & Culture of India*. Vol. 6. Delhi: Isha Books, 2004.

Gammel, W. A. M. *History of American Mission in Asia, Africa, Europe and North America*. Boston: Gould, Kendall and Lincoln, 1849.

Gori, Gulab Khan. *Changing Phase of Tribal Area of Manipur*. Delhi: B.R. Publishing Corporation, 1984.

Grierson, G. A. *Linguistic Survey of India*. Vol. V. Part 1. Delhi: Motilal Banarasidass, 1967.

Grimwood, Ethel. *My Three Years in Manipur*. Delhi: Vivek Publishing House, 1975.

____________. *My Three Years in Manipur: And Escape from the Recent Mutiny*. London: Richard Bentley and Son, 1891.

Hodson, T. C. *The Meitheis*. London: McMillan & Co, 1908.

____________. *The Meithies*. Delhi: Low Price Publications, 1984.

Imchen, Narola. *Remembering Our ForeMothers: The Influence of the American Woman's Movement on American Baptist Women Missionaries in North East India*. Women Study Series No. 2. Jorhat: Women Study Department ETC, 2003.

Irene, Salam. *The Muslims of Manipur*. New Delhi: Gyan Books Pvt. Ltd., 2010.

Jeyakumar, D. Arthur. *History of Christianity in India: Selected Themes*. Revised Edition. Madurai: Author, 2007.

Jeyaseelan, L. *Impact of the Missionary Movement in Manipur*. Delhi: Scholar Publishing House (P) Ltd., 1996.

Johnstone, James. *Manipur and Naga Hills*. Reprinted. New Delhi: Gyan Publishing House, 1971.

____________. *My Experiences in Manipur and Naga Hills*. London: Marston and Company, 1896.

Kabui, Gangmumei. *History of Manipur: Pre-Colonial Period*. Vol. I. New Delhi: National Publishing House, 1991.

Kipgen, Mangkhosat. *Christianity and Mizo Culture*. Aizawl: Mizo Theological Conference, 1996.

____________. *The Meitei Lai Haraoba*. Imphal: Rajo Maibi, 1953.

Kumar, B. B. *The Tribal Societies of India: A Macro Perception*. New Delhi: Omsons Publications, 1998.

Kumar, Kh. Ratan. *Lai Haraoba of Manipur: Indigenous Festival of the Meitei: A Socio-Historical Perspective*. Imphal: Smt. Ph. Pratima Devi, Mayang Imphal Konchak, 2001.

Kuriakose, M. K. Comp. *History of Christianity in India: Source Materials*. Madras: Christian Literature Society, 1982.

Lahiri, Rebati Mohan. *The Annexation of Assam, 1824-1854*. Calcutta: Firma K. L. Mukhapadhyay, 1975.

Laiba, M. T. *The Geography of Manipur*. Imphal: N. Priyokumar Singh, 1992.

Lainingthou Sanamahi Board. *Lainingthou Sanamahina Haying Khongbal Tolong Yumphamda Lengsillakpa. (Coming of Lainingthou Sanamahina at Tolong)*. Imphal: Lainingthou Sanamahi Board, 1987.

Lamdamsida Nupigi Ihou (Women's Movement of the Land). Imphal: The Manipur Chanura Leisem Marup, 1981.

"Langjeel": A Special Issue on the 91st Birth Anniversary of Laininghal Naoriya; Laininghal Phulo and Our Clan. Imphal: Malem Yaiphasang, 1988.

Lolly, R. R. *The Baptist Church in Manipur*. Imphal: R.R. Lolly, 1985.

Longchar, Wati. *The Tribal Religious Traditions in North East India: An Introduction*. Jorhat: W. Longchar, 2000.

Luikham, T. *A Short History of the Manipur Christian*. Ukhrul: North East Christian Association, 1948.

Mabry, Hunter P. *A Manual for Researchers and Writers*. Second Edition. Bangalore: The Board of Theological Education Senate of Serampore College, 2003.

Mackenzie, Alexander. *History of the Relation of the Government with the Hill Tribes of the North-East Frontier Bengal*. Calcutta: Home Office Department Press, 1884.

____________. *North-East Frontier of India*. Delhi: Mittal Publications, 1989.

Majumdar, R. C. Ed. *The History and Culture of the Indian People: British Paramountcy and Indian Renaissance*. Bombay: Bharatiya Vidya Bhavan, 1970.

Mangang, Ng. Kangjia. *Revival of a Closed Account: A Brief History of Kanglei Script and the Birth of Phoon (Zero) in the World of Arithmetic and Astrology*. Imphal West: Sanamahi Laining Amasung Punsiron Khupham, 1969.

Mattumana, Matthew. *Christianity in Assam and Inter-faith Dialogue: A Study on the Modern Religious Movements in North East India*. Pune: Satprakashan Sanchar Kendra, 1984.

McColloch, W. *Account of the Valley of Manipur and of the Hill Tribes with a Comparative Vocabulary of the Munnipore and other Languages*. Calcutta: Bengal Printing Co. Ltd., 1859.

____________. *Valley of Manipur*. Delhi: Gyan Publications, 1980.

Meitei Marup Hourakpagi Wari (*Story of the Origin of Meitei Marup*). Imphal: Meitei Marup, 1993.

Meitei, H. Ibopishak. Ed. *Bamon Khunthoklon* (*Immigration of Brahmin*). Imphal: Manipur Sahitya Parishad, 1987.

Meitei, Rajen & Ibohal Meitei, *Sakok Lamlel (The Land of Animal's Lead)*. Imphal: Rajen, 1973.

Minaketan, A. *Meitei Lairol.* Imphal: A. Minaketan, 1951.

Moorshead, Robert Fletcher. Heal th*e Sick: The Story of the Medical Mission Auxiliary of the Baptist Missionary Society*. Oxford: Oxford University, 1929.

Morris, J. H. *The History of the Welsh Calvinistic Methodists' Foreign Mission*: *To the End Year of 1903*. Reprinted. Delhi: Indus Publishing Company, 1996.

Nag, Chitta Ranjan. *The Mizo Society in Transition*. New Delhi: Vikas Publishing House Pvt. Ltd., 1993.

Nag, Sajal. *Contesting Marginality.* New Delhi: Manohar, 2002.

Naoriya, Laininghal. *Tengbanba Amusung Lainingthou Laipao, Creator and God's Message*. Cachar: Moirengjamba Munal, 1946.

Nilabir, Sairem. *Lainingthou Sanamahi Amasung Sanamahi Laining Hinggat Echou* (*Sanamahi the almighty and the Restoring weave of Sanamahism*). Imphal: Sairem Nilabir 2002.

Parekh, Manilal Chhotalal. *The Brahma Samaj: A Short History*. Michigan: Oriental Christ House, 1929.

Parratt, Saroj Nalini. *The Religion of Manipur: Belief, Ritual and Historical Development.* Calcutta: Firma KLM Private Limited, 1980.

Pemberton, R. Boileau. *Report of the Eastern Frontier of British India*. Guahati: Government of Assam, 1966.

Reid, Robert. *History of Frontier Areas Bordering on Assam, 1883-1941*. New Delhi: Eastern Publishing House, 1983.

Roy, Jyotirmoy. *History of Manipur*. Calcutta: Firma K.L. Mukhopadhyay, 1958.

Rudenko, Georgy. *Colonialism and Neo-Colonialism*. Moscow: Novosti Press Agency Publishing House, 1970.

Saha, Ranajit Kumar. *Valley Society of Manipur: A Cultural Frontier of Indian Civilization*. Calcutta: Punthi Pustak, 1994.

Sangma, Milton S. *History of American Baptist Mission in North-East India, 1836-1850.* Vol. I. Delhi: Mittal Publications, 1987.

Sarin, V. I. K. *India's North-East in Flames*. New Dellhi: Vikas Publishing House, 1980.

Sen, S. P. *Social and Religious Reform Movement in the Nineteenth and Twentieth Century*. Calcutta: International Book Trust, 1979.

Sen, Sipra. *Tribes & Castes of Manipur*. Delhi: Mittal Publications, 1992.

Shakespear, J. Manipur under British Management, 1891-1907. Shillong: n.p. 1907.

Sharma, Ph. Atombapu. *History of Manipur*. Imphal: Manipuri Sahitya Parishad, 1976.

Sharma, S. N. *The Neo-Viasnavite Movement and the Satra Institutions of Assam*. Gauhati: Department of Publications, Gauhati University, 1966.

Singh, Lairenmayum Ibungohal. & N. Khelchandra Singh. Ed. *Cheitharol Kumbaba* (*The Chronicle*). Imphal: Manipur Sahitya Parishad, 1967.

Singh, E. Nilakanta. *Fragments of Manipur Culture*. New Delhi: Omsons Publications, 1993.

Singh, K. B. *Traces of Pre-Hinduism in Meitei Society Folklore*. Vol. 5. Imphal East: Meitei Lup Publications, 1964.

Singh, K. M. *History of Christian Mission in Manipur and Other Neighbouring States*. Delhi: Mittal Publications, 1991.

Singh, L. Bhagyachandra. *A Critical Study of the Religious Philosophy of the Meeteis Before the Advent of Vaishnavism in Manipur*. Imphal: L. Jayantakumar Singh, 1991.

Singh, L. Ibungohal. *An Introduction to Manipur*. 3rd Print. Imphal: The Saraswati Printing Works, 1987.

__________. *Meaning of Mayang*. Imphal: Manipur Sahitya Parishad, 1962.

Singh, M. Kirti. *Religion and Culture of Manipur*. Delhi: Manas Publication, 1988.

__________. *Religious Development in Manipur in the 18th & 19th Centuries*. Imphal: Manipur State Kala Akademi, 1980.

Singh, N. Joykumar. *Social Movement in Manipur*. Second Ed. Delhi: Mittal Publications, 2005.

__________. *Colonialism to Democracy: A History of Manipur, 1819-1972*. Delhi: Spectrum Publications, 2002.

Singh, N. Khelchandra. *Ariba Manipuri Sahitya Itihas* (*Old Literary History of Manipur*). Imphal: Ningthoujam, 1969.

__________. *Battle of Khongjom*. Imphal: N. Khelchandra Singh, 1983.

Singh, N. Lokendro. *The Unquiet Valley*. Delhi: Mittal Publications, 1998.

Singh, N. Tombi. *Manipur and the Mainstream*. Imphal: Chitrebirentombichand Khorjeirup, 1975.

Singh, P. Gunindra. *Manipur Numismatic*. Imphal: Mutua Museum, 1983.

Singh, Pangambam Bharat. *Kangla: The National Heritage of Manipur*. Imphal: Pangambam Bharat Singh, 2008.

Singh, R. K. Jhaljit. *A Short History of Manipur: From 33 A.D. to the Present Time*. Imphal: The O. K. Store, 1965.

Singh, Ravindra Pratap. *Geography of Manipur*. New Delhi: National Book Trust, 1982.

Singh, W. Ibohal. *The History of Manipur: An Early Period.* Imphal: 1986.

Singh, W. Yumjao. *An Early History of Manipur.* Imphal: W. Lalmani Singh and other Brothers, 1966.

________________. *Religious Belief of Ancient Manipur*. Imphal: W. Yumjoa Singh, 1966.

Sircar, D. C. *Studies in the Geography of Ancient and Medieval India*. Delhi: Motilal Banarsidass, 1971.

Snaitang, O. L. *Christianity and Social Change in Northeast India: A Study of the Role of Christianity in Social Change among the Khasi-Jaintia Hill Tribes of Meghalaya.* Shillong: Vendrame Institute, 1993.

Solo, Jonah M. & K. Mahangthei. Ed. *Forty Years in Manipur, Assam: An Account of the Work of W. Pettigrew, the First Foreign Missionary in Manipur Landed in 1894*. Imphal: Christian Literature Center, 1986.

Solo, Johan M. & K. Mahangthei. Comp. *Forty Years Mission in Manipur: Mission Reports of Rev. William Pettigrew*. Imphal: Christian Literature Centre, 2006.

Srinivas, M. N. *Social Change in Modern India*. New Delhi: Orient Longmans, 1972.

Tarapot, Phanjoubam. *Bleeding Manipur*. New Delhi: Har-Anand Publications Pvt. Ltd., 2005.

Telem, Indra Kumar. Comp. *General Knowledge of Manipur 2010: Complete & Comprehensive*. Imphal: Sharmila Telem, 2010.

Thapar, Romila. *The Past and Prejudice*. Delhi: National Book Trust, 1967.

Wessels, C. *Early Jesuit Travellers in Central Asia: 1603-1721*. Delhi: J. Jetly, 1924.

Zeliang, Elungkiebe. *A History of the Manipur Baptist Convention*. Imphal: Manipur Baptist Convention, 2005.

Encyclopaedias & Dictionaries

Bareh, Hamlet. "Manipur." In *Encyclopaedia of North-East India*. Volume III. Delhi: Mittal Publications, 2007.

Bhushan, Indu. "Caste." In *Encyclopedia of Oriental Philosophy and Religion: Hinduism,* Vol. I. Edited by N. K. Singh, A. P. Mishra. New Delhi: Global Vision Publishing House. 2005.

Dimock, E. C. "Kirtana." In *Abingdon Dictionary of Living Religions*. Edited by Keith Crim, Roger A. Bullard Larry D. Shinn. Nashville: Abingdon Press, 1981.

Dimock, E. C. "Vaisavism." In *Abingdon Dictionary of Living Religions*. Edited by Keith Crim, Roger A. Bullard Larry D. Shinn. Nashville: Abingdon Press, 1981.

Hexham, Irving. "Varnas." In *Concise Dictionary of Religion*. Illinois: InterVarsity Press, 1993.

Kumar, S. S. & V. Dey. "Brahman and Brahmanism." In *Encyclopedia of Oriental Philosophy and Religion: Hinduism*. Vol. I. Edited by N. K. Singh, A. P. Mishra. New Delhi: Global Vision Publishing House, 2005.

Singh, Lisam Khomdon. *Encyclopaedia of Manipur*. Vol. 3. Delhi: Kalpaz Publications, 2011.

WordWeb. 2012 ed. Version 6.75. S.v. "Agni."

WordWeb. 2012 ed. Version 6.75. S.v. "Brahmins."

WordWeb. 2012 ed. Version 6.75. S.v. "Bhagavad-Gita."

WordWeb. 2012 ed. Version 6.75. S.v. "Bhakti."

WordWeb. 2012 ed. Version 6.75. S.v. "Brahminism."

WordWeb. 2012 ed. Version 6.75. S.v. "Dhoti."

WordWeb. 2012 ed. Version 6.75. S.v. "Durga."

WordWeb. 2012 ed. Version 6.75. S.v. "Hanuman."

WordWeb. 2012 ed. Version 6.75. S.v. "Indra."

WordWeb. 2012 ed. Version 6.75. S.v. "Kshatriya."

WordWeb. 2012 ed. Version 6.75. S.v. "Rama."

WordWeb. 2012 ed. Version 6.75. S.v. "Sakti."

WordWeb. 2012 ed. Version 6.75. S.v. "Siva."

WordWeb. 2012 ed. Version 6.75. S.v. "Sudra."

WordWeb. 2012 ed. Version 6.75. S.v. "Turban."

WordWeb. 2012 ed. Version 6.75. S.v. "varna."

WordWeb. 2012 ed. Version 6.75. S.v. "Vishnu."

CD-ROMs

Encyclopædia Britannica, 2007 edition. S.v. "Vaishnavism." CD-ROM.

Barbara A. Standley and Deryck O. Lodrick, "Manipur." *Encyclopædia Britannica*. 2002 edition. CD-ROM.

Online Sources (Author-wise)

Dena, Lal. "AMCO's Peace Efforts During the Kuki-Naga Conflict, 1992–1994." *Kuki International Forum*. http://kukiforum.com/2010/04/amcos-peace-efforts-during-the- kuki-naga-conflict-19921994-2/. (19 Feb 2013).

Lalit, P. "A Brief History of the Meitei of Manipur." http://themanipurpagm/history/pu- warimeitei.html (22 Feb 2013).

Singh, Pandit N. Khelchandra. "British Officers Who Served as Political Agents in Manipur: Table No. 2-2." http://books.epao.net/Heritage_Ma-nipur/epShow Chapte- r.asp?src=kangla/agents (17 Feb 2013).

____________. "Tracing Origin of Kangla in Pre-Pakhangba Or Khaba Era." http://books.e-pao.net/Heritage_Manipur/ (1 April 2013).

Online Sources (Caption-wise)

"*Abhisheka.*" http://www.answers.com/topic/abhisheka (22 Feb 2013).

"Ahom Dynasty." http://www.absoluteastronomy.com/topics/Ahom_Dynasty (24 Feb 2013).

"Aimol Tribe, Manipur." http://www.indianetzone.com/7/aimol.htm (13 Mar 2013).

"Alaungpaya Dynasty." *Encyclopedia Britannica.* http://www.britannica.com/EBchec- ked/topic/12381/Ala-ungpaya-Dynasty (20 Feb 2013).

"American Baptist International Ministries celebrates New Baptist Covenant." *International Ministries* (8 Feb 2008): http://www.internationalministries.org/read- /4870-american-baptist-international-ministries-celebrates-new-baptist-covenant (25 Feb 2013).

"Anal Tribe, Manipur." http://www.indianetzone.com/7/anal_manipur.htm (13 Mar 2013).

"Angami Tribe, North East India." http://www.indianetzone.com/8/angami.htm (13 Mar 2013).

"Aryans." http://www.answers.com/topic/aryans (22 Feb 2013).

"Bishnupur: The Land of the Dancing Deer." http://bishnupur.nic.in/history.htm. (21 Feb 2013).

"Burma." http://thesou- ndofhope.org/countries/burma/ (20 Feb 2013).

"Chaitanya." http://www.britannica.com/EBchecked/-topic/88591/Chaitan-ya (22 Feb 2013).

"*Cheiraoba.*" http://www.mapsofindia.com/manipur/society-and-culture/cheiraoba.html (19 Feb 2013).

"Chiru Tribe, Manipur." http://www.indianetzone.com/8/chiru_tribe.htm (13 Mar 2013).

"Chothe Tribe, Manipur." http://www.indianetzone.com/8/chothe_tribe.htm (13 Mar 2013).

"Definition of Sankirtan." http://dictionary.baby-lon.com/sankirtan/ (19 Feb 2013).

"Gandharvas." http://www.answers.com/topic/gandharva (23 Feb 2013).

"Gangte Tribe, Manipur." http://www.indianetzone.com/8/gangte_tribe.htm (13 Mar 2013).

"Garuda." http://www.britannica.com-/search?query=Garuda (22 Feb 2013).

"Gaudiya Vaishnavism." http://www.answers.com/topic/gaudiya-vaishnavism (22 Feb 2013).

"Gotra." http://www.britannica.com/search?query=Gotra (23 Feb 2013).

"Govinda." http://www.answers.com/topic/govinda (22 Feb 2013).

"Gsowamis." http://www.answers.com/-topic/goswami (23 Feb 2013).

"History of Manipur." http://www.answers.com/topic/history-of-manipur#-Anglo- Burmese_Advents (21 Feb 2013).

"History of Manipur." http://www.iitg.ernet.in/rcilts/phaseI/his_mnea.html (28 Feb 2013).

"Hmar Gospel Centenary: Southern Manipur Gospel Centenary (1910-2010)." http://hmargospelcentenary.blogspot.in/2011/11/birth-of-christianity-in-hmar- tribe.html (20 Mar 2013).

"Hmar Tribe, Tribes of Manipur." http://www.indianetzone.com/8/hmar_tribe.htm (13 Mar 2013).

"ISKCON Desire Tree-Devotee Network." http://www.iskcondesiretree. net/profiles/b-logs/bhagavatasaptaha-1 (18 Mar 2013).

"Jesuit." http://www.answers.com/topic/jesuit (25 Feb 2013).

"Kabui Tribe, Manipur." http://www.indianetzone.com/8/kabui_tribe.htm (13 Mar 2013).

"Kacha Naga Tribe, Manipur." http://www.indianetzone.com/8/kacha_naga_tribe.htm (13 Mar 2013).

"Khamtis." http://www.1911encyclopedia.org/Khamtis (25 Feb 2013).

"King Bagyidaw." http://www.journeysmyanmar.com/historical_timeline.htm (25 Feb 2013).

"Kirtan." http://www.answers.com/topic/kirtan (23 Feb 2013).

"Koirao Tribe, Manipur." http://www.indianetzone.com/8/koirao_tribe.htm (13 Mar 2013).

"Koireng Tribe, Manipur." http://www.indianetzone.com/8/koireng_tribe.htm (13 Mar 2013).

"Kom Tribe, Manipur." http://www.indianetzone.com/8/kom_tribe.htm (13 Mar 2013).

"Kshatriya." http://www.answers.com/topic/kshatriya (22 Feb 2013).

"Lai Haraoba.' http://www.indianetzone.-com/31/lai_haraoba_indian_ritual.htm (20 Mar 2013)

"Lakshmi: Goddess of Wealth and Beaty." http://hinduism.about.com/od/hindugoddess- es/p/lakshmi.htm (23 Feb 2013).

"Lushai Tribe, Manipur." http://www.indianetzone.com/8/lushai_tribe.htm (15 Mar 2013).

"Madhava." http://www.dlshq.org/saints-/madhva.htm (22 Feb 2013).

"Manipur Map." *Maps of India.Com* (12 Jan 2012): http://www.mapsofindia.com/ma-ps/manipur/ (2 Mar 2013).

"Manipuri Alphabet." http://www.omniglot.com/writing/manipuri.htm (21 Feb 2013).

"Maram Tribe, Manipur." http://www.indianetzone.com/8/maram_tribe.htm (13 Mar 2013).

"Maring Tribe, Manipur." http://www.indianetzone.com/8/maring_tribe.htm (13 Mar 2013).

"Mithila." http://www.britannica.com/search?query=Mithila (22 Feb 2013).

"Monsang Tribe, Manipur." http://www.indianetzone.com/8/monsang_tribe.htm (15 Mar 2013).

"Moyon Tribe, Manipur." http://www.indianetzone.com/8/moyon_tribe.htm (15 Mar 2013).

"Mundus: Gateway to Missionary Collections in the United Kingdom." http://www.m-undus.ac.uk/cats/10/1092.htm (25 Feb 2013).

"Nabadwip." http://www.answers.com/topic/nabadwip (23 Feb 2013).

"Nimbarka." http://www.newworldencyclopedia.org/entry/Nimbarka (22 Feb 2013).

"Poumai Naga Socio-cultural Aspects." http://thohepou.wordpress.com/category/pou-mai-naga-socio-cultural-aspects/ (15 Mar 2013).

"Poumai.com." http://poumai.tripod.com/ (15 Mar 2013).

"Record of the Baptist Missionary Society–Collection 223." *Billy Graham Centre Archives.* http://www.wheaton.edu/bgc/archives/-GUIDES/223.htm (24 Feb 2013).

"Sanamahism." http://www.answers.com/topic/sanamahism (22 Feb 2013).

"Saraswati." http://www.sanatansociety.org/hindu_gods_and_goddesses/saraswati.htm (26 Mar 2013).

"Sex Trade Thrives in Conflict-Ridden Manipur." (12 June 2007). http://www.indiatog- ether.org/2007/jun/wom-sxmanipur.htm (19 Feb 2013).

"Shaktism." http://www.experiencefestival.com/shaktism (23 Feb 2013).

"Singpho." http://www.srimanta-.net/contents_l3.php?q=3&ID=1&ID3=11&link_ca- ption=Singphos (25 Feb 2013).

"Sylhet." http://www.britannica.com/search?query=Sylhet (22 Feb 2013).

"Sylhet: The Home of Saints and Tea Gardens." http://www.betelco.com/bd/sylhet/syl- het.html (25 Feb 2013).

"Syncretism." http://www.answers.com/topic/syncretism (23 Feb 2013).

"Tangkhul Tribe, Manipur." http://www.indianetzone.com/8/tangkhul_tribe.htm (16 Mar 2013).

"Tantrism." http://www.philtar.ac.uk/encyclopedia/hindu/devot/tant.html (23 Feb 2013).

"Thadou Tribe, Manipur." http://www.indianetzone.com/8/thadou_tribe.htm (16 Mar 2013).

"The Anglo Manipur War 1891 and its Consequences." *Manipur State Archive* (1990) http://-archivesmanipur.nic.in/whoswho.htm#THE%20ANGLO. (16 Feb 2013).

"The Caste System." http://www.vepachedu.org/castemore.-htm. (23 Feb 2013).

"The People of Manipur." http://themanipurpage.tripod.com/culture/people ofmanipu- r.html (13 Mar 2013).

"Things to do in Manipur." http://www.thrillophilia.com/blog/things-to-do-in-manipur/ (13 Mar 2013).

"Translation Services in Meitei." http://www.tridindia.com/translat-ion-services-in-me-itei/ (18 Mar 2013).

"Treaty of Yandaboo, February 24, 1826." http://www.uprinfo.org/IMG/pdf/COHR_I- ND_UPR_S1_2008 anx_Annex_X_Treaty_of_Yandab -oo_1826.pdf (16 Feb 2013).

"Vaiphei Tribe, Manipur." http://www.indianetzone.com/8/vaiphei_tribe.htm (16 Mar 2013).

"Vaishnavism." http://www.britannica.-com/search?query=Vaishnavism (22 Feb 2013).

"Vrindavan." http://www.answers. com/topic/-vrindavan (23 Feb 2013).

"Vrindavan's Geographic Features." http://www.radhava-llabh.com/vrindavan. html (20 Feb 2013).

V., Jayaram. "Know All About Saivism." http://www.saivism.net/ (23 Feb 2013).

"Where and what is northeast India." http://www.northeast-india.com/information/wh- at_where.html (2 Mar 2013).

"Zou Tribe, Manipur." http://www.indianetzone.com/8/zou_tribe.htm (16 Mar 2013).